BEYOND THE
ARAB SPRING

BEYOND THE ARAB SPRING

Authoritarianism & Democratization in the Arab World

Rex Brynen
Pete W. Moore
Bassel F. Salloukh
Marie-Joëlle Zahar

LYNNE
RIENNER
PUBLISHERS

BOULDER
LONDON

Published in the United States of America in 2012 by
Lynne Rienner Publishers, Inc.
1800 30th Street, Boulder, Colorado 80301
www.rienner.com

and in the United Kingdom by
Lynne Rienner Publishers, Inc.
3 Henrietta Street, Covent Garden, London WC2E 8LU

Library of Congress Cataloging-in-Publication Data
Beyond the Arab spring: authoritarianism and democratization in the Arab
world / Rex Brynen ... [et al.].
  Includes bibliographical references and index.
  ISBN 978-1-58826-853-2 (hardcover : alk. paper)
  ISBN 978-1-58826-878-5 (pbk. : alk. paper)
  1. Arab countries—Politics and government. 2. Authoritarianism—Arab countries.
3. Democratization—Arab countries. I. Brynen, Rex.
  JQ1850.A58B49 2012
  320.917'4927--dc23   2012021783

British Cataloguing in Publication Data
A Cataloguing in Publication record for this book
is available from the British Library.

Printed and bound in the United States of America

The paper used in this publication meets the requirements
of the American National Standard for Permanence of
Paper for Printed Library Materials Z39.48-1992.

5 4 3 2 1

Contents

Preface

Whatever the ultimate outcome of the popular mobilization, uprisings, and regime transitions that shook the Arab world in 2011, there is little doubt that they mark a historic change in the political dynamics of the region. Authoritarian regimes that once seemed unchallengeable have been challenged, and many of them have been found to be much less formidable than their citizens once feared. Dictators who once seemed to assume a lifetime hold on power have found themselves in exile, on trial, or dead at the hands of victorious rebels. Corruption, nepotism, cronyism, and injustice have been the targets of mass protests. Appeals for dignity, human rights, and democracy have been among the protesters' most prominent slogans.

As will be clear in the pages that follow, we are well aware of the challenges that lie ahead. Most authoritarian regimes in the Arab world remain in power, working to reconsolidate their political control. Those countries where regime change has taken place are struggling to define their politics anew, and to construct more participatory politics. Whatever the hopes for democracy, there also arises the specter of possible authoritarian relapse or, in some cases, collapse into civil strife. Yet the very fact that the Arab political future has become contentious and undefined is a dramatic break from the stultifying, repressive politics of the previous decades.

This book has its earliest origins in a project on political liberalization and democratization in the Arab world undertaken at McGill University and the Université de Montréal in the mid-1990s, under the auspices of the Interuniversity Consortium for Arab and Middle Eastern Studies (ICAMES). At that time, Rex Brynen was the most junior member of an ICAMES research team led by Bahgat Korany and Paul Noble. Pete Moore, Bassel Salloukh, and Marie-Joëlle Zahar were then all PhD students, ICAMES graduate fellows, and research assistants for the project. In the two edited volumes that resulted (also published by Lynne Rienner Publishers), it was argued that the authoritarian edifices of the region were far from permanent. The growth of civil society, emerging Arab discourse on human rights and political democracy, the contradictions of political economy, and the global diffusion of norms and ideas all represented slowly growing pressures for change. Regimes would attempt to blunt these, whether through repression or limited reformism. We were unconvinced, however, that they could do so forever. There and in our other work we also placed great emphasis on the importance of what we termed "regional permeability," the extent to which ideas and movements and social forces could echo within and across the Arab world in powerful but changing ways.

It was shortly after the four authors of this present volume decided to revisit such issues that the Arab Spring erupted, starting in Tunisia, spreading to Egypt, and then reverberating across the region. None of us would have predicted in November 2010 how very different the next year would look, and certainly none of us were betting that Zine el-Abidine Ben Ali or Hosni Mubarak or Muammar Qaddafi were about to fall. Yet the existence of such forces of change waiting to be unleashed was no fundamental surprise, nor was it unexpected that events in one Arab country could have such powerful demonstration effects on others.

We would like to thank all of those who made this project possible. Friend, colleague, and ICAMES fellow-traveler Janine Clark (University of Guelph)—who also participated in the earlier democratization project—contributed Chapter 6. ICAMES graduate research fellow Merouan Mekouar (McGill University) coauthored Chapter 2. ICAMES research fellow Rob Stewart assisted us greatly with editing and comments. We would like to thank David Brynen, Shoghig Mikaelian, John Jeha, Lara Khattab, Rabie Barakat, Adam Chamseddine, and Jinan al-Habbal for research assistance. We also gratefully acknowledge research grant support from the Social Sciences and Humanities Research Council of Canada, the International Development Research Centre, and the Fulbright Scholar Program.

Fundamentally this volume is a collaborative endeavor that seeks to synthesize our various perspectives. Our thinking has been enriched by the many collective discussions and revisions that have contributed to the final product. We hope that the reader finds it equally useful in spurring their own reflections on the antecedents, causes, dynamics, and consequences of the Arab Spring.

We would also like to express a debt of gratitude to the two mentors who made this possible. Had it not been for Paul Noble and Bahgat Korany, it is unlikely that any of us would have found ourselves in Montreal two decades ago to begin this particular intellectual journey in the first place. What an interesting journey it has been—and as the Middle East continues to undergo the throes of change, how even more interesting it promises to become.

Rex Brynen
Pete Moore
Bassel F. Salloukh
Marie-Joëlle Zahar

BEYOND THE
ARAB SPRING

1

New Horizons in Arab Politics

For much of the past four decades, a central puzzle of Arab politics had been a striking persistence of authoritarianism. No other part of the world had proven quite so resistant to the so-called third wave of democratization, which transformed Latin America and Eastern Europe in the 1980s and 1990s and which also had significant effects in Asia and sub-Saharan Africa. In 2010, the advocacy organization Freedom House classified 59 percent of countries around the world as electoral democracies. Of these, not one was to be found in the Arab world.[1]

In 2011, however, the authoritarian status quo was shattered by the Arab Spring—a series of Arab uprisings that unseated long-standing dictators in Tunisia, Egypt, Libya, and Yemen, generated mass protests and countervailing repression in Bahrain and Syria, and affected almost every other regime in the region in some way.[2] Clearly something very important changed, with lasting repercussions for the politics of the region.

The Arab Spring will be the focus of a great deal of scholarly debate in the years to come, both because it emerged so suddenly out of a context of apparent authoritarian stability, and because of its widespread and lasting implications for Middle East politics. The affected societies will struggle with the challenges of transition to uncertain futures as contending political and social forces seek to influence the emerging political order. Some will undoubtedly prove difficult: democratic transitions do not always succeed, and violence often leaves legacies of continued civil strife. Some authoritarian regimes will weather the storm. Others may not. And still others, in adapting to the new regional environment, may change in significant ways.

This volume has emerged from a long-standing interest on the part of the authors in issues of authoritarianism and democratization in the Arab world, one that dates back to the early 1990s.[3] For reasons that will be explored later, we resist the temptation to treat the current wave of antiauthoritarian protest as disconnected from the dynamics of prior authoritarian maintenance, but instead treat them as fundamentally linked. Consequently this volume confronts two sets of questions. First, what have been the dynamics of authoritarian persistence in the region? Second, why did many of these systems so suddenly fail in 2011? In addition, we also identify some of the transitional challenges that newly emerging postauthoritarian regimes will face, although we do so only tentatively given the uncertainties of the current era.

Although we sometimes make reference to the broader Middle East, our focus is the Arab world.[4] In part this is because only so much can be dealt with in a single volume. More fundamentally however, it is because the existence of a common language, shared political narratives, and transnational Arabic media renders the Arab world especially permeable to transnational political influences, including the various demonstration and neighborhood effects associated with authoritarianism and democratization.[5] It was very much in this "public space" that the echoes of change reverberated so powerfully in 2011.[6]

In reflecting on these issues we are not inclined to offer any especially parsimonious theorizing about either the persistence or the collapse of Arab authoritarianism, and will similarly not offer a definitive account of the Arab Spring. For a start, we are far from convinced that there was or is a single Arab authoritarianism; rather, there is an array of political settings with histories, structural conditions, and dynamics that share both similar and strikingly dissimilar characteristics. The politics of Ben Ali's Tunisia were very different from those of Saleh's Yemen or the Khalifa monarchy in Bahrain, and nothing anywhere quite resembled Qaddafi's Libya. The dynamics of opposition and protest in those countries, although linked, have also been quite different.

We tend to the view that it was a complex multiplicity of factors (and interaction between them) that buttressed regimes and undermined them. We also believe that processes of change in the region have often been subtle and gradual, with pressures mounting until the point where new forms of politics suddenly become possible. As Ellen Lust has suggested, there is value in "shifting our focus from a search for immediate causal factors to a greater recognition of micro- and meso-level transitions—that is, gradual, interrelated changes in political, economic and social spheres that, like slowly moving tectonic plates, eventually create the conditions conducive to earth-shattering events."[7]

In doing so, our intellectual inspirations and methodological preferences are unabashedly eclectic. Too often scholars have, in their desire to set their work within a certain intellectual tradition, prioritized a focus on the Weberian state and its formal boundaries at the expense of the transnational, emphasized one set of causal factors to the exclusion of others, preoccupied themselves with formal politics at the expense of less formal processes, or looked for that which is quantifiable while ignoring the insights of qualitative research (or vice versa). While our eclecticism is probably more the result of personal orientation than anything else, we find some vindication in research that suggests that the predictive accuracy of political scientists is inversely proportional to their preoccupation with "one big idea."[8] We also recognize that, as Charles Kurzman has argued with regard to Iran, political upheaval is particularly resistant to theorizing. The collapse of the established and internalized rules of the game results in rapid and unpredictable shifts in political preference structures as individuals are suddenly called upon to respond to developments that once seemed almost unimaginable.[9] In the transition from authoritarian settings (where individuals have every reason to keep their political views private) to transitional ones (in which the individual risk of expressing dissent declines as increasing numbers of people do so), the character of public discourse and behavior can change quickly.[10] Perceptions of political opportunity structures change in unanticipated ways, and "informational cascades" reshape what people choose to do.[11]

Given this, and in light of the uncertainty in the region's political development, it seems wise for scholars to be appropriately humble about the analytical claims that they make. Instead, we should see the present moment as a historic opportunity for review, reflection, and critical dialogue about what the Arab Spring represents.[12] In this sense, we invite readers to disagree with us as well as agree, for it is such an intellectual and critical conversation that scholarship aims to develop. To the extent that this book reflects some of our own intellectual curiosity and excitement, we also hope to render the challenges of writing amid uncertain times into an asset rather than a liability.

From Authoritarian Persistence to Political Change in the Arab World

As noted earlier, the political history of the Middle East was hardly one of flourishing postcolonial democracy. Upon independence, those states that featured some form of elective, parliamentary, or quasi-democratic political system soon found these systems toppled by military coup (Syria, Egypt, Iraq, Sudan) or beset by civil war (Lebanon, Sudan). In others, independent states emerged firmly under the grip of authoritarian-constitutional monarchies (Jordan, Morocco, Kuwait, Bahrain) or absolutist monarchies (Saudi Arabia, Oman, Qatar, the United Arab Emirates). In still other cases, successful national liberation movements (Algeria, South Yemen) established single-party states in the aftermath of violent decolonization.

There was nothing particularly unusual in all of this. The decolonizations of the interwar and post–World War II years often resulted in authoritarian politics or produced the politics of fragility and internal violence—and in many cases a bit of both. What was somewhat striking, however, was how long it all lasted. Certainly, third wave democratization was far from universal, especially in Asia and Africa. Not all political transitions of the 1970s, 1980s, and 1990s resulted in real democracies. In many cases, old authoritarianisms recycled themselves as quasi-democracies in hybrid regimes that combined the trappings of pluralism and electoral process with deep-seated centers of authoritarian power that remained beyond the reach of popular control.[13] Nonetheless, the era did mark an important change in modern politics.

But that important change largely bypassed the Arab world; or put another way, the so-called third wave of democracy never really reached Arab shores. Indeed, in contrast to the regime changes in many other parts of the world, the four decades after 1970 were the most stable in the modern Middle East. The persistence of Middle Eastern authoritarianisms was fully evident in data published by Freedom House, which each year rates countries' political and civil liberties on separate 7-point scales, with 1 indicating the greatest freedom and 7 indicating the least. By this measure, Africa's combined Freedom House rating (the sum of both political and civil liberty scores) improved from 11.9 in 1980 to a high of 8.2 in 2006, before deteriorating somewhat to 8.6 in 2010. Asia improved from 8.4 in 1980 to 6.8 in 2010. Because of the transformation of authoritarian regimes in Latin America, the Americas overall shifted from a rating of 6.8 in 1980 to 4.6 in 2010. But in the Middle East and North Africa as a whole, the Freedom House rating changed hardly at all, from 10.5 in 1980 to 10.6 in 2010, marking this region the most authoritarian in the world.[14]

This is not to say, however, that the underlying politics of the region were unchanging. Indeed, a strong argument can be made that authoritarian persistence in the region was not simply due to immobilism and political stasis, but was rather an adaptive process of "authoritarian upgrading" whereby regimes responded to social, economic, technological, and international changes by modifying their modalities of rule and configurations of power.[15] In some cases this involved partial or periodic political openings—a controlled degree of political liberalization and limited political pluralism that was intended by regimes as a substitute for, rather than a step toward, fuller democratization.[16]

Such limited reforms became increasingly common from the late 1980s onward. In Egypt and Tunisia, the Mubarak and Ben Ali regimes promised more liberal politics than those of their predecessors. Jordan renewed parliamentary elections in 1989, legalizing a return to multiparty life soon thereafter. Algeria underwent a political opening too, one that commenced in November 1988 with the adoption of a number of political reforms that seemed to open the way for the dismantling of single-party rule. In Kuwait, parliament was reestablished after the Iraqi occupation ended in 1991, with some hope that this might encourage change elsewhere in the Gulf. A decade later, however, the limited nature of the reform processes had become clearly evident. Egypt's limited multipartyism remained tightly controlled. Tunisia soon clamped down against political opponents. Political opening in Jordan stalled, as it did in other countries, and then quickly eroded. Algeria had slipped into a decade of bloody civil war after the military aborted the electoral process. In Kuwait, limited parliamentarianism evolved slowly, but there was much less change elsewhere in the Gulf.

A second round of attention came in the aftermath of the September 2001 terrorist attacks and the subsequent wars in Afghanistan and Iraq. The Western world expressed a newfound interest in promoting democracy in the region. Thus in December 2002 the United States unveiled the US–Middle East Partnership Initiative, a series of programs intended to "support the expansion of political opportunity throughout the Middle East."[17] According to the George W. Bush administration, this—together with the overthrow of Saddam Hussein—would constitute part of a "forward strategy of freedom to promote democracy throughout the Middle East."[18] The European Union also placed greater emphasis on promoting political change in the region.[19] The June 2004 meeting of the Group of Eight (G8), the largest industrialized countries, saw the declaration of a common interest in reform in the Middle East. Greater funding also became available for research on the issue, and new research institutions and initiatives proliferated.

Sustained Western foreign policy emphasis on democratization of the Middle East would not last the decade, however. The importance of Arab cooperation in the global "war on terror" meant that Washington was reluctant to push its Middle Eastern allies too far or too fast. The Bush administration did little to protest fraud within the Egyptian government and its manipulation of the country's 2005 parliamentary elections—effectively, Egypt was deemed too important to alienate or risk instability, and there was little US or European desire to help the opposition Muslim Brotherhood, which likely would have been the biggest beneficiary of political reform. In the occupied Palestinian territories, the 2006 Palestinian Legislative Council elections led to the establishment of a Hamas-led cabinet. Almost immediately, Western donors, Israel, and the Fatah party (which had previously held a monopoly on power in the Palestinian Authority) worked to undermine the cabinet. In Iraq, the US invasion and occupation as well as subsequent generalized violence within the country hardly represented a shining example of the benefits of postauthoritarian politics.[20] Although a new US administration took to the world stage in 2009 without much of the regional baggage of its predecessor, it initially did little to highlight the issue of regional authoritarianism beyond offering a few rhetorical statements.[21] Up until the end of 2010, Barack Obama and his administration were largely silent on human rights abuses by Arab regimes. For example, when the November 2010 parliamentary elections in Egypt saw the ruling National Democratic Party strengthen its overwhelming majority through fraud and intimidation, Washington did little more than express dismay, calling it a "cause for concern."[22]

The ebbs and flows of the discourse on political reform in the Arab world were paralleled by similar shifts in the academic literature. Prior to the late 1980s, there was very little scholarly attention paid to the possibility of democratization in the Middle East. Scholars of the region tended to focus on other things, while scholars of democratic transition tended to ignore the region, or cast doubts on its potential for change.[23] Michael Hudson was among the first to suggest, in 1987, that state-society relations, political economy, and public attitudes were changing in a way that threatened to delegitimize authoritarian regimes and open up the possibility of eventual political transitions in the Middle East.[24] Thereafter, and especially following the 1990–1991 Gulf War, a growing number of scholars began to seriously examine the prospects for political liberalization and democratization.[25] This was paralleled, within the region itself, by increasing levels of political discourse framed in terms of human rights, political participation, civil society, and democracy.

Much of this literature quite explicitly hedged its bets, arguing that at best the prospects for democracy had entered the stage of "maybe" or "interesting possibilities" rather than representing an inexorable trend or an inevitable outcome. Nevertheless, by the end of the 1990s the failure of limited political reform to deliver much more than a reconfiguration of authoritarian power was generating ever-growing levels of analytical cynicism. Had scholars overreacted to the limited openings of the early 1990s? Had the attention to political liberalization and democratization been so much wishful thinking, underpinned by normative preferences? Or perhaps it had been driven by third wave "envy" of sorts, having more to do with academic fads than with real trends in the Arab world?

To take one example, Lisa Anderson suggested that scholars had been "searching where the light shines" in their treatment of the issue, driven more by the exigencies of US foreign policy and disciplinary preoccupations than by the actual content of politics in the region:

There is an old joke that captures the dilemma confronting political scientists who studied the Middle East. One evening, a passer-by chances on a fellow searching for his lost house key under a streetlight. Hoping to be helpful, the spectator asks the searcher where he dropped the key. "Across the street," comes the reply. Then why is he searching on this side of the street? "The light is so much better over here."

For more than fifty years, the policy and scholarly community of the United States looked for glimmers of democracy in the Middle East. And occasionally they found them—small traces of hope glinting in the bright light of US policy and American social science. . . .

Political science's disciplinary bias toward democracy and American foreign policy's emphasis on democratization cast a bright light that confused and distorted the research agenda in the study of Middle East politics, thereby preventing it from contributing as much as it might to a genuinely comparative science of politics.[26]

Other scholars characterized earlier scholarship as a "demo-crazy" era of "democracy spotting," suggesting that analysis needed to adopt a "post-democratization" approach that would focus on the real dynamics of politics-as-it-is rather than speculation on the absence of politics-as-it-might-be.[27] Much of the scholarly attention thus shifted from trying to understand the potential sources of reform in the Middle East to trying to understand the roots of authoritarian persistence in the region. Accordingly, a special issue of the leading journal *Comparative Politics* on the topic in 2004 explicitly asked: "Why have the Middle East and North Africa remained so singularly resistant to democratization?"[28] Questions were raised about the sources of the Middle East's "democracy deficit" and the region's apparent political exceptionalism.

Such oscillation between the tentative, hopeful literature of the mid-1990s and the authoritarian persistence–centric focus of a decade later was both helpful and unhelpful in terms of its contribution to scholarly understanding of Arab politics. At its most useful, it represented a thoughtful debate over how analysts might best appreciate the inevitable struggle between those social, economic, and political forces that might hasten the pace of change, and those factors (both structural and adaptive) that might preserve the authoritarian status quo. As Steven Heydemann noted:

Authoritarian upgrading consists, in other words, not in shutting down and closing off Arab societies from globalization and other forces of political, economic, and social change. Nor is it based simply on the willingness of Arab governments to repress their opponents. Instead, authoritarian upgrading involves reconfiguring authoritarian governance to accommodate and manage changing political, economic, and social conditions. It originated in no small part as a defensive response to challenges confronting Arab autocrats during the past two decades.[29]

In its more counterproductive form, however, this oscillation reflected the frequent tendency in academic debates to miscast and simplify earlier literatures so as to emphasize the newness and superiority of later accounts. After all, it was far from clear that a focus on the sources of political change in the Middle East necessarily came at the expense of understanding how those changes were managed, manipulated, controlled, or repressed. On the contrary, the two ought to have been intimately linked, and indeed they were in the work of a great many scholars.[30]

Consequently, instead of a sort of dialectic engagement of ideas that might have produced a superior analytical synthesis, the result was sometimes a firm attachment to the notion of authoritarian persistence that lost sight of the potential vulnerabilities and fragility of that construct. As Bahgat Korany presciently argued mere months before the Arab Spring erupted:

> Mainstream vision and analysis of the Middle East seem to disregard this dynamism and to insist that the region, one of the most internationally penetrated, does not change. Is this another case of the widely held belief in "Middle East exceptionalism"? On the surface, this static vision seems justified. . . .
>
> For some analysts, however, this overemphasis on continuity and the neglect of aspects of change are evidence of an inherently conservative bias in social analysis. Bias in favor of continuity also indicates an intellectual laziness, since it is easier to analyze the status quo than its counterpart, change and transformation.[31]

Part of the problem might also have been that scholars often lost sight of the role of politics at the level of citizens and potential protesters, or focused on the former without linking it to institutions and shifts in broader political economies. As Asef Bayat has shown, our understanding of politics needs to include the ways in which ordinary people make adjustments to their pattern of life that accommodate, challenge, or substitute for the power of the (authoritarian) state.[32] Ideational notions of legitimacy, which at one time had been central to many analyses of Arab politics, had fallen by the wayside, often reduced to more material incentives and disincentives.[33] Lisa Wedeen's focus on compliant, participatory, and identity-affirming acts at the individual and group level also pointed to the importance of everyday symbolic and ideational factors.[34] Such work has proven particularly significant in the light of Arab protest movements that started in large part from the bottom up and asserted the illegitimacy of authoritarian rule as a central part of their message, and in which symbols (such as atrocities or victories recorded by mobile phone, or the public mocking of authoritarian power) often proved important indeed.

Linking Past and Future: The Analytical Challenges

In the chapters that follow we are far more interested in the challenge of synthesis than in staking out a narrow postauthoritarian paradigm that would repeat some of the shortcomings of the earlier postdemocratization tendencies. Clearly authoritarianism flourished in the Arab world for decades, withstanding the effects of the third wave. Clearly many authoritarian regimes in the region continue to survive despite the tumultuous events of the Arab Spring. There is also the possibility that the difficult transitions under way in the region could in time become new authoritarianisms, whether populist, hybrid, Islamist, military, or nationalist. Understanding how Arab authoritarianism has functioned from both a regional perspective and a broader comparative perspective remains no less important despite the events of 2011. At the same time, the events of the Arab Spring ought to prompt reflection and indeed self-reflection, since clearly many analysts got many things wrong, the authors of this volume included. Clearly too, things have changed and new dynamics are being established across the region.

In Part 1 of the volume we examine the trajectories of authoritarianism and reform in the Arab world through a consideration of recent developments in selected countries in North Africa, the Mashreq, and the Arabian Peninsula. Our focus here is on social structures, elite and institutional structures, and immediate subregional settings. Institutions are particularly important because they reflect and embed social realities, as well as enabling and constraining the social and political choices that actors have within political systems. And because they differ from country to country, the precise dynamics of politics—while authoritarian—can vary in fundamentally important ways. To take but one of many possible examples, different institutional patterns and configurations of state security forces and civil-military relations proved to be of considerable importance in explaining the rather different trajectories of political developments in Tunisia and Egypt (where the military ultimately abandoned its president), Libya (where the military was weak, with part remaining loyal to the regime while others defected to the opposition), and Bahrain (where the security forces remained loyal and were buttressed by outside assistance from other Gulf states).[35]

In Part 2 of the book we turn our attention to key thematic and theoretical issues in the study of Arab authoritarianism, reform, democratization, and political transition. These are not necessarily exhaustive treatments of all potential topics, which would be far beyond the scope of a single volume. Rather they are framed more as a series of debates, inquiries, and conversations around our central questions of authoritarian stability and postauthoritarian change, aimed at teasing out what we feel are the most promising sets of explanations for the trajectories of contemporary Arab politics. Specifically, we have chosen to focus on eight main areas: debates over the relationship between culture and politics; the particular role that Islamist movements might play in political liberalization and democratization; processes of electoral politics; the particular dynamics of Middle Eastern monarchies; the political effects of oil wealth in the rentier economies; the effects of economic liberalization; the importance of satellite television and other Arab media; and the regional and international context of Arab authoritarianism and postauthoritarianism.

Finally, in Part 3 in our concluding chapter, we pull these various threads together, highlighting the complex and multidimensional ways in which various factors interacted to sustain Arab authoritarianisms in the decades preceding the Arab Spring. We revisit the myriad ways in which regimes used a range of institutionally embedded policy tools—from repression to patronage, controlled electoral process, and cultural symbolism—to foster social and political compliance, as well as the ways in which this matrix of control weakened or collapsed with the onset of Arab popular uprisings in 2011. We offer a limited look ahead to the challenges faced by transitional regimes, as well as to the social and political dynamics that will shape them.

We are fully aware of the immense challenges that still face those Arab populations still struggling to reform or end authoritarian regimes, for whom an Arab Spring has not yet come. We are equally aware of the challenges faced by postauthoritarian societies that must now construct new, and hopefully inclusive, political orders. It will undoubtedly be messy as contending views clash, or seek mutual accommodation. In some cases it might even fail.

However, it was for precisely these very processes—the freedom to debate, disagree, contend, compromise, and shape new futures—that so many have mobilized in defiance of long-standing dictatorships. Herein we hope to offer some insight into how this new historic juncture came to pass, and to reflect on where it might be headed.

Notes

1. Freedom House, Freedom in the World 2011 (Washington, DC, 2011), http://www.freedomhouse.org/template.cfm?page=594. While a number of issues can be raised about the categorization and assessment of "electoral democracy," the observation nonetheless highlights the lack of meaningful democratic politics in the Arab world at the time.

2. There has been considerable debate—both in general and among the authors of this volume—as to what term best describes the Arab upheavals of 2011. Commentator Rami Khouri, for example, has argued that "Arab Spring" underemphasizes the agency

of the protesters. He prefers "Arab revolution," noting that "revolution" (*thawra*) is the term that the protesters themselves have most often used. On the other hand, in many countries it is not clear that the events of 2011 have yet met the threshold of "revolution" in the way that many social scientists use the term. Other terms such as "Arab uprisings" and "Arab protests" are also inadequate for other reasons. Rather than impose the straightjacket of a single term, we have tended to use several (including "Arab Spring") depending on preference and context. Rami Khouri, "Spring or Revolution?" Agence Global, 17 August 2011, http://agenceglobal.com/article.asp?id=2618.

3. Rex Brynen, Bahgat Korany, and Paul Noble, eds., *Political Liberalization and Democratization in the Arab World, vol. 1, Theoretical Perspectives* (Boulder: Lynne Rienner, 1995); Bahgat Korany, Rex Brynen, and Paul Noble, eds., *Political Liberalization and Democratization in the Arab World, vol. 2, Comparative Experiences* (Boulder: Lynne Rienner, 1995).

4. Although part of the Arab world, this volume offers little attention to Sudan, where local political dynamics are deeply shaped by the secession of the south—an issue beyond the scope of our primary focus on authoritarianism and democratization. For reasons of space, we also devote little attention to Mauritania, and none to Arab League members Comoros (which really is not part of the political dynamics of the "Arab world") and Somalia (which is not "Arab" to begin with).

5. We have long emphasized the importance of political permeability in the region, and especially with regard to the Arab world. See, for example, many of the contributions in Bassel Salloukh and Rex Brynen, eds., *Persistent Permeability? Regionalism, Localism, and Globalization in the Middle East* (Aldershot: Ashgate, 2004).

6. For the role of satellite television in contributing to this Arab "public space," see Marc Lynch, *Voices of the New Arab Public: Iraq, Al-Jazeera, and Middle East Politics Today* (New York: Columbia University Press, 2006).

7. Ellen Lust, "Why Now? Micro Transitions and the Arab Uprisings," The Monkey Cage blog, 24 October 2011, http://themonkeycage.org/blog/2011/10/24/why-now-micro-transitions-and-the-arab-uprisings.

8. Philip E. Tetlock, *Expert Political Judgment* (Princeton: Princeton University Press, 2005).

9. Charles Kurzman, *The Unthinkable Revolution in Iran* (Cambridge: Harvard University Press, 2004).

10. On the issue of "preference falsification" under authoritarianism (or other conditions) and the role that changes in this can play in rapid political change, see Timur Kuran, *Private Truths, Public Lies: The Social Consequences of Preference Falsification* (Cambridge: Harvard University Press, 1997).

11. On the concept of informational cascades, see Sushil Bikhchandani, David Hirshleifer, and Ivo Welch, "A Theory of Fads, Fashion, Custom, and Cultural Change as Informational Cascades," *Journal of Political Economy* 100, 5 (1992); Susanne Lohmann, "The Dynamics of Informational Cascades: The Monday Demonstrations in Leipzig, East Germany, 1989–91," *World Politics* 47, 1 (October 1994).

12. For other such efforts, see F. Gregory Gause III, "Why Middle East Studies Missed the Arab Spring: The Myth of Authoritarian Stability," *Foreign Affairs* 90, 4 (July–August 2011); Eva Bellin, "Reconsidering the Robustness of Authoritarianism in the Middle East," *Comparative Politics* 44, 2 (January 2012).

13. Larry Diamond, "Elections Without Democracy: Thinking About Hybrid Regimes," *Journal of Democracy* 13, 2 (April 2002); Steven Levitsky and Lucan Way, *Competitive Authoritarianism: Hybrid Regimes After the Cold War* (Cambridge: Cambridge University Press, 2010).

14. Calculated from Freedom House's "Freedom in the World Comparative and Historical Data," with civil and political rights combined. Excludes occupied Palestinian territories and the Western Sahara.

15. Steven Heydemann, *Upgrading Authoritarianism in the Arab World* (Washington, DC: Brookings Institution, October 2007).

16. Elsewhere we have emphasized the important difference between political liberalization (understood as "the expansion of public space through recognition of civil and political liberties, particularly those bearing upon the ability of citizens to engage in free political discourse and to freely organize in pursuit of common interests") and political democratization (which entails "an expansion of political participation in such a way as to provide citizens with a degree of real and meaningful collective control over public policy"). Rex Brynen, Bahgat Korany, and Paul Noble, "Introduction: Theoretical Perspectives on Arab Liberalization and Democratization," in Brynen, Korany, and Noble, *Political Liberalization and Democratization in the Arab World, vol. 1*, p. 3.

17. US Department of State, fact sheet, US–Middle East Partnership Initiative, 18 June 2003. Reflecting the thrust of most post-9/11 Western democracy assistance, the initiative focused on liberal economic reform, support (liberal) for civil society, and promoting educational reform. Colin Powell, "The US-Middle East Partnership Initiative: Building Hope for the Years Ahead," speech to the Heritage Foundation, Washington, DC, 12 December 2002.

18. White House, Office of the Press Secretary, fact sheet, "President Bush Calls for a 'Forward Strategy of Freedom' to Promote Democracy in the Middle East," 6 November 2003. See also George W. Bush, "Remarks by the President at the 20th Anniversary of the National Endowment for Democracy," Washington, DC, 6 November 2003.

19. Richard Youngs, "The European Union and Democracy Promotion in the Mediterranean: A New or Disingenuous Strategy?" *Democratization* 9, 1 (2002).

20. On the negative effects of US intervention in Iraq on regional democratization, see Rex Brynen, "The Iraq War and (Non) Democratization in the Arab World," in Mokhtar Lamani and Bessma Momani, eds., *From Desolation to Reconstruction: Iraq's Troubled Journey* (Waterloo: Wilfrid Laurier University Press, 2010); Eric Davis, "History Matters: Past as Prologue in Building Democracy in Iraq," *Orbis* 49 (Spring 2005).

21. President Barack Obama, "Remarks by the President on a New Beginning," Cairo, 4 June 2009, http://www.whitehouse.gov/the_press_office/Remarks-by-the-President-at-Cairo-University-6-04-09.

22. US State Department, "State Department on Egypt's Parliamentary Elections," 29 November 2010, http://www.america.gov/st/texttrans-english/2010/November/20101130105621su0.6068951.html#ixzz1AZwx7m9c.

23. See, for example, Samuel Huntington, "Will More Countries Become Democratic?" *Political Science Quarterly* 99, 2 (Summer 1984), p. 216.

24. Michael Hudson, "Democratization and the Problem of Legitimacy in Middle East Politics," *MESA Bulletin* 22, 2 (December 1988).

25. See, for example, Michael Hudson, "After the Gulf War: Prospects for Democratization in the Arab World," *Middle East Journal* 45, 3 (Summer 1991); Ghassan Salamé, ed., *Democracy Without Democrats? The Renewal of Politics in the Muslim World* (London: Tauris, 1994); Augustus Richard Norton, *Civil Society in the Middle East, vols. 1–2* (Leiden: Brill, 1995); Brynen, Korany, and Noble, *Political Liberalization and Democratization in the Arab World, vol. 1, Theoretical Perspectives*; Korany, Brynen, and Noble, *Political Liberalization and Democratization in the Arab World, vol. 2, Comparative Experiences*.

26. Lisa Anderson, "Searching Where the Light Shines: Studying Democratization in the Middle East," *Annual Review of Political Science* 9 (2006), pp. 208–209.

27. Francesco Cavatorta, "The Convergence of Governance: Upgrading Authoritarianism in the Arab World, and Downgrading Democracy Elsewhere?" *Middle East Critique* 19, 3 (Fall 2010); Morten Valbjørn and André Bank, "Examining the 'Post' in Post-Democratization: the Future of Middle Eastern Political Rule Through Lenses of

the Past," *Middle East Critique* 19, 3 (Fall 2010). Some years earlier we had warned that "there is a danger that the democratic aspirations of scholars will lead them to read an unjustified democratic teleology into their subject matter, conceptualizing liberal democracy as a sort of natural 'endpoint' of political development rather than focusing on the underlying social struggles that comprise the real raw material of all politics." Rex Brynen, Bahgat Korany, and Paul Noble, "Trends, Trajectories, or Interesting Possibilities? Some Conclusions on Arab Democratization and Its Study," in Brynen, Korany, and Noble, *Political Liberalization and Democratization in the Arab World, vol. 1, Theoretical Perspectives,* p. 334.

28. Eva Bellin, "The Robustness of Authoritarianism in the Middle East: Exceptionalism in Comparative Perspective," *Comparative Politics* 36, 2 (January 2004), p. 139. Revised articles from this issue of *Comparative Politics,* together with other contributions, were later published as Marsha Pripstein Posusney and Michele Penner Angrist, eds., *Authoritarianism in the Middle East: Regimes and Resistance* (Boulder: Lynne Rienner, 2005).

29. Heydemann, *Upgrading Authoritarianism in the Arab World,* p. 1.

30. An example of this would be Richard Norton's pioneering work on the development of civil society in the Middle East. While some saw this as evidence of an excessive focus on the potential for change, Norton's project highlighted the interplay between both forces of social organization and the state's efforts to control, capture, and co-opt these. Martin Kramer, *Ivory Towers on Sand: The Failure of Middle Eastern Studies in America* (Washington, DC: Washington Institute for Near East Policy, 2001), pp. 66–70; Norton, *Civil Society in the Middle East,* vols. 1–2.

31. Bahgat Korany, introduction to Korany, ed., *The Changing Middle East: A New Look at Regional Dynamics* (Cairo: American University in Cairo Press, 2010), p. 1. The volume itself noted important changes in Arab civil society, the Arab media, and within previously radical Islamist groups—all of which would prove of importance in the events that followed.

32. Asef Bayat, *Life as Politics: How Ordinary People Change the Middle East* (Stanford: Stanford University Press, 2009).

33. Larbi Sadiki emphasized the importance of examining the role of "anomie, social upheaval, and political protest" in the context of a collapsing social compact between regimes and citizens, which well-describes many of the contours of the Arab Spring a decade later. Larbi Sadiki, "Popular Uprisings and Arab Democratization," *International Journal of Middle East Studies* 32, 1 (February 2000). The classic work on political legitimacy in Arab politics was Michael Hudson, *Arab Politics: The Search for Legitimacy* (New Haven: Yale University Press, 1977); whether his arguments were negated by the decades of authoritarian stability that followed, or validated by the role that issues of legitimacy played in an Arab Spring, remains an open issue.

34. Lisa Wedeen, *Peripheral Visions: Publics, Power, and Performance in Yemen* (Chicago: University of Chicago Press, 2008). On the importance of symbolic displays of authoritarian power in social compliance, see also Lisa Wedeen, *Ambiguities of Domination: Politics, Rhetoric, and Symbols in Contemporary Syria* (Chicago: University of Chicago Press, 1999).

35. For discussion of the importance of this, see the roundtable discussion "Rethinking the Study of Arab Militaries," *International Journal of Middle East Studies* 43, 3 (August 2011).

PART 1

The Context

2

North Africa:
Algeria, Egypt,
Libya, Morocco, Tunisia

While Egypt has often played a leading role in Arab politics—most notably in the 1950s and 1960s, when the pan-Arabism of Egyptian president Gamal Abdul Nasser influenced much of the region—the rest of North Africa has never been seen as being at the forefront of ideological and political change in the Arab world. That changed, however, over the course of a few weeks in late 2010 and early 2011. On 17 December 2010, a Tunisian street vendor named Mohamed Bouazizi was harassed by police in the provincial town of Sidi Bouzid. When his attempts to lodge a complaint were rebuffed, he set himself on fire in protest. He subsequently died of his injuries on 4 January 2011.

Bouazizi's actions set off an escalating series of antigovernment demonstrations in Sidi Bouzid and across the rest of Tunisia. By late December 2010, these protests had reached the capital, Tunis. On 14 January 2011, President Zine el-Abidine Ben Ali, who had ruled the country largely unchallenged for the previous twenty-three years, fled Tunisia for exile in Saudi Arabia.

Ben Ali's overthrow in turn set off a wave of antiauthoritarian mobilization elsewhere in the region that would become known as the Arab Spring. Popular protests were publicized through the sharing of pictures and video recordings on social networking Internet sites and were widely covered on Al Jazeera and other regional satellite television stations. In Egypt, activists occupied Cairo's Tahrir Square on 25 January, sparking nationwide protests that would culminate in the ouster of the Egyptian president two weeks later. In Libya, protests escalated in mid-February and soon sparked a popular uprising against the regime of Muammar Qaddafi that escalated into civil war. Anti-regime protests also spread to Yemen, Bahrain, and Syria.

The Arab Spring was a startling enough development in its own right. But what made it even more remarkable is that it started in Tunisia, a coun-

---

This chapter was coauthored with Merouan Mekouar, PhD candidate in the Department of Political Science at McGill University.

try that few would have identified as being ripe for regime change only a few months prior, despite some signs of economic strain and political discontent.

Tunisia

Since independence in 1956, Tunisia had really known only two political leaders. One was Habib Bourguiba, founder and leader of the anticolonial Neo-Destour party, who quickly sidelined King Muhammad VIII al-Amin to become the country's first president in 1957. Thirty years later, Bourguiba's own prime minister (and a former military officer), Zine el-Abidine Ben Ali, led the "soft coup" that removed the aging and increasingly infirm leader from power. Ben Ali thus became Tunisia's second president.

Under Bourguiba, Tunisian foreign policy tilted heavily toward the West, while domestically the president and his party saw themselves as agents of secular modernization and social development. Consequently, they sought to weaken the power-base of traditional rural and Islamic social forces and institutions by promoting wider access to education and launching some social reforms. Although the state played an important strategic role in economic development, it also left considerable space for private sector development. Politically, Bourguiba saw his ruling party, the Parti Socialiste Destourien (PSD, Socialist Destourian Party), as a corporatist mechanism for mobilizing social support for his regime. Consequently, little space was left for other formally organized political actors, or indeed for meaningful political participation from below.

Ben Ali came to power at a time of growing labor unrest, as well as at a time when an Islamist opposition was emerging. He reformed the PSD as the Rassemblement Constitutionnel Démocratique (RCD, Democratic Constitutional Rally), which seemed to suggest that there was an opening for competitive party politics. In practice, however, Ben Ali did the opposite, strengthening the coercive apparatus of the state, co-opting other groups (including the major trade union, the Union Générale de Travailleurs Tunisiens [UGTT, Tunisian General Labor Union], and clamping down on the moderate Islamist party Ennahda (al-Nahda). Like Bourguiba, he won repeated presidential terms over the following years, garnering as much as 99 percent of the "vote." Similarly, the RCD (like the PSD before it) won large majorities in parliamentary elections that were very far from being free and fair.

Economic policies under Ben Ali continued to be generally liberal in nature, and economic growth was quite impressive in aggregate terms. Growth of gross domestic product (GDP) averaged around 5 percent per year through most of the 1990s and 2000s, and most social indicators showed marked improvement over the decades following independence. Yet there were growing perceptions in the country that with such growth had come increased social inequality. This wasn't entirely true, since according to most indicators, economic inequality in Tunisia actually declined in the 1970s and 1980s, only to rise back almost to earlier levels in the first part of the 1990s and then remain largely unchanged for more than a decade.[1] At the same time, it was certainly the case that many of the primary beneficiaries of economic growth and of the regime's privatization policies were increasingly to be found among the coterie of crony capitalists close to the RCD and President Ben Ali. The president's extended family—especially his sons-in-law and the Trabelsi family of his wife, Leila—were particularly prominent beneficiaries of this. As the US embassy in Tunis noted in a classified cable to Washington in June 2008:

> Although the petty corruption rankles, it is the excesses of President Ben Ali's family that inspire outrage among Tunisians. With Tunisians facing rising inflation and high unemployment, the conspicuous displays of wealth and persistent rumors of corruption have added fuel to the fire. . . . This government has based its legitimacy on its ability to deliver economic growth, but a growing number of Tunisians believe those at the top are keeping the benefits for themselves.[2]

This situation was compounded by the fact that this very conspicuous consumption by the regime's elite was accompanied by widespread speculation that some family members hoped to eventually succeed to the presidency.[3]

In Tunisia and elsewhere, this combination of single-party institutional legacies, facade multipartyism, and patronage-based economic privatization had been pointed to as a major factor in the persistence of authoritarianism.[4] Paradoxically, however, perceptions of economic inequality, corruption, and cronyism, and the absence of meaningful political voice, were central elements of the social discontent that propelled the popular protests of 2011. Clearly, analysts and regimes alike had overestimated the efficacy of neopatrimonialism, or had perhaps failed to anticipate the point at which the benefits of patronage-based elite solidarity would be offset by declining popular legitimacy.

In addition to the historical and structural conditions that preceded the protests, more immediate political actions also had an effect. The initial reaction of the security forces was simply to suppress demonstrations, though this proved difficult in the face of growing numbers of demonstrators. It also antagonized the population and generated a growing sense of crisis.

Ben Ali visited the badly burned Mohamed Bouazizi in hospital a week after the initial incident in an apparent effort to show sympathy for his plight. Bouazizi was later moved to a better hospital, and the police officer involved in the initial confrontation was briefly arrested.

Despite these moves, the protests continued to spread, including to the capital, Tunis. Lawyers, other professional syndicates, trade unions, and civil society groups increasingly mobilized against the government. Once again the president sent mixed signals. On 10 January 2011, he outlined steps to increase employment, but also condemned "acts committed by hooded gangs who attacked public institutions at night, and even citizens in their homes through terrorist acts that cannot be tolerated."[5] A mere three days later, he pledged that security forces would show restraint, and indicated that he would not run for office again when his term expired in 2014. The police themselves received confused, even contradictory, orders—perhaps reflecting differences among their senior officers. Such vacillation projected more weakness than strength, highlighting not the deterrent power of the regime but rather the protesters' ability to win concessions through mass mobilization. As well, Ben Ali's promise to leave power in three years was judged by the protesters as being far too little, far too late.

As the civil uprising grew, senior Tunisian military officers seemed reluctant to employ the sort of force that might (or might not) quell the protests. Lacking support from key military commanders, Ben Ali had little option but to flee the country on 14 January for exile in Saudi Arabia. As would be the case in Egypt, Libya, Bahrain, Syria, and elsewhere, the nature of civil-military relations proved to be of considerable importance in shaping political trajectories in Tunisia.[6]

A caretaker government was quickly formed under Prime Minister Mohamed Ghannouchi, with Fouad Mebazaa (president of the Chamber of Deputies) serving as acting president. But the new cabinet was immediately criticized for its inclusion of RCD members. UGTT ministers resigned their newly appointed cabinet seats and demonstrations continued, forcing the RCD members to quit. Subsequently, Tunisian courts would order that the party itself be dissolved. In March 2011, a new transitional cabinet was announced under Prime Minister Beji Caid Essebsi. Elections were to be held for a Constituent Assembly tasked with both overseeing the executive and revising the Tunisian constitution. New parliamentary and presidential elections would then be held in 2013 under the new constitution.

The transitional process in Tunisia raised a host of new issues. For instance, what should happen to those individuals associated with the old regime? While Ben Ali and his wife were tried in absentia—and sentenced to thirty-five years in prison—others who had been associated with the regime (notably those among the business elite) might well have hoped to preserve or recycle some of their previous power.

There was also the question of what role Islam and Islamists would play in the politics of the new Tunisia. Ennahda founder Rachid Ghanouchi returned from exile, and the party was soon legalized. While Ennahda espouses a moderate Islamism, some leftist and secular Tunisians viewed the rise of Islamist politics with apprehension.[7] This split was to some extent further accentuated by the schism (also present in Morocco and Algeria) between urban francophones, Europhile elites, and the broader Arabic-speaking masses.

Elections to the Constituent Assembly proceeded smoothly in October 2011. Ennahda won by far the largest share of the vote (37 percent) of any party. It soon formed a coalition with the secular-leftist Congrès pour la République (CPR, Congress for the Republic) and the Democratic Forum for Labor and Liberties (Ettakatol), with CPR leader Moncef Marzouki subsequently selected by the Constituent Assembly as president, while Ennahda general secretary Hamadi Jebali was chosen to head the new government as prime minister.

Following the elections, attention turned to writing the new Tunisian constitution—a "critical juncture" of political institutionalization that would shape politics in the country for decades to come. The political process generally continued smoothly, a positive sign for Tunisia's transition to a pluralist, democratic political system. However, some political tensions arose over the boundaries of acceptable public discourse, with hard-line (Salafi) extraparliamentary religious groups seeking to halt what they saw as impious depiction of Islam by secular media and intellectuals—an issue on which Ennahda tried to steer a cautious course between the two sides. Socioeconomic conditions continued to generate grievances. The end of the dictatorship failed to deliver immediate economic improvement—especially in the economically marginalized center and northwest of the country, where periodic protests (and even self-immolations) continued. Despite its uneven benefits, previous Tunisian economic policy had produced positive economic growth and could not be quickly or easily improved upon. Addressing social demands through redistributive policies would present difficult political and fiscal challenges, with the added risk of capital flight if adjustments were made too hastily. In the meantime, the dislocations and uncertainties caused by transition, coupled with the general weakness of the global economy, deterred both investment and tourism.

The regime change in Tunisia soon sparked domino effects across the region. Key in this process were events in Egypt, which is the most populous country in the Arab world. Events there would soon impart even greater momentum to the Arab Spring.

Egypt

Egypt emerged from British colonial rule as a constitutional monarchy with an imperfect but functioning parliament, and problematic but competitive elections. This all came to an end in 1952, when King Farouk was overthrown in a military coup. The Free Officers, led by Gamal Abdul Nasser, were nationalists who condemned the corruption and inequalities of the old order. Despite their rhetoric, however, they also moved to ban other political parties and suppress political opposition.

Through the late 1950s and the 1960s, Egypt positioned itself as a regional champion of Arab nationalism. Domestically, a single political party was established, the Arab Socialist Union (ASU). Suspicious of rival power centers, Nasser never allowed the ASU to articulate popular sentiments in an effective or autonomous way. Instead, the party served the state's efforts to maintain domestic support.

After Nasser's death in 1970, his vice president and fellow army officer Anwar Sadat acceded to power. Sadat had rather different views on Egyptian domestic and foreign policy, leading him to conclude a peace deal with Israel in 1979, reorient Egypt's foreign policy toward Washington, and undertake a degree of economic liberalization. Because he saw the ASU as a potential source of Nasserite opposition to such moves, he broke up the organization and allowed the establishment of a limited multiparty system. Within this new political order, the National Democratic Party (NDP) served by design as the dominant, pro-regime political force. The NDP repeatedly "won" Egyptian elections, benefiting as it did from state patronage, the harassment of rival political forces, and a fair share of electoral fraud. Sadat also allowed the Muslim Brotherhood, repressed under Nasser, to gradually reemerge as a social movement (although not as a legal political party), although still subject to periodic bouts of repression.

Sadat was assassinated by Islamist radicals in 1981, and succeeded by vice president (and former air force commander) Hosni Mubarak. Mubarak continued most of his predecessor's policies, including close ties with the United States and continued economic reform and privatization, much of which benefited a coterie of business leaders close to the regime. Multiparty elections continued, always under conditions that ensured the overwhelming victory of the NDP. Presidential elections were, until 2005, uncontested referendums rather than genuine elections.

The regime had always faced some internal challenges over the years, from sources as varied as radical Islamist violence, periodic labor unrest, and judicial criticism of electoral irregularities. Domestic pressures for a greater political opening grew through the 1990s. The post-9/11 era also contributed to this, with somewhat greater support for reform from the West.

In 2004, the Kefaya (Enough!) protest movement emerged in opposition to Mubarak's rule, although it was rather narrowly based and would soon lose most of its momentum. In November 2005, opposition figures—including Ayman Nour of the Ghad (Tomorrow) party—were permitted to run against Mubarak. With state resources deployed to support the incumbent, and with less than 23 percent of the Egyptian electorate voting in what many regarded as a fixed election with a foregone conclusion, Mubarak won with an alleged 88.6 percent of the vote.[8] Nour, who had been arrested earlier in the year by the regime, was subsequently imprisoned (and later released on grounds of ill health in February 2009).

In November 2005 the regime also held somewhat freer parliamentary elections. The Muslim Brotherhood won most of the races it contested, securing around 88 of the 454 seats in the People's Assembly. Thereafter, the regime and ruling NDP did their best to stymie the Brotherhood's parliamentary delegation while continuing to harass the movement as a whole. The November–December 2010 parliamentary elections saw substantial vote-rigging and other measures to undercut opposition candidates. Some parties boycotted the election together, while the Muslim Brotherhood withdrew in the second round of voting after having only one of its members elected.[9]

The unsteady pace of Egyptian political reform was also accompanied by growing speculation as to who might eventually succeed the ailing Mubarak. Many believed that the president's younger son Gamal, who had risen rapidly within the ranks of the NDP as a self-styled reformer, was being groomed for the position. It also seemed that Mubarak's longtime intelligence chief and member of the army's old guard, Omar Suleiman, might be interested in the job. In any case, it seemed likely that even Hosni Mubarak's death would not lead to substantial democratization, but rather simply to a renewal of the status quo.

As in Tunisia, social and economic grievances were widespread. Although Egypt had achieved a quite respectable rate of economic growth in recent years—with GDP growth averaging 6.7 percent per year from 2006 to 2010, up from 3.5 percent per year in the first half of the decade[10]—unemployment, and especially youth unemployment, was high even among people with middle and higher levels of education, and had been so for some time. Many Egyptian workers were employed in the informal sector, with all of the attendant uncertainties. There were also significant increases in food prices in 2010 and 2011, which added to the general discontent. Although there is little evidence that economic inequality had increased dramatically in recent years, decades of crony capitalism had nonetheless contributed to a widespread public perception that the benefits of economic development were primarily accruing to those elites who were close to the regime.

Although the state took measures to limit civil society, authoritarian Egypt nonetheless featured a wide array of civil organizations. Formal groups were increasingly complemented by informal groups, many of them formed by a younger generation of activists who made use of e-mail, Facebook, Twitter, texting, and other newer communication and information technologies to organize and coordinate. Indicative of this was the campaign that emerged around the death of Khaled Mohamed Said, a young man who was beaten to death by police in Alexandria in June 2010. Mobile phone pictures of his battered corpse soon went viral across Egypt, and a "We are all Khaled Said" Facebook page attracted hundreds of thousands of supporters.

This was the context when the first Arab uprising erupted in Tunisia. Television images of President Ben Ali's fall undoubtedly galvanized the Egyptian opposition, especially given the parallels between the two regimes. On 25 January 2011, activists protested police brutality by organizing demonstrations in Cairo and elsewhere. These grew much larger than anticipated, resulting in thousands of protesters occupying Tahrir (Liberation) Square in the center of the capital. As disturbances spread across the country, Tahrir Square became a rallying point for the opposition—despite regime efforts at intimidation. The protesters were not mobilized by Egypt's established opposition parties, although such parties (including the Muslim Brotherhood) eventually threw their support behind the campaign. Instead, they represented a broad cross-section of society, especially urban youth, who mobilized through informal means and media coverage around the growing evidence that the authoritarian edifice of the Mubarak regime might not be quite as solid as it had long seemed.

At this point, in Egypt as in Tunisia, the role of the army became critical. Though the army was deployed in an effort to maintain public order, it was reluctant to use extensive force against the demonstrators. Instead, it was the police, Central Security Force, State Security Intelligence, and NDP thugs who were the primary tools of repression.

On 1 February Mubarak made a nationally broadcast speech in which he pledged vague political reforms and offered not to run again when his term expired. The next day, bands of government supporters stepped up their attacks against antigovernment demonstrators, and the military increasingly stepped in to separate the two sides. Washington, whose initial position had been uncertain as it watched yet another US ally under pressure, now pressed the Egyptian leader to compromise.

On 10 February Mubarak again addressed the country.[11] Once again, he seemed badly out of touch with the public mood. Despite expectations—and possibly at the urging of his son Gamal—the president refused to step down, but instead agreed to transfer some of his powers to Omar Suleiman, who was hurriedly designated as vice president.[12] Far from stabilizing the situation, the speech instead enraged protesters. The military, which may have believed that it had secured the president's agreement to step down, increasingly felt that Mubarak had become a growing liability who imperiled its own position. Washington too felt that it had been mislead by Mubarak, leading President Barack Obama to immediately call for a "credible, concrete and unequivocal path toward genuine democracy."[13]

The very next day, Suleiman announced that Mubarak was leaving power. He would be replaced by a Supreme Council of the Armed Forces (SCAF), headed by a senior Egyptian military commander, Field Marshal Mohamed Hussein Tantawi, until new elections could be held. With this, Egypt entered a new and uncertain stage.

Among the activist groups, political parties, and ordinary protesters who had united to bring the regime down, the common purpose that was evident in the struggle against authoritarianism soon gave way—quite naturally—to significant political differences. The Muslim Brotherhood emerged as the best-organized political force in the country, and certainly enjoyed considerable support among both the urban and the rural masses. They favored a quick transition, hoping to capitalize on their support and grassroots organization. Other established political parties, by contrast, drew on much less popular support. Many of the young liberal and secular activists who had played such an important role in galvanizing the "25 January Revolution" did not particularly feel at home in the established opposition parties, yet had not yet constructed national political organizations of their own that were capable of effectively competing for electoral power. Often from urban and middle-class backgrounds, they had only weak connections to Egypt's large rural population, or even to the urban poor. Large numbers of independent figures entered into the political fray, establishing political parties or hinting at presidential ambitions. These groups also tended to favor a slower transition, so that they might have time to build their strength. Meanwhile, the remnants of the former NDP and others closely associated with the old regime struggled to preserve their privileges.

The SCAF itself remained something of an enigma, with little information available on its internal processes. Clearly, however, it sought to simultaneously stabilize Egypt, shape the transitional process to its advantage, and protect the current and future status and privileges of the military. In doing so, it often had recourse to authoritarian measures, or adopted the timeworn approach of labeling its critics agents of foreign powers. It hinted at setting down supraconstitutional principles that would constrain any future constitution and government,[14] but later backed off the idea. At times it seemed to ally with liberals against the Islamists, and at other times with the Muslim Brotherhood against the liberals.

In turn, all of this took place against a backdrop of political disorder and the risk arising from the mounting unmet social expectations. In the absence of any institutionalized political process, much of politics continued to be played out in the form of street protests. As a result of public pressure, the NDP was dissolved by judicial order. In August 2011, Mubarak himself, together with his two sons, was placed on trial.

In March 2011 the SCAF held a referendum on a number of limited constitutional amendments. These would make it easier to nominate presidential candidates, revise eligibility criteria, limit the president's ability to declare a state of emergency, establish limits on presidential terms, and mandate an elected parliament to appoint a constituent committee to draft a new Egyptian constitution. The referendum passed overwhelmingly. Between November 2011 and February 2012, elections were then held for the lower (People's Assembly) and upper (Shura Council) houses of the Egyptian parliament. The Muslim Brotherhood's newly formed political party, the Freedom and Justice Party (FJP), did well, winning 213 of 508 seats in the People's Assembly. The more religiously conservative and fundamentalist (Salafist) al-Nour party also did well, winning 107 seats. Islamists thus composed about 70 percent of the new parliament.

When parliament subsequently appointed a constitutional committee to revise the constitution, critics complained that over half of those selected were Islamists. Secular liberals and Coptic Christians threatened to boycott the committee, which was also subjected to court challenges. Adding to the confusion, the Supreme Constitutional Court issued a ruling on June 14 dissolving the new parliament altogether, on the grounds that the electoral law had wrongly allowed members of political parties to run as independents. The SCAF also moved to limit the powers of any new president.

Presidential elections were to be held in May–June 2012. Several candidates—including Omar Suleiman and initial FJP candidate Khairat el-Shater—were disqualified. The first round saw support split quite widely among the leading candidates, with none winning more than one-quarter of the vote. This set the stage for a run-off election pitting former Mubarak prime minister Ahmed Shafik against FJP candidate Mohamed Morsi. Morsi secured a narrow victory, winning 51.7 percent of the vote, and was sworn in on June 30. He immediately found himself in a continuing political and legal tangle with the military, the courts, and other political forces.

The transitional process in post-Mubarak Egypt has thus been confused, unclear, and at times chaotic. However, it has also created new opportunities for participatory politics—although, with electoral turnout quite low (40–50%), many Egyptians have not availed themselves of these new openings. The military has certainly protected many of its privileges, but at the cost of growing unpopularity. The Muslim Brotherhood has shown both political adaptability (variously aligning itself with or against the SCAF, liberals, and Salafists as conditions dictate) and an ability to mobilize substantial popular support—although at some point too much political maneuvering could damage its political credibility. The establishment of a stable constitutional and political process may take years, especially if characterized by an ongoing power struggle between Islamists, liberals, the military, and the judiciary.

In addition, as in Tunisia, a weak global economy, the disruptions associated with the overthrow of the old regime, and continued political uncertainty have all had negative effects on business and investment even as citizens' demands for improvements in their daily lives are increasing. If anything, these problems are greater in Egypt, given the structural problems of both its economy and its bureaucracy. Regardless of their political complexion, therefore, future Egyptian governments are likely to face serious social and economic challenges for some time to come.

Libya

It is has never been fashionable in political science to offer interpretations of national politics that hinge upon the personality of a single leader. In the Libyan case, however, it is impossible to separate four decades of Libyan politics from the rule of Muammar Qaddafi, who first seized power in a military coup in 1969. Nominally, Qaddafi's Libya was a self-proclaimed "state of the masses" *(jamahiriya)* in which a pyramidal system of "people's congresses" provided an almost Athenian model of direct democracy. In practice, real power lay with the security services, the bureaucratic administration, and most especially with Qaddafi himself (together with his family and inner circle). Political parties were prohibited. While some nongovernmental organizations (NGOs) were allowed, their numbers were strictly limited and they were unable to effectively question, let alone challenge, regime policy. At times, various "revolutionary committees" appeared to play an active role in attempting to mobilize support for the regime, while at other times their role was unclear, even marginal.

Not only was Qaddafi central to this system, but his own behavior was subject to rapid changes as he variously embraced and abandoned issues in what one scholar characterized as "neo-Tarzanism."[15] Libyan politics and administration were dependent on the whims of the country's peculiar dictator and his apparent aversion to strong and permanent institutions.

Yet despite this, the system endured. There was some opposition, certainly. In the 1970s and 1980s, there were rumors of various coup plots, which were invariably followed by arrests and purges. The late 1980s and

1990s saw the rise of an Islamist opposition, including armed groups (of which the Libyan Islamic Fighting Group [LIFG] was the largest). The Libyan leader took few chances, however, especially given the bloody civil war between the government and Islamist opposition in neighboring Algeria. The LIFG was effectively suppressed, and its imprisoned members were "convinced" (through both coercion and selective inducements) to abandon violence.[16] Who might succeed the "Great Leader" and "King of Kings" was unclear, although many believed that his second eldest son, Saif al-Islam, was positioning himself to do so, adopting the mantle of a Western-educated reformer.

Libya's oil wealth—accounting for around 95 percent of export earnings and 25 percent of GDP, and providing for 60 percent of government wages—undoubtedly played a role in sustaining the Qaddafi dictatorship. It certainly helped to bring about substantial improvement in Libyan living conditions. In 2009 it was estimated that Libya had a GDP per capita of $13,400 (adjusted for purchasing power parity), by far the highest in Africa.[17] According to the United Nations, Libya also has the highest Human Development Index rating (0.755) of any country in Africa and the fifth highest in the Arab world (behind the United Arab Emirates, Qatar, Bahrain, and Kuwait, but ahead of Saudi Arabia).[18]

Oil wealth also fueled extensive Libyan military purchases, often well beyond what the regime was able to effectively use. The general standard of much of the Libyan military remained poor, however, as evidenced by its defeat in Chad in 1987. Some loyalist units (notably the 32nd Brigade, commanded by Qaddafi's youngest son, Khamis) were of higher quality, having been organized, equipped, and financed to act as the regime's praetorian guard.[19]

Oil wealth also financed political patronage. But benefits from this were often unevenly distributed within the country, with more resources being lavished on the capital, Tripoli, and on Qaddafi's home area, around Sirte, than on the eastern region of Cyrenaica. Unemployment, especially youth unemployment, was high, and there were frequent complaints about government corruption.

The Libyan uprising that erupted in February 2011 was fundamentally rooted in socioeconomic and political dissatisfaction, but was also clearly inspired by events in Tunisia and Egypt. Initially, the regime responded to demonstrations by announcing a $24 billion fund for housing and development, hoping to blunt discontent. In mid-February, protests in the east culminated in the regime losing control over the city of Benghazi and other towns. On 27 February, rebels announced the formation of a National Transitional Council (NTC), headed by Mustafa Abdul Jalil, which had as its aim the overthrow of the Qaddafi regime. Qaddafi responded with rambling speeches that condemned the protesters as drug addicts and stooges of al-Qaeda.

The Libyan dictator also struck back hard, unleashing loyal military units against rebel-held areas. By mid-March, regime forces had reached the very gates of Benghazi. In response, on 17 March the United Nations Security Council (with the support of the Arab League) approved Resolution 1973, authorizing "all necessary measures . . . to protect civilians and civilian populated areas under threat of attack."[20] Two days later, the North Atlantic Treaty Organization (NATO) began naval and aerial strikes against Qaddafi's forces.

Unlike in Tunisia and Egypt, where civilian protests and the unwillingness of the military to engage in widespread repression ultimately forced Ben Ali and Mubarak from power, Libya saw a much more violent response by the regime and a descent into civil war. While some military units collapsed or allied with the rebels, others (notably those commanded by Qaddafi's own family and close associates) remained loyal, once again highlighting the importance of military institutions and loyalties in the Arab Spring. NATO intervention certainly prevented the regime from overrunning Benghazi in March, but was unable to deliver a quick military victory for the opposition.

The rebels themselves demonstrated high morale, but had limited military expertise and competence. Despite popular expressions of national unity, the NTC itself was beset by tensions: political infighting, regional divisions, potential tribal or ethnic differences, and disagreements between civilian leaders and rebel combatants, as well as between longtime opposition activists and former Qaddafi aides. The idiosyncratic and dictatorial nature of the Qaddafi regime and the weaknesses of long-repressed Libyan civil society also meant that the rebels inherited few organizational resources upon which to build alternative state structures.

Events in Libya were also bound to have broader ramifications. Qaddafi's response to popular protests showed that some Arab leaders were willing to use widespread violence to preserve their positions, a pattern that would also be seen in Bahrain and Syria. Conversely, international sanctions and intervention highlighted the possible costs of repression. The willingness of so many ordinary Libyans to confront their brutal and dictatorial regime may have encouraged others to do so too, notably in Syria. Finally, it seemed likely that the civil war itself would have prolonged, long-term implications for Libya's political development, regardless of its ultimate outcome. On the one hand, it energized a sense of national purpose among many Libyans. Yet as wars inevitably do, it also brutalized and polarized the population. The proliferation of small arms and light weapons (most looted from Qaddafi's extensive arsenals) also had broader implications, making it easier for radical groups across the region to acquire weapons.

Postdictatorship Tunisia (and ordinary Tunisians) offered a significant degree of quiet humanitarian support to the Libyan rebels, although they could ill afford to be drawn into a direct confrontation with their unpredictable neighbor. Qatar offered military and relief supplies and joined the NATO contingent, conducting air strikes against Qaddafi's forces. Egypt, on the other hand, demonstrated little concern—despite being a leading regional power, it was far too absorbed by its own difficult political transition. Algeria was even more circumspect. Its regime worried about the consequences of a civil war on its borders, and was also anxious to avoid the sort of domestic challenges that other North African regimes had experienced.

In late August 2011 the rebels captured Tripoli. While the regime fought on in a few places for two more months, Qaddafi was ultimately killed by rebel fighters in Sirte on 20 October. The symbolism of a powerful dictator ending his days hiding in a drain was hardly lost in the region: in Syria that very evening, anti-regime protesters congratulated the Libyan people, clearly insinuating that they hoped their own leader might be next.

With the end of the civil war, an interim cabinet was established by the NTC in November 2011, with Abdurrahim Abdulhafiz el-Keib serving as prime minister. However, the new government continued to be plagued by poor administrative performance (in part a legacy of weak institutions under Qaddafi) as well as a proliferation of heavily armed local militias not under government control (a legacy of the civil war). Various tribal, regional, ideological, and personal tensions also continued to afflict post-Qaddafi politics. Periodically, these disputes erupted into localized violence. Some activists in the eastern part of the country called for the establishment of a federal political system.

Nonetheless, despite these difficulties, national elections were successfully held in July 2012 for a 200-member General Congress. This would act as an interim parliament, appointing a new cabinet and prime minister. Later, a constituent assembly is to be formed to draw up a new Libyan constitution.

Algeria

It is difficult to understand the postcolonial history of Algeria without examining the unique colonial trajectory of the country. Unlike Morocco and Tunisia, which faced relatively softer forms of colonial domination, the French ruled Algeria in a direct fashion, which involved the marginalization of traditional tribal forms of social organization, forced displacements of the native population, as well as the destruction of local precolonial economic institutions. While some scholars estimate the number of casualties due to colonialism in Morocco and Tunisia as numbering in the tens of thousands and a few hundred, respectively, the colonial subjugation of Algeria claimed hundreds of thousands of lives. The length of the colonial presence in Algeria, which lasted more than 135 years, is also unique among Arab countries.

Following the independence of the country in 1967, the Front de Libération Nationale (FLN, National Liberation Front) imposed itself as the sole political force in the country. That regime, shaped by the bloody liberation struggle, settled into decades of populist authoritarian rule. From 1967 to the late 1980s, the military establishment of the newly independent state worked to eliminate the opposition while adopting a strong socialist and pan-Arabist agenda. As in Libya, oil and gas revenues buttressed the Algerian state, at least until weaker oil prices, pressure from the street, and growing external debt propelled the country into economic crisis in the 1980s. The FLN's failed efforts to deal with the crisis through economic structural adjustment and a degree of political opening plunged the country into a more widespread crisis that saw the Algerian military and FLN old guard abort parliamentary elections in 1992. This triggered a vicious civil war with the Islamist opposition that left over 100,000 Algerians dead.

While the conflict gradually abated by the end of the decade, contemporary Algeria is very much a hybrid regime in which a degree of electoral participation and relatively open civil society coexist with what remains a nondemocratic regime controlled by a powerful political elite. In this latter respect at least, Algerian domestic politics bore some similarities to those of Egypt under Mubarak. Yet throughout 2011, the country seemed less affected by the Arab Spring than was most of North Africa. Why?

One answer may have to do with the decentralized nature of the political leadership of the country. That is, while political power in Egypt was mostly concentrated in the hands of Mubarak, power holders in Algeria comprise an unknown number of high-ranking military and security officials (often known as *le pouvoir,* or "the power") whose identity and murky relationship to each other and to the presidency are far from clear.[21] Heavily embedded in the country's economic structure, these officials participate in business and politics and engage in complex games of influence against each other. The complexity of the Algerian "deep state" makes the identification of the real power holders difficult, while also diluting the personal responsibility of the numerous members of the security apparatus. The opacity of the state is particularly beneficial to President Abdelaziz Bouteflika, who has been able to avoid criticism by distancing himself from the establishment and cultivating close relationships with local NGOs.[22] It is also beneficial to the wide network of local leaders (provincial governors and city mayors) who conveniently blame mysterious conspirators for the popular riots that have occurred regularly in the country since the end of the civil war.[23] However, despite the divisions between the different elements of the security apparatus, all members have a shared interest in the long-term survival of the regime. Thus, when confronted by existential challenges such as the Islamist terrorist wave of the 1990s, officials have been able to successfully overcome their differences and work together to guarantee the continuation of the regime. Under President Bouteflika in particular, the general strategic orientations of the country have been the result of a delicate consensual exercise designed specifically not to disturb the power dynamics among the various members of the security elite.

Promises of constitutional reform and the prompt lifting of the emergency law that had been in effect since 1992 also helped the regime navigate the first difficult months of the Arab Spring. Yet it is important to note that these gestures would not have succeeded in muting popular resentment without the crucial relief brought by oil and gas revenues since the early 2000s. Under President Bouteflika, the government took advantage of the high price of energy commodities and engaged in massive rent distribution through the building of social housing, the granting of generous loans for local investors, and the massive subsidization of staple products, all of which helped contain social pressure coming from the poorest segments of the population. Oil and gas revenues also meant that at least part of the population was finally enjoying the fruits of the economic recovery and therefore was unwilling to support protests that might renew instability in the country. Finally, the brutal civil war of the 1990s may also explain the reluctance of the population to engage in potentially destabilizing acts. That conflict had a profound impact on a society still deeply traumatized by its brutal violence.

At the same time, however, there is a deep feeling of social malaise that continues to linger among large parts of the Algerian population, and that is regularly expressed through violent riots, communal conflicts, and an overall increase in popular religiosity.[24] This underlines the fact that the situation in the country remains fragile, particularly as the government may not be able to sustain the massive (and often shortsighted) state investments upon which it relies so heavily to buy social peace. Indeed, despite the considerable revenues of their state, Algerians continue to share the same grievances related to poor economic performance, inequalities, and lack of political opening expressed elsewhere in the region, and are moreover increasingly dissatisfied with the undisputed hegemony of age-old FLN figures who have dominated the politics of the country since its independence. In 2010 alone the regime faced more than a thousand instances of popular protest (such as strikes, riots, and blockades) across the country.[25]

The generalized disillusionment with the regime has meant growing disaffection with the electoral process, which has caused electoral participation rates to decrease from 59 percent of eligible voters in 1991 to 36 percent in 2007.[26] This spectacular drop illustrates the widening divide between the general populace and political representatives, who are perceived as a simple extension of the regime's patrimonial networks. Using their organization as a venue for access to state resources, subservient and often corrupt party leaders are increasingly removed from the population and remain unable to translate street grievances into political leverage. Parliamentary elections in May 2012 again generated much more skepticism than popular enthusiasm.

In some respects, the future of Algeria is dependent on the ability of the regime to maintain elite cohesion while using petroleum rents to diminish political discontent. However, even the latter may not diminish the widespread feeling of relative deprivation shared by large parts of the population vis-à-vis Europe and other oil countries (in terms of standard of living) and vis-à-vis neighboring Morocco and Tunisia (in terms of the political change there). If Tunisia continues its relatively smooth transition to more democratic politics, increasing numbers of Algerians may question why they too should not enjoy a more accountable political system.

Morocco

In many ways, Morocco's postcolonial history can be seen as the history of its long-lasting monarchy. The three kings who have ruled the country since its independence in 1956 have all had a profound impact on the country's political trajectory.

Following Morocco's independence, King Mohammed V consolidated his rule by initiating three governance strategies that were later refined by his successors. First, the king relied heavily on rural notables, Sufi leaders, and a wide circle of French-trained military leaders to weaken the bourgeois leaders of the nationalist Istiqlal party, thereby strengthening the centrality of the palace. Second, the monarch portrayed himself as the guarantor of traditional values, by emphasizing his links with the rural notables and by using a sophisticated set of religious and symbolic ceremonies to transform his originally mostly symbolic status into a politically concrete one. Finally, the monarch took advantage of his close relationship with the French authorities to undermine the opposition.[27]

After the sudden death of Mohammed V in 1961, King Hassan II refined the set of strategies initiated by his late father. Throughout his thirty-nine years of rule, Hassan II used a sophisticated mix of repression, nationalist discourse, religious legitimization, and parliamentary maneuvering to tame the army, marginalize the opposition, and consolidate the domination of the palace. As discussed in Chapter 8, he was able to strengthen his position by encouraging the fragmentation of the political scene into numerous competing parties and by bolstering his role as an arbitrator above those political divisions. While the king continued to benefit from the tensions between rural notables and the members of the Istiqlal party originally encouraged by his father, he also exploited the rivalries between the nationalists and the socialists and, from the late 1990s, between both groups and the emerging Islamists. Although heavily rigged, regular elections also allowed the king to maintain his preeminent position by offering loyal elites an avenue to access state rents. At the same time, loyalist parties within parliament created by close associates of the king helped the palace to weaken the opposition by virtue of the institutionalization of a complex system of patronage through which government positions and official licenses were granted to regime supporters in exchange for their loyalty.

As noted, a final element crucial to the success of Hassan II's rule was repression. Thus his regime physically eliminated a number of political figures, carried out widespread torture of leftist activists in the 1960s and 1970s, and bloodily repressed popular riots in Casablanca (1965 and 1981), Nador (1984), and Fez (1990). Although the level of repression diminished once the socialists were tamed by the mid-1990s, the regime continued to resort to physical repression, particularly against the emerging Islamist activists.

Yet despite its longevity, the survival of the monarchy under Hassan II was also a question of luck. The king narrowly escaped two coup attempts in the early 1970s: the first time by hiding in a room while a number of cadets led by one of his close associates attacked his palace and killed dozens of guests, and the second time by tricking his attackers into thinking he was dead when his plane was shot at by dissident air force jets.

By the time his rule came to an end in the late 1990s, Hassan II had been able to tame the opposition almost completely. Thus, with the nationalists of the Istiqlal party and the socialists of the Union Socialiste des Forces Populaires (USFP, Social Union of Popular Forces) comfortably embedded in a complex patronage system, and with Morocco's main Islamist party, the Parti de la Justice et du Développement (PJD, Justice and Development Party), under control, Mohammed VI's accession to power occurred under very favorable circumstances.

Upon becoming king, Mohammed VI initiated a number of significant reforms that immediately bolstered his popularity. These included the adoption of a new family code—despite the opposition of various Islamist groups—that reinforced women's rights, severely constrained polygamy, and raised the legal age for marriage. The king also put in place a commission for equity and reconciliation that was aimed at compensating those who had been tortured under his father's rule, a move that sought to mark his break with the repressive legacy of the previous regime. And thanks in part to continued support from friendly Gulf monarchies, the king initiated an ambitious program of investments in public infrastructure and public housing, which boosted his popularity among the poorest segments of society.

Many of the reforms introduced by the new monarch came to an abrupt end when the country experienced its first suicide terrorist attacks in 2003. The regime began using torture when questioning suspected Islamist militants, and also limited freedom of the press and jailed a number of prominent independent journalists. With virtually no checks on his powers, the king's position became even more hegemonic. By the late 2000s, not only was the palace the heart of the country's political system, but also the king and his inner circle of family and friends were Morocco's most important economic actors.

In the latter half of 2011, however, the absolute power of the king was challenged when local activists who shared many of the grievances expressed elsewhere in the Arab world emulated the strategies used in neighboring countries and initiated a series of regular protests at a level unseen since the accession of the new king to the throne. Aided by the use of social networking tools, many Moroccan prodemocracy activists coalesced around the February 20 Movement in calling for more economic justice and political accountability. Mohammed VI responded to these demands by offering reforms, of which amendments to the constitution were the most significant. Those amendments, which were later endorsed by more than 98 percent of the voters in a referendum, introduced a number of changes. They strengthened the powers of the legislature while taking some steps to insulate the judicial branch from the executive. The prime minister was now to be selected from the party with the most seats in parliament, although the king retained the ability to veto decisions taken by the government. The constitution also reaffirmed the country's commitment to human rights and gender equality and the prohibition of torture. Finally, the king acquiesced to longtime demands from Berber groups by recognizing Amazigh as an official national language.[28]

Yet despite popular support for the king's reforms, the constitutional reforms brought only limited changes. The king retained authority over the country's most important institutions and the ability to dismiss the government (although no longer the prime minister) at will. Perhaps more important, the new constitution did not offer any mechanism to increase the accountability of the king's entourage, whose hegemonic position in the domestic economy is increasingly resented.

In response to regional unrest, Morocco moved elections forward to November 2011. The PJD made major gains, winning 107 of 395 seats and emerging as the largest party in parliament. In keeping with the recent constitutional changes, PJD leader Abdelilah Benkirane was appointed as prime minister of a coalition government. At the same time, other political figures were appointed as advisers to the palace, creating a shadow cabinet of sorts intended to manage relations with the elected government.

As elsewhere in the region, socioeconomic grievances are widespread and substantial. High urban unemployment, widespread perceptions of widening levels of inequality,[29] underdevelopment of the rural sector (which employs 40 percent of the population[30] and is highly dependent on uncertain rainfall), and increasing resentment over cronyism have led many to call for a better distribution of resources. Although Mohammed VI continues to portray himself as the "king of the poor" by personally distributing meals for the needy during the month of Ramadan or by investing heavily in symbolic projects such as public housing, it is increasingly difficult for him to justify his associates' spectacular wealth accumulation and apparent sense of entitlement.

In his responses to the uprisings of 2011, the king seems to have avoided the difficult decisions that would force him to confront the endemic corruption in Morocco and to prosecute local cronies. Moreover, the palace appears to have chosen constitutional maneuvering as a way to delegitimize the opposition and to avoid making significant political concessions and changes. Taken together, these failings represent a challenge to the king's legitimacy and moral authority, since they risk undermining his own personal popularity, which is still very high among the vast majority of Moroccans. If the tensions are not addressed, the continuation of the monarchy may perhaps be less certain than first appearances otherwise suggest.[31]

Conclusion

In both Tunisia and Egypt, long-standing hybrid regimes that had appeared quite stable were overthrown by the rapid mobilization of protests in early 2011. In both cases, economic grievances were a major component of the protests, even though neither economic performance nor income inequality had substantially worsened in recent years. But in both cases, issues of social equity were perceived through a public prism that had been heavily influenced by dissatisfaction with elite corruption, crony capitalism, and unresponsive public institutions.

In both countries, issues of legitimacy were also at the center of the political discourse. And in the face of protesters insisting on regime change, neither Zine el-Abidine Ben Ali nor Hosni Mubarak was able to frame an adequate defense of their right to rule. Both leaders seemed badly out of step with the demands and sentiments of their publics. In both countries, the trappings of multipartyism and elections were clearly an authoritarian sham. Both leaders sought to blame the protests on outside influences, and to justify the status quo by invoking the dangers of chaos. In neither case was this "après moi, le deluge" approach successful, however. Finally, both leaders showed poor rhetorical skills and political instincts at the very juncture when they most needed those things.[32]

Significantly, Islamist movements did not take the initial lead in the protests in either Egypt or Tunisia, a fact that might have made the protesters appear to be less threatening to the military (and thus to have persuaded the military to not stop the protests with force). In both countries, patterns of civil-military relations were of critical importance; concretely, this meant that neither the Tunisian nor the Egyptian army was willing to give up its mantle of national institution by undertaking its own version of "Tiananmen Square" and thus being forever tarred as an agent of mass repression. Instead, when the status quo became untenable, in each case the army preferred to protect its own interests by ushering the president from power.

In terms of understanding the relationship between events in the two countries and across North Africa, the similarities between Tunisia and Egypt made it more likely that the dramatic events in the former would have a demonstration effect in the latter. In turn, Egypt's size and importance virtually guaranteed that as the protesters held their ground in Tahrir Square and ultimately forced Mubarak from power, the repercussions would be amplified regionwide.

The cases of Libya, Algeria, and Morocco all underscore the particular importance of institutional settings and historical legacies. In Libya, the uprising and subsequent civil war were deeply shaped by the nature of Qaddafi's erratic personalistic regime, the particular patterns of patronage used to sustain it, the configuration of the security establishment, as well as underlying tribal, regional, and other social factors. These factors, and the legacies of the war itself, continue to shape the sometimes chaotic and uncertain transitional process. In Algeria, particular aspects of the regime may have diffused political responsibility, while the memory of that country's bloody civil war may act as a continued deterrent to protest. In Morocco, King Mohammed VI continues to use a degree of reformism to attenuate opposition, but his continued reliance on a close network of confidantes, associates, and palace cronies undermines his efforts.

Just as the birth of the Arab Spring in North Africa had dramatic effects across the Arab world, so too might its subsequent evolution. Networks of activists of various sorts continue to learn from each other's experiences—as do regional dictators. Islamists have been buoyed by the success of Islamist parties in North African elections, while their opponents have cited those same successes as a growing peril. Successful democratic transition in Tunisia—by far the most successful transitional process to yet emerge from the Arab Spring—could have positive demonstration effects, especially if it highlights the compatibility of a moderate, pluralist Islamism and democratic politics. Smooth and successful transition in Egypt could have an even greater effect in increasing pressures for reform elsewhere. On the other hand, difficult transitions in (possibly) Egypt and (probably) Libya would undoubtedly be cited by authoritarian leaders as evidence of the dangers of pursuing too much change too fast. Whatever the case, the events of 2010–2012 have clearly ushered in an era of much more fluid and dynamic politics across North Africa.

Notes

1. Branko Milanovic, "Inequality and Its Discontents: Why So Many Feel Left Behind," *Foreign Affairs*, 12 August 2011, http://www.foreignaffairs.com/articles /68031/branko-milanovic/inequality-and-its-discontents.

2. "Corruption in Tunisia: What's Yours Is Mine," Embassy Tunis to State Department, Washington, DC, SECRET TUNIS 000679, 23 June 2008, http://wikileaks.org/cable/2008/06/08TUNIS679.html. For a detailed account of the lavish lifestyle of the president's in-laws and extended family, see "Tunisia: Dinner with Sakher El Materi," Embassy Tunis to State Department, Washington, DC, SECRET TUNIS 000516, 27 July 2009, http://wikileaks.org/cable/2009/07/09TUNIS516.html.

3. Larbi Sadiki, "Bin Ali Baba Tunisia's Last Bey?" *Al Jazeera English*, 27 September 2010, http://english.aljazeera.net/indepth/opinion/2010/09/20109238338660692 .html.

4. See, for example, Stephen King, *The New Authoritarianism in the Middle East and North Africa* (Bloomington: Indiana University Press, 2009), pp. 169–182.

5. For a video of Ben Ali's speech, see http://www.youtube com/watch?v=BB8JR2l89U8.

6. For some preliminary discussion of this, see Zoltan Barany, "The Role of the Military," *Journal of Democracy* 22, 4 (October 2011).

7. One poll showed that for 76 percent of Tunisians, the secularism of a future Tunisian political system was important to them. However, respondents were split on the question of what that system should look like, with 54 percent favoring secularism and 40 percent opposing it. International Republican Institute, Survey of Tunisian Public Opinion, 14–27 May 2011, http://www.iri.org/sites/default/files/flip_docs/Tunisia %202011/HTML/index.html#/1/zoomed.

8. Jeremy M. Sharp, Egypt: 2005 Presidential and Parliamentary Elections, Congressional Research Service, 21 September 2005, http://fpc.state.gov/ documents/organization/54274.pdf.

9. "Egypt Election Routs Popular Muslim Brotherhood from Parliament," *Christian Science Monitor*, 1 December 2010, http://www.csmonitor.com/World/Middle-East/2010/1201/Egypt-election-routs-popular-Muslim-Brotherhood-from-parliament.

10. World Bank data, from http://data.worldbank.org.

11. Video and translated text of speech on *Al Jazeera English*, 10 February 2011, http://english.aljazeera.net/video/middleeast/2011/02/2011210234022306527.html.

12. "Gamal Mubarak Behind Leader's Surprise Attempt to Retain Power," *The Australian* (from Associated Press), 13 February 2011, http://www.theaustralian.com.au

/news/world/gamal-mubarak-behind-leaders-surprise-attempt-to-retain-power/story-e6frg6so-1226005194176. See also, "Alaa, Gamal Mubarak Argued During Dad's Final Speech," Al Arabiya News, 14 February 2011, http://www.alarabiya.net/articles/2011/02/13/137490.html.

13. Barak Obama, "Statement of President Barack Obama on Egypt," White House, Washington, DC, 10 February 2011, http://www.whitehouse.gov/the-press-office/2011/02/10/statement-president-barack-obama-egypt.

14. Omar Ashour, "Mubarak's Last Laugh," *Project Syndicate*, 5 August 2011, http://www.project-syndicate.org/commentary/ashour5/English.

15. Abdul-Qader Shareef, "Neo-Tarzanism: Gaddafi's Legendary Petulance," Khaleej Times, 10 December 2006, http://www.khaleejtimes.com/DisplayArticleNew.asp?col=&section=opinion&xfile=data/opinion/2006/December/opinion_December32.xml.

16. Omar Ashour, "De-Radicalizing Jihadists the Libyan Way," *Sada* (Carnegie Endowment for International Peace), 7 April 2010, http://www.carnegieendowment.org/sada/2010/04/07/de-radicalizing-jihadists-libyan-way/6bak.

17. "Libya," *CIA World Factbook*, https://www.cia.gov/library/publications/the-world-factbook/geos/ly.html.

18. United Nations Development Programme, *Human Development Report 2010* (New York, 2010), p. 142, http://hdr.undp.org/en/media/HDR_2010_EN_Tables_reprint.pdf. Since statistics are reported by national authorities, however, it may be that Libya was exaggerating some of its improvements in health and education.

19. "Saif al-Islam's Staff Reaches Out on Pol-Mil Issues," Embassy Tripoli to State Department, Washington, DC, SECRET TRIPOLI 000960, 14 December 2009, http://www.wikileaks.ch/cable/2009/12/09TRIPOLI960.html.

20. United Nations Security Council, Resolution 1973, adopted by the Security Council at its 6,498th meeting, 17 March 2011, http://daccess-dds-ny.un.org/doc/UNDOC/GEN/N11/268/39/PDF/N1126839.pdf?OpenElement.

21. Jon Marks, "Nationalist Policy-Making and Crony Capitalism in the Maghreb: The Old Economics Hinders the New," *International Affairs* 85, 5 (2009), p. 961.

22. Thierry Desrues and Miguel Hernando de Larramendi, "S'Opposer au Maghreb," in Thierry Desrues and Miguel Hernando de Larramendi, eds., *L'Année du Maghreb 2009* (Paris: CNRS Éditions, 2009), p. 22.

23. Chérif Bennadji, "Révision de la Constitution: Vers une Présidence à Vie," in Desrues and de Larramendi, *L'Année du Maghreb 2009*, p. 231.

24. Ibid.

25. Abed Charef, "Algeria: Revolutionary Factors and Their Limitations," *Al Jazeera*, 17 August 2011, http://www.aljazeera.net/NR/exeres/DA2C6503-4342-48DE-A245-440F8D785F9F.htm.

26. Louisa Dris-Ait Hamadouche, "L'Abstention en Algérie: Un Autre Mode de Contestation," in Desrues and de Larramendi, *L'Année du Maghreb 2009*, p. 272.

27. Pierre Vermeren, *Histoire du Maroc Depuis l'Indépendance* (Paris: La Découverte, 2002), p. 26.

28. Driss Bennani, Mohammed Boudarham, and Fahd Iraqi, "Nouvelle Constitution, Plus Roi que Jamais," *Telquel Online*, 2 August 2011, http://www.telquel-online.com/479/couverture_479.shtml.

29. "Distribution of Family Income: Gini Index," *CIA World Factbook*, https://www.cia.gov/library/publications/the-world-factbook/fields/2172.html.

30. Economist Intelligence Unit, Country Report: Morocco 2011, http://www.eiu.com/report_dl.asp?issue id=588308243&mode=pdf.

31. Merouan Mekouar, "The Last Moroccan King?" *Open Democracy*, 8 August

2011, http://www.opendemocracy.net/merouan-mekouar/last-moroccan-king.

32. Hamit Bozarslan "Réfléxions sur les Configurations Révolutionnaire Égypti-enne et Tunisienne," Mouvements, 17 August 2011, http://www.mouvements.info/Reflexions-sur-les-configurations.html.

3

The Mashreq:
Iraq, Jordan,
Lebanon, Palestine, Syria

Historically considered as the heartland of ideological and political developments in the Arab world, the Mashreq has been partially eclipsed by the developments in North Africa that triggered the 2011 uprisings.[1] Had it not been for the eruption of protest in Syria and the decision of the Assad regime to use heavy-handed repression against demonstrators, there would have been relatively little to discuss in terms of the impact of the uprisings in a region of the Arab world still convulsed by ongoing unresolved conflicts and security issues, including continued Israeli occupation of Palestinian territories, the aftereffects of the 2003 US invasion of Iraq, and the endemic crisis of governance in Lebanon.

Although the Mashreq countries share a number of structural similarities with North Africa and the Gulf region, including young populations and high levels of unemployment, there are important differences between them as well. With the exception of Iraq and Syria, most Mashreq countries are not oil producers. Unlike North Africa, there is a much higher degree of societal heterogeneity in the Mashreq. Lebanon is divided along sectarian lines; religion and ethnicity have taken on increasing significance as political markers in Iraq, Syria, and Jordan. In the West Bank and Gaza, the division between secular and religious Palestinians has been instrumentalized for political purposes. The region stands out when it comes to the entanglement of domestic and international dimensions, particularly the extent to which debates over political reform have become wrapped up with not only regime but also state and regional security.

That Mashreq countries sit somewhere between North Africa and the Gulf is reflected in the manner in which they were affected (or not) by the 2011 uprisings. As its regime attempts to maintain itself in power, Syria has gone the way of Libya and Yemen. Unlike Libya, however, in Syria violence has not elicited foreign military intervention. Jordan might be compared to Morocco in terms of the monarchy's ability to maneuver around demands for reform and preempt violence. The ripples of the 2011 uprisings seem to have bypassed Lebanon, Iraq, and the Palestinian Authority, but this is mostly due to the fact that these societies are in the grips of serious and already extremely destabilizing problems of their own.

Violent Uprisings: Syria

To the casual observer of the 2011 uprisings, Syria, one of the Arab world's most repressive police states, could have seemed an unlikely candidate to follow in the footsteps of either Tunisia or Egypt. But when trouble erupted in the southern city of Daraa on 19 March 2011, it started a downward spiral into violence. And although President Bashar al-Assad tried to stay ahead of the revolts sweeping neighboring countries by offering a string of concessions,[2] these were not enough to stem the tide of protests that spread to Latakia, engulfed the cities of Homs and Hama, and even triggered fighting in the capital, Damascus, the bastion of the regime. Initially, President Assad blamed the events on foreign conspirators, claiming "satellite television and propaganda had incited demonstrators." Then Assad added that the chaos in Syria had an Israeli agenda.[3] By mid-April, as violence escalated across the country, Assad conceded that reform was needed and brought forty-eight years of emergency law to an end. This was too little too late, as more than 5,000 antigovernment protesters took over the main square of Homs, Syria's third largest city, vowing to stay until their demands for change were met. While human rights organizations and activists reported an increasing human toll, hundreds of Baath party members resigned in protest against the bloody crackdown that followed.[4] By mid-May, several Western states had passed sanctions against top officials of the regime. As the scale of protests increased further, the United States pressed Assad to consider a genuine transition to democracy and to launch a constructive dialogue with the opposition. But opposition members boycotted a "national dialogue" conference on reform, vowing not to meet with the regime in the shadow of the ongoing crackdown. At the end of July, as the might of Syria's armed forces was being felt in the rioting cities of Homs, Hama, and Latakia, the country's cabinet approved a draft law reintroducing multipartyism. The law was described as an empty gesture by regime opponents.

In spite of growing condemnation and although world leaders called on Assad to resign, the regime continued with its heavy-handed repression tactics. In August 2011, the Syrian National Council (SNC) was established to coordinate opposition to the regime. Composed largely of exiled figures, the SNC had difficulty projecting leadership over the disparate protest movement within the country. Not surprisingly, as repression continued, some protesters (and defecting members of the security forces) took up arms against the regime.

As the country began sliding into a full-fledged civil war, outsiders were hamstrung in their efforts to steer the course of events. In the fall of 2011, the European Union imposed an embargo on oil imports, Turkey announced sanctions, and the Arab League followed suit by suspending Syria from the organization, but to no avail. In December 2011, as the United Nations put the death toll in the uprising beyond the 5,000 mark, Damascus accepted the deployment of an Arab League monitoring mission, but this initiative was suspended a mere month later because of worsening violence. In spite of votes in the UN's Human Rights Commission (22 November) and General Assembly (19 December) condemning the human rights situation in the country, the Assad regime was bolstered by two Sino-Russian vetoes against UN Security Council draft resolutions in October 2011 and February 2012 condemning the repressive tactics of the regime and calling for an immediate cessation of hostilities.

While his armed forces continued to bomb rioting cities, on 15 October Assad announced the establishment of an ad hoc committee to revise the constitution. In November and again in January 2012, the regime released political prisoners. On 12 December, municipal elections were held in the shadow of violence and the opposition described them as a sham. On 26 February, a referendum was held on the new constitution, which was accepted by 89 percent of voters. On 7 May 2012, Syria held its first multiparty elections against a background of ongoing violence and in a climate shrouded by the boycott of the vote in opposition strongholds. Meanwhile, the violence had reached new heights. In Damascus and Aleppo, boobytrapped cars repeatedly sowed death and destruction. The Syrian armed forces launched a massive attack on neighborhoods in Homs, the bastion of the opposition, which fell on 29 February. As for the United Nations, it declared in late January that it was henceforth unable to provide casualty tolls. In this context, UN Secretary-General Ban Ki-moon dispatched his predecessor, Kofi Annan, to Damascus on 10 March 2012. On 27 March, Syria accepted Annan's peace plan, which sought to bring an immediate end to all violence and human rights violations, secure humanitarian access, and facilitate a Syrian-led political transition through dialogue between the regime and the opposition. This paved the way for Russian and Chinese acceptance of UN Security Council Resolution 2043 of 21 April 2012, which established the UN Supervision Mission in Syria to monitor and support the implementation of Annan's peace plan. However, in light of escalating violence and against the background of ongoing divisions at the Security Council, by mid-July, Kofi Annan declared the plan a failure.

Looking back at the decade since Bashar al-Assad became president, it is possible to discern growing signs of discontent in Syrian society. In the winter of 2000, the new president was credited with encouraging the

"Damascus Spring," or the emergence all over Syria of dozens of forums where intellectuals publicly criticized the political system of the country and signed petitions calling for liberal and democratic reforms. A mere two months after Assad came to power, 99 prominent public figures issued the "Statement of 99," which argued that administrative, economic, and legal reform would not achieve real change if not complemented by political reform. In terms strikingly similar to the demands of protesters in 2011, the 99 called for the lifting of martial law; an amnesty for political prisoners, deportees, and exiles; the establishment of the rule of law; political pluralism; the respect of all basic personal and political freedoms; and an end to censorship.[5] According to Ellen Lust, "The political fervor of the 'Damascus Spring' inspired hope that the president could garner sufficient support and enthusiasm to stand up to hard-line, anti-reform figures within the regime."[6]

When he took power, Bashar al-Assad portrayed himself as a potential reformer and a self-styled modernizer.[7] But by mid-2001, the new president was clamping down on would-be reformers, accusing them of seeking "to undermine Syria's internal stability from within."[8] This followed the publication of the "Statement of 1000," a critical document that called for an end to the Baath Party's monopoly on political life and the restoration of multiparty politics. Following its publication, civil society forums were closed, and activists and prominent journalists were arrested and tried, while others were forced into exile.[9]

While the president's favorable disposition toward civil society may not have lasted long, Assad maintained his gradualist approach to reform. In its first five years, his regime oversaw substantial economic and administrative reform. Private banks and universities were established; customs duties were significantly reduced and foreign investment opportunities increased; and hundreds of laws and presidential decrees were signed to reform the economy and administration.[10] According to Raymond Hinnebusch, this prompted a struggle between the government and the more socialist old guard of the ruling Baath Party, to the point that the president sought to decrease the number of senior party figures in his later cabinets. Thus, when the United States invaded Iraq, Assad attempted to rid his cabinet of those, including then–prime minister Mustafa Miro, whom he saw as "a coterie of crony capitalists enriching themselves on monopoly licenses for the delivery of goods to Iraq."[11] But as a result of the highly unstable regional environment and in the face of mounting international pressure, the Baath regional command refused to curtail the party's role in government or to launch a major liberalization program.

In another attempt to secure greater control, one that would have major consequences for the unfolding of events in 2011, Assad inserted close allies into positions of power and leadership within the military and the security services. He made wide use of his constitutional powers to appoint and promote his own men while dismissing and retiring old-guard officials. By the end of 2002, "three-quarters of the top 60-odd officials in political, security and administrative ranks were replaced."[12] Assad benefited from the fact that his father had purged hostile security and military officers before his death, and appointed their successors, including his brother Maher as head of the Republican Guard and his brother-in-law Asef Shawkat as head of military security. In the army, the president promoted second-rank Alawi officers who were beholden to him. This trend accelerated as international pressure began to mount on Syria, first in 2003–2004 when the George W. Bush administration supported and signed the Syria Accountability and Lebanese Sovereignty Restoration Act, then in 2004 when the United States and France jointly endorsed UN Security Council Resolution 1559, which called for Syria's withdrawal from Lebanon, and finally in 2005 when the UN Special Tribunal for Lebanon implicated the Syrian regime in the assassination of former Lebanese prime minister Rafiq al-Hariri.

The tenth regional congress of the Baath Party would become a battleground between advocates of reform and the regime. The debate over reform—including the fate of the martial law of 1963; of Law 49, which outlawed membership in the Muslim Brotherhood; and of Article 8 of the Syrian constitution, which underpinned the Baath Party's monopoly on power—had taken place in the state-controlled press, stirring the hopes of reformers. But when the congress took place in June 2005, it became clear that no reform would be forthcoming. Instead, President Assad defended the ideas of Baathism, locating problems in their implementation. The congress endorsed a "social market economy" and the privatization of certain sectors.[13] Perhaps most significant, the congress finalized the consolidation of Assad's personal power as he removed "the last major Sunni barons in the inner circle."[14]

The regime had already signaled the existence of "red lines" ahead of the congress when it arrested members of the last remnant of the Damascus Spring, the Jamal Atassi Forum. Nor was it pleased by the Damascus Declaration of October 2005, in which Syrian opposition forces blamed the regime for the rending of the Syrian national social fabric, precipitating an economic collapse, exacerbating crises of every kind, and isolating the country internationally.[15]

Beginning in 2006, the regime "seemed to act against its internal opponents with greater impunity."[16] Syrian authorities arrested, tried, and sentenced a number of political activists, including signatories of the Damascus Declaration. Throughout 2007 and 2008, security forces clamped down on Internet use.[17]

By the end of the decade, not only was political reform dead but the economic situation had reached levels that were "dangerous for social stability."[18] As many as 30 percent of the population were living under the poverty line,[19] an estimated quarter of a million people were entering the labor force each year, and unemployment rates had soared to as high as 22 percent. These problems were greatly exacerbated by the country's declining oil production and the economic sanctions, which limited growth of gross domestic product. They were amplified by Syria's population growth rate, which was one of the highest in the region at 2.2 percent. Dealing with the various challenges became more difficult in the face of rising social tensions that, given the increased exploitation of communal ties and the reinforcement of sectarian identities, took on sectarian and ethnic tones, most notably in the Kurdish areas.[20] They were also harder to deal with due to widespread corruption—and popular anger over that corruption—which continued despite the ousting of the old guard, since "the revitalized private sector [created] new monopolies controlled by members of the governing elite."[21] In one (admittedly rather egregious) example, the president's cousin Rami Makhlouf, who became a focal point for social frustrations in 2011, "amassed a fortune estimated at $3 billion through his ownership of two mobile phone companies, the port of Latakia, and numerous factories, hotels, and duty-free shops."[22]

In hindsight, all the ingredients for an explosion were in place. At the same time, the ability of the Syrian regime to deal with such an explosion was limited by what Ellen Lust has aptly described as a Catch-22: it needed to reform to stay in power, but any moves in that direction threatened it with collapse.[23] The hesitant reactions of President Assad to the early mobilizations against his regime illustrate this quandary.

That he ultimately chose repression could also have been anticipated, due to the narrowing of his political base. Certainly the regime enjoyed support in some quarters, including among party cadres who had benefited from the system and among many Alawis and religious minorities who feared the potential Sunni majoritarianism of a post-Assad regime. Key units of the security forces, designed to safeguard regime security, could be counted upon to be much more reliable than those in Egypt or Libya.[24] Still, poor training for crowd control and weak command and control left security personnel poorly prepared to limit the brutality of their response. Moreover, far from intimidating protesters (whose perception of regime power and political opportunities had been fundamentally reshaped by the popular overthrow of dictatorships in Tunisia, Egypt, and Libya), such brutality only further delegitimized the regime and narrowed its constituency.

Managed Protests: Jordan

The 2011 uprisings in Jordan were a relatively peaceful affair. With the exception of an attack on a weekly pro-reform vigil by progovernment loyalists on 25 March 2011 in Amman, they did not become an occasion for violent clashes nor did they bring down the monarchy. Still, thousands took to the streets demanding better employment prospects, cuts in food and fuel costs, and an end to corruption. The opposition Islamic Action Front, the political arm of the Muslim Brotherhood, demanded sweeping reforms and a parliamentary system of government.

After King Abdullah II sacked the cabinet of Prime Minister Samir al-Rifai, he asked the new prime minister, Marouf al-Bakhit, to take "practical, swift and tangible steps to launch a real political reform process."[25] In a televised speech to the nation, the king signaled his readiness to implement reform,[26] saying that future cabinets would be formed according to the results of parliamentary elections. He also expressed support for a new electoral law and for active political-party representation in parliament, though he warned that sudden change could lead to chaos and unrest. Yet the monarchy also appeared to use social cleavages to undermine pressures for change. On several occasions, groups of loyal East Bank and tribal supporters of the monarchy clashed with reformist protesters.[27]

The story of Jordan's attempts at reform since the early 1990s is a seesaw of advances and setbacks largely determined by considerations of regime security in a troubled regional environment. From the 1989 "bread riots" until the events of 2011, liberalization has been used as a pressure valve to help the regime deal with threats to its security—what some have labeled "defensive democratization"[28]—while outside pressures have been used to justify stalls and backsliding in the liberalization process.

In 1989, Jordanians went to the polls for the first time in twenty-three years following an acute crisis of Jordanian neopatrimonialism. The end of the "seven fat years" of the Arab petroleum economy had had a deep impact on Jordan's economy, which depended heavily on workers' remittances and petrodollar foreign aid.[29] When it finally resigned itself to seeking help from the International Monetary Fund, the Jordanian government agreed to a five-year stabilization program. In spite of its initial reluctance to cut subsidies on essential goods, the government decreed price increases for a range of goods including cooking gas, gasoline, diesel fuel, and kerosene.[30] Rioting ensued in Transjordan, the traditional area of bedrock support for the monarchy. In response, King Hussein announced elections to be held later that year. Although they were initially managed,[31] these elections were ultimately free of interference. Notably, they resulted in the election of twenty-one members of the Muslim Brotherhood and of thirteen other independent Islamists.

No sooner had Jordan held its elections than Iraq invaded Kuwait. The Gulf crisis presented the regime with the first major challenge on the path to liberalization. The king elected to declare Jordan "neutral" and, though opposed to the invasion of Kuwait, decided not to participate in the US-led multinational coalition. This move was a political necessity given Jordanian society's overwhelming support for Saddam Hussein's anti-Western stance.[32] In the meantime, a commission appointed by King Hussein to draft a national charter that would outline the goals and parameters of the country's democratization efforts came back with a document that emphasized "democratic rights, intellectual pluralism, tolerance, and equality."[33] In 1992, political parties were legalized. The Law on Political Parties made the granting of a license conditional on abiding by the constitution and respecting the principle of pluralism, and expressly forbade parties from having foreign financial or organizational ties (Article 21).[34] In 1993, the Law on Press and Publications was also adopted. However, Article 40 of the latter law "gutt[ed] the very press freedoms the law was supposed to guarantee. It made illegal any news item that offends the king or the royal family; insults Arab, Islamic or 'friendly' heads of state, or accredited diplomats in Jordan; is contrary to public morals; may offend the dignity of any individual or damage his reputation, or offends the armed forces or security organs."[35]

The king's stance on the Gulf crisis might have won him broad support at home; it seriously hurt the country's economy and foreign relations. In regard to the former, the remittances of workers were key to the health of the Jordanian economy; yet many of them fled Kuwait when fighting broke out and those who remained behind were later expelled. This loss was compounded by the fact that the port of Aqaba was blockaded to prevent supplies from reaching Iraq through the Jordanian-Iraqi border. Politically, the George H. W. Bush and Bill Clinton administrations made the "rehabilitation" of Jordan conditional on the country's willingness to sign a peace treaty with Israel "prior to the latter's agreement to withdraw from the occupied Palestinian territories," and only once Jordan had assisted efforts to topple Iraqi president Saddam Hussein.[36]

Peace with Israel provided the background for the first sustained setback in Jordanian liberalization. Concerned with popular opposition to the signing of the peace treaty, the regime sought to weaken potential opponents.[37] In August 1993, the king dissolved parliament and ratified a temporary amendment to the electoral law that instituted the principle of "one person, one vote," which curtailed the ability of political parties to win support.[38] Although officially Jordan's first multiparty electoral contest, the 1993 parliamentary elections yielded a more regime-friendly tribal parliament where opposition figures could not successfully act as watchdogs of government policies.[39] By the time the peace treaty with Israel was signed on 25 October 1994, the regime had renewed restrictions on the press, using the full might of Article 40 of the Law on Press and Publications. Efforts were also made to clip the wings of Islamists. Municipal councils with strong Islamist representation were dissolved, and Islamists were able to win only 8 of the 259 councils contested in the elections of July 1995.

In 1996 the king entrusted Abdul Karim al-Kabariti with forming a new government. It would boast the worst record on human rights of any Jordanian government since 1989, particularly after bread riots erupted in Karak in August following the lifting of subsidies on wheat.[40] Events abroad poured oil on the fire—the September 1996 "tunnel incident," in which Israelis opened a tunnel beneath the Western Wall near the al-Aqsa Mosque in Jerusalem, and the 1997 Israeli decision to proceed with the construction of the Har Homa settlement in East Jerusalem, provided the background to an incident in which a Jordanian soldier fired at Israeli schoolgirls in the Jordan Valley. When Kabariti criticized Israeli prime minister Benjamin Netanyahu and then publicly disagreed with King Hussein's decision to visit the families of the dead schoolgirls, he was dismissed.

At the end of the 1990s, deliberalization was the name of the game in Jordan. The government had "carefully craft[ed] the legal codes that structure politics to serve its own interests," thus successfully weakening domestic political opponents.[41] Not only did the government narrow the existing political space, but beginning in 1997 it also asserted control over associational space. With parliamentary elections due later that year, the king worried about the ability of Jordan's professional associations (nearly all controlled by the opposition) to unite in opposition to normalization of relations with Israel.[42] The Law of Societies and Social Organizations (Law 33 of 1996) defined the activities of voluntary organizations as the provision of social services, what John Clark has called "supply NGOs,"[43] limiting them from becoming involved in political mobilization. As Quintan Wiktorowicz documents, "conflict between the regime and cultural organizations accelerated after 1997, after a series of moves by the Ministry of Culture to curtail overtly political activities in civil society."[44] Meanwhile, demonstrations and protests were routinely discouraged and actively contained. In February 1998, as the United States was preparing to strike Iraq, the Jordanian regime prohibited demonstrations altogether in the name of national security. Attempts to defy this decision were met with force. When King Hussein died of cancer in 1999, his son Abdullah inherited a country that was outwardly politically stable but that had paid the price for this stability with steady deliberalization.

Abdullah II has walked in the footsteps of his late father. The new king has pursued economic liberalization. He has sought to advance political reforms, only to suspend them when convinced that they pose a risk to stability. Finally, he has not hesitated to curb public expressions of dissent by using the state's security services and riot police.

Abdullah II initially focused on the economy, securing Jordan's accession to the World Trade Organization in 1999 and the first ever free trade agreement between an Arab state and the United States in 2000. While the king indicated his interest in political reform in his letter of designation to his first ever prime minister, Abdul Rauf al-Rawabdeh, the latter apparently convinced the young monarch that the combination of political and economic reform "carried major threats for stability."[45] Tensions in the Palestinian territories and later in Iraq provided the justification to dismiss parliament in June 2001, which resulted in the postponing of elections and the passage of over 200 provisional laws that curbed freedom of the press and public protests. Following the start of the second Palestinian intifada (uprising) in the occupied territories in September 2000, Jordan was rocked by "its most extensive and violent demonstrations since April 1989."[46] The regime responded by arresting and detaining protesters and by making it more difficult for them to stage demonstrations, which now required permits instead of simple notification. Much like King Hussein had done in 1997, Abdullah II proceeded to limit the space available to civil society. In 2002, for the first time ever, the regime shut down a civil society organization for having criticized government policies. It also banned the Anti-Normalization Committee of the Union of Professional Associations.[47] In the meantime, the king launched the Jordan First initiative, which was intended to articulate a comprehensive vision of reform. But the committee charged with articulating the vision did not include members of the opposition, and it only succeeded in securing the adoption of a recommendation on implementing a six-seat parliamentary quota for women. The initiative failed to address the growing tensions and economic pain that were behind recurrent rioting, particularly in the southern city of Maan.

In 2003 the king had to devise a reaction to the domestically hugely unpopular US invasion of Iraq. Against a background of demonstrations, the country's political forces were starkly divided, with one camp seeing democratization as a threat to stability and the other seeing it as the only option for long-term stability.[48] The king ultimately decided to hold elections in June of that year, and he tasked his new prime minister, Faisal al-Faiz, with accelerating the pace of reform. The momentum for reform seemed to increase with the Tunis Declaration of 2004, the Arab League's first ever document on political reform, which was produced in reaction to the George W. Bush administration's Greater Middle East Initiative. Yet the gerrymandering and the problems arising from the one-person, one-vote system plagued the elections, resulting in a weak and very traditional parliament.[49] Then, under pressure from the intelligence services, Faiz "shifted gears and started talking about 'administrative reform.'"[50] By March 2005, the interior minister had introduced a bill in parliament further restricting associational space. This triggered sit-ins, protests, and, in parallel, crackdowns and arrests.

This was the context in which the National Agenda initiative of 2005 emerged. In contrast with the Jordan First committee, the twenty-seven-member National Agenda committee included regime stalwarts, opposition members, and civil society representatives. Tasked with drafting "a national agenda that embodies the vision of all of us and specifies strategic programs and national policies whose realization should be binding to all successive governments,"[51] the committee reflected the depth of divisions as its members locked horns over contentious issues such as the election law. The old guard sought to maintain the one-person, one-vote formula that guaranteed their power and their access to state rents; political liberals sought the introduction of a mixed electoral system. In the crossfire that ensued, liberals were accused of "participating in a conspiracy to weaken the Jordanian state" and the king was faulted for "prioritizing 'merit over loyalty'" by pushing the National Agenda.[52] The agenda's draft program was completed at the most inauspicious of times: Jordan had just experienced its first spate of al-Qaeda bombings, while parliamentary contests in Egypt and the West Bank and Gaza had empowered Islamists. Taken together, these events ensured that security concerns trumped pressure for reform.

From 2006 until the November 2010 parliamentary elections, nothing much changed in the tempo of reform efforts. Every advance, such as the November 2006 anticorruption and financial disclosure laws, either was met with or was soon followed by a setback, as happened in July 2008 when parliament passed a highly restrictive law on nongovernmental organizations (NGOs) that severely curtailed the ability of civil society to seek foreign funding and gave the government a wide margin of maneuver in accepting or refusing the registration of NGOs. Elections in 2007 were perceived to have been rigged by the intelligence services. In the absence of any meaningful reform of the election law, the Islamic Action Front suffered its worst ever defeat at the polls, losing eleven of the seventeen parliamentary seats it had previously held. In 2010 the king dissolved the parliament, and the new prime minister, Samir al-Rifai, produced an election law that introduced only minor changes and triggered a decision by the Muslim Brotherhood to boycott the parliamentary contest of November 2010.

Given the history of liberalization efforts in Jordan, the reaction of the head of the Islamic Action Front's political office, Zaki Bani Rsheid, to the king's June 2011 speech to the nation, took on added significance. Said Rsheid: "There was nothing new in the speech. The King has expressed hopes, as we have heard several times in the past, but he did not give specifics and there were no guarantees."[53]

Subsequently a very limited package of constitutional changes was announced. Abdullah II once more changed prime ministers in October 2011, appointing Awn Shawkat al-Khasawneh in an attempt to project an aura of renewed reform. Clearly, however, the strategy of the Hashemite monarchy remained one of trying to placate demands with reformist rhetoric, coupled with minor incremental changes that would leave the existing political system largely intact.

The Primacy of Security: Iraq, Lebanon, and Palestine

Since 2000, Iraq and Palestine have shared the dubious distinction of heading the list of the most unstable areas of the Middle East, closely followed by Lebanon. The 2003 US invasion of Iraq and the subsequent insurgency against US troops, the 2006 Israel-Hezbollah war, and the December 2008–January 2009 war in Gaza all underscore the extent to which the dynamics of local politics are wrapped up with security considerations. Unlike most Arab states, which before 2011 boasted (seemingly) strong authoritarian governments and weak and divided oppositions, these three cases featured weak and somewhat representative governments (in Iraq after 2005, in Lebanon after Syria's 2005 withdrawal, and in Palestine from 1996 through to the Fatah-Hamas clashes of 2007) and powerful internal political undercurrents. More than anything, it has been this combination of security and political considerations that has both underpinned attempts at, and severely limited the scope for, reform in all three instances. It is also the reason why, in spite of echoes of the protests that have engulfed other Arab regimes, little has come of the 2011 uprisings in Iraq, Lebanon, or Palestine.

Iraq

Had it not been for demonstrations that erupted at the end of February and in early March in several Iraqi cities to protest corruption and poor service delivery, there would have been no signs of the 2011 uprisings in Iraq. Rather, daily life in the country continues to be marked by episodic violence. The preeminence of security concerns was illustrated by the reaction of Prime Minister Nuri al-Maliki, who warned demonstrators that they would "become victims of al-Qa'ida and pro-Saddam violence."[54] In a country emerging from life under a brutal authoritarian regime—the forceful removal of which did not usher in an era of prosperity but one of insecurity and civil strife—this illustrates the extent to which the security situation can be (and has been) used to justify a certain status quo.

Following the occupation of Kuwait in 1990 and the popular uprisings against Saddam Hussein in 1991—which according to Eric Davis almost led to the collapse of his regime[55]—Hussein proceeded to put family members in top positions and purged army and Republican Guard commanders suspected of disloyalty, including associates from his home town of Tikrit and Baath Party members. Throughout the 1990s, increased reliance on his immediate family and clan members transformed national politics into "a pronounced family affair,"[56] or what sociologist Falih Abd al-Jabar has called "the family-party state."[57] UN sanctions requiring that all transactions with Iraq be channeled through the government unwittingly contributed to increasing its hold over the population.[58] In the meantime, the northern provinces of Kurdistan, which were protected by the provisions of UN Security Council Resolution 688 (1991), established the foundations of a semidemocratic system including the establishment of a parliament and the holding of elections.[59]

When the United States invaded Iraq in 2003, it did not simply depose the regime of Saddam Hussein; it fundamentally shaped the course of post-Saddam Iraqi politics. The mission of the Coalition Provisional Authority (CPA), which was established soon after US troops entered Baghdad on 9 April, was "to restore conditions of security and stability, to create conditions in which the Iraqi people can freely determine their own political future (including by advancing efforts to restore and establish national and local institutions for representative governance), and facilitating economic recovery, sustainable reconstruction and development."[60] The CPA took a number of key decisions that shaped the future political evolution of the country: it outlawed the Baath Party and barred members from taking up positions in the state; it enshrined the principle of sectarian representation; it disbanded (and then reformed) the Iraqi army; and it favored those parties and NGOs whose goals seemed consistent with US interests.[61]

Almost a decade after the US invaded Iraq, these decisions continue to reverberate on the Iraqi political scene. The security vacuum created by disbanding the Iraqi army has produced conditions favorable to insurgency and to terrorist activities. In 2004, the bulk of clashes saw US troops facing Sunni insurgents, as well as the Mahdi Army of radical Shiite cleric Muqtada al-Sadr. By 2006, the then-head of the US Central Command, General John Abizaid, warned the US Congress that the risks of civil war in Iraq were increasing.[62] By 2008, violence had abated as a result of the unilateral cease-fire declared in August 2007 by al-Sadr, and also as a result of the counterinsurgency effort of the Sunni Sahwa (Awakening) committees, which had turned against al-Qaeda and other Sunni jihadist groups.[63]

Nevertheless, in 2009, Anthony Cordesman underlined that, in comparative terms, the number of casualties occurring under conditions of "peace" and within a context of improved security in Iraq were equivalent to those occurring under conditions of "war" in Afghanistan.[64] This highlighted the degree to which restoring security and ensuring stability remained tall orders in the country.

On the political front, the CPA opened the door for Iraq's previously marginalized Shiite and Kurdish communities to reach positions of power in the state. Yet the new political realities in Iraq and the rules laid out in the early years of the transition enshrined sectarian logics that continue to affect political dynamics. Inaugurated in July 2003, the US-sponsored Iraqi Governing Council (IGC) included representatives of the most prominent political parties selected on a sectarian basis. The IGC's close ties to the CPA and its broadly secularist orientation elicited critiques from Grand Ayatollah Ali al-Sistani and from Muqtada al-Sadr alike. In the 2005 elections to the Transitional National Assembly (TNA), the Supreme Council of the Islamic Revolution in Iraq (SCIRI, later the Islamic Supreme Council of Iraq, ISCI), the Party of the Call to Islam (al-Da'wa al-Islamiya), and the two Kurdish parties, the Kurdistan Democratic Party (KDP) and the Patriotic Union of Kurdistan (PUK), emerged victorious, with PUK leader Jalal Talabani becoming the first Kurdish president of Iraq and Ibrahim al-Jafari of al-Da'wa becoming prime minister.

The year 2005 was also notable for the drafting of, and subsequent referendum on, the Iraqi national constitution. The constitution granted de jure recognition to the autonomous Kurdistan Regional Government (KRG), thus creating a highly asymmetric federal Iraq.[65] Against a background of mutual mistrust, disagreements between Kurds and Arabs over the extent of Kurdish autonomy remain unsettled. Arabs fear that Kurds are laying the ground for full independence; Kurds fear that Arabs are attempting to recentralize decisionmaking in Baghdad. Contentious issues include the management of the country's oil resources, many of which are located in Iraqi Kurdistan, as well as the status of the disputed Kirkuk governorate.[66]

Nor have tensions between Shiite and Sunni Arabs fully abated. Sunnis boycotted elections for the 2005 TNA. They were underrepresented in the assembly, and then–prime minister al-Jafari blocked those in parliament from holding senior ministerial positions.[67] Sunni political forces ultimately participated in the December 2005 elections for the permanent Iraqi National Assembly, winning 44 of the 275 seats. By 2007, Sunni tribal leaders were forming "Awakening Councils," committees of fighters who were credited with helping stem the tide of violence in the country by launching a successful counterinsurgency against al-Qaeda cells. Nevertheless, and in spite of promises to the contrary, the government of Prime Minister Nuri al-Maliki failed to integrate Awakening's fighters into the country's security and armed forces. Nor did he carry through on implementing the January

2008 law that lifted the ban on the participation of former Baathists in government. While the 2010 parliamentary elections saw the rise of (sometimes nominally) cross-sectarian coalitions—notably al-Maliki's State of Law coalition and the Iraqi National Movement (INM) of Iyad Allawi—the prime minister's support for the decision of the Supreme National Commission for Accountability and Justice to bar 511 candidates from running in the elections because of their Baathist past dealt a blow to the fragile reconciliation process. In spite of the INM's electoral victory, al-Maliki received a renewed mandate as prime minister in December 2010 after months of political paralysis. But while his government has sought to reestablish security, there are signs that the prime minister is trying to concentrate power in his own hands. A number of previously independent commissions are now controlled by the executive. Al-Maliki has also put himself in charge of overseeing the organization of elections, the allocation of funds by the central bank, and the investigation of human rights abuses and corruption in what a member of his State of Law coalition, member of parliament Laila al-Khafaji, has called a "coup."[68]

Last but not least, economic developments also affect the dynamics of reform in Iraq. The oil sector is the victim of unresolved tensions between Kurds and Arabs. The Iraq Oil and Gas Law, the draft of which was first sent to parliament in 2007, was set aside by parliament in April 2012 and competing proposals were still under consideration. The first round of bidding for oil and gas field developments in 2009 yielded disappointing results as insecurity tempered the temptations of profit, and oil fields in the relatively stable south were snapped up while those in the north and on the edge of Baghdad's Sadr City were snubbed. Although it might not have created the conditions under which the war economy emerged in Iraq, the CPA did ensure the regulatory vacuum that arrayed existing networks of smugglers—which had been established during the long years of war and sanctions before 2003, and which were mostly tied to the lower echelons of tribal clans across the country—against US allies backed by the US military. All of these actors attempted to benefit from Iraq's openness to business, with the result that the central state institutions did not control the market. Rather, it was carved up among various militias that depended on control of local areas for resources and did not hesitate to use violence to maintain that control.[69] Not only has this given insurgent groups the means to sustain themselves, but it has also hampered the ability of the central state to use the economy and service delivery as a way of building ties to citizens across the nation. Instead, various political forces have asserted their control over parts of the economy. For example, the ISCI established its dominion over construction permits and transportation as well as Iranian retail imports into southern towns that it controlled around Basra, while Prime Minister Nuri al-Maliki's Da'wa Party has profited from "control of federal ministries and their business dealings with Iran."[70] As a result, while rehabilitating factories that were destroyed in the course of the war against Saddam Hussein's regime might be the sound developmental approach to restoring Iraq's economy, the personal benefits and the political gains arising from the current market configuration decrease the likelihood of any radical change in the near future.

A final factor that is important for understanding the current sociopolitical context in Iraq is the high level of discomfort with public unrest on the part of government authorities. For example, the Iraqi Federation of Trade Unions (IFTU) pushes for improved working conditions. But it attracted the attention of US commanders, who "considered worker unrest to be a threat to local security"[71] and thus occupied and shut down the IFTU headquarters. In August 2005 the al-Jafari government further restricted the work of the IFTU by entrusting the Committee for Labor and Social Rights with "authority over all aspects of the activities of worker organizations."[72] Similarly, in the Kurdistan region, popular mobilizations against the inefficiency and corruption of local authorities, such as the March 2006 mass demonstration of Halabja massacre survivors, have been met by force.

These examples make clear that there have been protests in Iraq against such things as corruption and poor service delivery—with many of them predating the 2011 uprisings in the Arab world—but that they have been primarily managed by invoking considerations related to "security" or "communal cohesion." As such, they seem to point toward the conclusion that the dynamics of authoritarianism and reform in Iraq will be more affected by internal developments, especially following the withdrawal of US combat forces from the country in December 2011. Moreover, the trend has hardly been a positive one: on the contrary, patronage, corruption, and the consolidation of executive power have been the general pattern.

Palestine

In the West Bank and Gaza, the dynamics of reform have fluctuated with the ebb and flow of relations with Israel. Following the signing of the 1993 Oslo Accords, Palestinians set up the Palestinian National Authority (also known as the Palestinian Authority [PA]), and in 1996 they elected Palestine Liberation Organization (PLO) leader Yasser Arafat as the first PA president, while also making his party, Fatah, the largest winner in the first ever PA parliamentary elections. Assessment of the 1996 elections has been mixed, with some arguing that they should be evaluated as foundational elections intended to legitimate a new political order on the road to peace and reconstruction,[73] while others expressed fears that they would pave the way to one-party rule.[74] In support of the latter position, the PA did seem in its early years to be "emerging as a state that resembled other Arab political systems."[75] Among contributing factors, analysts have singled out three particularly harmful and mutually reinforcing elements: Arafat's personalized and heavily neopatrimonial leadership and his tendency to divide and rule;[76] the unintended consequences of the economic arrangements put in place by the Oslo Accords, under which Israel collects taxes and delivers them to the PA, which has fostered a system of monopolies and border crossings that put a lot of money into the hands of the president and his allies;[77] and last but not least, the international community's belief that the success of the peace process was contingent on political stability, a belief that translated into support for a strong central authority and particularly for buttressing the PA's capacity to meet its security obligations.[78] On the ground, the vibrant civil society that had developed in the West Bank and Gaza during the first intifada was weakened by lack of international support.[79] The PA also sought to contain civil society organizations that had emerged as some of the strongest critics of its authoritarian tendencies. Military security courts were established in February 1995 to deter Hamas and Islamic Jihad from attacking Israeli targets and to demonstrate the PA's seriousness about combating terrorism. Every major attack on Israeli targets became an occasion to arrest opposition leaders and activists, without charge or trial. Many of them complained of being tortured, and several died during interrogations. The PA also took repressive measures against the press, including temporarily closing opposition papers and banning the circulation of papers that published anti–Oslo Accord views. Yet as Nathan Brown argues, Palestinian authoritarianism operated in an "atmosphere of intellectual openness" in which critics and indeed the Palestinian Legislative Council (PLC) itself tested the limits of the system; for example, the PLC took the "Basic Law" drafted by the PLO's legal committee and "transform[ed] it into the most liberal constitutional document in Arab history before passing it in 1997."[80] Ironically, the limited liberalizing success of PLC efforts was a primary reason for authoritarianism moving outside legal channels (and thus becoming harder to regulate). In any case, such moves were rendered moot by the failure of Israeli-Palestinian permanent status negotiations in 2000–2001, eruption of the second intifada in September 2000, and Israeli reoccupation of many PA areas, all of which caused reform to be temporarily shelved.

The reform movement regained momentum in 2002 at the prodding of the United States—which sought to clip the wings of Arafat, whom it considered to be responsible for the intifada—as well as of European donors convinced of the need for a capable Palestinian Authority as a partner in the peace process.[81] The "Roadmap for Peace," spelled out in President George

W. Bush's Rose Garden speech, made support for a Palestinian state conditional on Arafat's removal and on reform of the PA, particularly of its fi-
nances and judiciary and security services.

By summer 2003, Palestine had perhaps the most transparent and efficient fiscal apparatus of any Arab state. The Basic Law was amended to
transfer executive authority from the office of the president to a cabinet
headed by a prime minister who was fully accountable to the parliament.
Other reform projects—such as the Judicial Law—were similarly revived
and approved. Internal security was placed under the authority of the cabinet, theoretically ending its isolation from parliamentary oversight.[82]

Yet the implementation of reforms stumbled over a number of obstacles: the intifada had seriously harmed the institutions of the PA; domestic
support for reform did not extend to the masses, who were preoccupied with
daily survival under difficult conditions; and the agendas of outside donors
contained only a shallow commitment to reform—indeed, even the
Roadmap to Peace "linked a 'Rebuilt and refocused Palestinian Authority
security apparatus' exclusively to 'sustained, targeted, and effective operations aimed at confronting all those engaged in terror and dismantlement of
terrorist capabilities and infrastructure.'"[83] The main test for reform would
be the 2006 elections, which were labeled by Arafat's successor, Mahmoud
Abbas, "as a way of renewing Palestinian institutions."[84]

The 2006 elections illustrate both the depth of reform and its intrin-
sic dependence on security agendas. The campaign was fairly clean, with
the parties respecting a code of conduct mostly focused on fair play.
Hamas had been enticed to participate in the electoral process, and had
disavowed the use of violence. Although reform was not its priority,
Hamas ultimately focused on deficits in governance and on the PA's harsh
security practices. The movement's credibility relative to the PA earned it
the votes of disenchanted Palestinians, and it emerged victorious. This
marked "the first time in Arab history [that] a governing party had lost
power through democratic means."[85] But the victory of Hamas rang the
death knell for reform. Mahmoud Abbas, who had spearheaded reform efforts when he was still prime minister, now sought to dissolve the Hamas-
dominated PLC, in clear violation of Article 47 of the Basic Law, which
set the term of an elected PLC at four years from the date of its election.
Western donors simultaneously imposed sweeping sanctions on the Palestinians. And while efforts at rehabilitating the PA security forces were renewed, this was "only as part of a regime change strategy intended to deny
the new government control over the [security forces] and to turn the latter into a countervailing force against Hamas."[86] Responsibility for paying the security forces was diverted back to the office of the president,
thereby undermining progress in fiscal transparency. Although some of

the independent bodies that had been responsible for the organization of the 1996 elections—such as the Central Elections Commission—continued to operate, most suffered from lack of funding.[87] As Hamas and Fatah dug in, Palestinian institutions became divided between the two parties, with Fatah retaining the presidency and much of the administration and Hamas controlling the cabinet and holding a majority in the PLC. According to Yezid Sayigh, "By seeking to reverse the outcome of the parliamentary elections, the United States and the European Union weakened the notion of constitutional government, effectively encouraging the emergence of rival armed camps and the militarization of national politics."[88] By 2007, Fatah and Hamas were embroiled in a civil war that resulted in the de facto division of the Palestinian territory between the Fatah-controlled West Bank and the Hamas-controlled Gaza Strip.

With the standstill in negotiations with Israel and the security escalation between Israel and Hamas—which resulted in the January 2009 Gaza war—reform took a backseat to security developments. It would therefore come as no surprise that in the West Bank and Gaza, the 2011 uprisings became an occasion for Palestinian activists to call for unity of ranks and an end to Israeli occupation rather than for reform of the PA. Indeed, the PA's September 2011 initiative to seek recognition of statehood at the United Nations, although driven in part with frustration at the moribund peace process, appears to have also been driven by Abbas's desire to blunt any Arab Spring–inspired reformist pressures on his government by adopting a more proactive and populist position on Israeli-Palestinian issues.

Lebanon

In 1989, Lebanese parliamentarians hammered out an agreement to end the country's fifteen-year civil war. The Document of National Accord (also known as the Taif Agreement) recalibrated the division of powers, one of the contentious issues that had triggered the war, weakening the presidency, transferring many of its powers to cabinet in its collective capacity, and strengthening the power of the speaker of parliament.[89] This was intended to depersonalize rule and to strengthen institutions. By providing for the demobilization of militias, the agreement paved the way for reform of the security sector. While by no means a perfect blueprint for democratization—it did not for example tackle the sectarian nature of Lebanese politics—the agreement nevertheless held out the promise of making reform possible. Yet under Syria's custodianship of Lebanon, the promise would not come to fruition. The Taif Agreement was implemented piecemeal, with priority given to those aspects that contributed to furthering Syrian objectives in Lebanon. In an environment where peace talks between Syria and Israel had gone nowhere, security considerations were key. Syria wanted a stable Lebanon, as an unstable one would be a liability in the conflict with Israel and could potentially harbor critics of the Assad regime.

Critics of the Syrian custodianship were politically marginalized or coercively muzzled.[90] The new redistribution of power did not strengthen institutions; instead it created a system in which "the relationship between members of this troika [i.e., the president, the prime minister, and the speaker of parliament] overshadow[ed] the role of any institution."[91] The troika saw themselves mostly as representatives of their communities, and they perceived their ability (or lack thereof) to legislate or implement policies in terms of communal gains or losses. In the absence of a national institution capable of adjudicating between them, they increasingly turned to Syria to play that role, thereby giving the authorities in Damascus even greater sway over Lebanese politics. The use and abuse of elections to bring Syrian allies to power was consistent with practices in other Arab authoritarian states. Whereas the Taif Agreement sought to use elections as an instrument of mutual peaceful coexistence and as a guarantor of proper political representation, in practice every electoral contest was held under a different law and with different rules (particularly in terms of redistricting) that sought to constrain or even to eliminate the political opportunities of opponents of Syria's custodianship of the Taif Agreement.[92] This nullifying of the spirit of Taif was echoed in a deal struck between Syria and Iran that allowed Hezbollah to eschew demobilization and to continue to function as a resistance movement in South Lebanon and the eastern Bekaa Valley.[93]

In 2000, developments raised hopes that the space for political dissent and for discussion of reform would widen. Israel withdrew from Lebanon and President Hafez al-Assad of Syria died, to be replaced by his son Bashar. Public criticism of the Syrian presence in Lebanon and of the quality of governance in the country "reached new heights," and the debate was both heated and open. Even erstwhile Syrian allies, such as Progressive Socialist Party leader Walid Jumblatt, joined the fray.[94] The window of opportunity closed very quickly, however, in light of developments in the security realm both regionally (the second intifada) and internationally (the 9/11 terrorist attacks). In February 2001, President Assad "affirmed that Syria had no plans to withdraw from Lebanon before regional peace was achieved."[95] Instead, Assad drew closer to the Lebanese military and security services, and in 2004 his regime forced the reinstatement of its ally, President Emile Lahoud, to another term in office by amending the Lebanese constitution. Syria quickly found itself on a collision course with the United States and France, which retaliated by spearheading the adoption of UN Security Council Resolution 1559, which called for "the strict respect of Lebanon's sovereignty, territorial integrity, unity, and political independence under the sole and exclusive authority of the Government of Lebanon throughout the country."[96] Syria's primacy in Lebanon was thus formally challenged.

In this context, new hopes for reform were raised when, in 2005, Lebanese from all sectarian backgrounds poured into Martyrs Square in downtown Beirut in reaction to the assassination of former prime minister Rafiq al-Hariri. The "Beirut Spring"—as this mass mobilization was called—received unequivocal and very public Western support, with US assistant secretary of state William Burns calling for the immediate implementation of Resolution 1559.[97] A month later, Syrian troops withdrew from Lebanon. The Lebanese people would soon become divided by their attitudes toward developments on the ground, with two rival coalitions emerging: the March 14 coalition, led by Hariri's son Saad and his Future Movement, and the March 8 coalition, led by Hezbollah, which opposed Western intervention and Syria's withdrawal from Lebanon. Nevertheless, for the first time since Syria took over implementation of the Taif Agreement, Lebanese leaders were discussing key issues that impeded reform. An independent national commission was formed in August 2005 to consider the possibility of electoral reform, to address the flaws in Lebanon's electoral law, and to tackle serious concerns about practices during electoral campaigns and on election day.[98] A national dialogue launched in March 2006 shattered many taboos by focusing on "issues that had been barred from discussion since the close of the civil war, from sectarian relations and the distribution of powers to the question of Hizballah's arms and the status of armed Palestinian refugees."[99]

Once again, developments in the security realm would derail the momentum for reform. The reason was the thirty-four-day war between Israel and Hezbollah that took place in July 2006, as well as the subsequently tense domestic climate, which saw Hezbollah accuse the March 14 coalition of having collaborated with Israel in an attempt to destroy the party, and the March 8 coalition withdraw its members from the cabinet. The confrontation effectively took reform off the table, as disagreements were taken into the streets. Members of the two coalitions clashed multiple times between December 2006 and May 2008, with the most violent clash taking place on 8 May 2008, when Hezbollah forces seized locations in West Beirut. This fighting reawakened fears of civil war and led to the negotiation of the Doha Agreement. That agreement included a principle pushed for by the March 8 coalition, that minorities in government should have a "blocking tier" consisting of one-third of seats plus one. The principle was aimed at ensuring that no important decision touching upon issues of national interest could be taken unilaterally by one faction or the other, and was seen as a way of ending the paralysis gripping the executive and as paving the way for the election of a new president to replace Lahoud, whose second term in office had ended in November 2007.

Parliamentary elections in 2009 highlighted the extent to which, in Lebanon as in Palestine, democratic electoral exercises could be wrapped up in and potentially subverted by strategic considerations. When advance polling indicated that support for the two coalitions was extremely close, the United States threatened to suspend its military aid to the Lebanese army if Hezbollah and its allies prevailed. This did not come to pass, however, as the March 14 coalition gained a majority of seats in parliament, though not a majority of the popular vote.[100] It would subsequently take five months for Saad al-Hariri to form a unity government, which in December 2009 endorsed Hezbollah's right to maintain its arsenal.

Looking back at the decade since Israel withdrew from Lebanon, three factors emerge as constant impediments to reform in Lebanon: the primacy of sectarianism and the inability and unwillingness of communal leaders to think beyond narrow and immediate communal interests; the growing entanglement between domestic and international issues;[101] and last but not least, the veto power that Hezbollah holds over events because of its special status as the only armed political faction in the country. The importance of the latter factor was underlined by the fact that as nearby Arab countries were convulsed by the 2011 uprisings, it was Hezbollah's staunch opposition to the Special Tribunal for Lebanon—set up by the UN to investigate the murder of Rafiq al-Hariri—that resulted in the January 2011 fall of the government of Saad al-Hariri. Hezbollah called for a boycott of the tribunal, describing it as an instrument of the United States and Israel. And given that Hezbollah and its allies hold a majority of seats in the government of Prime Minister Najib Mikati at the time of writing, it seems clear that once again, key control over the way forward in Lebanon rests in the organization's hands.

Conclusion

The examination of the push and pull of authoritarianism and reform in the Mashreq has underscored the extent to which this region is not only geographically but also politically situated halfway between North Africa and the Gulf. There has to date been no regime change in the Mashreq. Rather, one country has descended into violence, another has successfully contained and managed popular mobilization, and the uprisings seem to have largely bypassed three other countries. Three sets of factors can be invoked to explain the similarities and differences between the cases: the nature of societal cleavages, the institutional bases of the regimes and the nature of civil-military relations, and the entanglement of domestic and external issues.

In Lebanon and Iraq, the depth of societal cleavages and their prior instrumentalization by the regimes have so far prevented the kind of mass upheaval that occurred in Tunisia and Egypt, even as populations toil under similarly harsh social and economic conditions. In Syria, Iraq, Jordan, and to a lesser extent the West Bank, armed forces are loyal to the regime and unlikely to turn against it. Two factors account for such loyalty: the regimes' ability to staff the higher ranks of the armed forces with officers who have a personal loyalty to leaders based on political affiliation or common sectarian identity, and the economic opportunities and benefits afforded to members of the armed forces, particularly but not exclusively to the officers corps, which create a vested economic interest in the survival of the regimes. Finally, all Mashreq countries—with the partial exception of Jordan—are in the throes of upheavals caused as much by their domestic politics as by their external environment. From the outbreak of the second intifada to the 2006 conflict between Hezbollah and Israel, the scope of these upheavals has provided regimes with a broader margin for maneuver in the sense that they have been able to put off calls for reform in the name of pressing security issues.

Taken together, these factors suggest that mass mobilization in support of regime change is less likely in the Mashreq than it was in either Egypt or Tunisia. This is due to the combined impact of deep societal divisions and pressing domestic and international threats. The factors also suggest that, much as we have seen in Syria, most regimes are more likely to use their coercive capabilities to maintain themselves in power.

Notes

1. The Mashreq refers to the region extending north of Egypt to the Arabian Peninsula. It comprises the West Bank and Gaza, Jordan, Syria, Lebanon, and Iraq.
2. Including heating-fuel subsidies, access to previously banned social media, a three-month cut in military service, and the release of political prisoners.
3. Katherine Marsh and Martin Chulov, "Syrian President Blames Foreign Conspirators for Inflaming Protests," *The Guardian,* 31 March 2011.
4. Katherine Marsh, "Syria Crackdown: Hundreds Resign from Ba'ath Party," *The Guardian,* 28 April 2011.
5. Flynt Lawrence Leverett, *Inheriting Syria: Bashar's Trial by Fire* (Washington, DC: Brookings Institution, 2005), p. 91.
6. Ellen Lust-Okar, "Reform in Syria: Steering Between the Chinese Model and Regime Change," Carnegie Papers, Middle East Series, no. 69 (Washington, DC: Carnegie Endowment for International Peace, 2006), pp. 4–5. See also, Eyal Zisser,

"What Does the Future Hold for Syria?" *Middle East Review of International Affairs* 10, 2 (June 2006), pp. 96–97.

7. Roschanack Shaery-Eisenlohr, "From Subjects to Citizens? Civil Society and the Internet in Syria," *Middle East Critique* 20, 2 (Summer 2011), pp. 128–129. See also David W. Lesch, *The New Lion of Damascus: Bashar al-Asad and New Syria* (New Haven: Yale University Press, 2005).

8. Zisser, "What Does the Future Hold for Syria?" p. 98.

9. Leverett, *Inheriting Syria*, pp. 93–94.

10. Lust-Okar, *Reform in Syria*, p. 7.

11. Raymond Hinnebusch, "The Ba'th Party in Post-Ba'thist Syria: President, Party and the Struggle for 'Reform,'" *Middle East Critique* 20, 2 (Summer 2011), p. 116.

12. Ibid., pp. 113–114.

13. Lust-Okar, *Reform in Syria*, p. 8.

14. Hinnebusch, "The Ba'th Party in Post-Ba'thist Syria," p. 121.

15. Lust-Okar, *Reform in Syria*, pp. 9–10.

16. Mona Yacoubian and Scott Lasensky, "Dealing with Damascus: Seeking a Greater Return on U.S.-Syria Relations," Council Special Report no. 33 (Washington, DC: Council on Foreign Relations, 2008), p. 7.

17. Ibid., pp. 7–8; Shaery-Eisenlohr, "From Subjects to Citizens," p. 135.

18. Lust-Okar, *Reform in Syria*, p. 13.

19. Heba el-Laithy and Khalid Abu-Ismail, *Poverty in Syria, 1996–2004: Diagnosis and Pro-Poor Policy Considerations* (Damascus: United Nations Development Programme, 2005), http://www.planning.gov.sy/SD08/msf/PovertInSyriaEnglishVersion.pdf.

20. Lust-Okar, *Reform in Syria*, p. 13.

21. Ibid., p. 7.

22. Yacoubian and Lasensky, "Dealing with Damascus," p. 10.

23. Lust-Okar, *Reform in Syria*.

24. The regime could not be certain of the loyalty of all personnel, however. In particular, it likely foresaw that too much brutality against Sunni protesters might cause defections among the predominately Sunni rank-and-file of the army. For this reason, the most active role in repression was often assigned to particularly loyal units, the security and intelligence communities, or to gangs of hired criminal thugs known locally as the *shabbiha* ("ghosts").

25. Ian Black, "Jordan Denies Report About Attack on King Abdullah," *The Guardian*, 14 June 2011, p. 20.

26. Ibid.

27. While support for political reform can be found in both the Palestinian and East Bank communities, there are certainly those in the latter population (notably among tribal conservatives and former military officers) who fear that any political democratization might increase the influence of the former.

28. Glenn E. Robinson, "Defensive Democratization in Jordan," *International Journal of Middle East Studies* 30, 3 (August 1998), p. 13.

29. See Rex Brynen, "Economic Crisis and Post-Rentier Democratization in the Arab World: The Case of Jordan," *Canadian Journal of Political Science* 25, 1 (March 1992), especially pp. 84–91.

30. Ibid, p. 90.

31. The government initially maintained Article 18, Paragraph E, of the election law, which prohibited candidates from belonging to parties that either were illegal or held aims, objectives, and principles that clashed with the Jordanian constitution. The paragraph was suspended only three weeks before the election, thus hampering the ability of smaller opposition forces to mobilize. The whole process took place under martial law, which would not be repealed until 1991. See Linda Shull Adams, "Political Liberalization in Jordan: An Analysis of the State's Relationship with the Muslim Brotherhood," *Journal of Church and State* 38, 3 (1996).

32. Adams, "Political Liberalization in Jordan," p. 513. See also Beverly Milton-Edwards, "Façade Democracy and Jordan," *British Journal of Middle Eastern Studies* 20, 2 (1993), pp. 196–197.

33. Robinson, "Defensive Democratization in Jordan," p. 394.

34. Article 5 of the law also barred party members from claiming a non-Jordanian nationality or seeking foreign protection. Robinson, "Defensive Democratization in Jordan," p. 395.

35. Robinson, "Defensive Democratization in Jordan," p. 396.

36. Lamis Andoni and Jillian Schwedler, "Bread Riots in Jordan," *Middle East Report* 201 (October–December 1996), p. 41.

37. For more detail, see Laurie A. Brand, "The Effects of the Peace Process on Political Liberalization in Jordan," *Journal of Palestine Studies* 28, 2 (Winter 1999).

38. The 1989 electoral law had granted each voter multiple votes to select the representatives for each of the seats in their districts.

39. Robinson, "Defensive Democratization in Jordan," pp. 397–399.

40. Brand, "The Effects of the Peace Process," pp. 59–62; Andoni and Schwedler, "Bread Riots in Jordan," pp. 40–42.

41. Quintan Wiktorowicz, "The Limits of Democracy in the Middle East: The Case of Jordan," *Middle East Journal* 53, 4 (Autumn 1999), p. 617.

42. Russel E. Lucas, "Deliberalization in Jordan," *Journal of Democracy* 14, 1 (January 2003), p. 141.

43. John Clark, "The State, Popular Participation, and the Voluntary Sector," *World Development* 23, 4 (1995). See also, Quintan Wiktorowicz, "The Political Limits to Nongovernmental Organizations in Jordan," *World Development* 30, 1 (2002).

44. Wiktorowicz, "The Political Limits to Nongovernmental Organizations in Jordan," p. 610.

45. Marwan Muasher, "A Decade of Struggling Reform Efforts in Jordan: The Resilience of the Rentier System," Carnegie Papers (Washington, DC: Carnegie Endowment for International Peace, 2011), p. 5.

46. Jillian Schwedler, "More Than a Mob: The Dynamics of Political Demonstrations in Jordan," *Middle East Report* 226 (Spring 2003), p. 18.

47. Ibid., p. 22.

48. Muasher, *A Decade of Struggling Reform Efforts in Jordan,* p. 9.

49. See Curtis R. Ryan and Jillian Schwedler, "Return to Democratization or New Hybrid Regime? The 2003 Elections in Jordan," *Middle East Policy* 11, 2 (June 2004).

50. Muasher, *A Decade of Struggling Reform Efforts in Jordan,* p. 12.

51. Ibid.

52. Ibid., p. 14.

53. Black, "Jordan Denies Report About Attack on King Abdullah."

54. Harriet Sherwood and Tom Finn, "Thousands Join 'Day of Rage' Across the Middle East," *The Guardian,* 25 February 2011.

55. Eric Davis, "History Matters: Past as Prologue in Building Democracy in Iraq," *Orbis* 49 (Spring 2005), p. 235.

56. Fred H. Lawson, "Iraq," in Michele Penner Angrist, ed., *Politics and Society in the Contemporary Middle East* (Boulder: Lynne Rienner, 2010), p. 263.

57. Falih Abd al-Jabbar, "Min Dawlat Hizb al-Wahid ila Dawlat al-Hizb/al-Usra" [From the One Party State to the Family-Party State], *al-Thaqafa al-Jadida* 267 (December 1995–January/February 1996), quoted in Davis, "History Matters," p. 235.

58. Abbas Alnasrawi, *The Economy of Iraq* (Westport: Greenwood, 1994), p. 213, quoted in Lawson, "Iraq," p. 272.

59. See Gareth R. V. Stanfield, *Iraqi Kurdistan: Emergent Democracy* (London: Routledge Curzon, 2003).

60. US Office of Management and Budget, *Report to Congress Pursuant to Section 1506 of the Emergency Wartime Supplemental Appropriations Act, 2003* (Public Law 108-11), 2 June 2003, p. 2.

61. Lawson, "Iraq," p. 275.

62. John Diamond, "Civil War Risk Up, So No Cut in Troops," *USA Today,* 8 March 2006, http://www.usatoday.com/news/washington/2006-08-03-pentagon-congress_x.htm.

63. The shifting alignment occurred because of both the provocative behavior of jihadist groups, as well as a growing Sunni fear of Shiite military power and majoritarianism. A US troop "surge" in 2007 also played a role, as did changing US counterinsurgency tactics.

64. Anthony Cordesman, *Iraq Trends in Violence and Civilian Casualties, 2005–2009* (Washington, DC: Center for Strategic and International Studies, 5 May 2009), http://csis.org/files/media/csis/pubs/090504_iraq_patterns_in_violence.pdf.

65. See David Cameron, "Inching Forward: Iraqi Federalism at Year Four," in Mokhtar Lamani and Bessma Momani, eds., *From Desolation to Reconstruction: Iraq's Troubled Journey* (Waterloo: Wilfrid Laurier University Press, 2010).

66. See David Romano, "The Struggle for Autonomy and Decentralization: Iraqi Kurdistan," in Lamani and Momani, *From Desolation to Reconstruction.*

67. Ahmed S. Hashim, *Insurgency and Counter-Insurgency in Iraq* (London: Hurst, 2006), p. 78.

68. Nizar Latif and Phil Sands, "Critics Attack al Maliki's 'Power Grab' over Iraq State Institutions," *The National,* 26 January 2011, http://www.thenational.ae/news/worldwide/middle-east/critics-attack-al-malikis-power-grab-over-iraq-state-institutions.

69. Pete Moore and Christopher Parker, "The War Economy of Iraq," *Middle East Report* 37, 243 (Summer 2007).

70. Pete Moore, "Making Big Money on Iraq," *Middle East Report* 252 (Fall 2009).

71. Lawson, "Iraq," p. 269.

72. Ibid.

73. As'ad Ghanem, "Founding Elections in a Transitional Period: The First Palestinian General Elections," *Middle East Journal* 50, 4 (Autumn 1996); Khalil Shikaki, "The Palestinian Elections: An Assessment," *Journal of Palestine Studies* 25, 3 (Spring 1996).

74. Lamis Andoni, "The Palestinian Elections: Moving Toward Democracy or One-Party Rule?" *Journal of Palestine Studies* 25, 3 (Spring 1996).

75. Brown, "The Palestinian Authority," p. 374.

76. Rex Brynen, "The Neopatrimonial Dimension of Palestinian Politics," *Journal of Palestine Studies* 25, 1 (Autumn 1995). For a broader analysis of elite formation, see Rex Brynen, "The Dynamics of Palestinian Elite Formation," *Journal of Palestine Studies* 24, 3 (Spring 1995).

77. Brown, "The Palestinian Authority," p. 377; Nathan Brown, "Requiem for Palestinian Reform," in Marina Ottaway and Julia Choucair-Vizoso, eds., *Beyond the Façade: Political Reform in the Arab World* (Washington, DC: Carnegie Endowment for International Peace, 2008), p. 96.

78. Khalil Shikaki, "The Peace Process, National Reconstruction, and the Transition to Democracy in Palestine," *Journal of Palestine Studies* 25, 2 (Winter 1996).

79. Details are culled from ibid., pp. 9–11.

80. Brown, "Requiem for Palestinian Reform," p. 97.

81. For a history of the movement, see International Crisis Group, "The Meanings of Palestinian Reform," *Middle East Briefing* (Washington, DC: International Crisis Group, 12 November 2002).

82. Brown, "Requiem for Palestinian Reform," p. 100.

83. Yezid Sayigh, "'Fixing Broken Windows': Security Sector Reform in Palestine, Lebanon, and Yemen," Carnegie Papers no. 17 (Washington, DC: Carnegie Endowment for International Peace, October 2009), p. 15.

84. Brown, "The Palestinian Authority," p. 372.

85. Ibid., p. 375.

86. Sayigh, "'Fixing Broken Windows,'" p. 15.

87. Brown, "Requiem for Palestinian Reform," pp. 107–108.

88. Sayigh, "'Fixing Broken Windows,'" p. 15.

89. This amounted to a redistribution of powers between Lebanon's three main communities. Ever since the 1943 National Pact, which laid the basis for Lebanese independence, the presidency had been the preserve of Christian Maronites, the post of prime minister had gone to a Sunni, and that of house speaker to a Shiite. See Joseph Maila, "The Ta'if Accord: An Evaluation," in Deirdre Collings, ed., *Peace for Lebanon? From War to Reconstruction* (Boulder: Lynne Rienner, 1994); Marie-Joëlle Zahar, "Peace by Unconventional Means: Lebanon's Ta'if Agreement," in Stephen J. Stedman, Donald Rothchild, and Elizabeth Cousens, eds., *Ending Civil Wars: The Implementation of Peace Agreements* (Boulder: Lynne Rienner, 2002).

90. Zahar, "Peace by Unconventional Means," pp. 579–583.

91. Choucair-Vizoso, "Lebanon," p. 118. See also Hassan Krayem, "The Lebanese Civil War and the Ta'if Agreement," in Paul Salem, ed., *Conflict Resolution in the Arab World: Selected Essays* (Beirut: American University of Beirut Press, 1997), pp. 426–427.

92. See Bassel F. Salloukh, "The Limits of Electoral Engineering in Divided Societies: Elections in Postwar Lebanon," *Canadian Journal of Political Science* 39, 3 (2006).

93. Alan Cowell, "Syria and Iran Agree Militias Can Remain in Parts of Lebanon," *New York Times,* 30 April 1991, p. 6.

94. Marie-Joëlle Zahar, "Liberal Interventions, Illiberal Outcomes: The United Nations, Western Powers, and Lebanon," in Edward Newman, Roland Paris, and Oliver P. Richmond, eds., *New Perspectives on Liberal Peacebuilding* (Tokyo: United Nations University Press, 2009), p. 298.

95. Marie-Joëlle Zahar, "Liberal Interventions, Illiberal Outcomes," p. 298.

96. United Nations, Press Release no. SC/8181, "Security Council Declares Support for Free, Fair Presidential Election in Lebanon; Calls for Withdrawal of Foreign Forces There: Resolution 1559 (2004) Adopted by Vote of 9 in Favour, to None Against, with 6 Abstentions," 2 September 2004, http://www.un.org/News/Press/docs/2004/sc8181.doc.htm.

97. Bureau of Information Programs, US Department of State, "Transcript: State's Burns Calls for Investigation into Hariri Assassination," 16 February 2005, http://usinfo.org/wf-archive/2005/050216/epf306.htm.

98. Benedetta Berti, "Electoral Reform in Lebanon," *Mideast Monitor* 4, 1 (July–August 2009), http://www.mideastmonitor.org/issues/0907/0907_4.htm. See also Choucair-Vizoso, "Lebanon," pp. 125–130.

99. Choucair-Vizoso, "Lebanon," p. 121.

100. Elias Muhanna, "Deconstructing the Popular Vote in Lebanon's Election," *Mideast Monitor* 4, 1 (July–August 2009), http://www.mideastmonitor.org /issues/0907/0907_3.htm.

101. Zahar, "Liberal Interventions, Illiberal Outcomes," pp. 292–315.

4

The Arabian Peninsula: Bahrain, Kuwait, Saudi Arabia, Yemen

The Arab societies and states of the Arabian Peninsula have some of the region's most unique sociopolitical histories. Not only are they the youngest countries in terms of achieving political independence, but the area is also one of the first in the world to experience globalization, as a result of the arrival of Western oil companies in the nineteenth century.[1] Since that time, the hackneyed description of the region as moving rapidly from "tradition to modernity" has endured, though telling us less and less about it. In fact, of all parts of the Arab world, the Gulf societies attract some of the most pejorative stereotypes, whether they be references to tribes with flags, spoiled nouveau riche, or reactionary conservatives. Like stereotypes of Americans as gun-wielding fast-food patrons, locals may agree with some of these characterizations, but caution that they also miss much. Similarly, the stereotypical view of Gulf politics as uniformly nondemocratic or thoroughly traditional tells us a little but also misses much. While none of the Gulf monarchies meet the procedural definition of democracy, grouping all the countries into the same nondemocratic category fails to take into account the evolving pockets of political pluralism or to capture differences in how rulers maintain centralized political power.

The 2011 mass uprisings in Bahrain and Yemen and smaller though still significant demonstrations in Kuwait, Oman, Saudi Arabia, and the United Arab Emirates (UAE) demonstrated that not all of the region's residents were content with their restricted political voice. In Yemen, which is geographically not a Gulf country, peaceful protests against President Ali Abdullah Saleh progressively became overshadowed by organized violence. The fate of that struggle has implications for the rest of the Gulf, particularly Saudi Arabia, whose leaders are loath to see regime change anywhere in the neighborhood. And the fierce reaction of rulers to their own people demonstrates the lengths that political leaders are willing to go to preserve the privileges of their centralized systems. Indeed, the maturation of Saudi Arabia and the UAE into "super-rentier powers" willing to spend money and spill blood beyond the Gulf region to preserve authoritarianism suggests a new global role for the

Gulf's big oil exporters. Or put another way, authoritarianism seems to have gone transnational in that the preservation of authoritarianism in such Arab countries as Jordan and Morocco is perceived as a requisite for maintaining political control at home.[2] This chapter begins by considering several general themes: pressures for change in the Arab world in the past several decades, and changes in both formal and informal mechanisms of political participation. It then examines in more detail the cases of Bahrain, Kuwait, Saudi Arabia, and Yemen in light of the events of 2011, and offers some thoughts on major trends in these countries.

On the Way to 2011

According to the "tradition versus modernity" trope, conservative Gulf rulers struggle to resist social and economic changes in their societies. While this refrain has an element of truth, Gulf politics can hardly be reduced to a uniform, binary opposition between the traditional and the modern. This is because over time, pressures for political change have been harnessed and used by rulers as well as the opposition for diverse purposes. Consider that Dubai has liberalized and opened up its economy and society far more than any of its neighbors. Foreigners can own land, and behind the closed doors of five-star resorts, foreigners and Gulf citizens can cavort and imbibe in ways that rival life in Beirut, the region's other great tourist magnet. Yet at the same time, organized political opposition and participation in Dubai are absent, as the ruling al-Maktoums have maintained absolute control. Contrast this with Kuwait, which has some of the broadest forms of political participation in the region, including an elected parliament and a vibrant tradition of public debate—yet Kuwait's society has gradually become more socially conservative and resistant to Dubai-style social liberalizations.[3] Pressures for change, then, are complex.

Overlapping with this authoritarian political diversity is the fact that events in one country affect others. Distinctions such as Shia, Sunni, Arab, Muslim, and tribal are not fixed traditional bindings but rather dynamic transnational identities shaped by societies and rulers alike. Just as political oppositions have at times adopted these labels to advance their claims, monarchs have been quick to stoke sectarian fears to justify their centralized rule.[4] Moreover, the events of 2011 will likely have a lasting impact on the Gulf's transnational links. For the ruling families, however, the more immediate impact may well be the most serious threat to their continued political dominance seen in decades. Understanding that threat requires unpacking how monarchical authoritarianism took root and how efforts to resist it have evolved.

One way in which observers have come to simplify and explain factors for change is by categorizing them as external or internal, though these labels should not be seen as mutually exclusive. Internally, pressures for change have been driven by the evolution of rentier states expanding their rule over societies with previously weak or transitioning institutions of political rule. Absolute hereditary monarchies as a form of political rule were not indigenous to the Gulf. It was European dominance, specifically that of the British, that introduced and protected monarchical rule. Quelling of political opposition, creation of borders, and early infrastructure were all mediated, nurtured, or—in the case of infrastructure—put in place by external imperial powers. Timing is important in this case, as the arrival of oil monies occurred at roughly the same time that rulers embarked upon the project of constructing new states and political institutions. The expenditure of that oil money made possible the rapid institutionalization of monarchical rule along lines that often preserved traditional mechanisms of control, such as elite consultation and patronage. Consequently, many aspects of the region's perceived tradition, particularly in terms of tribe and religion, have been harnessed by rulers to preserve modern political power.[5]

As oil profits far in excess of what could be domestically invested arrived year after year in the 1970s, expenditures and economic expansion really took off. Ruling families, after taking their own cut of course, distributed oil money throughout society in the form of infrastructure, education, and higher standards of living. According to rentier-state arguments, this may be one reason why greater political participation has lagged over the decades: societal groups and potential oppositions are simply bought off. However, observers of Gulf politics stress two caveats: one, that distribution can in fact give rise to political demands, since all may not benefit evenly;[6] and two, that growth and economic expansion have helped to generate the very foundations for future participation demands.[7] This is because a reduction in oil prices in the 1980s curtailed economic expansion and reduced distribution. For example, Kuwait went into debt for the first time in the mid-1980s, while Saudi Arabia began a long, slow decline in per capita income at that time due to its population continuing to expand while revenues stagnated. Since long-held public expectations that the socioeconomic pie and state largess would continually increase were seemingly being violated, publics wanted answers. Thus demands voiced through petitions, media campaigns, and even public mobilization increased. Not all of these demands were aimed at political liberalization per se; rather, many were pushing for more input into decisions previously reserved for the ruling families. Consequently, there is good reason to believe that rentier economies, while easing the maintenance of centralized power in the short term, may have actually contributed to the kinds of demands for participation that culminated in the uprisings of 2011.

Externally, the Gulf is a region subject to dynamic transnational politics. If we recall that the Gulf region experienced one of the first waves of economic globalization in the nineteenth century, it becomes apparent that external powers have been dominant players in the area for some time. Regarding political liberalization, however, the story is more recent. That is, while the economic downturn of the 1980s coincided with the so-called waves of democratization in other parts of the developing world, the monarchies of the Gulf found themselves a glaring exception. Petitions and demands of that time were put forward amid global expectations for more liberalization. It was during this period that rulers in Saudi Arabia, Kuwait, Bahrain, and Qatar began, rhetorically at least, to commit themselves to various reforms. What then of direct external pressure to liberalize? Here one could highlight the role of international human rights and professional organizations whose reports and media campaigns constitute reform pressure, but these are hardly direct and are easily ignored. More consequential might be pressure coming from external allies, principally the United States in the past two decades. US democracy rhetoric, at least since the Jimmy Carter administration, has not spared Gulf allies, even Saudi Arabia. But this only goes so far, as former secretary of state James Schlesinger infamously admitted in the early 1990s: "An even deeper question is whether we seriously desire or prescribe democracy as the proper form of government for other societies. Perhaps the issue is more clearly posed in the Islamic world. Do we seriously want to change the institutions of Saudi Arabia? The brief answer is no."[8]

Contrast, for example, the muted reaction of Washington to the violent crackdown on and abuse of protesters during Bahrain's 2011 uprisings with its forceful reaction to Libya in the same year. But this is not to argue that all domestic events are externally controlled. The Gulf is a region at the crossroads of not only the global economy but also vexing regional political conflicts. Since the 1980s, the region has experienced a devastating interstate war (Iran-Iraq), a civil war in Yemen, a short-lived violent annexation (Iraq-Kuwait), two US invasions (1991 and 2003), periodic interstate violence (United States–Iran), and persistent, low-intensity substate violence (Saudi Arabia, Bahrain, and Yemen). While it is beyond the scope of this chapter to explore all the possible connections, war and violent political conflict have been credited with sparking subsequent political openings in other regions (such as Argentina's political transition following the Falklands War). Yet not all violent conflict is similar or takes place within similar contexts. While external powers may not manipulate all events, they have been able to limit the effects of interstate war in the region—limits that can act to forestall political development that might entail political liberalization.[9] As well, conflict in the past decade has been of a substate nature, characterized, to use a term that was popularized under the George W. Bush administration after the events of 11 September 2001, as a "war on terror." Within this framing, encouraging reform that might weaken allied rulers could embolden "the extremists." Furthermore, increased security cooperation between Gulf rulers and US government agencies has resulted in the transfer of technologies and skills that can also be used against political opponents. Thus recasting the preceding Schlesinger quote in the context of Washington's 2011 support for Gulf autocrats might lead one to question how much has really changed.

Regardless of whether reform pressures have weighed heavily on one side or the other, there has certainly been political change in recent decades. Procedural definitions of democracy emphasize free and fair elections for leaders, and though there has been no change on this front, other changes in formal institutions and consultative mechanisms have taken place, albeit very deliberatively. In 1980, one could identify only two Gulf countries that had experience with national parliamentary elections, Kuwait and Bahrain. Since then, however, formal mechanisms legalizing, promising, or enacting wider participation have included constitutional reforms (Bahrain), appointed consultative councils (Saudi Arabia), free elections for some professional associations like chambers of commerce, creation of state-sponsored human rights organizations, female suffrage (at least in Kuwait), and some subnational and municipal elections. Seen from this vantage point, one might posit that some of the Gulf's citizen protests in 2011 were animated by the perception that further promised reform had not materialized.

This perception has perhaps been reinforced by the fact that most formal mechanisms of monarchical power have changed very little. In one sense, rulers have enacted formal shifts with little or no societal engagement, and none of these changes actually limit ruler prerogatives. Kuwait's parliament may be lively, but its legislative powers are as circumscribed as they were in the 1970s. In all Gulf Arab states, ruling family members continue to dominate important government and security ministries; political parties and independent labor unions remain illegal; issues of leadership succession continue to be matters internal to the regime; court systems are tied to executive power; and new constitutions (in Qatar and Bahrain) reserve little power for elected bodies. Ironically, outright election rigging is often not needed, because the electoral stakes are so low, and with the exception of parliamentary elections in Kuwait, voter participation has been anemic. If and when the political opposition oversteps formal boundaries, security forces have proven effective at repression. Why then hold elections if everyone knows that they are not about genuine political representation? This is a question that will be pursued in the chapter's case studies, but one potential answer is to look beyond the formal mechanisms of governance.

Many observers of Gulf politics note that genuine political power lies outside formal bodies. After all, a defining characteristic of any monarchical arrangement is that the king or ruler exists above or outside politics, shaping decisions beyond the public view. And regardless of whether an existing constitution qualifies this monarchical privilege to some extent or not, the fact of the matter is that rulers have been able to fashion informal institutions that allow a type of mediated participation that has preserved centralized power. Rulers buoyed by oil monies have adapted traditional (tribal or religious) forms of consultation, or have crafted new ones.[10] Termed "informal corporatism" to differentiate them from types found in Western Europe, these institutions do not have membership lists or official recognition. Instead, merchants, tribal leaders, religious heads, and other important groups have intermediaries who communicate their demands or advice to rulers through royal courts or councils. Often these interactions concern access to patronage and privilege that the ruler exclusively manages. Sometimes rulers may use these venues to gauge public reaction or to gain nonbinding participation in policies or ideas. Because there are no formal rules, rulers can also encourage competition and divisiveness among corporate intermediaries.

Though formal political parties are not allowed in most Gulf Arab states, chambers of commerce and other professional syndicates have in some cases come to take on party roles by mobilizing opposition and providing venues for political voice. So-called traditional social gatherings such as Kuwait's *diwaniyya* have increasingly become important stages upon which citizens engage and debate. And the links between the youth of Gulf societies and growing transnational movements, coupled with their use of communication technologies and new media, suggest that the difficulty of limiting participation will only increase. Political pluralism comes in many forms, and while Gulf citizens cannot directly choose their representation, this does not mean that representation, debate, and voice are absent.[11] In this respect, an intriguing area of informal politics is the growing, and in many cases permanent, ranks of foreign labor. Since Gulf countries have built economies far larger than the native population base can service, large numbers of blue- and white-collar laborers have come to live, work, and participate in societies in which they themselves are not citizens. Indeed, in every Gulf country except Saudi Arabia, the native citizens constitute very small minorities. Could future demands by foreign workers for increased protection and rights be part of greater overall political participation?

Perhaps the most consequential informal institution ensuring centralization of political power in the Gulf is the ruling families themselves. Ruling families have proven adept at crafting and preserving intrafamily cohesion through placement of family members in government positions. This is key, because in many studies of regime transition or democratization, defections from or splits within ruling groups usually herald more significant change. So the contrast of opposition disorganization with ruler cohesion is stark and consequential. All of which brings us to what Samuel Huntington termed "the King's Dilemma." According to this formulation (discussed in further detail in Chapter 8), what should doom monarchical rule are growing societal complexity and demands for participation that are too significant for rulers to satisfy or to quash. One response to Huntington's dilemma is worth recalling: "In the less than long run, however, monarchy is particularly well suited to the requirements of state formation, especially in its early stages."[12] The question today, especially in light of the events of 2011, is: How near are we to the "less than long run"?

Kuwait

In a region of unique politics, Kuwait really stands out. It possesses the region's oldest and strongest elected parliament; it pioneered forms of revenue distribution and welfare provision that have come to define all of the Gulf states; its political oppositions are among the best organized in the region; and outside formal channels, pluralistic forms of debate and participation are well developed. On the other hand, while politics in the country remains contentious, Kuwaitis were notable for their lack of participation in the kind of mass protests that swept the region in 2011.[13] In a number of ways, the country shares aspects of political centralization common to those of its neighbors: the ruling al-Sabah family has final say in all important decisions, political parties are illegal, rulers can and have disbanded parliament, and nonparliamentary branches of government are not independent from the ruling family.

The role played by parliament in Kuwaiti political life is not new. Most observers agree that the al-Sabahs and other prominent families came to what is now called Kuwait City in the eighteenth century. The al-Sabahs were considered the first among equals, taking up political power but in alliance with the other prominent merchant families, thus creating a sort of balance of power. Things eventually came to a head in 1938. In that year, prominent merchants elected among themselves a legislative council, a majlis. Members quickly moved to take over local municipalities, organize public services, and eventually take control of the public budget, including oil royalty payments. These moves, particularly the effort to take control of oil royalty payments, were too much for the members of the al-Sabah family, who banded together and, with the acquiescence of British authorities, shut down the majlis and exiled some of its leaders. From this point, members of the ruling family would lead important government ministries such as finance and interior, though the precedent set by the elected parliament was not forgotten. When Kuwait gained its political independence in 1961, it faced an immediate challenge to its sovereignty by Iraq (a more violent version of which would be repeated in 1990). Within this context, the ruling al-Sabahs agreed to elections and to the writing of a constitution. What has since prevailed in Kuwait is a formal system of limited participation.

In formal terms, parliament is composed of members freely elected by Kuwait's citizens. However, the emir appoints the prime minister (historically the crown prince), who then appoints the government ministers, sixteen in all, who also serve in parliament. Not only do these formal privileges allow ruling-family control of the important ministries, but appointments to parliament also give the government a controlling voting bloc in parliament. Legislation can only be submitted by the prime minister, though parliament can amend, approve, or disapprove the legislation. Many of these elements can be found in other parliaments (such as in Jordan), but where Kuwait's majlis is different is in the power that elected members have to question and to vote their nonconfidence in individual ministers, including ruling-family members and the prime minister.[14] And though in practice this rarely occurs, the threat of it provides important public leverage on policy in two ways: the emir avoids appointing family members to the government who might risk losing a vote of confidence, and appointed members of parliament tend to acquiesce to elected parliamentary blocs to avoid questioning.[15] According to the country's constitution, parliament also has a unique role to play in leadership succession. In January 2006, then-emir Shaikh Jaber died, spurring a debate within the ruling family about who should succeed him. Ultimately and for the first time, parliament voted on the successor and approved Shaikh Sabah. This choice was admittedly in line with the wishes of a majority of the ruling family, yet it nonetheless was significant because it underscored the legitimizing effect of approval by parliament. Taken together, these formal elements make Kuwait's parliament the strongest in the region, but there are other formal limits to parliamentary power.

The emir has the power to dissolve parliament, though according to the constitution he must then call elections within two months. Dissolution has occurred six times (in 1976, 1986, 1992, 1999, 2006, and 2009), with the first two instances deemed unconstitutional because elections did not follow within the required time limit. The 1986 and 2009 dissolutions occurred in the wake of calls to question and to vote nonconfidence in ruling-family members who were sitting ministers. While political parties are illegal in the country, groupings and informal candidate lists spanning the political spectrum have long existed. In the most recent elections, political blocs included

Sunni Islamists within the Islamic Constitutional Movement; merchants, liberals, and nationalists in the National Action bloc; and more conservative nationalists and some Shiite Islamists in the Popular Action bloc. Government-allied candidates (outside the sixteen appointed ministers) run as independents. The result is parliaments that are not short on debate, drama, and openness.

Elections to Kuwait's parliament are equally turbulent. Since 2006, women have been allowed to vote, and in the May 2009 elections following the last dissolution, four women were elected. This marks a procedural advancement in women's rights, but limits persist regarding such things as inheritance and citizenship. Election rules, and struggles over their design, have been an area of particular dispute. Kuwait's earliest elections took place under rules specifying ten electoral districts with five representatives each, thereby allowing election of more cohesive opposition groups. In 1980, the emir sought to curb the opposition's power by changing the rules to specify twenty-five districts with two representatives each, effectively diluting the opposition and favoring the election of government-allied candidates.[16] Long-standing opposition efforts to reduce the number of districts came to a head in May 2006, when opposition parliamentarians led protests demanding an end to delays in electoral reform. Eventually the emir gave in, allowing passage of a new law reducing the number of districts to just five.

Outside the ruling institutions and parliament, Kuwaitis enjoy an array of social organizations that enhance pluralism in the small country. Perhaps because parties have been banned, professional associations like the national chamber of commerce, as well as local cooperatives, have served as institutional venues for political and social voice.[17] And long before the advent of regional media outlets like Al Jazeera, Kuwait's press had a history of joining in the country's public debates. Media of all political persuasions must still be licensed by the government and have at times been shut down, yet compared to its neighbors, Kuwait's media enjoy a large degree of autonomy. In sum then, the formal aspects of Kuwait's political participation set it apart from the region, though once we look at less measurable, less overt mechanisms of power, we see some elements of centralized control similar to that found in other Gulf states.

Kuwait's 1938 majlis and the adoption of a constitution and elected parliament at independence masked strong protections of centralized ruling-family power. One way to understand this dynamic is as an "unwritten contract" in which the traditionally most powerful political opposition, merchant elites, acquiesced to the ruling family's centralized rule in exchange for merchant autonomy in areas of business and the economy. An expression of this was the fact that by the 1980s, about 90 percent of Kuwait's citizen labor force had come to work for the government. For the merchants' part, they were free to mobilize, critique, and run candidates against government loyalists, but an informal line has persisted. No direct critique of the emir or challenge to the political position of the ruling family would be tolerated.

As part of this informal standoff, vigorous forms of societal debate and participation have evolved. The *diwaniyya*—a traditional male gathering in homes—is another institutional practice that has come to define Kuwait's political pluralism. Semi-regular meetings that increase in frequency during periods of national debate or election take place in a person's home, with extended family members or professional colleagues drinking tea, smoking, and discussing current events. Many meetings are small and local and may not be politically inclined, but others can serve as quasi-parliaments, with intense debate and exchange. Like the national chamber of commerce, these meetings provide institutional autonomy and space for opposition debate and strategizing, especially when parliament is not in session. Moreover, mobilization through these meetings has at times played key roles in national politics, such as the petitions that grew out of opposition *diwaniyyas* in the late 1980s demanding a reinstitution of parliament. Ignored by the emir at first, these petitions laid the groundwork for a reinstitution of parliament in the aftermath of the liberation of Kuwait from Iraq in 1991.[18]

Utilization of informal means to contest power is not, however, solely an opposition tactic. While the constitution stipulates that oil monies are remitted directly to the government and not to the ruling family—unlike in other Gulf countries—Kuwaitis recognize that the al-Sabahs maintain significant flexibility in how public resources are distributed. Indeed, many see this as part of the unwritten contract in that an unsupervised public purse affords Kuwait's rulers a myriad of tools to route money and privilege in exchange for political acquiescence. The ruling family funds and organizes its own *diwaniyyas,* directs informal patronage to allies, and cuts benefits to rivals. Elections to parliament are a good example of this formal/informal dichotomy. On paper, Kuwaiti elections are free contests, but in reality a lot of money is at play. Rulers and the opposition fund election *diwaniyyas,* make promises of patronage in exchange for votes, and influence media coverage. And while political parties are not allowed, candidates from tribal backgrounds (often progovernment) gain advantage through informal and illegal "tribal primaries" that enhance their chances of winning at the expense of opposition candidates.

The 2011 protests did not hit Kuwait with the same force as elsewhere in the region, yet the country has not been completely quiet. While events in Egypt's Tahrir Square were grabbing world attention, Kuwait's parliament for the first time in its history questioned a sitting prime minister, Shaikh Nassar. Hundreds of Kuwaitis subsequently gathered in protest, and in March 2011 the cabinet resigned rather than face more parliamentary questioning. Clearly, however, the scale of such protests is significantly smaller than in other countries of the region, a fact that is somewhat surprising given that Kuwait is the one Gulf country that has a long experience with political participation as well as having the best-organized political opposition. On the other hand, some have argued that it is precisely Kuwait's comparatively robust experience with political participation that has given the ruling family some room. Or perhaps it is the fact that the ruling family quickly distributed billions in public sector patronage to stave off citizen protest once events in Egypt had gathered steam. For now at least, Kuwait appears to have achieved a degree of political stability situated somewhere between lively parliamentary participation and stubbornly centralized monarchical rule.

Bahrain

Prior to 2011, Bahrain was considered to be the one Gulf Arab country moving toward a Kuwait-style form of more participatory politics. But in the wake of the government's violent repression of protesters in March and April 2011 with the assistance of troops from Saudi Arabia and the United Arab Emirates, and the continued repression of protesters, this is no longer true. The killing of peaceful protesters and the subsequent mass arrests of doctors and professionals have proven watershed events in Bahraini history. Though protesters mostly came from depressed Shiite villages in the country and were demanding political reform, the ruling al-Khalifa family, along with the other ruling families, exploited the fear of a Shiite uprising "directed from Tehran," all without evidence. Observers and critics countered that the real threat posed by Bahrain's protests was to ruling-family reign and privilege across the region. By the summer of 2012, Bahrain's political future appeared dark.

Shortly after Bahrain gained its independence in 1971, the emir decreed that an elected Constituent Assembly would be formed. In 1972 the country held its first national elections—which were restricted to male citizens—and in 1973 the assembly approved a constitution remarkably similar to that of Kuwait. The document allowed the assembly to alter and approve legislation (though not to submit it), provided for questioning and votes of nonconfidence of individual ministers, and gave the emir the power to dissolve the assembly provided that elections were called shortly after. This was a short-lived experiment, however. In August 1975, the emir shut down the

Constituent Assembly and ruled by various emergency decrees until the ascension of a new emir, Shaikh Hamad ibn Isa al-Khalifa, in 1999.

While Bahrain is often depicted as a majority-Shiite country ruled by a Sunni monarchy, the country's politics should not be viewed as flowing from a "mere religious divide." Other divisions, socioeconomic and historical in origin (Arab Shiites versus Shiites from Iran, for instance), have also influenced the country's politics.[19] And divisions, of course, can and have figured into ruler strategies of practicing divide-and-rule politics. Given a steady decline in Bahrain's petroleum resources and its simultaneously increasing population, a reinforcing cycle of complex sectarian and socioeconomic tensions grew. The culmination came in the form of mass social unrest and violence in the mid-1990s. Termed Bahrain's "intifada" (or uprising, a term borrowed from the Palestinian phenomenon), the period witnessed running street battles between police and poor Shiite youth that roiled the country for several years. When the new emir, Shaikh Hamad, ascended the throne in 1999, the most violent demonstrations had ended but tensions remained high. The emir's announcement of his intention to initiate political reform produced considerable relief and hope.

A number of positive changes followed. The emir released political prisoners, abolished state security laws, relaxed restrictions on the press, and extended "full citizenship" to Bahraini women. A plan for further reform, a national action charter, was overwhelmingly approved by a plebiscite in 2001. The charter pledged to reinstate the 1973 constitution, paving the way for a new, elected legislative body. For many observers, Bahrain looked to be on the way to putting in place a "constitutional monarchy," which would have been a not inconsequential first in the Middle East.[20]

But by 2002, implementation of the actual constitutional reforms revealed a different story. Shaikh Hamad used the reforms to centralize political power, declaring himself "king" and "protector of religion and homeland."[21] In particular, the creation of a bicameral legislature—in which a lower house would be comprised of elected members, while an upper house would be made up of ministers appointed by the king—effectively rendered elected representatives powerless. In October 2002, the monarch pushed forward with elections to the lower house. As in Kuwait, political parties in Bahrain are outlawed, so informal societies and groups assumed that role by acting as quasi-parties. Significant portions of these groups representing the Shiite opposition decided to boycott the elections, which depressed the voter turnout and resulted in a parliament that was dominated by pro-monarchy representatives. Social unrest mounted.

In 2005, a new antiterrorism law was passed with very broad parameters for what constituted a threat to the country, while another law curtailed rights of assembly. In reaction, the major Shiite opposition movements decided to reverse their previous election boycott and participate in the 2006 lower-house elections. The largest of these blocs, al-Wifaq, won seventeen out of the forty seats in an election that saw significantly higher voter turnout than in 2002. According to several observers, it seemed as if the opposition had decided to change the system from within, despite its limitations.[22]

In a foreshadowing of how external actors would respond in 2011, fears over Shiite political power accompanied Bahrain's political turmoil of the period. Regime supporters as well as other Gulf monarchs were quick to suggest that nefarious interference from neighboring Iran was fomenting unrest among the country's Shiite communities. As headquarters of the US Fifth Fleet, Bahrain's ruling family is also a key Washington ally. A free trade agreement between Bahrain and the United States in 2006 was widely interpreted not as an economic agreement (trade is insignificant between the two) but rather as a symbol of continued US political support for King Hamad. Such support has meant that aside from occasional human rights reports, Washington has generally avoided criticizing its Bahraini allies.

As struggles over formal avenues of political participation narrowed, shifts in informal politics suggested a similar narrowing. As a typical Gulf rentier state, though less well off than its neighbors, Bahrain has long supported despotic power through its top-down patronage. Indeed, while the country's oil reserves are the region's most modest, King Hamad's ascension was fortuitously timed with the rise in oil prices of the 2000s; as well, the monarchy receives significant, though unaccounted for, financial support from Saudi Arabia. These revenues facilitated the placement of the king's allies into senior government positions. Ruling-family members reportedly saw their monthly stipends increase, while other local elites enjoyed generous housing grants in new developments near the capital, Manama.[23] While there have been parliamentary investigations into allegations of fraud in the public pension system, with efforts to question several ministers in 2004, royally imposed limits on the questioning of ministers effectively blocked further inquiries and thus limited accountability. Another method the monarchy has employed to offset the opposition and its numerical advantage has revolved around citizenship. In 2002, the cabinet of ministers enacted a new law that grants Bahraini citizenship to other Gulf nationals.[24] This law allows the king to grant citizenship not only to previously stateless Bedouins, but also to expatriate Arab workers from majority-Sunni countries, as a means of countering the predominantly Shiite opposition. It was little surprise that some of these nationalized Arabs reportedly served in units responsible for some of the worst abuses in 2011.

In a sense, one can view the violence in Bahrain as part of regional contagion, though it must also be underlined that the regime-opposition struggle was particularly Bahraini and was linked to the country's own past. Prior to 2011, procedural advancements were not followed by substantive or genuine political participation; monarchy and opposition were deeply distrustful of one another. What is precedent-setting beginning with the events of 2011 is overt Saudi and Emirati intervention. Bahrain's internal politics, or for that matter most Gulf politics, can no longer be considered just a local affair. Moving forward, it is depressing to conclude that Bahrain's trajectory of reform has come to an end. The country's varied opposition and the monarchy remain far apart; few believe that the monarchy will open up in any meaningful way; few doubt the opposition will continue to demand justice and equal treatment; and none question the lengths to which the Gulf's rulers will go to ensure al-Khalifa primacy.

Saudi Arabia

The kingdom of Saudi Arabia is in many ways the archetypal rentier state. Since the state's founding in 1933, the ruling al-Saud family has used proceeds from the world's largest oil reserves to co-opt political dissent or has used the various tools purchased by those proceeds to repress its population. This does not mean that the country's citizens have been quiet; indeed, resistance to centralized rule has been expressed through a variety of means, some violent, most not. Since the 1990s, formal procedures of political participation that were long promised by the monarchy have gradually evolved. However, many have viewed these steps as tentative at best, since informal arrangements and relations remain a cornerstone of absolute rule by the al-Sauds. It is within this context that the fall of Egypt's Mubarak regime and of Tunisia's Ben Ali regime, coupled with similar dynamics in neighboring Bahrain and Yemen, shook the Saudi monarchy to its core. In response, Saudi authorities deployed men and money to defend nondemocratic rule across the region. No longer just a rentier state, Saudi Arabia has matured into a global player that some are crowning "leader of the counter-revolution."[25]

The Saudi royal family has ruled the country in ways that are different from those employed by its Kuwaiti and Bahraini neighbors. Perhaps the most important difference is in how the ruling family came to solidify its rule. The ruling family expanded its power through an eighteenth-century alliance with a puritanical form of Islam propagated by the preacher Muhammad ibn Abd al-Wahhab. Since that time, Wahhabis (as followers of this inerpretation of Islam are known) have been the country's official religious leaders and have enjoyed influence in shaping the country's social institutions. This religious grounding is an integral component of the al-Saud family's claims to political rule over an area in which Islam's two holiest cities are located. The al-Sauds also expanded their power through domestic conquest; hence there was little history of bargaining with political rivals or of the creation of constitutional bodies as in Kuwait and Bahrain. That being said, municipal elections did take place between 1954 and 1964 throughout the kingdom. Recent research has documented the struggles of reformers to push the envelopes of modernization and reform in this period. Ironically, however, Crown Prince Faisal's announced reforms in 1962 actually sounded the death knell for further advancement. Instead of establishing a basic law, a consultative council, and broader elections, the soon-to-be king centralized authority, ended elections, and never followed through with a basic law or constitution.[26] Promise without implementation would become a pattern in the kingdom.

The country's massive capital inflows and infrastructure development in the 1970s drove educational and social advancements. By the 1980s, a new stratum of religiously educated Saudis came to contribute to an Islamic resurgence in the country. Nonviolent and not explicitly political in their early development, these movements would form the foundation for a more distinct political opposition in the following decades. The Gulf War of 1990–1991 provided a spark for this movement. Initial criticism focused on the stationing of US troops in the country, but ultimately expanded to include a variety of socioeconomic complaints. Petitions to the king were the most common form of dissent and were used by various groups to call for action against corruption, creation of an independent judiciary, and more equitable distribution of oil monies. Public demonstrations—quite rare in the country's history—occurred, as did arrests of dissidents and of prominent shaikhs. Of importance in these petitions was their cross-societal nature; that is, these were complaints shared by a broad section of Saudi society, not the grumblings of a discontented minority,[27] something the royal family could hardly ignore.

In March 1991, the response from King Fahd was to implement the long-promised 1962 Basic Law. Most important, the law authorized the formation of a consultative council and reform of provincial governance. But like many procedural advancements, the devil was in the details: members of the council were appointed by the king, thus actual legislative powers were quite limited, and reform of local governance entailed devolving more power to provinces in which ruling-family members governed. In short, the reforms actually centralized power in the monarchy. This of course did little to satisfy critics and the opposition. Mounting socioeconomic inequality in the kingdom, combined with broader opposition to the country's foreign policy throughout the 1990s, emboldened the evolution of an unofficial grouping of reform-minded and religiously conservative clerics collectively termed the Sahwa (Awakening) movement. Many of these Islamist reformers were arrested or pushed into exile.

Following the 9/11 attacks in the United States, regional and international attention focused on the kingdom much as it had a decade earlier. Secularists, Islamists, and Shiite groups all submitted their own petitions, and though they emphasized different elements, all generally agreed on reforms that would curb the power of the ruling family.[28] Crown Prince Abdullah, the de facto ruler since the incapacitation of King Fahd in 1995, responded by setting up organized debates, termed "national dialogue" sessions. This move was followed by renewed promises for municipal elections, which took place to great media and international fanfare in 2005. Unfortunately, many Saudis did not share this optimism and very small numbers of them showed up to vote. Low voter turnout was at least partly a reflection of the fact that only half of the seats were up for election and that municipal powers remained limited. Additionally, while the rhetoric of reform was at a high pitch, arrests of dissidents and opposition figures accused of "terrorism" increased.[29] The experiences of 1961, 1991, and 2005 appeared to solidify a pattern of procedural reform followed by substantive crackdown.

Against these formal limits on political participation, there have been signs of more informal change. Clearly the public discourse on reform is now legitimate and accepted in a manner that contrasts with that of earlier decades. The kingdom's Islamist opposition "has fundamentally altered the terms of political debate in [the] kingdom, forcing the royal family to take them seriously." And while opposition figures in the country risk arrest if they go too far in critiquing the regime, opposition movements outside the country, such as the London-based Movement for Islamic Reform in Arabia, are now well established. Prior to 2011, the general consensus was that—at least in rhetorical terms—King Abdullah was continuing to advocate a reform agenda, while his main rival, Prince Nayif, the interior minister, argued "no to change, yes to development."[30] Of course, more long-standing and informal means for maintaining royal power endure, particularly the patronage links that extend from the royal family. In these informal areas, observing change is difficult. On the one hand, the growth of the Saudi economy and a genuine expansion of the private sector suggest a political economy that might be growing beyond the webs of simple patronage politics. On the other hand, an evolving facet of rule in the kingdom has been the type of informal corporatism that ensures that business interests are heard. For example, Saudi Arabia's national chamber of commerce acts as an unofficial political party of business, commenting on draft legislation and regularly meeting with political leaders. Since 2000, other groups of professionals such as lawyers and engineers have sought a similar institutional path. Thus what was once a truly informal system of individual consultation between representatives (usually chosen by the ruler) of important social groups and the monarch may be gradually transitioning to more institutionalized terrain.[31]

On 11 March 2011 the regional uprisings came to Saudi Arabia in the form of small demonstrations in Shiite neighborhoods across the Eastern province. Protesters' calls for an end to discrimination and the release of political prisoners were met by the deployment of security forces and by accusations from the country's leadership that the opposition was following Tehran's bidding. Days after these demonstrations, Saudi leaders took a cue from Kuwaiti leaders and announced significant new public expenditures to placate a nervous public. But unlike their Gulf neighbors, Saudi leaders also expanded support to conservative religious institutions and clergy. For many, this was interpreted as a show of strength by Prince Nayif and the regime's more conservative, unyielding elements. It seems quite clear that many Saudi royal-family members see the regional protests as an existential threat. Assertive intervention in Bahrain and hands-on involvement in Yemen and elsewhere suggest that Saudi's rulers view the stability of the region's remaining rulers as a requisite for their own.

Yemen

While also located on the Arabian Peninsula, Yemen is a Gulf country neither by geography nor in terms of its socioeconomic and political development. On the contrary, it stands very much at the other end of a spectrum: an unstable authoritarian republic and one of the poorest countries in the Arab world. Here the Arab Spring had very different effects, sparking far more widespread public protests, splits in the security forces, violence, and a challenge to the three-decade rule of President Ali Abdullah Saleh that ended in his resignation. In the lead-up to 2011, Yemeni society had been afflicted by frequent violence: past civil wars and conflict between the former North and South Yemen, the more recent Houthi rebellion in the northwest of the country, and continuing separatist sentiment in the south. At the same time, many of the factors that shape Yemeni politics are not dissimilar to those that shape politics in its much richer neighbors. Tribal and kinship politics remains important. Oil income, although insufficient to lift the country from poverty, has nonetheless shaped both development and politics. Yemen is a country that is often described as traditional, and yet according to a closer reading: "One of the enduring myths about Yemen is that change has been very slow."[32] The country, which only five decades ago was largely inaccessible to the outside world, is now "embedded in global trends," whether through communications technology, dependence on world food prices, or its entanglement with US counterterrorism campaigns.

In Yemen, tribes play a key role in defending and challenging the state. Their military power and prowess were harnessed at several key junctures, including during the civil war of 1994 when southerners rebelled in protest against the unbalanced terms of unification. Tribes are all the more important, as the regime has had only partial control of the country's periphery, with analysts estimating that in 2010 "the state could not reliably access significant parts of seven of its 21 governorates."[33] The harnessing of tradition can also be seen in the Houthi rebellion in the northern governorate of Sadah. The leadership of the Houthi rebellion has used its roots—the al-Houthi family are descendants of the prophet Muhammad—as an instrument to mobilize followers; likewise, the regime has equally attempted to delegitimize the movement by describing it as merely a sectarian phenomenon serving Iran's geopolitical objectives.[34]

North Yemen's per capita income increased during the 1970s and 1980s, when the country was not an oil-producing state, in large part due to remittances from Yemeni workers employed elsewhere in the Gulf, but especially in Saudi Arabia. However, while foreign remittances were central to the North Yemeni economy before 1990,[35] the government paid a dear price for its decision to call for an Arab solution to the August 1990 Iraqi invasion of Kuwait. Almost overnight, nearly 1 million Yemeni workers were expelled from Saudi Arabia and Kuwait; the Gulf Cooperation Council (GCC) states also suspended much of their development aid. Meanwhile, in South Yemen, aid from the Soviet Union declined sharply in the 1980s, and the country suffered from a violent internal conflict within the ruling party in 1986. Indeed, South Yemen's political and economic crisis played a key role in its decision to enter unification with North Yemen in 1990. Southern dissatisfaction with unity arrangements, in turn, led to a brief unsuccessful secessionist civil war (backed by Saudi Arabia) in 1994.

Oil has played an important role in Yemen's political dynamics since unification and leading up to the 2011 uprising. Yemen began exploiting oil fields on its territory in the 1990s. Oil has served to change the balance between state and society. With oil revenues accounting for up to 70 percent of the state budget, the regime has used such revenues to finance its neopatrimonial networks in society, and consequently bolster its social control. Oil income did not trickle down in sufficient amounts to promote dramatic social and economic development, however. As society remained poor, the state became richer. The particularly egregious characteristics of Yemeni rentier-financed patronage likely contributed to the swelling of public disenchantment against the Saleh regime, culminating in the Yemeni uprising of 2011. Moreover, the government expropriated land in the oil-rich south of the country, thus contributing to the dissatisfaction of many southerners with unification. It also distributed socioeconomic benefits unequally, with lower-level members of the president's Hashid tribe enjoying disproportionate access to employment in the military and in the security services, at a time when estimates put unemployment at around 40 percent and malnourishment at 42 percent of the child population.[36]

In the early 1990s, Yemen's unification and its initial wave of political liberalization were both influenced by events elsewhere in the world, and were used by the regime to build credibility with Western donors and secure much needed international aid. Yemen was subsequently pegged by some as "a vibrant transitional democracy."[37] Yet as a keener observer has shown, the regime deployed the 1999 presidential elections and the May 2000 tenth anniversary of national unification as spectacles "to announce and enact its political power."[38] In 2005, and as part of its post-9/11 "Forward Agenda for Freedom," the George W. Bush administration admonished Saleh for the rising levels of corruption in his government and pressed him to introduce some pluralism into the political process. Yemen was also taken off the Millennium Challenge Corporation's threshold program and the World Bank cut its aid to the country, citing concerns with transparency and good governance.

With the reversals in the Freedom Agenda after 2006, the Saleh regime moved again toward recentralizing power. Transnational security threats provided a new discourse upon which to anchor the foundations of Yemen's collaboration with Western governments and Saleh's authoritarian grip. The latter battled an exaggerated threat from al-Qaeda in the Arabian Peninsula (AQAP) in Yemen, ostensibly siding with the Bush administration in its "war on terror." Additionally, Saleh used Riyadh's geopolitical confrontation with Tehran to invite a limited Saudi military intervention against the Houthi rebels when the crisis threatened to spill over the border with Saudi Arabia in 2009. Riyadh, but especially the late Prince Sultan bin Abdulaziz, also bankrolled Yemeni tribal shaikhs to maintain the status quo at the border and provided Yemen financial aid to weather growing domestic pressures.

Yemen's uprising began in January 2011, with mounting local discontent being catalyzed into protests by similar events in Tunisia and Egypt. In the months that followed, protests became larger and more frequent, with protesters taking over some areas of the capital, Sanaa, and other towns. By May, GCC mediators seemed to have negotiated a deal whereby Saleh would step down—but at the last moment the president refused to sign. This led the head of the Hashid tribal federation, Sadiq al-Ahmar, to announce his support for the opposition protests and provoked armed clashes in Sanaa and elsewhere. While some military personnel allied with the opposition, others remained loyal to the regime. On 3 June, President Saleh was seriously wounded in an explosion at his presidential compound and left the country to receive medical treatment in Saudi Arabia.

When in September 2011 Saleh returned to Yemen, he did so in spite of continuing popular mobilizations calling for his departure and continued defections among members of the ruling elite and military formations. Henceforth the regime began orchestrating bloody confrontations with the opposition in an attempt to derail the uprising in Yemen from its peaceful tactics. Saleh's decision to return to Yemen and stand up to the protesters cannot be explained without reference to three key elements. As already discussed, Saleh believed he could still count on the loyalty of many tribesmen and close associates in the military and security services. He also hoped that the potential reverberations of regime change in Yemen would be perceived as too risky by key outside powers, but primarily Saudi Arabia and the United States, which might continue to support Saleh and his purported war against AQAP. Last but not least, Saleh was cognizant that some Yemeni opposition parties were still hedging their bets. Like opposition forces in other authoritarian countries, Yemen's opposition Joint Meeting Parties (JMP) coalition wanted political reform but hesitated to call for unbridled change. Weakened by the politics of divide and rule that Saleh so masterfully deployed, opposition parties have tended to focus on maintaining unity even at the cost of efficacy. In the case of the JMP, fears that the Islamist Islah party might dominate others have led to the adoption of decisionmaking by consensus.

In February 2012, the GCC eventually succeeded in persuading Saleh to hand over power to his deputy, Abdrabbuh Mansour Hadi. Yet much of Saleh's regime remained in place, prompting protesters to continue their calls for a more inclusive and civil state.

Conclusion

Even while heralding momentous change, the 2011 uprisings nevertheless highlight some enduring aspects of the struggle over political participation in the Arab Gulf states. First, the oil-exporting states have been able to rely on the use of typical rentier tools, revenue distribution and political repression. These strategies have clearly expanded beyond borders as Saudi and Emirati rulers struggle to put out uprisings with cash and resources. Second, beyond the material inducements, rulers have played on regional identities and rivalries to frighten citizens and secure their rule. This in turn has hardened minority views and emboldened opposition. Third, though a common vision of political participation is lacking, political oppositions and societies have not been quiescent in the face of the changes around them. Like in other parts of the Arab world, the onset and core of protests have been peaceful; violence in Yemen and Bahrain was largely exogenous to the protest movements themselves. Fourth, external intervention and the role of Washington in Gulf politics remain consequential for any future political participation. Much like the Sunni monarchs, Washington seems frozen by fear of change rather than giving serious attention to protester demands. Going forward, the ominous specter hovering over regional politics is that if decades of promised reform have failed and means of peaceful protest are blocked, how will political oppositions and citizens react?

Notes

1. Robert Vitalis and Ellis Goldberg, "The Arabian Peninsula: Crucible of Globalization," Working Paper RSC no. 2002/9, Mediterranean Programme Series (Florence: European University Institute, 2002); Timothy Mitchell, "McJihad: Islam in the US Global Order," *Social Text* 20, 4 (Winter 2002).

2. In reaction to the 2011 uprisings beyond the Gulf, the Gulf Cooperation Council offered membership to Jordan and Morocco, fellow monarchical regimes. For further discussion, see Chapter 8.

3. Michael Herb, "A Nation of Bureaucrats: Political Participation and Economic Diversification in Kuwait and the United Arab Emirates," *International Journal of Middle East Studies* 41, 3 (2009).

4. F. Gregory Gause III, *The International Relations of the Persian Gulf* (Cambridge: Cambridge University Press, 2010), pp. 241–243.

5. F. Gregory Gause III, *Oil Monarchies: Domestic and Security Challenges in the Arab Gulf States* (New York: Council on Foreign Relations Press, 1994), pp. 10–41.

6. Gwenn Okruhlik, "Rentier Wealth, Unruly Law, and the Rise of the Opposition: The Political Economy of Oil States," *Comparative Politics* 31, 3 (April 1999).

7. Gause, *Oil Monarchies*.

8. James R. Schlesinger, "Quest for a Post–Cold War Foreign Policy," *Foreign Affairs* 72, 1 (Winter 1993), p. 20.

9. Ian Lustick, "The Absence of Middle Eastern Great Powers: Political 'Backwardness' in Historical Perspective," *International Organization* 51, 4 (1997).

10. Khaldun Naqib, *Society and State in the Gulf and Arab Peninsula: A Different Perspective* (London: Routledge, 1990).

11. For an elaboration of these informal trends in Yemen, see Lisa Wedeen, *Peripheral Visions: Publics, Power, and Performance in Yemen* (Chicago: University of Chicago Press, 2008), pp. 103–147.

12. Lisa Anderson, "Absolutism and the Resilience of the Monarchy in the Middle East," *Political Science Quarterly* 106, 1 (1991), p. 4.

13. Kristin Diwan, "Kuwait's Impatient Youth Movement," Middle East Channel, *Foreign Policy Magazine,* 29 June 2011, http://mideast.foreignpolicy.com/posts/2011/06/29/kuwait_s_youth_movement.

14. The contrast of course is with standard parliamentary systems in which members can vote no-confidence in the entire government.

15. Herb, "A Nation of Bureaucrats," p. 379.

16. Mary Ann Tétreault, *Stories of Democracy: Politics and Society in Contemporary Kuwait* (New York: Columbia University Press, 2000), pp. 107–110.

17. Pete W. Moore and Bassel F. Salloukh, "Struggles Under Authoritarianism: Regimes, States, and Professional Associations in the Arab World," *International Journal of Middle East Studies* 39, 1 (February 2007).

18. Tétreault, *Stories of Democracy,* pp. 68–75.

19. Laurence Louer, *Transnational Shia Politics: Religious and Political Networks in the Gulf* (New York: Columbia University Press, 2008), pp. 24–33.

20. Neil Quilliam, "Political Reform in Bahrain: The Turning Tide," in Anoushiravan Ehteshami and Steven Wright, eds., *Reform in the Middle East Oil Monarchies* (Reading, UK: Ithaca Press, 2008), pp. 82–86.

21. Previously, only Morocco, Jordan, and Saudi Arabia were ruled by self-described kings.

22. Quilliam, "Political Reform in Bahrain," p. 93.

23. Abd al-Hadi Khalaf, "Political Reform in Bahrain: End of the Road," *Middle East International,* 19 February 2004.

24. Nadeya Sayed Ali Mohammed, "Political Reform in Bahrain: The Price of Stability," *Middle East Intelligence Bulletin* 4 (September 2002).

25. Toby Jones, "Counterrevolution in the Gulf," Peace Brief no. 89 (Washington, DC: US Institute of Peace, 15 April 2011).

26. Robert Vitalis, *America's Kingdom: Mythmaking on the Saudi Oil Frontier* (Palo Alto: Stanford University Press, 2006), pp. 228–251.

27. Gwenn Okruhlik, "Understanding Political Dissent in Saudi Arabia," *Middle East Report Online,* 24 October 2001, http://www.merip.org/mero/mero102401.

28. Andrezej Kapiszewski, "Elections and Parliamentary Activity in the GCC States: Broadening Political Participation in the GCC States," in Abdulhadi Khalaf and Giacomo Luciani, eds., *Constitutional Reform and Political Participation in the Gulf* (Dubai: Gulf Research Center, 2006), pp. 92–95.

29. Toby Jones, "Seeking a 'Social Contract' for Saudi Arabia," *Middle East Report* 228 (Fall 2003).

30. Ibid.

31. Steffen Hertog, *Princes, Brokers, and Bureaucrats: Oil and the State in Saudi Arabia* (Ithaca: Cornell University Press, 2010).

32. Sarah Phillips, "Yemen and the Politics of Permanent Crisis," Adelphi Paper no. 420 (London: International Institute for Strategic Studies, 2011), p. 14. See also Sheila Carapico, "Yemen Between Civility and Civil War," in Augustus Richard Norton, ed., *Civil Society in the Middle East,* vol. 2 (Leiden: Brill, 1996), p. 287.

33. Phillips, *Yemen and the Politics of Permanent Crisis,* p. 26.

34. See in particular the excellent analysis of Samy Dorlian, "The Sa'da War in Yemen: Between Politics and Sectarianism," *The Muslim World* 101, 2 (April 2011).

35. Kiren Chaudhry, "The Price of Wealth: Business and State in Labor Remittance and Oil Economies," *International Organization* 43, 1 (Winter 1989).

36. Phillips, *Yemen and the Politics of Permanent Crisis,* p. 30.

37. Sarah Phillips, "Foreboding About the Future in Yemen," *Middle East Report Online,* 3 April 2006, http://www.merip.org/mero/mero040306.

38. Lisa Wedeen, "Seeing Like a Citizen, Acting Like a State: Exemplary Events in Unified Yemen," *Comparative Study of Society and History* 45, 4 (October 2003), p. 688.

PART 2

The Issues

5

Political Culture Revisited

The three chapters in Part 1 of this volume all highlighted the abrupt transformation experienced by the Middle East from early 2011, from persistent authoritarianism to widespread popular protests, instability, regime change, and possible transitions to democracy. With Part 2, attention now turns to the major explanations for this. What characteristics, structures, institutions, social and economic forces, and other factors might account for these developments? And more broadly, what have been the major theoretical debates among scholars with regard to these questions? How can explanations address both decades of political immobilism, and yet also the dramatic changes represented by the Arab Spring?

This chapter addresses perhaps the most controversial set of explanations for the Middle East's long-standing "democracy gap," namely those that emphasize the possible role played by cultural characteristics. At first glance, the apparent appeal of such approaches is clear. Emphasis on cultural factors might offer an explanation as to why authoritarianisms in the Middle East were so persistent for so long, in contrast to those parts of the world that experienced so-called third wave democratization. Surely so much repression for so long cannot simply be attributed to unusually smart dictators, or to especially clever regime survival strategies that were somehow beyond the grasp of other, less-gifted authoritarians elsewhere in the world.

At the same time, political-culture approaches suffer from serious potential drawbacks, and as a result have faced substantial criticism from most scholars of the region. Some have charged that such explanations risk lapsing into ethnic or religious stereotyping, or the sort of "Orientalism" decried by Edward Said and others. Others argue that existing attitudinal data actually suggest broad popular support for democratic governance in the region. Important questions can also be raised about attitudinal variation across state, generation, and social class lines. Political culture explanations also risk being a residual category of sorts, offered up to explain political behaviors that do not seem to be accounted for by other, more tangible factors.

Doubts about the value of political-culture explanations of Arab authoritarianism grew even stronger in the wake of the Arab Spring. If political
culture is truly cultural—that is, embedded more deeply than merely a set
of fleeting or ephemeral attitudes—how can we explain the sudden change
in Arab politics represented by the events of 2010–2011?

Complicating the issue further, few if any scholars of the contemporary Middle East would argue that culture is irrelevant to politics. Cultural factors—rooted in history and social experience—help to shape how
people think about themselves, the groups with which they identify, the
nature of communication, and the value that people place on certain political processes and outcomes. One could hardly explain the permeability of the Arab world to transnational politics and ideological
appeals—including the remarkable regional demonstration effect of
protests in Tunisia in December 2010—without reference to the region's
linguistic and cultural heritage. Equally, one cannot explain the salience
of Jerusalem, the Palestinian question, Arab nationalism (or for that matter, Kurdish or Berber nationalisms), or the importance of political Islam
without recognizing that nonmaterial values can become deeply entrenched and reproduced over time.[1]

What is in dispute, therefore, is how important cultural orientations are,
how and under what conditions they make themselves felt, and the extent
to which culture is predeterminant, or rather arises from other more structural or situational factors such as political economy, opportunities, institutions, material incentives, and political manipulation. Should political
culture be an entry point for investigation of Arab politics, or at best a marginal consideration?

Essentialists, Contextualists, and Critics

Generally speaking, the existing literature on Middle Eastern political culture has fallen into three broad (if rather fuzzy and overlapping) categories:
the essentialists, the contextualists, and the critics.

Essentialist Perspectives

Essentialist approaches to political culture see culture as important, determinative, and at least semi-primordial—that is, so deeply rooted in history,
religion, and social organization as to be highly resistant to change. They
also tend to see the Middle East as a single historical unit, with its cultural
commonalities more salient in explaining regional politics than the varied,
internal characteristics of individual states. In policy terms, most essential-

ist approaches—although by no means all—have been quite pessimistic about the prospects for political reform in the region.

Raphael Patai's *The Arab Mind,* first published in 1973, was a classic (and much criticized) example of this approach. Patai used various personal and second-hand observations and anecdotes to emphasize a relatively homogeneous Arab psychology stretching across the Middle East, rooted in past tribal-survival practices, reinforced by childrearing practices, and evident in sexual, personal, and social and group behaviors. The result, he argued, is a society prone to conflict and extreme emotion, and unwilling to accept institutional authority.[2]

Elie Kedourie addressed the issue of Middle Eastern political culture and the prospects for political reform even more directly, arguing that what he saw as the pillars of Western democracy—popular sovereignty and suffrage, the rule of law, pluralism, and the secular state—were all "profoundly alien to the Muslim political tradition."[3] Samuel Huntington, in both *The Third Wave: Democratization in the Late Twentieth Century* and even more so in *The Clash of Civilizations,* seemed to attribute considerable scope for violence, and little prospect for democratization, to the Islamic world.[4] According to Huntington, the Islamic culture/civilization is inherently prone to violence: "Islam," he asserted, "has bloody borders."[5] Moreover, like Kedourie, he felt that it lacked the cultural foundations (such as separation of religious and secular authority) upon which Western democracy emerged. Another author who follows the essentialist approach, Daniel Pipes, has long argued that violence is endemic in Arab and especially Muslim political culture.[6]

In addition to focusing on what they see as Islam's nonseparation of religion and state, the rigidity of sharia (Islamic law), and the primacy of the religious-divine over popular sovereignty, essentialist scholars also emphasize discrimination against women and religious minorities, limited pluralism, a preference for order over *fitna* (social chaos), and a long historical tradition of authoritarianism during the caliphates. Ernest Gellner was especially influential in arguing that there are long-standing and recurrent characteristics of Muslim societies that have shaped their political evolution through the centuries. In particular, he suggested that within Muslim societies, political power and legitimacy is always tenuous, challenged first by tribes who resist the rule of urban areas, and later by urban-based ulama (religious scholars). The latter, while often accepting the political power of the day, see themselves as the guardians of religious law and legitimacy. The net result is one of a weak state faced by a strong society, with the political order vulnerable to fundamentalist challenges.[7]

Others also emphasize aspects of the region's tribal or Bedouin roots. Philip Salzman, for example, has emphasized what he calls the "tribal

DNA" of Middle Eastern societies. In his view, the imperatives of past no-madic and tribal existence led to a deep-seated impulse for predatory expan-sion, which in turn was subsumed and spread by Islam.[8] He suggests that enduring conflict and feuds between kinship groups therefore characterize Middle Eastern societies, precluding constitutionalism and a universal rule of law.[9] This view of the peoples of the region is one in which violence and despotism seem almost inevitable. Others see things rather differently, how-ever. Lawrence Rosen also focuses on the influence of a "tribal ethic" in Middle Eastern politics, with concepts of time, memory, the person, and re-lationships that are significantly different than those in the West. He notes a tendency to focus on persons and personal relationships rather than for-malized rules and roles ("persons make institutions, and not the other way around").[10] At the same time, he is careful to emphasize the "enormous flex-ibility" of multifaceted Arab political culture. His argument, therefore, is not that these cultural traits make democratic good governance possible, but rather that the limitation of government authority and the protection of freedoms may involve constitutional models that are somewhat different than those that accompanied the emergence of liberal democracy in the West.

Perhaps the most influential voice among essentialists has been Bernard Lewis. His views on the relationship between Middle Eastern cul-ture and democracy have undergone significant changes over time, how-ever. Long dubious about democratic prospects in the region[11] and emphasizing the importance of religious-cultural tradition in most of his work, Lewis later came to shift his position and argue that such traditions should not be seen as implacably hostile to political reform. On the con-trary, he suggested that Islam also contains notions of justice and popular consultation, rejection of despotism, and limits on state power. He argued that contemporary Middle Eastern authoritarianism "is alien, with no roots in either the classical Arab or the Islamic past, but it is by now a couple of centuries old and is well entrenched, constituting a serious obstacle." More recently, he also asserted that "positive elements of Islamic history and thought could help in the development of democracy."[12] With the overthrow of the Ben Ali and Mubarak dictatorships in Tunisia and Egypt, Lewis suggested that "the tyrannies are doomed. . . . The real question is what will come instead." Indeed, he went so far as to argue, "The whole Islamic tradition is very clearly against autocratic and irresponsible rule. . . . There is a very strong tradition—both historical and legal, both prac-tical and theoretical—of limited, controlled government." At the same time, and in keeping with his culturalist lens, he warned against rapid elec-tions or attempts to establish parliamentary democracy: "We have a much better chance of establishing—I hesitate to use the word democracy—but some sort of open, tolerant society, if it's done within their systems, according to their traditions."[13]

Most essentialists focus on the qualitative analysis of historical, textual, or anthropological data in making their case. However, there have also been a few efforts to assess these issues quantitatively. M. Steven Fish, for example, undertook a cross-national regression analysis of the impact of "Islamic religious tradition" (operationalized as a predominately Muslim population), as well as other possible explanations (economic development and performance, sociocultural divisions, British or Communist political heritage), on authoritarianism versus democracy.[14] He found that Islam, along with level of economic development, is a significant and substantial predictor of authoritarianism versus democracy. He did not find that Muslim societies have higher levels of violence or lower levels of interpersonal trust (both of which are associated with lower levels of democracy by the literature). He did find, however, less equality of women in Muslim societies and a statistical correlation between the status of women and democratic politics. The causal mechanism that would link these is unclear, although Fish did provide several preliminary suggestions. Daniela Donno and Bruce Russett reexamined Fish's conclusions on the basis of their own cross-national quantitative analysis. They agree that Islamic countries appear to be less amenable to democracy, but note that the effect is much stronger in Arab than non-Arab countries. They found that Islam impacts negatively on the equality of women, especially in Arab countries (and much less so elsewhere), but did not find any particular linkage between gender equality and (authoritarian or democratic) regime type.[15]

While scholars undertaking cross-national quantitative analysis tended to provide evidence that culture matters, they did not necessarily reach the conclusion that this means that the Middle East was doomed to an authoritarian future. Donno and Russett, for example, stressed that their results uphold a "weak culturalist" view, whereby "while certain elements of democratic culture are required for democracy to take hold, this political culture is not incompatible with any particular religious tradition, since such traditions are malleable or at least subject to reinterpretation."[16] A number of scholars have pointed to the experience of Catholicism to demonstrate the point: although once associated with persistent authoritarianism in southern Europe, Latin America, and elsewhere, these regions went on to experience widespread democratic transitions and consolidations.[17] In many ways, both these empirical findings and the Catholic experience point to the sorts of more contingent cultural explanations offered by contextualist scholars of the political culture of the Middle East.

Contextualist Perspectives

Contextualist approaches to political culture still hold that political culture is important in explaining politics, but tend to see culture as more varied and changeable, and operating on politics in ways that are often subtle and mediated. They typically reject the notion of an "Arab" or "Islamic" culture as a gross overgeneralization, and instead place emphasis on subcultures and the often contradictory and complex ways in which cultural influences are felt on politics. In this view, cultural influences are important, but traditions and doctrines are far from immutable. Contextualists also see the interplay between ideas, ideologies, cultural symbols, and material conditions as being important.[18]

Contextualists also often differ substantially from essentialists in their views on the content of religious and other traditions, suggesting that these are rather less definitive than many essentialists imply. Islam, for example, not only contains elements that may seem antidemocratic, but also contains contending principles of consultation (*shura*), social justice, and political responsibility.[19] They note that the past secularism of European society is often exaggerated (as evidenced by the historical role played by state churches and official religion), as is its past tolerance (as can be seen in the historical subordination of women, or the Holocaust). Similarly, they suggest that the supposed nonseparation of religion and state in the Middle East is also overemphasized. Beyond this, however, contextualists argue that how culture operates on social and political behavior is very much shaped by immediate circumstances, with individuals, political movements, and leaders potentially able to draw upon a broad array of cultural elements in determining or legitimating their actions.[20] In short, they differ not only on the extent of cultural determination, but also with regard to its very nature.

Dale Eickelman and James Piscatori are typical of scholars who emphasize the complex and multifaceted nature of Islam, and the extent to which individuals and elites are able to draw from a broad range of potential symbols in expressing very different positions. "Doctrine," they suggest, "is of secondary importance. Muslim politics is not determined by a template of ideas; it is influenced by a number of factors, which, while including scripturally defined precepts, also include national identities, economic circumstances, and social status."[21] A similar point has been made by Gudrun Krämer, who emphasizes that the political behavior of Islamist movements, and their particular orientation toward issues of pluralism and democracy, are shaped as much or more by the political context within which they operate as by the "theoretical" position of Islamic doctrine on such issues.[22] Her emphasis on the importance of political context appears to have been validated by the political flexibility shown by the Ennahda party in Tunisia or the Muslim Brotherhood in post-Mubarak Egypt.

Among contextualists, Michael Hudson, in his seminal 1977 study *Arab Politics: The Search for Legitimacy,* integrated political-culture factors (and, in particular, attitudes to group identity and authority) into a broader political analysis. Hudson pointed to both authoritarian and potentially democratic aspects of tribal and Islamic traditions, and emphasized the ways in which modernization and social mobilization had fractured these traditional authority structures. In this analysis, political-culture change, as well as the multiplicity and complexity of subcultures, was one (but not the only) driving force of politics. Hudson has been critical of many of the analyses offered by essentialists, but at the same time has differed with other critics in his assertion that political-culture analysis does have much to offer in understanding Middle Eastern politics.[23] He has also long held out the potential for reform and democratic change in the region, arguing that authoritarian regimes were bound to face a growing crisis of political legitimacy.

Fouad Ajami might be classified as a contextualist, despite the tendency of many of his critics to ascribe to him essentialist views.[24] Ajami has argued that the Arab world is trapped within dysfunctional intellectual traditions and political cultures. He says that in the course of interactions and confrontations with a rapidly modernizing West (and the dislocations of its own modernizing experiences), it initially clung to (or invented) a misguided Arab nationalism, followed by Islamist ideologies and movements.[25] He does not, however, view this situation as so fundamentally deep-seated as to be resistant to change, even rapid change, in response to both internal and external developments. For this reason, he was a strong supporter of the George W. Bush administration's declared (if somewhat transitory) support for Arab democratization, and was critical of those who attributed to the Middle East either immutable Islamic antidemocratic values or Arab exceptionalism.[26] Ironically, Ajami eventually grew deeply disenchanted with the immediate prospects for political change, noting in a December 2010 opinion piece that "we can now unequivocally admit that the forces of Arab autocracy have turned back the challenge to their dominion."[27] He could not have been more wrong, of course: less than a week later, Mohamed Bouazizi would set himself on fire in Tunisia, setting in motion a series of events that would transform the politics of the Middle East.

A number of authors have sought to tease out the ways in which cultural and noncultural factors interact in shaping political outcomes. Some of the literature on civil society in the Arab world, for example, has emphasized the way in which cultural and noncultural factors (such as state policy) have interacted to stunt its growth.[28] New modes of economic production could also be expected to interact with cultural legacies.[29] It could be hypothesized, for example, that preexisting sociocultural patterns render the "rentier" distribution of state revenues (explored in Chapter 9) more effective than might otherwise be the case. It certainly seems reasonable to assume that the corporatist and neopatrimonial mechanisms of resource control and political management that are so common in the region will function especially effectively when they map on to earlier, culturally rooted patrimonialism, or where they are able to build upon and manipulate existing social formations (such as tribe or clan). Unfortunately, this possible interface of political economy and political culture has been only sporadically examined by scholars of the region, and rarely in any detailed way.

One of the most interesting examinations of the role of ideational factors in modern Arab politics is offered by Lisa Wedeen, in her examination of the cult of personality constructed by the Assad dictatorships in Syria. In explaining the power of public spectacles of obedience, Wedeen does not emphasize preexisting cultural attitudes, and indeed is critical of the notion of political culture. Instead she looks at the ways in which symbolic reassertions of hegemony help to sustain political control. By demonstrating its ability to force citizens to engage in acts of public obedience, the regime indicates and perpetuates its power.[30] Conversely, Wedeen's analysis implicitly suggests that when the facade of hegemony begins to crumble, regimes might find their ability to deter protest rapidly diminishing. Thus, although her work on Syria long predated the widespread protests in that country in 2011, her theoretical argument seemed to be validated by the way in which initial challenges to the authority of the regime revealed it to be far less omnipotent than its carefully constructed public image had sought to project.

Critical Perspectives

Critical perspectives tend to doubt the feasibility or value of political-culture analysis. Typically, they argue that cultural variables are not only hard to assess, but also secondary to more structural determinants like political economy and institutional legacies.

Perhaps the most powerful and influential critique of an essentialist cultural approach to explaining the Middle East was that offered by Edward Said in *Orientalism*.[31] There he suggested that Western study of the Middle East had been characterized by a perception of the region and its peoples as an alien, unchanging, ahistorical "other." Methodologically, Orientalism as a discipline involved excessive reliance on philology, textual accounts of classical Arab-Islamic history, and formal Islamic theology, reflecting an assumption that described patterns of behavior from centuries earlier were innate Middle Eastern characteristics that also explained contemporary politics and society. Said also stressed the extent to which the production of

Western knowledge had been shaped by the exigencies of colonial rule and imperial interest, and the ways in which the Middle East had been "represented" through a Eurocentric lens rather than allowed to represent itself.

While Said's main focus was on the Orientalist literature of the nineteenth century, the implications for some contemporary scholarship were clear. What was less clear, however, was how Said proposed that the region be understood instead. That is, while he was a literary scholar with deep appreciation for cultural content, he also offered little guidance to social scientists regarding how to build a better understanding of the region, beyond the need to question one's assumptions and interpretive lenses.

Greater attention to these issues has been offered by Lisa Anderson. In contrast to the grand sweep of Said's reading of intellectual history, her point of departure is very much contemporary social science. Anderson condemned what she viewed as the simplistic stereotypes of a crude essentialist approach. She warned that although "unusually susceptible to distortions and bias," political-culture perspectives "can be very seductive, particularly to policy-makers looking for short, neat explanations of the complexities they face." As a consequence, "if we are not careful to specify its context and limits, we not only risk analytical confusion, we set the stage for sloppy, self-indulgent, or even damaging [policy] prescription."[32] In her view, scholars are far better off first focusing on the role of political economy, social class, political institutions, and other structural variables before examining the possible role of psychological and attitudinal factors.

The debate over what role political culture does or does not play in shaping Middle Eastern politics—and, in particular, its possible role in shaping trajectories of authoritarianism and political change—was given heightened salience by the terrorist attacks of 11 September 2001, subsequent US intervention in Afghanistan and Iraq, and the announcement of the Forward Agenda for Freedom in the Middle East by then–US president George W. Bush in November 2003.[33] Some critics charged that the Bush administration's policy was driven by an excessive reliance on political-culture stereotypes,[34] and sustained by a close relationship between leading neoconservatives and scholars such as Lewis and Ajami.[35] Lewis shot back with the charge that Middle Eastern studies had become afflicted by a combination of "political correctness and multiculturalism" that resulted in an "imposed orthodoxy" that made "scholarly discussion of Islam . . . dangerous" and provided Islam and "Islamic values" with "immunity from criticism."[36] Amid the heightened political sensitivities of the post-9/11 era, therefore, debates over scholarship became bound up with polemics over Middle East policy, to the detriment of both.[37]

Lost in the fray were many of the analytical issues at stake. What can political culture approaches explain—and not explain—about Middle Eastern politics in general, and about the dynamics of authoritarianism and democratization in particular? To what extent are cultural variables region-wide and slow to change, or to what extent are they variegated, changing, and contextually dependent? Perhaps most important, how do we demonstrate and measure this? These methodological issues ought to be at the core of debates over Middle Eastern political culture—yet they have been oddly absent.

Methodology, Attitudes, and Politics: Knowing What We Know (and Don't)

How do we "know" another culture and the ways in which that culture shapes political behavior? Perhaps the most obvious way is through the written content a culture produces: histories, religious documents, literature, political statements, and so forth. But the dangers in assessing political culture this way are twofold. First, by focusing on religious and historical texts, there is a danger of reading into contemporary society attitudes that have long ago changed. It is also far from clear that classic texts reflect the broader canvas of varying cultural attitudes across social groups, or give adequate voice to disadvantaged groups. Would a close textual reading of Old Testament prescriptions regarding, for example, the correct treatment of women and slaves, provide much insight into the politics of the (predominantly Judeo-Christian) United States? Why, then, would one presume that a similar reading of the Quran provides insight into how modern culture interacts with politics in the contemporary Middle East? Do the classic works of Shakespeare provide insight into the lives of seventeenth-century English peasants, let alone contemporary British workers? (Indeed, reading Shakespeare one might incline to the view that Britain is a treacherous and murderous society incapable of democracy.)

This, of course, was part of the methodological foundation of Said's criticism of Orientalism: that by focusing on philology, theology, and classical history, and moreover by doing so in a Eurocentric way, scholars had painted a static, distorted, and inaccurate view of the Middle East. Ironically, however, much the same criticism can and has been made of Said's own work, namely that he selected his textual examples of nineteenth-century (and twentieth-century) Western observation and scholarship with a view to making his case, ignoring evidence that might have painted a rather different picture.[38]

Some of the weaknesses of a textual reading of Middle Eastern culture can be minimized by more systematic sampling techniques and by focusing on materials that might be more representative of the attitudes and prefer-ences of a variety of groups within the mass public. Doing so has been in-hibited in the past by censorship and self-censorship of published materials. Only with the advent of direct broadcast satellite television (discussed in depth in Chapter 11) and later the Internet has the Arab public found a rel-atively open vehicle for information and debate, in what Marc Lynch in-sightfully characterized as a new, emerging "Arab public sphere."[39]

In addition to inferring political culture from largely textual and the-ological sources, one can also examine it qualitatively using more anthro-pological research techniques. Ethnography of this sort provides a potentially far richer description, and—if done well—is far less suscepti-ble to formal and elite biases. Often, close and sustained observation re-veals patterns of everyday behavior, rooted in the interaction of culture, institutions, and political economy, that would not otherwise be evident. It also can be keenly sensitive to the ways in which culture is mediated and interpreted through the lenses of gender, social class, and locale, and is hence cognizant of the many subcultures (and broader cultural repertoires) that are at play.

Methodologically, two potential problems arise here. The first is whether the initial ethnography is done well. To what extent can individual observation and anecdotal evidence provide a firm enough basis from which to develop broader theories of political psychology? The second issue—and for the study of regional authoritarianism and reform, one that is par-ticularly important—is the extent to which one can generalize from the sociocultural dynamics of one element of society to society as a whole. Some of the work on "tribalism" in Middle Eastern politics falls prey to this, using ethnographies of small groups to draw shaky conclusions about the region as a whole. While there is no doubt that clan politics and tribal dynamics shape some aspects of Middle Eastern politics in some countries, it is also the case that only a tiny proportion of the region's population have any significant links to a nomadic or Bedouin past. The majority of modern Middle Easterners are urban, and many have traditions of urban or seden-tary social organization that stretch back centuries or even (as in the case of Egypt) millennia. Conversely, much of the initial analysis of protest move-ments in Tunisia, Egypt, and elsewhere has placed primacy on the voices of protest organizers, Internet activists, and human rights commentators. To what extent, however, are such views typical of the majority of protesters, let alone the public at large? The degree to which many observers underes-timated support for Salafist Islamist candidates in Egypt before the 2011 parliamentary elections underscores the point.

One way of addressing these problems is to complement qualitative po-litical ethnography with quantitative data drawn from opinion surveys. Done properly, attitudinal survey data allow one to see how attitudes relate to a variety of social and economic variables, how clusters of attitudes vary within larger population groups, and how sets of attitudes might be related.

The application of these techniques to the Middle East was long limited by dictatorship and the resultant difficulties of public opinion polling. Indeed, until the 1990s, many opinion survey–based attitudinal studies were forced to depend upon data drawn exclusively from university students, because it was difficult to secure the necessary permissions from authorities to conduct wider studies. The cross-national World Values Survey (WVS) project, for example, included no Middle Eastern countries at all in its initial wave of polls in 1981–1984, while in the 1989–1993 and 1994–1999 waves it featured only one Middle Eastern country (Turkey), as well as a few predominantly Muslim countries elsewhere.[40]

One important early exception to this pattern was the Palestinian territories, where the onset of the Oslo peace process led to the establishment of a number of institutions and nongovernmental organizations (NGOs) undertaking frequent opinion surveys on a broad range of issues.[41] The result is a rich body of opinion data—certainly the most extensive in the Arab world—on political and social attitudes, now stretching back more than a decade.

Lately, more data have become available, both because of a degree of political liberalization in some countries and due to increased interest in Arab and Muslim attitudes on the part of researchers, NGOs, and governments alike in the wake of the 9/11 terrorist attacks. International pollsters, such as Gallup, began to undertake large, multicountry surveys on attitudes in the Muslim world, as did research projects such as the Pew Global Attitudes project.[42] The 1999–2004 wave of the WVS included no fewer than eight Middle Eastern countries (Turkey, Egypt, Iran, Iraq, Israel, Jordan, Morocco, and Saudi Arabia). The United Nations Development Programme's groundbreaking 2004 *Arab Development Report* sought to map how Arab publics conceptualized and prioritized various political, social, and economic freedoms by drawing upon extensive opinion survey data from across the region.[43] The University of Maryland, in conjunction with the polling firm Zogby International, has conducted annual polls since 2003 in several Arab countries, largely focusing upon foreign policy issues.[44] In 2005, the Arab Barometer project was established at the University of Michigan, in collaboration with counterpart institutions in the Arab world and with other regional Barometer projects based in Africa, Asia, and Latin America.[45] Considerable polling has been done in Iraq, whether by the US military, aid agencies, or the media. In those countries where the Arab Spring has brought greater political freedom, it is likely that even richer data will be forthcoming.

Questions can be raised about some of the available survey data, in terms of both reliability and validity.[46] Some social groups—for instance, women, households without telephones, and rural populations—may be underrepresented due to poor research designs. In authoritarian countries and countries with little experience of opinion surveys, respondents may be reluctant to share their real views with a pollster. Survey questions and responses may be poorly translated from English to Arabic or vice versa, while the questions themselves may be poorly designed.

More fundamentally, basic questions can be raised about what expressed attitudes represent—are they deep-seated and hence causative of political action, or are they themselves a product of underlying political constraints and opportunities? In the former instance, as both essentialists and contextualists would argue, it is worth looking at attitudes to understand current and future politics. In the latter case, however, attitudes become more epiphenomenal, and one would expect them to change significantly as underlying structural and institutional conditions change. This debate has been particularly germane to the issue of legitimacy, which Michael Hudson (among others) made a centerpiece of his analysis of Arab politics.[47] To understand politics, must we primarily focus on how populations view authority and therefore what sorts of leaders they regard as legitimate and choose to obey? Or is legitimacy irrelevant to stable authoritarianism, in that it is repression, fear, and the lack of viable political alternatives—rather than respect for authority—that lead to compliant behavior?[48] With an eye to recent events, did 2011's political transitions occur because regimes lost credibility with the masses, or because they were no longer able to intimidate or otherwise deter protesters?

Quantitative attitudinal analysis cannot fully resolve these questions, although it does shed some light on them. Certainly it helps us to dispense with the notion that democratic governance has only weak popular support in the Middle East. Using WVS data, Ronald Inglehart has found that support for democracy is actually higher in Arab countries than in any other region of the world.[49] He has also found that support for democracy is high across the broader Muslim world but with significant differences between countries, which suggests the important contingent impact of other factors (as contextualists would argue). Using WVS attitudinal data to examine Huntington's thesis about Islam and the "clash of civilizations" in particular, Inglehart and Pippa Norris found only minimal differences between the Islamic and Western worlds on issues of democracy, with much greater differences between Western European and Islamic countries on the one hand and post-Soviet countries on the other. In the Islamic world, there was greater support for religious authorities playing a strong societal role, but this differed little from similar attitudes in Africa and Latin America. Finally, they found a very strong difference between the West and other societies, especially Islamic ones, on attitudes toward gender and sexual orientation.[50]

Drawing upon data from both the WVS and the Arab Barometer project, Amaney Jamal and Mark Tessler drew similar conclusions, noting that the proportion of respondents favoring democratic government in their own country ranged from a low of 81 percent in Algeria to a high of 92 percent in Morocco in 2006.[51] There is also little evidence from attitudinal survey data that Islamic religiosity is a strong predictor of attitudes toward democratic governance[52] or that most Arabs see any incompatibility between Islam and democracy.[53] Indeed, the relationship between religious orientations and political views appears to be stronger in the West than in the Middle East.[54] In short, systematic use of polling data helps to explain why antiauthoritarianism so quickly emerged as a central theme of Arab protests in 2011 and why there was such a wide postauthoritarian consensus in countries like Tunisia and Egypt in favor of democratic elections and reform.

Resolving the Debate?

Where do we stand, therefore, after this brief review of approaches, debates, and recent methodological advances in the study of political culture in the Middle East? Moreover, what are the implications of this for future trajectories of authoritarianism and political reform? Several observations can be made.

The first is that the debate over the impact of political-culture variables had become rather stale over the past two decades. Essentialists stress elements of Islamic doctrine (the sovereignty of God, the relatively unchanging nature of sharia, a lack of secularism and separation of church and state, attitudes toward women and non-Muslims) and Arab/Middle Eastern culture (tribalism, kinship-based politics, patrimonialism, ethno-sectarianism), and attributing much of the region's enduring authoritarianism to them. Contextualists emphasize a broader array of cultural values, many of them potentially conducive to democratic politics (principles of consultation in Islam and limits on the power of rulers; notions of reciprocal social obligation and accountability in tribal politics; the global spread of democratic norms). They also underline that the salience of cultural variables is contextually dependent and that effects can only be understood in tandem with noncultural variables.

While good scholarship ought to be able to determine which claims are stronger, until recently neither side was much swayed by the qualitative case studies of the other. The almost universally antiauthoritarian orientation of

Arab protests in 2011 does, however, cast profound doubt on the essentialist view. Contextualists can point to the Arab Spring as evidence that attitudes and conditions interact in complex ways that make the former changeable, to the point that authoritarian compliance rapidly dissolved into opposition and even regime change. Critics might take this a step further, arguing that the very rapidity of political transformations in 2011 undermined the notion that culturally embedded political values played a significant causal role.

The quantitative turn in comparative politics, although not without pitfalls, also offers an opportunity to cast new light on this debate. The consistent attitudinal finding that the degree of a respondent's religiosity has no significant impact on their views about democracy[55] suggests there is no necessary connection between Islam and political authoritarianism versus democracy, and that the effects of cultural factors are heavily mediated by other, noncultural variables, even allowing for the different ways respondents may conceptualize democracy. It is also striking the degree to which individual attitudes toward pluralism and citizen involvement vary substantially from country to country,[56] something that we would not expect to find if essentialist arguments about the weight of regionwide Islamic, tribal, or other cultural determinants were accurate. Indeed, such findings stress the contingent nature of "political culture."

In other respects, however, some of the findings from large–sample size quantitative research and from attitudinal surveys appear hard to reconcile. Cross-national studies using country-level data seem to suggest that Islam is somewhat associated with more authoritarian political systems, particularly in the Arab world. These findings hold true even when variables such as level of economic development, oil rents, and militarized conflict are accounted for. On the other hand, attitudinal data show a different picture: neither Muslims nor Arabs are hostile to democratic governance—on the contrary, they are strongly supportive of it. How can this apparent paradox be explained?

Part of the explanation flows from the fact that cross-national country studies tend to conflate cultural group with geographic region. In other words, some of the authoritarian persistence that was evident in the Middle East may have been due more to neighborhood influences than shared political culture. This explanation is strongly consistent with the striking pace of change the region experienced over a few short months in 2011.

Demonstrations, Dominoes, and Democratization: The Importance of Regional Permeability

That democratic openings can have "demonstration" or "domino" effects is well established, evident (for example) in the wave of democratization that swept Latin America in the 1980s and Eastern Europe a decade later. In such cases, the toppling of the once-solid and apparently unassailable edifice of dictatorship alters perceptions of opportunity and cost in neighboring societies as well, indicating that democratic change is possible and even providing examples as to how such change might be achieved. Such effects are likely to be especially significant when, due to cultural, historical, or linguistic ties, populations feel a special affinity for, or understanding of, the "demonstrators."

Given this, it seems equally likely that dramatic repression (such as was used against the Hama uprising in Syria in 1982) or failed political transitions (such as the over 100,000 dead in the Algerian civil war, 1991–ca. 2006) would have the effect of deterring neighboring populations from risking political change. Bloody strife in Iraq (2003–), which has killed some 100,000 civilians and either displaced or made refugees out of more than 4 million others, was hardly likely to have acted as a positive model either.[57] Certainly the dictators of the region have little interest in encouraging democratic change among their neighbors, and indeed have cooperated to discourage it.[58]

Through the 1970s, 1980s, and 1990s, therefore, many Arab citizens may have had little inclination to risk their relatively stable, secure, but authoritarian status quo for an uncertain future, whatever the abstract appeal of democracy—especially in a region where the *mukhabarat* (secret police) state can be so brutally efficient. This attitude of "better the devil we know than the devil we don't" would, anecdotally at least, appear to have been a significant component of past political stability in many countries in the region. The result was an appearance of widespread public acquiescence to the status quo. Political opportunities seemed limited, if not closed off altogether.

Yet this stability was not absolute, of course. Some groups did challenge the political status quo, and were repressed for doing so. Moreover, this was a stability based in equal parts on fear and deterrence (with dissent equaling punishment), a vague social contract (stability and a basic of standard of living in exchange for quietism), and a widespread feeling that "resistance was futile" and that oppositional activity could bring no real change. In a very real sense, therefore, it was a facade encouraged by regimes to hide their fundamental weaknesses. The persistence of Arab authoritarianism was also rooted in what Antonio Gramsci labeled "hegemony"—that is, a sort of conventional wisdom about the way the world is and can be that is broadly accepted and serves to maintain the power of dominant elites while demobilizing potential opposition.[59]

Whether these ideational factors should be seen as "political culture" is an open question. Our own analysis in this volume has suggested that the primary "cultural" component of the ideational elements in Arab authoritarianism were related to the cultural symbolisms of political discourse and high degrees of regional permeability (that is, the ease with which ideas and information moved across state borders), and not to particular antidemocratic values associated with ethnicity or religion.

Moreover, and in contrast to the presumption of cultural essentialists, the ideational elements of Arab authoritarianism were vulnerable to being perceived in new ways. As one of us wrote in July 2009, "what has been lacking in the region is a galvanizing event that shifts passive but prodemocratic citizens into a more activist frame."[60]

That "galvanizing event" came with the self-immolation of Mohamed Bouazizi in December 2010, the subsequent mounting protests in Tunisia, and President Zine el-Abidine Ben Ali's departure from power the following month. If such an apparently stable regime could be toppled in less than a month by the force of popular protests, perhaps Arab authoritarianism in general was a facade. The authoritarian emperor, it seemed, had rather fewer clothes than he claimed.

As protests spread, the mobilization of opposition to the Mubarak regime in Egypt took on additional importance in the political and cultural echo chamber that is the Arab world. Tunisia, after all, is hardly at the center of the Arab order. Egypt is. Mubarak's ouster seemed to indicate that anything was possible—even the eruption of protests and armed resistance in the brutal authoritarian strongholds that were Muammar Qaddafi's Libya and Bashar al-Assad's Syria. Mass movements of citizens began to imagine new and achievable futures, pursuing ideas that had seemed depressingly unrealistic and unobtainable only a few months earlier.

In short, attitudinal factors—the "imagination of the possible"—were critical to the Arab Spring. Demonstration effects were crucial in sustaining this paradigm shift. Arab political culture found within itself notions of freedom, justice, dignity, accountability, and even democracy around which to mobilize and build coalitions. The growth of democracy as an increasingly globalized ideal undoubtedly played a role too: Arab populations knew that their present authoritarian regimes were not the only way of organizing politics and that many other peoples (including many with lower levels of development) had made successful democratic transitions. Dictatorship was not only stultifying and linked to social injustice—at a certain level it had become embarrassing too. Protesters had little trouble reaching out across the supposed boundaries of culture to invoke broader notions of rights and resistance.

This momentum for change spread as a result of the shared cultural and linguistic connections within the Arab world, and was further strengthened by the effect of regional media (notably satellite television) as well as even newer technologies (particularly the Internet and social media). The very regional permeability that had helped to reinforce authoritarian deterrence for decades in the Arab world—a permeability rooted in cultural factors of widely shared language, religion, and bonds of identity—therefore acted to transmit and reverberate the momentous change of the Arab Spring.[61] Simply put, had Mohamed Bouazizi set himself on fire in protest in (nearby, but non-Arab) Niger, or had the governments of Mali or Chad fallen to antiauthoritarian protests, it is extremely unlikely that we would have witnessed the same results in North Africa and the broader Arab world. Even the massive "Green Movement" protests in Iran that followed manipulation of the 2009 Iranian presidential elections had virtually no repercussions in nearby Arab countries.

Structural conditions—political exclusion, economic deprivation, inequality, the dynamics of crony capitalism—all played fundamental roles in setting the stage for protest and change. So too did the agency of proreform actors and the networks they had created. However, in seeking to understand how the protests erupted and spread, it is clear that addressing attitudinal, ideational, and nonmaterial factors is essential too.

Notes

1. On transnational permeability in Arab politics, see Rex Brynen, "Palestine and the Arab State System: Permeability, State Consolidation, and Responses to the Intifada," *Canadian Journal of Political Science* 24, 3 (September 1991); Bassel Salloukh and Rex Brynen, eds., *Persistent Permeability? Regionalism, Localism, and Globalization in the Middle East* (London: Ashgate, 2004).

2. Raphael Patai, *The Arab Mind,* rev. ed. (New York: Hatherleigh, 2002).

3. Elie Kedourie, *Democracy and Arab Political Culture* (London: Cass, 1994), pp. 5–6.

4. Samuel Huntington, *The Clash of Civilizations and the Remaking of World Order* (New York: Simon and Schuster, 1998); Samuel Huntington, *The Third Wave: Democratization in the Late Twentieth Century* (Norman: University of Oklahoma Press, 1991).

5. Samuel Huntington, "The Clash of Civilizations?" *Foreign Affairs* 72, 3 (Summer 1993).

6. See, for example, Daniel Pipes, *The Long Shadow: Culture and Politics in the Middle East* (New Brunswick, NJ: Transaction, 1989), as well as many of his essays at http://www.danielpipes.org.

7. Ernest Gellner, *Muslim Society* (Cambridge: Cambridge University Press, 1983).

8. Philip Salzman, "The Middle East's Tribal DNA," *Middle East Quarterly* 15, 1 (Winter 2008), http://www.meforum.org/1813/the-middle-easts-tribal-dna.

9. Philip Salzman, *Culture and Conflict in the Middle East* (Amherst, NY: Prometheus, 2007), pp. 16–17.

10. Lawrence Rosen, "Expecting the Unexpected: Cultural Components of

Arab Governance," *Annals of the American Academy of Political and Social Science* 603 (January 2006), p. 170.

11. Ian Buruma, "Lost in Translation: The Two Minds of Bernard Lewis," *The New Yorker,* 14 June 2004, http://www.newyorker.com/archive/2004/06/14 /040614crbo_books.

12. Bernard Lewis, "Freedom and Justice in the Middle East," *Foreign Affairs* 84, 3 (May–June 2005), pp. 44–45. For a characteristically pithy statement of the doubts that most other essentialists hold about the democratization agenda in the Middle East, see Martin Kramer, "Should America Promote a Liberal, Democratic Middle East?" lecture delivered to the Weinberg Founders Conference, Washington Institute for Near East Policy, 2002, http://www.geocities.com/ martinkramerorg/Landsdowne2002.htm.

13. "The Tyrannies Are Doomed," interview with Bernard Lewis, *Wall Street Journal,* 2 April 2011, http://online.wsj.com/article/ SB10001424052748703712504576234601480205330.html?mod=rss_opinion_mai n.

14. M. Steven Fish, "Islam and Authoritarianism," *World Politics* 55 (October 2002). It must be said that Fish is a limited and reluctant essentialist, having drawn his conclusions about the importance of cultural variables on the basis of his data analysis rather than *a priori.*

15. Daniela Donno and Bruce Russett, "Islam, Authoritarianism, and Female Empowerment: What Are the Linkages?" *World Politics* 56 (July 2004). This question of an "Arab" versus "Muslim" democracy gap has also been addressed by Alfred Stepan and Graeme Robertson. They argue (like Donno and Russett) that the data suggest that it is far more the former than the latter. Indeed, they note that the significant difference between Arab and non-Arab Muslim societies suggests that religion per se had only a very limited role to play in explaining the lack of meaningful electoral competition in so much of the Middle East. Alfred Stepan with Graeme Robertson, "An 'Arab' More Than 'Muslim' Electoral Gap," *Journal of Democracy* 14, 3 (July 2003). A similar point is made by Arthur Goldsmith, who argues that "individual variation dwarfs many aggregate similarities among Islamic polities." Arthur Goldsmith, "Muslim Exceptionalism: Measuring the 'Democracy Gap,'" *Middle East Policy* 14, 2 (Summer 2007), p. 95.

16. Donno and Russett, "Islam, Authoritarianism, and Female Empowerment," p. 594. They draw the concept of a "semiculturalist" approach from Adam Przeworski, José Cheibub, and Fernando Limongi, "Culture and Democracy," in *World Culture Report: Culture, Creativity, and Market* (Paris: UNESCO, 1998).

17. The question remains open as to whether the democratization of these societies was due to the reforms in the Catholic Church during the Second Vatican Council (1962–1965), or to changes in global, regional, and economic contexts. While the hierarchical nature of the Catholic Church makes it more amenable to reform-from-above than does the more decentralized religious authority of Sunni Islam, the latter also provides more opportunities to generate and disseminate alternative theological and political views. Shia Islam falls somewhere between the two in this regard.

18. With regard to Gellner's notion of a "Muslim society," for example, Sami Zubaida has argued: "Of course, there are certain cultural themes common to the Muslim lands and epochs, arising from religion and common historical reference, much like the common culture arising from Christian religion and history. It would be a mistake, however, to think that these cultural items and the entities they spec-

ify are sociological or political constants: they are assigned different meanings and roles by different socio-political contexts." Sami Zubaida, "Is There a Muslim Society? Ernest Gellner's Sociology of Islam," *Economy and Society* 24, 2 (May 2005), p. 153.

19. John L. Esposito and James P. Piscatori, "Democratization and Islam," *Middle East Journal* 45, 3 (Summer 1991).

20. See, for example, Mark Tessler's attitudinal survey work on Arab political culture, which notes the substantial cross-national variation (hence underscoring the importance of contextual factors). Mark Tessler, "Democracy and the Political Culture Orientations of Ordinary Citizens: A Typology for the Arab World and Beyond," *International Social Science Journal* 59, 192 (June 2008).

21. Dale Eickelman and James Piscatori, *Muslim Politics,* rev. ed. (Princeton: Princeton University Press, 2004), p. xvii.

22. Gudrun Krämer, "Islam and Pluralism," in Rex Brynen, Bahgat Korany, and Paul Noble, eds., *Political Liberalization and Democratization in the Arab World,* vol. 1, *Theoretical Perspectives* (Boulder: Lynne Rienner, 1995), pp. 113–123.

23. Michael Hudson, "The Political Culture Approach to Arab Democratization: The Case for Bringing It Back In, Carefully," in Brynen, Korany, and Noble, *Political Liberalization and Democratization in the Arab World,* vol. 1, *Theoretical Perspectives.* See also Michael Hudson, *Arab Politics: The Search for Legitimacy* (New Haven: Yale University Press, 1977).

24. Ajami's highly rhetorical writing style tends to reinforce perceptions of him as an essentialist. See, for example, Fouad Ajami, "Iraq and the Arab's Future," *Foreign Affairs* 82, 1 (January–February 2003).

25. Fouad Ajami, *The Arab Predicament: Arab Political Thought and Practice Since 1967,* updated ed. (Cambridge: Cambridge University Press, 1993); Fouad Ajami, *The Dream Palace of the Arabs: A Generation's Odyssey* (New York: Random, 1999).

26. See, for example, Fouad Ajami, "Bush Country: The Middle East Embraces Democracy—and the American President," *Wall Street Journal,* 22 May 2005, http://www.opinionjournal.com/editorial/feature.html?id=110006721; "The Promise of Liberty: The ballot Is Not Infallible, but It Has Broken the Arab Pact with Tyranny," *Wall Street Journal,* 7 February 2006, http://www.opinionjournal.com/editorial/feature.html?id=110007932.

27. Fouad Ajami, "The Strange Survival of the Arab Autocracies," *Defining Ideas,* 13 December 2010, http://www.hoover.org/publications/defining-ideas/article/58836.

28. Meran Kamrava, *Democracy in the Balance: Culture and Society in the Middle East* (London: Chatham, 1998).

29. Hisham Sharabi, *Neopatriarchy: A Theory of Distorted Social Change* (Oxford: Oxford University Press, 1992); Brigitte Weiffen, "The Cultural-Economic Syndrome: Impediments to Democracy in the Middle East," *Comparative Sociology* 3, 3–4 (2004).

30. Lisa Wedeen, *Ambiguities of Domination: Politics, Rhetoric, and Symbols in Contemporary Syria* (Chicago: University of Chicago Press, 1999).

31. Edward Said, *Orientalism,* rev. ed. (New York: Random, 1994).

32. Lisa Anderson, "Democracy in the Arab World: A Critique of the Political Culture Approach," in Brynen, Korany, and Noble, *Political Liberalization and Democratization in the Arab World,* vol. 1, *Theoretical Perspectives,* p. 90.

33. George W. Bush, "Remarks by the President at the 20th Anniversary of the National Endowment for Democracy," Washington, DC, 7 November 2003, http://www.ned.org/events/anniversary/20thAniv-Bush.html.

34. Lee Smith, "Inside the Arab Mind: What's Wrong with the White House's Book on Arab Nationalism," *Slate,* 27 May 2004, http://slate.msn.com/id/2101328/; Brian Whitaker, "Its Best Use Is As a Doorstop," *The Guardian,* 24 May 2004, http://www.guardian.co.uk/world/2004/may/24/worlddispatch.usa.

35. Michael Hirsh, "Bernard Lewis Revisited: What If Islam Isn't an Obstacle to Democracy in the Middle East but the Secret to Achieving It?" *Washington Monthly,* November 2004, http://www.washington-monthly.com/features/2004/0411.hirsh.html; Adam Shatz, "The Native Informant," *The Nation,* 28 April 2003, http://www.thenation.com/doc/20030428/shatz.

36. Bernard Lewis, "Studying the Other: Different Ways of Looking at the Middle East and Africa," keynote address at the annual conference of the Association for the Study of the Middle East and Africa, 25 April 2008, http://asmeascholars.org.

37. See, for example, Martin Kramer's highly polemical *Ivory Towers on Sand: The Failure of Middle Eastern Studies in America* (Washington, DC: Washington Institute for Near East Policy, 2001). For a very different view, see Zachary Lockman, *Contending Visions: The History and Politics of Orientalism* (Cambridge: Cambridge University Press, 2004).

38. Malcolm Kerr, "Review: Edward Said, Orientalism," *International Journal of Middle East Studies* 12 (December 1980).

39. Marc Lynch, *Voices of the New Arab Public: Iraq, Al-Jazeera, and Middle East Politics Today* (New York: Columbia University Press, 2006).

40. On the World Values Survey project and data, see http://www.worldvaluessurvey.org.

41. See, for example, the Palestinian Center for Policy and Survey Research (http://www.pcpsr.org), the Jerusalem Media and Communications Centre (http://www.jmcc.org), and Near East Consulting (http://www.neareastconsulting.com). However, data from these and other sources has often been underused by scholars of Palestinian politics.

42. For Gallup's work in this area, see Gallup Center for Muslim Studies, http://www.gallup.com/consulting/worldpoll/26410/Gallup-Center-Muslim-Studies.aspx. For the findings of the Pew Global Attitudes project, see http://pewglobal.org.

43. United Nations Development Programme, *Arab Development Report 2004: Towards Freedom in the Arab World* (New York, 2005).

44. For these, see the website of the Anwar Sadat Chair for Peace and Development, University of Maryland, http://sadat.umd.edu/surveys/index.htm.

45. For further information on the Arab Barometer project, see http://www.arabbarometer.org.

46. The *reliability* of survey data refers to whether the results of a poll or finding are consistent over multiple opinion samples, or whether the results might be distorted by small sample sizes, poor sampling, biases generated by the interview, or other weaknesses of research design. The *validity* of survey data refers to whether the result actually represents what it is the researcher claims it represents.

47. Hudson, *Arab Politics,* pp. 82–106.

48. Adam Przeworski, *Transitions from Authoritarian Rule: Comparative Perspectives* (Baltimore: Johns Hopkins University Press, 1986), pp. 50–53. For

a different critique, see the discussion in Wedeen, *Ambiguities of Domination,* pp. 5–11.

49. Ronald Inglehart, "The Worldviews of Islamic Publics in Global Perspective," in Mansoor Moaddel, ed., *Worldviews of Islamic Publics* (New York: Palgrave, 2005). See also http://margaux.grandvinum.se/SebTest/wvs/SebTest/wvs/articles/folder_published/publication_487/files/5_islamview.pdf.

50. Pippa Norris and Ronald Inglehart, "Islamic Culture and Democracy: Testing the 'Clash of Civilizations' Thesis," *Comparative Sociology* 1, 3–4 (2002), pp. 259–260.

51. Amaney Jamal and Mark Tessler, "Attitudes in the Arab World," *Journal of Democracy* 19, 1 (January 2008), pp. 97–98.

52. Mark Tessler, "Do Islamic Orientations Influence Attitudes Toward Democracy in the Arab World? Evidence from Egypt, Jordan, Morocco, and Algeria," *International Journal of Comparative Sociology* 43 (2002). The same study found only relatively weak or sporadic associations between demographic variables (such as gender, age, residential locale, education, and income) and attitudes to democracy. Gallup's polling of attitudes in the broader Muslim world found often strong support for a variety of what might be considered democratic principles, and a general view among Muslims that Islam and democracy are compatible. John Esposito and Dalia Mogahed, *Who Speaks for Islam? What a Billion Muslims Really Think* (New York: Gallup, 2007).

53. Mark Tessler, "Religion, Religiosity, and the Place of Islam in Political Life: Insights from the Arab Barometer Survey," *Middle East Law and Governance* 2, 2 (2010).

54. Mark Tessler, "Islam and Democracy in the Middle East: The Impact of Religious Orientations on Attitudes Toward Democracy in Four Arab Countries," *Comparative Politics* 34, 3 (April 2002).

55. Tessler, "Do Islamic Orientations Influence Attitudes Toward Democracy in the Arab World?"

56. For the differences on orientations toward pluralism and political involvement in Algeria, Jordan, and Palestine, see Mark Tessler and Eleanor Gao, "Democracy and the Political Culture Orientations of Ordinary Citizens: A Typology for the Arab World and Beyond," *International Social Science Journal* 59, 192 (June 2008).

57. For a more detailed discussion of this, see Rex Brynen, "The Iraq War and (Non) Democratization in the Arab World," in Bessma Momani and Mokhtar Lamani, eds., *Iraq's Desperation: Realities of Desolation* (Waterloo: Wilfrid Laurier University Press, 2010).

58. On the positive effects that democratic and democratizing neighbors can have, see Jon Powerhouse, *Democracy from Above: Regional Organizations and Democratization* (Cambridge: Cambridge University Press, 2005); Daniel Brinks and Michael Coppedge, "Diffusion Is No Illusion: Neighbor Emulation in the Third Wave of Democratization," *Comparative Political Studies* 39, 4 (2006).

59. Antonio Gramsci, *Selections from the Prison Notebooks,* edited and translated by Quentin Hoare and Geoffrey Nowell Smith (New York: International Publishers, 1971), pp. 12–13.

60. Rex Brynen, "Political Culture and the Puzzle of Persistent Authoritarianism in the Middle East," paper presented at the annual conference of the International Political Science Association, Santiago, July 2009.

61. For further discussion of the importance of transnationalism and permeability in Middle East politics, see Bassel Salloukh and Rex Brynen, eds., *Persistent Permeability? Regionalism, Localism, and Globalization in the Middle East* (London: Ashgate, 2004).

6

Islamist Movements
and Democratic Politics

Almost one year after Hosni Mubarak resigned from Egypt's presidency, the Islamist Freedom and Justice Party (FJP) swept to power in the country's first postrevolution parliamentary elections. During the campaign, the FJP stated that it was committed to a modern state, democracy, women's rights, and national unity and insisted that it did not wish a monopoly of power or to dominate parliament. In a gesture aimed at calming the fears of Egypt's secularists, it furthermore stated that it would not compete for more than half of parliamentary seats. However, the FJP did just that. It ran for significantly more than half of the seats and won 47 percent of the 498 seats in the lower house of parliament. Once in power, the FJP stated that it would ensure that the country's new constitution would not exclude anyone or institute Islamic law. Yet when the Islamist-dominated parliament voted on the membership of the panel that would write the constitution, the result was a panel with more than 50 percent Islamist membership. The FJP's seemingly contradictory actions present political scientists and policymakers with important questions regarding the relationship between Islamism and democratic politics. To what extent will Islamist parties use democratic elections in order to gain power and then dismantle the pluralist system that brought them to power? To what extent do Islamist organizations promote values, norms, and practices that foster democratic reform? Does participating in elections ideologically moderate illiberal or undemocratic beliefs of Islamist parties? Under what conditions do Islamists moderate their beliefs? Does moderation lead to democratization? With whom does the responsibility for reform lie?

The questions presented by Islamist postrevolutionary electoral successes are not new. The relationship between Islamist movements—movements that aim, broadly speaking, to apply Islam to public and private life—and democratic politics has been a subject of ongoing and

This chapter was written by Janine A. Clark, associate professor in the Department of Political Science at the University of Guelph. The author gratefully acknowledges the contributions of Stacey Philbrick-Yadav and Jillian Schwedler.

heated debate since the early 1990s. It is complicated by the fact that some Islamists—radical Islamists—employ decidedly undemocratic means, such as violence, to achieve their ends, while others—commonly termed moderate Islamists—have established political parties and entered electoral politics. Some Islamists further muddy the distinction by doing both. Furthermore, those Islamist organizations that have entered electoral politics have generally not clearly outlined their understanding of Islam, for example of the role that it would play should they gain power or their explicit views on the rights of women and minorities.

Research on Islamist movements and democratic politics generally falls into two broad and overlapping areas. The first looks at Islamism and political participation, with scholars largely examining, among other issues, Islamist political parties, their relations to the state, the conditions under which they enter elections, and the impact of political participation upon the parties. The second broad area of research looks more closely at Islamism and civil society, with scholars examining other types of Islamist organizations and activities, such as their role in professional associations, and questioning the political and social impact of these organizations and, for example, the degree to which they help promote democratization. Both areas of research share methodological debates concerning what exactly we should look at when examining Islamist movements, such as the extent to which we should look at Islamist movements' ideologies and practices.

Questions concerning Islamist movements and democratic politics have led many scholars who are interested in political participation to examine how Islamist organizations operate, how they are structured, how their leaders are selected, and what their main policy concerns are, in order to determine whether or not they are internally democratic.[1] In response, however, a growing majority of scholars argue that we cannot examine Islamist movements in isolation from their contexts, since such movements—along with their political parties—respond and adapt to their surrounding environments. In other words, if policymakers want Islamists to be democrats, they must provide the sort of environment that will foster Islamist support for democratic ideals and actions. For this latter group of scholars, the primary question concerns the conditions and mechanisms that cause Islamists to moderate their beliefs and to support democratic reform. While they may debate the specifics of both the conditions and the mechanisms, these scholars generally agree that political inclusion can ideologically moderate Islamists.

As with the literature on Islamist parties and political participation, the literature on Islamism and civil society also questions the degree to which and the conditions under which these values, norms, and practices foster democratic reform. Early scholarship on civil society in the Arab world was strongly divided between those who optimistically saw civil society as playing a leading role in democratization and, in contrast, those who regarded civil society in the Arab world as uncivil, largely as a result of the strong presence of Islamists. This latter school of thought indicated weak prospects for substantive democratization in the region. Today, few scholars view Arab civil society as uncivil, although some do question the degree to which certain civil society groups can be considered liberal. Arab civil society is recognized as vibrant, and many scholars, writing both before and after the 2011 Arab Spring, argue that civil society organizations are of greater political significance than formal political organizations such as political parties. Scholars further observe that it is within civil society that Islamists and the secular authoritarian states of the region are culturally, symbolically, and politically contesting values, norms, and practices. As a consequence, Islamist organizations are seen by many to be positively contributing to political change.

These two basic lines of inquiry—examining Islamist movements' ideologies on the one hand and their contexts and practices on the other—underlie some of the most important research that is being conducted on Islamism and democratic politics. With the uprisings and revolutions of the 2011 Arab Spring, the debates between and within the two have become more relevant than ever as scholars question Islamists' role during the uprisings and their electoral victories in postrevolution Tunisia and Egypt. The outcomes of these debates will have far-reaching policy implications both for these two countries and for reformers elsewhere in the region. If political scientists and policymakers believe, for example, that Egypt's Freedom and Justice Party is falsely portraying its commitments and is seeking to dismantle the democratic rules and principles that brought it to power, they are likely to adopt policies that exclude Islamists from political participation, such as running in elections, in the future. They also would be less likely to support policies of political liberalization in general, fearing that political liberalization would grant Islamists the opportunity to grow in popularity and size. If, however, they believe that Islamist beliefs and practices are influenced by the context in which they operate, that they are impacted by their alliance partners, the institutional structures within which they operate, and even their international trade partners, they are more likely to support the political inclusion and political liberalization of Islamists. If Islamists moderate as a result of interactions in and with the broader political field, it behooves policymakers to support their participation in democratic elections.

Debates over Islamist movements and democratic politics remain unresolved. However, emerging from the literature is a growing consensus that under the appropriate institutional conditions, Islamists can and do strategically moderate their ideologies and play a role in democratic reform. Policywise, this shifts attention to the regimes in the region—not only to the newly elected Islamist parties in Tunisia and Egypt but also to those regimes that remain in place despite the Arab Spring and the degree to which Islamists can depend on them to be democratic. The question is the degree to which *either* incumbent regimes or Islamists in the region can be counted on to act democratically.

What Is an Islamist? What Are Islamist Organizations and Islamist Movements?

What exactly is an Islamist? What is an Islamist organization? And how do they differ from Islamist movements? An Islamist is a Muslim who seeks to actively extend the purview of Islam beyond the private realm by also applying it in the public realm, so that Islam guides all spheres of life, including political life. Thus an Islamist seeks to Islamize society and, for many, also the state. For some Islamists, enacting or applying Islam means establishing a faith-based charity, while for others it may mean joining a political party that is established in the name of Islam, or simply teaching others to be better Muslims.

Throughout the Arab world today, one can find an abundance of Islamist organizations, including charities, daycare facilities, schools, and banks, as well as Islamist-dominated organizations, such as professional associations and university clubs. Islamist and Islamist-dominated organizations constitute the dominant sector within Arab civil society.[2] The same can be said of Islamist political parties, which in most Arab countries typically win the largest percentage of votes of any party (in countries where they are allowed to compete freely). The impact of Islamist organizations at the social, economic, and political levels is immense. Large numbers of Muslims in the Arab world have adopted aspects of the Islamic dress code, such as the veil, and are now sending their children to Islamist schools, having their teeth checked at Islamist medical clinics, keeping their money in Islamist banks, having their pensions managed by professional associations that are led by elected boards of Islamists, and voting for Islamist political parties. It is little wonder that some scholars refer to Islamist organizations as states within states.

The roots and causes of Islamist organizations are subjects of immense research and debate. While these are dealt with briefly here, they are largely beyond the scope of the chapter. Suffice it to say that the dominance of such Islamist organizations can largely be attributed to regimes' repression of other previously dominant political organizations, such as leftist political parties, as well as to the retreat of the state from socioeconomic service provision due to economic restructuring, and to the limited political openings—including the legalization of political parties and the institutionalization and expansion of electoral politics—that resulted from political liberalization and the democratic reforms of the early 1990s.

Like other kinds of political actors, Islamists seek societal and political change. From the perspective of those who establish them, Islamist organizations such as charities or banks are more than a mere alternative to their secular counterpart institutions; they are viewed as the foundations for a new society based on Islam. Islamist organizations claim to be governed differently than secular organizations, and to be providing an inspirational model for others to follow. The organizations themselves and their activities take different forms, and while they are always political in that they are struggling over the appropriate distribution of power, their external form may not always appear to be overtly political. Indeed, what makes them Islamist may sometimes lie more in their intention or spirit rather than in their shape or form.[3]

How Islamist organizations seek to achieve political change is one of the issues that differentiates a particular Islamist organization from another. While Islamists are quite diverse and a typology of multiple types according to different criteria could be drawn, Islamism is generally categorized into one of two broad types: moderate Islamism and radical (or violent) Islamism.[4] As the name implies, moderate Islamists are those who seek to achieve an Islamized state and society through nonviolent means. Politically, they support pluralist political competition and create parties that participate in elections. Morocco's Justice and Development Party is one example of such a party. By contrast, radical Islamists are those who employ violence. They seek the establishment of theocracies and view violence as the only means to achieve that goal. Egypt's Jihad and Algeria's Jama'a Islamiya fall into this category.[5] There are generally also ideological distinctions between moderate and radical Islamists. Thus a moderate Islamist movement can be defined as one that ideologically accepts electoral democracy and political and ideological pluralism, and aims for gradual social, political, and economic changes. Behaviorally, moderate Islamists accept the principle of working within the established state institutions, regardless of their perceived legitimacy, and shun violent methods to achieve their goals. Conversely, a radical Islamist movement is one that ideologically rejects democracy as well as the legitimacy of political and ideological pluralism; aims for revolutionary social, political, and economic changes; refuses to work within the established state institutions; and utilizes violent means to achieve its goals.

The distinction between moderate and radical Islamism has had its objectors, with one scholar arguing that if all Islamists imagine a fundamental restructuring of state and society, then they are all radicals.[6] To be sure, the distinction between the two is not always clear-cut. Lebanon's Hezbollah, for example, participates in parliamentary elections, has entered into pragmatic electoral alliances with non-Muslims, and has accepted election results even when defeated, but it also has a military wing. Today, however, scholars agree that distinguishing between moderate and radical Islamism helps to provide researchers with a more accurate understanding of the relationship between Islamism and democratic politics. As a result of such violent events as the terrorist attacks of 11 September 2001, policymakers have tended to pay a disproportionate amount of attention to radical Islamism. But it is moderate Islamist organizations that are having and almost certainly will continue to have the greatest impact on the future political evolution of the Middle East. Their importance extends beyond Egypt and Tunisia, where post-2011 Arab Spring Islamists are finding full inclusion in the transitional political system. Even in the authoritarian regimes of the region, their immediate goal of becoming a powerful force by participating in the normal politics of their countries is not an impossible one. While radical Islamists have goals that are largely unrealistic (such as reestablishing the Islamic caliphate) and employ violent tactics that do not appeal to the mainstream Arab public, moderate Islamists have already had a powerful impact on social customs in many countries, halting and reversing secularist trends and changing the way many Arabs dress and behave.[7] Moderate Islamists furthermore are large in number, well organized, and financially autonomous from the state.[8] It therefore behooves researchers to look closely at moderate Islamists as distinct from radical Islamists.

The Paradox of Democracy in the Middle East

The greatest concern raised by scholars and policymakers about constructing a typology of Islamist organizations according to whether they are moderate or radical is that it will not address the worry that certain organizations may adopt moderate behavior in order to hide radical agendas. This dilemma goes right to the heart of what is often called the paradox of democracy in the Middle East: the fear that democratic elections might bring to power an antidemocratic regime.[9] Will moderate Islamists use the democratic system in order to win power and then eliminate democracy?[10]

Are They or Aren't They? The Search for True Values

In trying to determine whether or not apparently moderate Islamist organizations are truly moderate, scholars often examine how they operate, how they are structured, how their leaders are selected, and what their main policy concerns are.[11] Scholars examine, for example, the statements and speeches of the Muslim Brotherhood, the type of parliamentary inquiries that is has made, the actions of the civil society organizations that it controls, the internal structure of the Brotherhood, and the types of political alliances that it pursues as well as how it treats its alliance partners.[12]

These scholars and policymakers thus engage in what Francesco Cavatorta calls the search for "true values" or the true essence of moderate Islamism—in other words, the search for indicators of what moderate Islamists really believe. Yet while this approach has been the dominant one, an increasing number of scholars, such as Cavatorta and Daniel Brumberg, argue that this search for true values is flawed.[13] First of all, an underlying assumption that often accompanies this approach is that Islamist ideology is unchanging: once the true values are identified, they are not subject to change. Second, studies that take this approach rarely take into account that while Islamist organizations have an ideology that they would like to propagate and policies that they would like to implement, they also must deal with institutional constraints such as electoral and constitutional rules, the presence of other political parties, and the decisions of courts. In dealing with these constraints, Islamists will be forced to adapt and potentially change. Finally, if the "true nature" of Islamists is interpreted in isolation from the surrounding institutional setting and in a political vacuum, the result will be highly influenced by the scholar's own preconceptions and biased selection of evidence. Effectively, scholars will either consciously or subconsciously focus upon those documents, statements, structures, and past behaviors that most support their own preconceived opinions.[14] Increasing numbers of scholars thus reject the approach that assumes it is possible to determine a priori the true ethos of a political actor by analyzing documents, statements, structures, and past behaviors.[15] Rather, they argue that the surrounding environment or context matters, since it influences the choices Islamist movements make and the strategies that they adopt. Indeed, as they adapt to it, the surrounding context may in fact moderate Islamists. As Jillian Schwedler states: "The idea that political inclusion leads to moderation now has emerged as *the* issue at stake in debates about Islamist political participation."[16]

Islamism and Civil Society

To a large extent, these same debates can be found in the literature on civil society. Within the literature on the Middle East, civil society is most commonly defined as comprising voluntary groups, associations, or organizations that lie between society, the state, and the market. Theoretically speaking, civil society is understood as an important bulwark against authoritarianism, as playing a dominant role in socializing citizens in the values and practice of citizenship, as contributing to the delivery of social services for the needy, and as giving voice to people's concerns and pressuring the government for change in line with those concerns. Much of the early scholarship regarded the democratizing function of civil society in the Arab world as weak at best, arguing that Islamist organizations—which constitute a significant, if not the dominant, sector within civil society—do not agree with the values that underwrite a democracy.[17]

Scholars today, however, have rejected a priori assumptions about the presumably uncivil and therefore undemocratic nature of Arab civil society due to its having been "Islamized." Scholars examine the values and practices in Islamist civil society organizations, the ways in which they are political, their relationship to the state, and how they contribute to or hinder democratization. As with the scholars who examine Islamist political parties, scholars who examine Islamist civil society organizations engage in the same sort of debates as those concerning Islamist political parties, and how and the degree to which Islamist activities in civil society, many of which are conducted at least partly in the name of greater democracy, are contributing to democratization. A number of these studies argue that the values and practices in Islamist organizations or in those organizations that are dominated by Islamists not only are civil, but also contribute to democratization.

Studies of Egyptian professional associations (the latter of which have been largely under the control of the Islamists since the 1980s)[18] in the 1990s and early 2000s, for example, argue that under Islamist leadership, Egyptian professional associations became new arenas for collective claimsmaking and sites of bargaining with state agents.[19] Bargaining occurred over both concrete material benefits, such as pensions and healthcare plans, as well as rules governing associational autonomy and freedoms. As a consequence, Islamist activities contributed to political and institutional change, such as the broadening of relations between citizens and state agents, a degree of equalization in terms of influence between citizens and state agents in decisionmaking, and a degree of protection for citizens from state agents. Although Islamist activities in the professional associations did not directly contribute to greater democratization or regime change, they nonetheless became important sites of political innovation in which official norms and practices were challenged.

In addition, by introducing new values and developing new repertoires of collective action, Islamists may have helped to pave the way for increased levels of citizen engagement in public life.[20]

Other scholars have shifted the grounds of the debate and questioned the degree to which Islamism can be considered the primary determinant of relations between the state and civil society.[21] They argue that relations between the state and civil society are determined more by the historical social bases of the regime and of civil society actors and the degree to which these social bases, be they ethnic or tribal, are in opposition to each other. In other words, while ideology (in this case, Islamism) can in no way be discounted, social identities such as tribalism are greater determinants of relations between the state and civil society. Thus the issue is not whether Islam is compatible with democracy, but whether other social identities are.

Gray Zones: The Bumpy Path to Moderation

Increasing numbers of scholars acknowledge that moderate Islamists not only are becoming increasingly receptive to democratic politics, but also are respecting the rules of political participation.[22] Moderate Islamists see themselves as democrats, firmly committed to free and fair electoral processes, whatever outcomes they may bring. While much of the Islamist leadership was late in officially joining the Arab Spring, many moderate Islamists participated as individuals in various demonstrations. Furthermore, as Stacey Philbrick Yadav points out in the case of Yemen, the ability of grassroots organizers to effectively build and sustain the 2011 protest movement was contingent partly on the prior articulation of a common oppositional identity created through the cooperation and networking of activists across ideological divides over several years.[23] The same can be said of Egypt. Moderate Islamists, however, continue to be ambiguous about their positions on many issues. These gray zones include issues that are pivotal to answering the questions this chapter began with. Are Islamists democrats? To what extent do they believe in the values that are the foundations of a liberal democracy? And will they use democratic elections in order to gain power but then dismantle the very system that brought them to power?

Nathan Brown, Amr Hamzawy, and Marina Ottaway identify six gray zones: Islamic law, the use of violence, political pluralism, civic and political rights, rights of women, and rights of religious minorities.[24] They press for Islamist groups to offer a precise understanding of Islamic law and to clarify their conception of political pluralism and tolerance and their understanding of freedoms, and point out, for example, that while moderate Islamists reject violence as a means of achieving their political goals, this is not the case when it comes to the issue of Israel and Palestinian rights. They furthermore note that Islamists have not accepted universal citizenship and that women's rights continue to be second to those of males, particularly in the area of personal law (such as divorce).

Brown, Hamzawy, and Ottaway, along with other scholars, view Islamist ambiguity as the result of the tension between the old goal of creating Islamic states and the new goal of becoming influential players in a pluralist, democratic society. As political organizations, Islamist movements must be flexible and pragmatic. As religious organizations, however, they are more inclined to use the dogmatic, absolutist language of the preacher and to focus on moral issues of good and evil.[25] Ambiguous stances ensure that they do not alienate any constituency. Yet for others, particularly policymakers, the gray zones do not merely reflect the bumpy path of moderation—rather, they reflect the fact that, at heart, Islamists do not believe in democratic values.

Islamist Movements as Context-Dependent

As stated earlier, in contrast to the literature that looks for true values, there is a growing literature that attempts to explain the behavior of Islamists by looking at how institutions and interactions with other actors shape behavior.[26] In a vein similar to the essentialist versus contextualist debate over political culture discussed in Chapter 5, this literature argues that Islamist actions are not entirely dictated by ideology but are also shaped by contextual factors, which may even modify Islamist ideology.[27] In other words, Islamism is context-dependent, with that context inevitably constraining the actions and modifying the beliefs of Islamists.[28] Cautioning against overgeneralizing the similarities between Islamist movements, scholars who share this perspective stress the differences between such movements and organizations, as a result of their contexts. Despite their ideological similarities, Islamist movements—including their parties and other organizations—operating in different political settings, may be confronted by radically different instrumental calculations.[29] These calculations in turn determine the extent to which Islamism may or may not act as a force for democratization.

Why, for example, did Morocco's Justice and Development Party and Jordan's Islamic Action Front take significantly different positions on their respective states' attempts (2004) to amend legislation dealing with the rights of women.[30] Women's rights often are an issue that divides Islamist parties internally, with what are perceived to be more ideologically hard-line members within the parties being opposed to women being granted rights that are equal and similar to those of men.[31] Women's rights thus are seen by many academics and policymakers as an important indicator of the extent of Islamists' beliefs in liberal democratic values. While the Justice and Development Party voted in support of vast revisions to Morocco's Family Code, including the regulation of polygamy, the right of women to contract their own marriages (rather than do so through a male), and the right of women to divorce on demand, the Islamic Action Front voted against attempts in parliament to change Jordan's Personal Status Laws. The difference between the two Islamist parties' actions is all the more puzzling given the fact that, while they were just as controversial and included the right of women to divorce on demand, the proposed changes to the Personal Status Laws were far less extensive in number and scope than the proposed changes to the Family Code. Three contextal factors explain the difference: the different relationships the two parties had at the time of the reforms with their respective monarchs, the strength of the two countries' leftist parties and nongovernmental organizations (NGOs), and the differing ways in which the respective reforms were introduced and defended by the two monarchs. Thus, while ideology cannot be discounted, a full understanding of Islamist political parties requires an examination of the larger political context and how they respond to it.

Scholars have analyzed the impact of a wide range of contextual factors, both international and domestic, upon Islamist movements and their ideological and political positions. These factors can include institutions, such as the European Union and how Islamists in Turkey have responded to their country's bid to be included in the European Union,[32] socioeconomic factors,[33] and even societal diversity and how Islamists located within pluralistic societies are forced to expand their discourse to include concepts of good governance, transparency, and the eradication of corruption in order to convince or persuade a broad range of citizens.[34]

Thus Islamist ideologies "are shaped by and encapsulated within a *multitude* of ideal social, political, and cultural identities and interests that can contradict as well as complement one another."[35] Consequently, many scholars, such as Mona el-Ghobashy, now reject conjectural, aimless "are they or aren't they?" debates about Islamists' commitment to democracy and argue that we should be analyzing how Islamists actually behave.[36] The real debate is not whether or not Islamism is truly democratic but rather the conditions or mechanisms under which Islamists can and do moderate their views and democratize.[37]

The Inclusion-Moderation Hypothesis

Shifting the debate in this direction has significant policy implications. With the creation of Islamist parties and the entry of Islamists into parliamentary politics, beginning largely in the early 1990s, scholars and policymakers began questioning whether the exclusion or the inclusion of Islamists from the formal political sphere would best moderate them.[38] The majority of scholars today argue that moderate Islamists need to be included in the political process, for it is only by participating in that process that they will have both the incentive and the compulsion to moderate their beliefs. At the heart of this argument lies the inclusion-moderation hypothesis, the idea that political groups and individuals may become more moderate as a direct result of their inclusion in pluralist political processes, even within less-than-democratic states.[39]

In formulating this hypothesis, scholars of the Middle East looked toward the literatures on comparative politics, modernization, and democratic transitions in particular. The moderation theory draws upon such work as studies of socialist parties in Western Europe, which essentially argue that parties espousing radical beliefs moderate their positions once they realize that adhering to radical positions will cost them votes. As a result, radical socialist movements were transformed into political parties representing the working classes. The democratic transitions literature refers to this as the "participation-moderation trade-off."

Scholars of Islamism have adapted this literature to address the question of whether inclusion of Islamists into the formal political sphere will moderate them. While such scholars define moderation differently, their definitions all essentially aim to capture indicators of a shift in actions and beliefs that is reflective of the values that are deemed important to liberal democracies. Carrie Rosefsky Wickham, for example, defines ideological moderation as the abandonment, postponement, or revision of radical goals that enables an opposition movement to accommodate itself to the give-and-take of "normal" competitive politics. It entails a shift toward a substantive commitment to democratic principles and to citizenship rights.[40]

An examination of the literature indicates that scholars generally understand Islamist moderation as coming about according to three basic dynamics.[41] The first involves electoral incentives. Upon entering party politics, Islamists must broaden and moderate their positions in order to attract votes beyond their narrow, extremist core constituency. The second dynamic relates to institutional structures. Working within the political system, Islamist parties must mount campaigns, raise and distribute funds, and develop policies. Their campaigns also require practical leaders and good administrators to run them. This means that Islamist parties must shift their energy and resources away from traditional revolutionary activities such as underground cells and away from radical ideological leaders. Finally, the third dynamic by which Islamists moderate is what can be called the "pothole theory of democracy." Once in power, Islamists must fulfill the demands of their constituents and deliver services, such as repairing potholes in the streets. The thinking here is that as Islamists are busy doing such things as filling potholes and upgrading sewage systems, they have little time for ideology, political rigidity, and radicalism.

The impressive electoral successes of Turkey's Justice and Development Party in 2002, for example, have been attributed to the party's response to voter preferences.[42] The Islamist movement in Turkey moderated itself in response to both perceived opportunities and constraints; that is, the movement was given credible opportunities for power within the political system, while simultaneously being forced to work within institutional constraints (judicial and military, for example). Once having decided to work within the political system, the most important reason for the party's dramatic success was a series of decisions by its leaders to moderate the party's message and image in an attempt to appeal to the more secular-minded, center-right voters. Inclusion thus resulted in strategic moderation.

The participation of Egypt's Muslim Brotherhood in elections for seats in parliament, for leadership of the professional unions, and for positions on municipal councils similarly has been attributed to having had a profound effect on the Brotherhood's political thought and organization.[43] As a result of its participation, the Brotherhood experienced internal splits along generational lines, intense internal debates about strategy, and an ideological shift in its understanding of politics, away from one that viewed politics as a sacred mission to one that viewed politics as a public contest between rival interests. Organizationally, these changes began when a younger generation of Islamists who gained their political experiences in university politics entered leadership positions in the Muslim Brotherhood. Based on their reading of the political context, they pressured the older generation to make changes in the types of activities and political projects pursued by the group. Ideologically, there was a shift in the types of religious thinkers upon which the Brotherhood based its beliefs and actions. Thus the group increasingly began using the writings of moderate Islamists thinkers, many of whom use Islamic concepts to authenticate democracy. The end result was that, by the mid-2000s, the Muslim Brotherhood had taken a more prodemocratic turn.

Other scholars, such as Wickham, turn to the literature on political learning, according to which the experience of dictatorship produces important cognitive changes, in order to better understand how moderation occurs.[44] She uses the political learning model (derived largely from studies of southern Europe and Latin America) to explain how the founders of Egypt's centrist, Islamist al-Wasat party moderated their views to embrace the concepts of pluralism and democracy and then, as a consequence, broke away from the Muslim Brotherhood in order to form their own Islamist party. Al-Wasat's founders left the Brotherhood largely as a result of their experiences of being elected to and working within Egypt's professional associations. As Muslim Brotherhood candidates in the elections for professional associations, they had to seek votes and, after being elected, had to satisfy an electorate, and most importantly had to work together with non-Islamist activists. Through the exposure to the ideas of non-Islamists, the founders effectively underwent a process of political learning that moderated their views. Once this democratic learning had taken place, they created their own party. Thus, according to this view, formal political participation does not in and of itself trigger ideological moderation. Rather, "democratic learning is most likely when institutional openings create incentives and opportunities for radical opposition leaders to break out of the insular networks of movement politics and engage in sustained dialogue and cooperation with other groups."[45]

Not all scholars agree with political learning as the mechanism by which Islamist parties moderate.[46] Schwedler's influential study points to a very different kind of mechanism to explain ideological moderation, arguing that Islamist parties moderate as a result of an internal shift in the "boundaries of justifiable actions."[47] Moderation occurs when Islamist parties engage in serious internal party debates about whether political participation (such as the decision to participate in elections) can be justified on Islamic grounds. Once justifying actions that had been deemed religously unacceptable previously, such as the establishment of political parties and their participation in elections, their ongoing participation in democratic politics requires further religious justifications (for members of parliament to participate in a government-appointed committee, for example) and, consequently, further shifts in the red lines and further moderation.

These analyses thus put the onus of reform on the regime. Rather than demanding that Islamists moderate before they are allowed to participate in electoral politics, the inclusion-moderation hypothesis essentially advises that inclusion comes first and moderation later.[48] As a consequence, "the challenge is not to figure out whether Islamism is 'essentially' democratic versus autocratic, or liberal versus illiberal. Instead, it is to see whether this or that Islamist group is acting within a hegemonic political arena where the game is to shut out alternative approaches, or else within a competitive . . . arena where Islamists, like other players, find themselves pushed to accommodate the logic of power-sharing."[49] In other words, are the incumbent regimes in the region acting democratically?

It is not surprising, therefore, that studies testing the inclusion-moderation hypothesis across state types find that there is a direct correlation between Islamist groups' ability to participate unhindered in the political process and their level of political maturity.[50] Islamists operating in Middle Eastern states categorized as stable or as "oases of incorporation"—where the same rules of the game apply to all political players, where members of political parties do not suffer from threats of arrest or have their party meetings disrupted by the police, and where political parties can feel confident that their elected candidates will be allowed to participate in parliament and that their parties will not be prevented from participating in future elections if they are successful at the polls—are more likely to respect the institutional framework of the state in which they operate and accept political plurality. In more inclusive states, Islamists have gradually retreated away from ideological debates and moved toward more pragmatic agendas that are primarily concerned with influencing public policies.

Yet it bears underlining that the inclusion-moderation hypothesis is just that, a hypothesis. Even sympathetic scholars do not all completely agree with it. They point out an important shortcoming of the causal relation posited by the inclusion-moderation thesis. As Michaelle Browers states, by formulating the question in terms of how changes in practice (inclusion) impact changes in thinking (moderation), scholars neglect the modes of thinking and the character of individuals necessary to bring about the interactions in the first place.[51] Inclusion and cooperation require moderates. Stated differently, which comes first, moderates or moderation? These scholars thus question the sequence of events that scholars attribute to the so-called moderation process and whether moderates are drawn to the idea of inclusion rather than inclusion making them moderate.

This discussion underlines that the inclusion-moderation hypothesis is far from being fully agreed upon by academics. Scholars differ in whether the analytical focus is on Islamist groups, individuals, or both; they also differ in whether they emphasize changes in behavior or changes in ideology.[52] Disagreements exist over precisely what is being explained and which mechanisms (and in what order) lead to moderation. As a consequence, questions remain as to the causal factor, whether moderation occurs as a result of inclusion or whether moderates decide to enter political processes. If moderation is occurring, then under what conditions and exactly how does it occur? Does the political system make a difference? Do the structure and conditions of the alliance itself dictate whether moderation occurs? Does moderation occur as a result of shifting the boundaries of justifiable actions? Does it occur through political learning? What is the role of individuals within the organizations? While the inclusion-moderation hypothesis offers important avenues for further research, the debate over the relationship between Islamist movements and democratic politics is far from being resolved.

Despite these questions, scholars generally agree that, at a very minimum, the inclusion of Islamists helps elevate moderate actors on the political scene and denies radicals a large support base by providing alternative voices working within the system. Thus, regardless of whether groups become more moderate as a result of inclusion, the encouragement of inclusion may discourage radicalism in a way that produces an overall political effect of more moderation.[53]

Consequences of Inclusion

Scholars today increasingly treat Islamists as actors who strategically respond to changing circumstances. As stated earlier, the policy implications of much of this research are that moderate Islamists should be included in the political system and that Islamists will rationally respond to the political opportunity structure of political inclusion by moderating their views as they do such things as work with non-Islamist actors and seek a larger voter base. But taking these assumptions as a given, we are still left with the question as to whether moderation leads to democratization. A number of critics of the inclusion-moderation hypothesis do not criticize the hypothesis itself, but rather whether moderation is even desirable.

Studies indicate, for example, that if Islamist moderation leads to an increase in votes (which is often the motivation behind moderation), authoritarian leaders halt processes of liberalization and democratization.[54] Beginning in the 1980s, Egyptian professional associations, for example, increasingly became targets of governmental control as a result of the Islamist takeover of the associations' elected councils. Effectively, therefore, Islamist victories gave the state an opportunity to justify further tightening its grip on civil society organizations. Furthermore, under certain conditions, the moderation of radical parties implies that they lose their capacity and perhaps even desire to reform the authoritarian characteristics of the regimes. Thus the moderation of a party may mean its domestication or "taming," as electoral concerns and the threat of state repression may cause it to cease pressuring for democratic reforms. Electoral calculations, fear of state repression, and organizational constraints all may make Islamists politically risk-averse. Consequently, Islamists may seek accommodation with authoritarian regimes.[55] Indeed, studies have shown that Islamist parties generally are reluctant to do well in elections under authoritarian regimes.[56] They go out of their way to avoid exceeding what they perceive to be the regime's acceptable threshold of seats in order to not invite an adverse reaction from the regime.

Other scholars, such as Holger Albrecht, have pointed out that political opposition in the authoritarian states of the Middle East (which is dominated by, but not limited to, the Islamists) is more of a political ally to the authoritarian regime than an opponent.[57] Albrecht argues that the "authoritarian opposition" ultimately contributes to authoritarian stability by performing five functions. First, this bestows a degree of legitimacy on authoritarian regimes through the opposition's participation in political systems that grant only a limited degree of political freedoms. Second, this legitimacy helps the authoritarian regimes to attract development funds from Western governments and organizations. Third, opposition parties and NGOs constitute "transmission belts" for the co-optation of social groups that are not represented in elitist circles. In other words, they help to bring more people into the system, and as a result help to support the system. Fourth, an authoritarian opposition performs a channeling function, since the opposition is in effect an institution through which societal dissent is organized. Finally, an authoritarian opposition performs a moderating function. The more accessible the state, the less likely the opposition will unify behind a violent strategy. Thus, the emergence and persistence of opposition does not necessarily mark the emergence of a likely vehicle for democratization. In other words, inclusion may lead to moderation, but moderation does not necessarily lead to democratic reform.

Not all scholars agree with this negative view, since many view political parties as some of the most important societal forces for democratic change and political reform.[58] However, scholars concur that there is an unequal power balance between the state and opposition parties, with the two sides reinforcing and depending upon each other.[59]

Islamists as Rational Actors

Underlying much of the growing literature that argues that scholars need to look at the contextual or environmental opportunities and constraints under which Islamists operate is the assumption that Islamists are rational political actors. The reason why Islamists moderate their ideologies in response to specific contexts or conditions is that they behave rationally. As Cavatorta states, the fact that Islamists have a religious dimension should not blind researchers to the fact that the objectives Islamist organizations want to achieve and the transformation of society that they envisage are very political, and require a rational understanding of their context.[60]

The incorporation of social movement theory—which was originally developed by looking primarily at movements in the United States and in Europe—into the study of Islamism has been pivotal to this understanding of Islamists as rational political actors. Its use began as early as 1996, but became far more prevalent in the 2000s, particularly with the publication of Quintan Wiktorowicz's influential book *Islamic Activism: A Social Movement Theory Approach.*[61] Scholars who employ social movement theory in order to better understand Islamist movements argue that there are patterns that arc common to movements of all types in terms of how they articulate their interests, frame their grievances, organize and mobilize support, pressure the state, seek allies, and respond to opportunities and constraints. While Islam as an ideological worldview marks out Islamist movements from other social movements, Islamist movements share the same dynamics and mechanisms as movements elsewhere. In this sense, they are not unique.[62] Social movements are similar because they are made up of rational actors who respond in similar ways if presented with similar opportunities and contraints.

Among other aims, scholars use social movement theory to help better understand why and how Islamist movements attract members and mobilize supporters, as well as to understand their decision to use moderate or violent tactics. In so doing, scholars such as Wiktorowicz challenge and refute arguments that label Islamist movements as fundamentalist—that is, as movements that take the sources of Islam literally. They furthermore challenge theories that label Islamist movements as coping mechanisms (for dealing with economic, political, and social change) and Islamists as dysfunctional or as deviant and in need of comfort in the face of (modernization's) dislocation and change.[63]

Scholars using social movement theory to better understand Islamist movements (and to help advance social movement theory) largely focus on three dominant concepts: political opportunity structures, resource mobilization, and framing.[64] They use the concept of opportunity structures to help explain when and how Islamist movements mobilize, and assume that Islamists are rational actors who take advantage of opportunities in order to mobilize. For example, Mohammed Hafez and Wiktorowicz argue that fluctuations in the degree of Islamist violence are a result of the prevailing political opportunity structures.[65] When state repression is indiscriminate, Islamists are more likely to engage in violent tactics; but when it is used selectively against radical (and not moderate) Islamists, state repression has an effect on the choice of strategy and tactics that Islamists use.

The concept of resource mobilization assumes that social movements (in this case, Islamist movements) can only form when strategic resources and organizational structures are available. Resources and organizations turn individual grievances into a movement. In other words, Islamist movements are not irrational outbursts but organized movements requiring money, skills, and infrastructure. At the same time, movements offer selective incentives to entice individuals to join. Studies have detailed, for example, how informal social networks underlie Islamist movements and are an important resource for movement building.[66] Wickham notes that youth initially join Islamist movements due to the material, psychological, and emotional benefits that they receive as a result of joining.[67]

Finally, other scholars turn to the concept of framing in order to better understand, for example, why people join Islamist movements despite the high risks, such as being jailed. Frames represent interpretive schemata that offer a language and cognitive tools for making sense of experiences and events in the "world out there."[68] Frames help the members of movements interpret and evaluate the world around them, including its problems and potential solutions, and provide them with a rationale for supporting the movement. Most important, frames are strategically calculated to provide an interpretation of the world that will resonate with people and their everyday life experiences. Islamists' framing of activism as a moral obligation that demands self-sacrifice and unflinching commitment to the cause of religious transformation encourages youth to view their activism in the movement as a religious duty and to participate in high-risk activities.[69]

Social movement theory thus goes to the heart of the issue of Middle East exceptionalism—the belief that the Middle East is somehow unique or different largely as a result of Islam (and, by extension, Islamism). It has helped shift our attention from ideology to rationality and opened the door to new research directions regarding Islamist movements, as well as to democratization and the challenges facing democratization in the region more generally.

Conclusion

The literature on Islamist movements and democratic politics is a vast one. Yet to a large extent it has been dominated to one degree or another by a few basic questions. For many of the policymakers and scholars who argue that Islamists do not hold democratic beliefs, the way forward is to exclude them from the political system for fear that they will use that system to gain power and then to dismantle the very system that brought them to power. Others focus less on the ideological pronouncements of Islamists and more on their rational calculations and actions. They generally argue that inclusion will moderate Islamists ideologically, even if they enter the political system for purely strategic reasons. In other words, democratization may take place even without committed democrats. The trick is to find and understand the right conditions and mechanisms under which moderation occurs. The path of inclusion is complicated by the fact that scholars disagree on what those conditions and mechanisms are, the fact that the road to moderation is a very bumpy one, and the view held by some scholars that moderation in fact aids authoritarianism and not democratization.

As stated at the beginning of this chapter, these questions are all the more acute given the success of Islamist political parties in postrevolutionary Tunisia and Egypt. It remains too early to determine whether inclusion is in fact having a moderating effect on Islamists in the two countries (or whether that moderation means greater democracy). The Islamist Freedom and Justice Party in Egypt leads a powerless parliament in a country that remains under military rule. If democratic inclusion moderates Islamists, the political system in Egypt, as of yet, does not fulfill the criteria of a democracy. While Tunisia is not under military rule, its transition also is far from complete—indeed, it has yet to complete the drafting of a new constitution. The Ennahda party campaigned on a platform of democracy and the protection of political liberties, human rights, and a free market economy. It furthermore promised that while being religiously oriented, it would not introduce Islamic law or other Islamic concepts to what was and will continue to be a secular constitution. Approximately a year after the revolution in Tunisia, many secularists are expressing fears regarding the future of the country and the degree to which the goals of the revolution will be safeguarded.[70] Demonstrations and strikes are continuing, if not increasing, in the streets of Tunis, both as a result of the flagging economy but also, and most importantly, as a result of the growing culture war between secularists and Islamists. These fears are based both on what appears to be the growing numbers of radical Islamists and, in particular, their actions on university campuses and in local communities, where they attempt, often violently, to enforce the segregation of sexes, the wearing of the *niqab*, and other Islamic practices, and also on Ennahda's perceived lenient response to these events. Most important, secularists fear the strength of radical Islamists within Ennahda and question the degree to which Ennahda was sincere in its campaign promises or is able to maintain these promises in the face of mounting pressures from within and without. Yet as noted in Chapter 2, Ennahda chose to form a coalition or unity government with two secular parties. Freedom of speech is flourishing in Tunisia, as is civil society. And while its decision was slow in coming, Ennahda rejected a proposal that the country's legislation be based on Islamic law and instead chose to keep the wording of the old constitution that proclaimed Islam as the state religion. Time will tell if Ennahda will safeguard the revolution's goals; however, whatever the outcome, it will be shaped by Ennahda's interactions with other political, social, and economic forces and not by ideology alone.

By focusing on whether or not Islamists are or can be democrats, we neglect the fact that until the very recent outpouring of demands for the removal of authoritarian regimes and for democratic reforms that were spearheaded by Middle Eastern youth in 2011, Islamists were often the strongest and the only critics of the region's authoritarian regimes. It is the weakness of moderate Islamism—as opposed to its strength—that should perhaps be of greater concern to analysts, for without any other real opposition—at least in the form of political parties—in the majority of Middle Eastern states, the authoritarian regimes risk being the only beneficiaries should moderate Islamist organizations further weaken or cease to exist. On the whole, Islamists have not won the overwhelming majorities that many in the West have feared,[71] though this observation should be tempered with the realization that past elections were not free and fair, and that as a result we do not have a definitive idea of what their true level of popular support is. In particular, with low turnouts in elections and without any real opposition from other political parties, their popularity may in fact be less strong than it appears to be. In some cases, Islamists have been punished at the polls for their lack of clear policy proposals; the phrase "Islam is the solution" is simply not enough.[72] In addition, Islamists are being weakened by internal tensions.[73] Even prior to the revolution there were splits along both generational and strategic lines within the Egyptian Muslim Brotherhood. The same can be said of the Jordanian Muslim Brotherhood.[74] Given the lack of political alternatives, perhaps the question should be about whether we can afford not to include moderate Islamists.

The debate over whether or not to include Islamists and the degree to which Islamists will ideologically moderate is far from over. Islamists, even moderate Islamists, are highly heterogeneous as a result of the contexts within which they operate and, as a result, their internal dynamics. While post-2011 Tunisia and Egypt may not prove that Islamists are democrats, they also do not prove that all Islamists are autocrats. Yet it is important to note that, historically, the emergence of all religious parties and movements has provoked fear. As scholars have pointed out, when the first Christian Democratic organizations were formed in the late nineteenth century, they were seen by many as dangerous organizations seeking to overthrow established political systems in order to open the way up for the domination of the Catholic Church. They too were accused of seeking to use democratic political processes to come to power but then rejecting them once they had achieved that power.[75]

Notes

1. Francesco Cavatorta, "Neither Participation Nor Revolution: The Strategy of the Moroccan Jamiat al-Adl wal-Ihsan," *Mediterranean Politics* 12, 3 (November 2007), p. 382.

2. Amy Hawthorn, "Is Civil Society the Answer?" in Thomas Carothers and Marina Ottaway, eds., *Uncharted Journey: Promoting Democracy in the Middle East* (Washington, DC: Carnegie Endowment for International Peace, 2005), p. 85.

3. Quintan Wiktorowicz, *The Management of Islamic Activism: Salafis, the Muslim Brotherhood, and the State in Jordan* (Albany: State University of New York Press, 2001), p. 85.

4. Saad Eddin Ibrahim, "Anatomy of Egypt's Militant Groups," *Journal of Middle East Studies* 12 (1980); Ali E. Dessouki, *Islamic Resurgence in the Arab World* (New York: Praeger, 1982); Leonard Binder, *Muslim Liberalism* (Chicago: Chicago University Press, 1988); Giles Kepel, *The Prophet and the Pharaoh* (London: al-Saqi, 1985); John L. Esposito and John O. Voll, *Islam and Democracy* (New York: Oxford University Press, 1996); John L. Esposito, ed., *Political Islam: Revolution, Radicalism, or Reform?* (Boulder: Lynne Rienner, 1997); Azza M. Karam, "Islamist Parties in the Arab World," Ambiguities, Contradictions, and Perseverance," *Democratization* 4, 4 (1997); Charles Kurzman, ed., *Liberal Islam: A Sourcebook* (New York: Oxford University Press 1998); Denis Sullivan and Sana Abed-Kotob, *Islam in Contemporary Egypt: Civil Society Versus the State* (Boulder: Lynne Rienner, 1999); Daniel Brumberg, *Reinventing Khomeini: The Struggle for Reform in Iran* (Chicago: University of Chicago Press, 2001); Graham Fuller, *The Future of Political Islam* (New York: Palgrave Macmillan, 2003).

5. Amr Hamzawy, "The Key to Arab Reform: Moderate Islamists," policy brief (Washington, DC: Carnegie Endowment for International Peace, 2005), pp. 1–2.

6. Daniel Pipes, "There Are No Moderates: Dealing with Fundamentalist Islam," *The National Interest* 41 (Fall 1995), pp. 48–52, 54.

7. Nathan J. Brown, Amr Hamzawy, and Marina Ottaway, "Islamist Movements and the Democratic Process in the Arab World: Exploring the Gray Zones," Carnegie Papers, Middle East Series, no. 67 (Washington, DC: Carnegie Endowment for International Peace, March 2006), p. 3.

8. Holger Albrecht and Eva Wegner, "Autocrats and Islamists: Contenders and Containment in Egypt and Morocco," *Journal of North African Studies* 11, 2 (June 2006), p. 123. In their examination of Muslim Brotherhood members of parliament in Egypt, Samer Shehata and Joshua Stacher, for example, note that in order to fulfill all their legislative duties, their role as government watchdog, and the demands for constituent services, the Brothers created a "parliamentary kitchen," as they call it, an organ that is part research arm and part think tank. The "kitchen" has people with knowledge and experience and consults with civil society and experts. The authors argue that this has made the Brothers more representative of Egyptians' concerns. Samer Shehata and Joshua Stacher, "The Brotherhood Goes to Parliament," *Middle East Report* 240 (Fall 2006).

9. Jillian Schwedler, "A Paradox of Democracy? Islamist Participation in Elections," *Middle East Report* 209 (Winter 1998), pp. 25, 27. See Judith Miller, "The Challenge of Radical Islam," *Foreign Affairs* 72, 2 (Spring 1993): 52.

10. To a certain extent, this question is unfair and unreasonable as it is not asked of other political currents and actors, a point that underlines the prejudices with which many analysts approach the question of political participation by Islamist organizations.

11. Cavatorta, "Neither Participation Nor Revolution," p. 382.

12. Magdi Khalil, "Egypt's Muslim Brotherhood and Political Power: Would Democracy Survive?" *Middle East Review of International Affairs* 10, 1 (March 2006).

13. Cavatorta, "Neither Participation Nor Revolution," p. 382; Daniel Brumberg, "Islamists and the Politics of Consensus," *Journal of Democracy* 13, 3 (2002).

14. Cavatorta, "Neither Participation Nor Revolution," p. 382. Jason Brownlee looks at the issue of moderation from a different perspective and argues that even if Islamists were to deal with their commitment issue—their clear commitment to democratic principles—there is not enough pressure, international or do-

mestic, on authoritarian regimes for them to be forced to respond to these commitments positively. Jason Brownlee, "Unrequited Moderation: Credible Commitments and State Repression in Egypt," *Studies in Comparative International Development* 45 (2010).

15. Cavatorta, "Neither Participation Nor Revolution," p. 383.

16. Jillian Schwedler, "Democratization, Inclusion, and the Moderation of Islamist Parties," *Development* 50, 1 (2007), p. 59.

17. Francesco Cavatorta, "Civil Society, Islamism, and Democratisation: The Case of Morocco," *Journal of Modern African Studies* 44, 2 (2006), p. 204.

18. Early studies on professional associations include: Mustapha K. El Sayed, "Professional Associations and National Integration in the Arab World, with Special Reference to Lawyers Associations," in Adeed Dawisha and I. William Zartman, eds., *Beyond Coercion: The Durability of the Arab State* (London: Croom Helm, 1988); Robert Bianchi, *Unruly Corporatism: Associational Life in Twentieth-Century Egypt* (New York: Oxford University Press, 1989); Elisabeth Longuenesse, "Ingenieurs et Marche de l'Emploi en Jordanie," in Elisabeth Longuenesse, ed., *Batisseurs et Bureaucrates: Ingenieurs et Societe au Maghreb et au Moyen-Orient, Etudes sur le Monde Arabe 4* (Lyon: Maison de l'Orient Mediterranée, 1990); Ninette S. Fahmy, "The Performance of the Muslim Brotherhood in the Egyptian Syndicates: An Alternative Formula for Reform?" *Middle East Journal* 52, 4 (Autumn 1998); Hani Hourani, "The Development of the Political Role of the Professional Associations: A Historical Survey, 1950–1989," in Warwick M. Knowles, ed., *Professional Associations and the Challenges of Democratic Transformation in Jordan* (Amman: al-Urdun al-Jadid Research Center, 2000), pp. 17–62.

19. Mona el-Ghobashy, "Constitutional Contention in Contemporary Egypt," *American Behavioral Scientist* 51, 11 (July 2008).

20. Carrie Rosefsky Wickham, *Mobilizing Islam: Religion, Activism, and Political Change in Egypt* (New York: Columbia University Press, 2002), p. 213.

21. Pete W. Moore and Bassel F. Salloukh, "Struggles Under Authoritarianism: Regimes, States, and PAs in the Arab World," *International Journal of Middle East Studies* 39, 1 (2007), p. 55; Mamoun Fandy "Tribe vs. Islam: The Post-Colonial Arab State and the Democratic Imperative," *Middle East Policy* 3, 2 (1993).

22. Hamzawy, "The Key to Arab Reform"; Amr Hamzawy, Marina Ottaway, and Nathan Brown, "What Islamists Need to Be Clear About: The Case of the Egyptian Muslim Brotherhood," policy outlook (Washington, DC: Carnegie Endowment for International Peace, February 2007), p. 3.

23. Stacey Philbrick Yadav, "Antecedents of the Revolution," *Studies in Ethnicity and Nationalism* 11, 3 (December 2011).

24. Brown, Hamzawy, Ottaway, "Islamist Movements and the Democratic Process in the Arab World," p. 8.

25. Brown, Hamzawy, Ottaway, "Islamist Movements and the Democratic Process in the Arab World," p. 7. See also Hamzawy, Ottaway, and Brown, "What Islamists Need to Be Clear About"; Nathan J. Brown and Amr Hamzawy, "The Draft Party Platform of the Egyptian Muslim Brotherhood: Foray into Political Integration or Retreat into Old Positions?" Carnegie Papers, Middle East Series, no. 89 (Washington, DC: Carnegie Endowment for International Peace, January 2008); Amr Hamzawy and Nathan Brown, "A Boon or a Bane for Democracy?" *Journal of Democracy* 19, 3 (July 2008); Marina Ottaway and Amr Hamzawy, "Islamists in Politics: The Dynamics of Participation," Carnegie Papers no. 98 (Washington, DC: Carnegie Endowment for International Peace, November 2008).

26. Cavatorta, "Neither Participation Nor Revolution," p. 384. See, for example, Ellen Lust-Okar, *Structuring Conflict in the Arab World: Incumbents, Opponents, and Institutions* (New York: Cambridge University Press, 2005).

27. Berna Turam, "The Politics of Engagement Between Islam and the Secular State: Ambivalence of 'Civil Society,'" *British Journal of Sociology* 55, 2 (2004).

28. Francesco Cavatorta and Azzam Elananza, "Political Opposition in Civil Society: An Analysis of the Interactions of Secular and Religious Associations in Algeria and Jordan," *Government and Opposition* 43, 4 (2008), p. 564.

29. Francesco Cavatorta, "Civil Society, Islamism, and Democratisation: The Case of Morocco," *Journal of Modern African Studies* 44, 2 (2006), p. 205.

30. Janine A. Clark and Amy E. Young, "Islamism and Family Law Reform in Morocco and Jordan," *Mediterranean Politics* 13, 3 (November 2008).

31. For the role of women's issues for internal party dynamics and for alliance behavior, see Janine A. Clark and Jillian Schwedler, "Who Opened the Window? Women's Struggle for Voice within Islamist Political Parties," *Comparative Politics* 35, 3 (April 2003); Michaelle L. Browers, *Political Ideology in the Arab World: Accommodation and Transformation* (Cambridge: Cambridge University Press, 2009); Stacey Philbrick Yadav and Janine Clark, "Disappointments and New Directions: Women, Partisanship, and the Regime in Yemen," *HAWWA: Journal of Women of the Middle East and of the Islamic World* 8, 1 (2010); Vincent Durac, "The Joint Meeting Parties and the Politics of Opposition in Yemen," *British Journal of Middle Eastern Studies* 38, 3 (December 2011); Yadav, "Antecedents of the Revolution."

32. Ziya Onis and E. Fuat Keyman, "Turkey at the Polls: A New Path Emerges," *Journal of Democracy* 14, 2 (April 2003); Burhanettin Duran and Engin Yildirim, "Islamism, Trade Unionism, and Civil Society: The Case of Hak-Is Labour Confederation in Turkey," *Middle Eastern Studies* 41, 2 (March 2005).

33. Asef Bayat, *Making Islam Democratic: Social Movements and the Post-Islamist Turn* (Palo Alto: Stanford University Press, 2007). Ayse Bugra also takes a "context-dependent approach" and compares Islamist associations in Turkey. She argues that the social projects they support are different as a result of their class differences. Ayse Bugra, "Class, Culture, and the State," *International Journal of Middle East Studies* 30, 4 (1998); Ayse Bugra, "Labour, Capital, and Religion: Harmony and Conflict Among the Constituency of Political Islam in Turkey," *Middle Eastern Studies* 38, 2 (2002).

34. Stacey Philbrick Yadav, "Understanding 'What Islamists Want': Public Debate and Contestation in Lebanon and Yemen," *Middle East Journal* 64, 2 (Spring 2010).

35. Brumberg, "Islamists and the Politics of Consensus," pp. 111–112.

36. Mona el-Ghobashy, "The Metamorphosis of the Egyptian Muslim Brothers," *International Journal of Middle East Studies* 37, 3 (2005), p. 375.

37. Jillian Schwedler, *Faith in Moderation: Islamist Parties in Jordan and Yemen* (New York: Cambridge University Press, 2006); Jillian Schwedler, "Can Islamists Become Moderates? Rethinking the Inclusion-Moderation Hypothesis," *World Politics* 63, 2 (April 2011).

38. See, for example, Gudrun Krämer, "The Integration of the Integrationist: A Comparative Study of Egypt, Jordan, and Tunisia," in Ghassan Salamé, ed., *Democracy Without Democrats? The Renewal of Politics in the Muslim World* (London: Taurus, 1994); Augustus Richard Norton, "The Challenge of Inclusion in the Middle East," *Current History,* January 1995.

39. Schwedler, *Faith in Moderation,* pp. 11–26; Schwedler, "Democratization, Inclusion, and the Moderation of Islamist Parties"; Schwedler, "Can Islamists Become Moderates?"

40. Carrie Rosefsky Wickham, "The Path to Moderation: Strategy and Learning in the Formation of Egypt's Wasat Party," *Comparative Politics* 36, 2 (January 2004), p. 206.

41. Sheri Berman, "Taming Extremist Parties: Lessons from Europe," *Journal of Democracy* 19, 1 (January 2008), p. 6.

42. R. Quinn Mecham, "From the Ashes of Virtue, a Promise of Light: The Transformation of Political Islam in Turkey," *Third World Quarterly* 25, 2 (2004), p. 353.

43. el-Ghobashy, "The Metamorphosis of the Egyptian Muslim Brothers," p. 374.

44. Wickham, "The Path to Moderation," p. 214; Nancy Bermeo, "Democracy and the Lessons of Dictatorship," *Comparative Politics* 24, 3 (April 1992); Omar Ashour, "Lions Tamed? An Inquiry into the Causes of De-Radicalization of Armed Islamist Movements: The Case of the Egyptian Islamic Group," *Middle East Journal* 61, 4 (Autumn, 2007); Omar Ashour, *The De-Radicalization of Jihadists: Transforming Armed Islamist Movements* (New York: Routledge, 2009).

45. Wickham, "The Path to Moderation," p. 225. Joshua Stacher similarly points to the experience of the Wasat members in professional syndicates and their frustration with the leadership of the Muslim Brotherhood as two of the most important variables. In addition, he cites government repression as a third variable. Joshua A. Stacher, "Post-Islamist Rumblings in Egypt: The Emergence of the Wasat Party," *Middle East Journal* 56, 3 (2002).

46. Schwedler, *Faith in Moderation;* Schwedler, "Can Islamists Become Moderates?" pp. 363–364. Other studies note that Islamist parties have strict ideological "red lines" that are not open for discussion or cooperation. Janine A. Clark, "The Conditions of Islamist Moderation: Unpacking Cross-Ideological Cooperation in Jordan," *International Journal of Middle East Studies* 38, 4 (2006); Dina Shehata, *Islamists and Secularists in Egypt: Opposition, Conflict, and Cooperation* (London: Routledge Press, 2009); Francesco Cavatorta, "'Divided They Stand, Divided They Fail': Opposition Politics in Morocco," *Democratization* 16, 1 (February 2009); Maha Abdelrahman, "'With the Islamists?—Sometimes; With the State?—Never!' Cooperation Between the Left and Islamists in Egypt," *British Journal of Middle Eastern Studies* 36, 1 (April 2009); Rikke Hostrup Haugbolle and Cavatorta, "Will the Real Tunisian Opposition Please Stand Up? Opposition Coordination Failures Under Authoritarian Constraints," *British Journal of Middle Eastern Studies* 38, 3 (December 2011); Cavatorta and Elananza, "Political Opposition in Civil Society"; Durac, "The Joint Meeting Parties," p. 359.

47. Schwedler, *Faith in Moderation.* Schwedler argues that her approach addresses the paradox of democracy conundrum—a serious internal discussion of inclusion is strong evidence that inclusion is not being used as a ploy to overthrow democracy. Schwedler, "Democratization, Inclusion, and the Moderation of Islamist Parties," p. 60.

48. Berna Turam takes a different approach and argues that Islamist moderation in Turkey must be understood in conjunction with moderation of non-Islamists, including the state, as well. She argues that Islamist actors and the state reshape each other. Berna Turam, *Between Islam and the State: The Politics of Engagement* (Stanford: Stanford University Press, 2007), p. 9.

49. Brumberg, "Islamists and the Politics of Consensus," p. 112.

50. Ottaway and Hamzawy, "Islamists in Politics." See also Hamzawy and Brown, "A Boon or a Bane for Democracy?" p. 51 Both studies were conducted prior to the 2011 Arab Spring.

51. Michaelle Browers, "Origins and Architects of Yemen's Joint Meeting Parties," *International Journal of Middle East Studies* 39, 4 (November 2007), p. 583. See also Günes Murat Tezcür, "The Moderation Theory Revisited: The Case of Islamic Political Actors," *Party Politics* 16, 1 (2010), p. 73.

52. Schwedler argues that most studies adopt one of three focal points: the behavioral moderation of groups, the ideological moderation of groups, or the ideological moderation of individuals. Schwedler, "Can Islamists Become Moderates?" p. 348.

53. Schwedler, "Democratization, Inclusion, and the Moderation of Islamist Parties," p. 59.

54. Eva Wegner and Miquel Pellicer, "Islamist Moderation Without Democratization: The Coming of Age of the Moroccan Party of Justice and Development?" *Democratization* 16, 1 (February 2009).

55. Tezcür, "The Moderation Theory Revisited," pp. 72, 83. See also Günes Murat Tezcür, *The Paradox of Moderation: Muslim Reformers in Iran and Turkey* (Austin: University of Texas Press, 2009).

56. Michael Willis, "Morocco's Islamists and the Legislative Elections of 2002: The Strange Case of the Party That Did Not Want to Win," *Mediterranean Politics* 9, 1 (2004); Shadi Hamid, "The Islamist Response to Repression: Are Mainstream Islamists Radicalizing?" policy brief, Brookings Doha Center of the Saban Center for Middle East Policy, Brookings Institution, August 2010; Shadi Hamid, "Arab Islamist Parties: Losing on Purpose?" *Journal of Democracy* 22, 1 (January 2011).

57. Holger Albrecht, "How Can Opposition Support Authoritarianism? Lessons from Egypt," *Democratization* 12, 3 (June 2005), p. 394. See also I. William Zartman, "Opposition in Support of the State," in Dawisha and Zartman, *Beyond Coercion;* Holger Albrecht, "Political Opposition and Arab Authoritarianism: Some Conceptual Remarks," in Albrecht, ed., *Contentious Politics in the Middle East: Political Opposition Under Authoritarianism* (Gainesville: University of Florida Press, 2010).

58. Marsha Pripstein Posusney, "Multi-Party Elections in the Arab World: Institutional Engineering and Opposition Strategies Studies," *Comparative International Development* 36, 4 (2002); Vickie Langohr, "Too Much Civil Society, Too Little Politics," *Comparative Politics* 36, 2 (2004); Ellen Lust-Okar and Seloua Zerhouni, eds., *Political Participation in the Middle East* (Boulder: Lynne Rienner 2008); Hendrik Kraetzschmar, "Opposition Alliances Under Electoral Authoritarianism," in Albrecht, *Contentious Politics in the Middle East.*

59. I. William Zartman, "Concluding Remarks: Opportunities in Support of the Arab State," in Albrecht, *Contentious Politics in the Middle East,* p. 230.

60. Cavatorta, "Neither Participation Nor Revolution," p. 385.

61. Quintan Wiktorowicz, ed., *Islamic Activism: A Social Movement Theory Approach* (Bloomington: Indiana University Press, 2004). See also Mohammed Hafez, *Why Muslims Rebel: Repression and Resistance in the Islamic World* (Boulder: Lynne Rienner 2003); Wiktorowicz, *The Management of Islamic Activism;* Wickham, *Mobilizing Islam;* Janine A. Clark, *Islam, Charity, and Activism* (Bloomington: Indiana University Press, 2004); Janine A. Clark, "Social Movement Theory and Patron-Clientelism: Islamic Social Institutions and the Middle Class in

Egypt, Jordan, and Yemen," *Comparative Political Studies* 37 (2004); Asef Bayat, "Islamism and Social Movement Theory," *Third World Quarterly* 26, 6 (2005); Schwedler, *Faith in Moderation;* Abdelrahman, "With the Islamists?"; Joel Beinin and Frederic Vairel, *Social Movements, Mobilization, and Contestation in the Middle East and North Africa* (Stanford: Stanford University Press, 2011). Some precursors of and earlier examples of social movement theory as applied to Islamist movements include Gehad Auda, "The Islamic Movement and Resource Mobilization in Egypt: A Political Culture Perspective," in Larry Diamond, ed., *Political Culture and Democracy in Developing Countries* (Boulder: Lynne Rienner 1993); Charles Kurzman, "Structural Opportunity and Perceived Opportunity in Social-Movement Theory: The Iranian Revolution of 1979," *American Sociological Review* 61, 1 (February 1996); Dale F. Eickelman and James Piscatori, *Muslim Politics* (Princeton: Princeton University Press, 1996); Asef Bayat, *Street Politics: Poor People's Movements in Iran* (New York: Columbia University Press, 1997); Saul Mishal and Avraham Sela, *The Palestinain Hamas: Vision, Violence, and Coexistence* (New York: Columbia University Press, 2000); Ziad Munson, "Islamic Mobilization: Social Movement Theory and the Egyptian Muslim Brotherhood," *Sociological Quarterly* 42, 4 (2001).

62. Quintan Wiktorowicz, "Islamic Activism and Social Movement Theory: A New Direction for Research," *Mediterranean Politics* 7, 3 (Autumn 2002), p. 189.

63. Quintan Wiktorowicz, "Introduction: Islamic Activism and Social Movement Theory," in Wiktorowicz, *Islamic Activism,* pp. 1–33.

64. Roel Meijer, "Taking the Islamist Movement Seriously: Social Movement Theory and the Islamist Movement," *International Review of Social History* 50 (2005); Oded Haklai, "Authoritarianism and Islamic Movements in the Middle East: Research and Theory-Building in the Twenty-First Century," *International Studies Review* 11 (2009).

65. Mohammed M. Hafez and Quintan Wiktorowicz, "Violence as Contention in the Egyptian Islamic Movement," in Wiktorowicz, *Islamic Activism,* pp. 61–88.

66. Diane Singerman, "The Networked World of Islamist Social Movements," in Wiktorowicz, *Islamic Activism,* pp. 143–163; Clark, *Islam, Charity, and Activism.*

67. Quintan Wickham, "Interests, Ideas, and Islamist Outreach in Egypt," in Wiktorowicz, *Islamic Activism,* pp. 231–249.

68. Wiktorowicz, *Islamic Activism,* p. 15.

69. Wickham, "Interests, Ideas, and Islamist Outreach in Egypt," in Wiktorowicz, *Islamic Activism,* p. 232.

70. According to a 2012 poll, 62 percent of those surveyed felt that the government was not guaranteeing the equality and rights of citizens, 53 percent believed that the government had not succeeded in guaranteeing democracy, and that 70 percent felt the country was more divided than before the revolution. See http://www.tekiano.com/ness/politik/5042-sigma-conseil-les-100-jours-du-gouvernement-tous-les-voyants-sont-au-rouge-.html.

71. Charles Kurzman and Ijlal Naqvi, "Do Muslims Vote Islamic?" *Journal of Democracy* 21, 2 (April 2010).

72. For the case of the Jordanian Islamic Action Front, see Janine A. Clark, "Questioning Power, Mobilization, and Strategies of the Islamist Opposition: How Strong Is the Muslim Brotherhood in Jordan?" in Albrecht, *Contentious Politics in the Middle East,* pp. 117 137.

73. See Hamid, "The Islamist Response to Repression."

74. Mohammad Abu Rumman, *The Muslim Brotherhood in the Jordanian Par-*

liamentary Elections, 2007: A Passing "Political Setback" or Diminishing Popularity? (Amman: Friedrich Ebert Stiftung, 2008); Clark, "Questioning Power, Mobilization, and Strategies."

75. Hamzawy, Ottaway, and Brown, "What Islamists Need to Be Clear About," p. 2.

7

Electoral Politics

Competitive elections have finally returned to a number of Arab states on the morrow of the 2011 popular uprisings. Starting in Tunisia's historic post–Ben Ali elections to the National Constituent Assembly and culminating in Egypt's People's Assembly elections, the ballot box has reemerged as a site for hard battles between political parties and groups possessing widely different visions of the emerging social and political orders. This is in stark contrast to past decades when Arab regimes considered elections an institutional mechanism serving authoritarian endurance.

When they held or reintroduced legislative elections,[1] authoritarian Arab regimes did so in the past only grudgingly, whether to co-opt opposition and ruling-party members through the dispensation of patronage,[2] to produce and display their political power by disciplinary spectacles,[3] as part of a reversible "democratic bargain" offered to their societies to offset socioeconomic and political tensions generated by the fiscal crisis of the Arab state from the late 1970s onward,[4] to absorb and manage domestic pressures caused by external invasion (as was the case in Kuwait after the Iraqi invasion of 1990), or, finally, in response to post–11 September 2001 calls by the United States for domestic reforms.[5]

Nor, as some comparativists claim,[6] have elections under authoritarianism engendered a gradual democratizing effect, measured by an improvement in civil liberties. As Table 7.1 shows, repeated legislative elections in the Arab world did not correlate in past years with improved civil liberties scores, with the possible exception of Kuwait and Morocco. Instead, the wave of political liberalization that spread throughout the Arab world in the late 1980s and early 1990s was soon reversed, as regimes reconfigured control over the domestic arena whether to smash a more assertive Islamist opposition, pass domestically unpopular peace treaties, or engage in more structural—read, painful—economic reforms.[7] Despite the fact that elections continued to be held throughout these deliberalization years, they signified little in terms of political empowerment and control over public policy. Instead, they became part of the institutional ensemble organized by Arab regimes to avoid democratization and reproduce authoritarianism.

Table 7.1 Repeated Legislative Elections and Civil Liberties Ratings for Selected Arab Countries, 1976–2010

	First Election		Second Election		Third Election		Fourth Election		Fifth Election		Sixth Election		Seventh Election		Eighth Election		Ninth Election	
	Year	Rating	Year	Rating	Year	Rating	Year	Rating	Year	Rating	Year	Rating	Year	Rating	Year	Rating	Year	Rating
Algeria	1992	6	1997	6	2002	5	2007 (2010)	5 (5)										
Egypt	1976	4	1978	4	1979	5	1984	4	1987	4	1990	4	1995	6	2000	5	2005 (2010)	5 (5)
Jordan	1989	5	1993	4	1997	4	2003	5	2007 (2010)	4 (5)								
Kuwait	1992	5	1996	5	1999	5	2003	5	2006	5	2008	4	2009 (2010)	4 (4)				
Morocco	1993	5	1997	5	2002	5	2007 (2010)	4 (4)										
Tunisia	1989	3	1994	5	1999	5	2004	5	2009 (2010)	5 (5)								
Yemen	1993	5	1997	6	2003	5	2006 (2010)	5 (5)										

Sources: Freedom House, "Freedom in the World Country Ratings, 1972–2006" (spreadsheet), http://www.freedomhouse.org/uploads/fiw/FIWAllScores.xls; Freedom House, *Freedom in the World: Selected Data from Freedom House's Annual Global Survey of Political Rights and Civil Liberties*, various years.

Note: Civil liberties ratings range from 1 to 7, with 1 representing the most free and 7 the least free.

Moreover, and contrary to regime wishes, and academic assumptions,[8] elections have failed to immunize authoritarian Arab regimes from mass protests. Popular uprisings have swept across Arab states with closed political systems—Tunisia, Syria, and Libya—as well as in "hegemonic authoritarian regimes"—Egypt, Jordan, Morocco, Yemen, and Bahrain—that deployed elections for authoritarian maintenance.[9] In fact, managed elections and the unaccountability that comes with them may have even exacerbated popular discontent with authoritarian regimes. Not surprisingly then, free and fair elections via truly representative electoral systems have emerged as central popular demands.

This chapter opens with an analysis of the causes and dynamics of successive election waves under authoritarianism in the Arab world. It then examines how authoritarian Arab regimes used elections and manipulated the electoral institutional repertoire to maintain—albeit unsuccessfully—their hold on power. It closes with an examination of the electoral challenges and contests unleashed by the 2010–2011 popular uprisings.

Explaining Past Electoral Waves in the Arab World

After a long hiatus during which multiparty elections were suspended by fiat, many authoritarian regimes in the Arab world reintroduced legislative elections in the face of political crises triggered by government measures aimed at containing state fiscal crises and the resultant socioeconomic upheavals. Until then, Arab regimes had sought to organize loyal socioeconomic and political coalitions through populist authoritarian bargains. In return for skirting political representation and accountability, regimes subsidized primary commodities, offered free education, medical services, and housing, guaranteed employment for university graduates and the professional middle class in the increasingly bloated and inefficient public sector, created or alternatively co-opted the petite bourgeoisies, and recruited strategic sectors of the rural population into the *mukhabarat* (secret police) and praetorian military formations. These populist authoritarian bargains obviated the need for any liberalizing measures as long as the income generated from domestic rents and remittances, as well as strategic external aid, was available. However, as discussed in Chapter 9 in greater detail, when revenues began decreasing in the mid-1980s, Arab regimes had to incur evergreater foreign debts to finance their authoritarian bargains, which soon made structural adjustment policies unavoidable. The socioeconomic crises that followed forced regimes to introduce legislative elections as part of a regime-controlled political liberalization strategy aimed at maintaining authoritarian control. In Egypt, Algeria, Jordan, Yemen, and Tunisia, elections were the hallmark of a new democratic bargain "in which citizens were given more political voice in exchange for accepting both the short-term costs of economic liberalization and the longer-term uncertainty of life in a market economy."[10]

Nowhere was the close affinity between economic crisis, the need for economic reforms, resultant social upheaval, and subsequent elections more clear than in Jordan. Parliamentary elections had been suspended since 1957, but were reintroduced by the Hashemite regime immediately after the bloody clashes of 18 April 1989. Those clashes were rooted in an economic crisis generated by years of overspending on the Hashemite regime's populist rentier authoritarian bargain with strategic sectors of the population, one that was financed by Arab petrodollar budgetary grants and workers' remittances. But as world oil prices declined, budgetary aid dropped from a peak of $1.3 billion in 1980 to $427 million in 1988; remittances by Jordanian workers also dropped, from $1.2 billion in 1984 to $980 million in 1988.[11]

In spite of these drops, the Jordanian regime decided to maintain its populist bargain through foreign borrowing. The country's externally scheduled debt-service payments increased to around $1.4 billion in 1989, at which point the government negotiated a structural adjustment program with the International Monetary Fund aimed at reducing the budget deficit. It was austerity measures, and especially an increase in the price of petroleum products, that triggered the April clashes, led by the kingdom's hitherto loyal southern population, which had benefited the least from the economic boom of the early 1980s. King Hussein subsequently decided that parliamentary elections should be held as part of a controlled process of political liberalization initiated from above.

The parliamentary election of 8 November 1989 was a stunning victory for Islamist candidates, who by then had emerged as the main opposition in the kingdom.[12] Islamists won thirty-two seats, of which twenty-two went to candidates fielded by the Muslim Brotherhood, while the rest went to independent Islamists. Arab nationalists and leftists won thirteen seats, raising the total number of opposition deputies to forty-five. The remaining thirty-five seats went to an assortment of conservative and centrist candidates.

A similar pattern transpired in Algeria, though with much more disastrous consequences. There, the populist authoritarian "ruling bargain" was financed by the sale of oil and natural gas, foreign remittances, and foreign aid, and guaranteed Algerians social welfare benefits and job security in exchange for one-party rule.[13] As the global oil glut hit in 1985, Algeria's hydrocarbon and remittance earnings plummeted, with foreign revenues dropping from $13 billion in 1985 to $8 billion in 1982. The deficit between government spending and revenues was covered by foreign borrowing, thus raising Algeria's foreign debt to $23 billion in 1988.[14] The Algerian regime responded to this with economic reforms that initially encouraged privatization and private investment, but ended up slashing subsidies on basic consumer commodities, increasing taxes, and reducing price controls on industrial and agricultural products. The socioeconomic tensions generated by these measures exploded in October 1988, when violent protests pitted students and unemployed youth against the army, leaving some 500 demonstrators dead and wounded. A beleaguered President Chadli Bendjedid responded with a program of political liberalization in which citizens were offered a new, democratic ruling bargain: greater political voice in exchange for acquiescence to difficult economic reforms.

A new constitution was subsequently promulgated in February 1989. It institutionalized multiparty politics, established a market economy, dismantled the one-party authoritarian state, and inaugurated competitive multiparty elections. In the ensuing parliamentary elections of 26 December 1991, the Front Islamique du Salut (FIS, Islamic Salvation Front) won outright 188 of 430 seats, and was leading in 150 other ridings. But the army decided to suspend the election results and cancel the second round of voting, scheduled for 16 January 1992.[15] This move plunged Algeria into a protracted civil war.

This first post–fiscal crisis wave of elections was soon reversed by regimes desiring greater control over the political arena in order to roll back Islamist penetration of civil society, introduce deeper economic restructuring measures, and in at least one case pass a domestically unpopular peace treaty. Egypt's flirtation with parliamentary elections after 1976 coincided with President Anwar Sadat's policy of economic openness *(infitah iqtisadi)*. But it was during the early phase of President Hosni Mubarak's tenure that parliamentary elections were used (in 1984 and 1987) to defuse socioeconomic and political pressures generated by the regime's economic liberalization policies. Later, as the regime grew increasingly wary of the power of Islamist groups in society and in the professional syndicates, and as the need to implement deeper and hence more painful economic reforms grew more urgent, it manipulated electoral laws to deliberalize the political arena and to organize a new sociopolitical coalition that was sympathetic to prospective economic reforms.[16]

Similarly, the Jordanian regime grew increasingly wary of the 1989 opposition-dominated parliament. King Hussein dissolved it on 4 August 1993, four months before the end of its mandate. Then on 17 August, over the objections of most political parties in the kingdom, the king ratified an amendment to the existing 1986 election law that replaced the

1989 unlimited-vote system with the single nontransferable vote (SNTV). Given Jordan's complex sociological anatomy, the former system was much more representative of the kingdom's political topography. But it had also worked to the advantage of the well-organized Muslim Brotherhood in the 1989 elections, because voters were able to vote along tribal, familial, *and* political-ideological lines. The 1993 amendment, which was labeled the "one citizen, one vote" law, limited the number of votes cast by each voter in multiseat constituencies to one. Consequently, most voters opted to vote for their tribal or familial candidate. This electoral ruse was aimed at ensuring the election of a pliant parliament that would serve as a rubber stamp for royal decisions, especially given that the king was preparing to sign a domestically unpopular peace treaty with Israel.

The SNTV system ensured that voting in Jordan's 8 November 1993 parliamentary elections followed along tribal lines.[17] Consequently, the total number of opposition deputies dropped to a mere twenty-three (compared to forty-five in 1989), of whom sixteen were part of the Muslim Brotherhood's political arm, the Islamic Action Front (compared to twenty-two in 1989). Leftists and Arab nationalists won six seats (compared to thirteen in 1989), while another opposition seat went to an independent Islamist. Of the remaining fifty-seven deputies, at least fifty were pro-regime. The 1993 election thus marked the beginning of deliberalization through elections in Jordan. As Table 7.2 shows, the SNTV system provided the Jordanian regime with a comfortable parliamentary majority in consecutive elections.

The terrorist attacks of 11 September 2001 and subsequent US calls for political and social reforms under the banner of George W. Bush's "Forward Strategy of Freedom" for the Middle East contributed to a second wave of elections under authoritarianism in the Arab world.[18] As Bush later explained in his memoirs, Washington "would advocate for freedom while maintaining strategic relationships with nations like Saudi Arabia . . . [and] Egypt."[19] Not without contradictions, the new policy meant that from 2002 until 2006, the Bush administration encouraged Arab regimes to undertake the kind of institutional reforms that implied respect for the trappings of political pluralism without jeopardizing regime control. Local and legislative elections played a central role in this new policy.[20] Hitherto closed Arab countries such as Saudi Arabia were encouraged to introduce formal plural practices and to reform their educational systems, while other countries with established electoral cycles—for instance, Egypt—were asked to make the electoral process more plural and to permit civil society monitoring.[21] The pressure resulted in a fresh wave of municipal and legislative elections aimed at silencing domestic reformers and containing external pressures.

Interrupted since 1964, municipal council elections in Saudi Arabia were reintroduced in 2005. A male-only electorate selected half of the representatives in 178 municipal councils, with the balance appointed by the government. The elections were won by moderate Islamists in respective Sunni and Shiite-dominated areas.[22] The councils possessed no real powers, however. Tellingly in terms of the government's commitment to electoral politics, the next round of municipal elections, scheduled for 2009, was postponed. As will be discussed later, municipal elections were subsequently held in September 2011 in reaction to the Arab uprisings.

Similar demonstration elections were held in the United Arab Emirates (UAE) in December 2006, and involved a handpicked group of 6,689 elites from the seven emirates—including 1,189 women—choosing half of the forty members of the country's powerless advisory panel-cum-parliament, the Federal National Council. The remaining members were appointed by the government.[23] As in Saudi Arabia, these elections were a sham and carried little value in terms of representativeness and accountability.

The electoral experiences of Qatar and Bahrain are a pre-9/11 phenomenon. They were part of efforts by new rulers to smooth the transition from father to son, and in the case of Bahrain were also aimed at cementing the transition to a kingdom in 2002.[24] Qatar was the first Gulf state to introduce universal suffrage, holding free municipal elections in 1999, 2003, 2007, and 2011. Elections for Qatar's hitherto appointed parliament (Majlis al-Shura) were first scheduled for 2008 but then postponed to 2010. In No-

Table 7.2 Legislative Elections in Jordan, 1989–2010

		Number of Elected Deputies	
Year	Electoral System	Regime Opposition	Loyalists
1989	Unlimited vote	45	35
1993	Single nontransferable vote	23	57
1997	Single nontransferable vote	12[a]	68
2003	Single nontransferable vote[b]	22	88
2007	Single nontransferable vote	6	104
2010	Single nontransferable vote	17	103

Source: International Institute for Democracy and Electoral Assistance (IDEA) and Arab NGO Network for Development (ANND), Building Democracy in Jordan: Women's Political Participation, Political Party Life, and Democratic Elections, 2005, http://www.idea.int /publications/dem_jordan/upload/Jordan_country_report_English.pdf; and International Foundation for Electoral Systems (IFES). IFES Election Guide-Country Profile: Jordan.

Notes: a. The Islamic Action Front, Jordan's main opposition party, boycotted the 1997 elections. b. A new election law was approved in 2001, Election Law no. 34, that maintained the SNTV system, but added six new seats for women, lowered the required voting age from nineteen to eighteen years, resized electoral districts (they grew in number from twenty to forty-five), and increased the number of seats in the Chamber of Deputies from 80 to 110.

vember 2011, Qatar's emir announced that they would finally take place in the second half of 2013. When they do take place, these elections will have little impact on the balance of political power in the country, given parliament's highly constrained powers relative to the emir. For example, under a new constitution approved in an April 2003 referendum, parliament needs a difficult two-thirds majority to withhold confidence in ministers. And with the emir appointing fifteen out of a total of forty-five deputies, this means that there would need to be unanimity among the opposition for such confidence to be withheld over the emir's objections. Moreover, the emir can promulgate laws when parliament is not in session, which it can only reject via a two-thirds vote. Future Qatari deputies "will have little power to constrain the monarchy," with parliament effectively a mere "soapbox."[25]

In Bahrain, unlike Saudi Arabia, the UAE, and Qatar, experience with parliamentary elections dates back to 1972. This initial experience proved short-lived after the ruling al-Khalifa family suspended the legislative body in 1975 when parliament refused to pass a restrictive state security law. Reforms to the system began in 1999, and were part of a gradualist liberalizing and reconciliation drive by Shaikh (later King) Hamad to win support for the new monarchical order. The United States supported these efforts after 9/11 as part of its so-called Freedom Agenda to fight terrorism.[26] Concurrent municipal and legislative elections were held in 2002 and 2006. However, Bahrain's new constitution, promulgated in 2002, constrained parliament compared to the powers that it had been assigned under the 1972 constitution. It also allowed for the lower house's already minimal legislative prerogatives to be checked and often blocked by an appointed forty-member upper house, the Consultative Council (Majlis al-Shura). Despite being headed by a Shiite—Ali bin Saleh al-Saleh—Shiite representation in the Consultative Council amounts to only twenty members, although the Shiite sect constitutes around 78 percent of the population.

To protest the restrictions on parliament's powers that were imposed by the regime, the main Shiite parties—the al-Wifaq National Islamic Society (Jam'iyat al-Wifaq al-Watani al-Islamiya) and the Islamic Action Association (Jami'yat al-'Amal al-Islami)—boycotted the October 2002 parliamentary elections. These elections saw a drop in Shiite representation from sixteen out of forty deputies in 1972 to twelve deputies.[27] By the time of the November 2006 elections, Sunni-Shiite tensions had reached a boiling point. The election saw al-Wifaq win a majority of the popular vote but not a parliamentary majority, due to government malapportionment practices and interventions in the voting process. The 2006 parliament was thus composed of two antagonistic sectarian blocs: a progovernment Sunni bloc of twenty-two deputies and al-Wifaq's eighteen-member bloc (made up of seventeen deputies plus a secular ally).[28]

Prior to the October 2010 elections, the regime, but especially the Royal Court faction headed by Khaled bin Ahmad al-Khalifa, unleashed a clampdown against Shiite activists aimed at redrawing the boundaries of licit political activity, thus jeopardizing the reform process started in 2001.[29] Nevertheless, al-Wifaq secured eighteen out of forty seats in the first round of voting. Sunni Islamist groups managed to win only seven seats compared to fifteen in 2006, with the balance of seats going to pro-regime Sunni parties and independents.[30] However, al-Wifaq's deputies later resigned their seats in response to the regime's violent crackdown against Shiite protesters in March 2011. Unperturbed, the regime instructed parliament to accept the resignations of only eleven al-Wifaq deputies, and scheduled by-elections on 24 September 2011 to fill the vacant seats. The by-elections were subsequently boycotted by al-Wifaq, however; only independent candidates contested the seats, and voter turnout was a meager 17.4 percent.[31]

In a departure from its neighbor Gulf states, Kuwait's experience with parliamentary elections is rather old, and driven mainly though not exclusively by indigenous factors rooted in the country's social and economic structures. Electoral politics in Kuwait date back to 1963, but have been interrupted by intermittent periods of royal rule by fiat (1976–1981 and 1986–1992) when the emir practices his constitutional right to dissolve parliament. The most recent drive for democratic representation and reform via elections belongs to the period following the 1990–1991 Gulf War, when domestic and US pressures forced the emir to reverse a 1986 decision to dissolve parliament. Since then, parliamentary elections have been held in 1992, 1996, 1999, 2003, 2006, 2008, 2009, and February 2012. The elections were organized either as part of the regular electoral cycle or after periods of political crisis triggered by a parliamentary vote of confidence in a minister (or the threat of such a vote) that led to the cabinet resigning or the emir dissolving parliament. Although the 2009 vote did see four women elected to parliament, the 2012 elections gave the Islamist-dominated opposition a majority of seats (thirty-four out of fifty), witnessed a decrease in the number of liberal deputies (from five to two), and saw the defeat of all female candidates.[32] Elections in Kuwait have hitherto failed to produce real political change, to institutionalize effective governance practices, or to curb corruption, all perennial demands of the parliamentary opposition and of Kuwaitis. The ruling al-Sabah family thus continues to wield substantial executive powers, to retain control over policy, and to check parliamentary initiative, while "cabinet acts as if it is more answerable to the amir [*sic*] than to the people's elected representatives."[33]

With the exception of Kuwait, the post-9/11 electoral wave in the oil-rich Gulf countries resulted in "election fetishism—elections with limited substance."[34] But among the non-oil Arab states, whether Egypt, Tunisia,

Yemen, Sudan, Algeria, Jordan, or Morocco, and in typical hegemonic authoritarian fashion, legislative elections were part of a regime-organized institutional mechanism to maintain authoritarian rule.

In Egypt, the "Freedom Agenda" had an ephemeral but real impact on electoral politics. Electoral laws and practices governing parliamentary elections had been a perpetual bone of contention between the regime and the opposition throughout Mubarak's long tenure. Opposition demands centered on judicial oversight of elections, and on replacing the list system used in the 1984 and, with slight changes, 1987 elections with an individual-candidacy system, so as to allow independent candidates to run for office.[35] The 1990 elections saw the list system abolished and an individual-candidacy system put in place, while the 2000 parliamentary elections were the first to be conducted under judicial supervision, which according to many observers explains the drop in the National Democratic Party's (NDP) share of parliamentary seats from a high of 94 percent in 1995 to 87 percent.[36]

Post-9/11 US policy pushed Egyptian reforms to new levels, at least for a short time. Thus between 2002 and 2006, the US administration added its voice to domestic calls for political reforms in Egypt. This led to the promulgation in 2005 of a package of constitutional amendments pertaining to presidential and parliamentary elections.[37] The amendments opened the way for direct, multicandidate presidential elections, created an electoral commission for parliamentary elections, and altered the procedures for party formation. The 2005 reforms unleashed a contest between the judiciary and the regime over "the quest for clean elections and the quest for judicial independence."[38] When the election results were in, the opposition had won its largest share of parliamentary seats ever—28 percent—with most of them going to the regime's nemesis, the Muslim Brotherhood, rather than to the secular opposition parties (see Table 7.3). Moreover, only 145 official NDP candidates won their electoral races; the remaining 166 deputies were independents who supported the NDP. Taken together, the NDP and its supporters made up a super-majority of 311 elected deputies. There were also 10 appointed deputies, which brought the NDP's share of parliament's 454 seats to 71 percent.[39]

But this electoral success for the Egyptian opposition proved short-lived. US interest in the "Freedom Agenda" waned after the 2006 Hamas electoral victory and Washington's increased preoccupation with regional crises, whether in Iraq, Yemen, Lebanon, Palestine, or Iran.[40] The Egyptian regime responded by promulgating a new wave of constitutional amendments that reversed the 2005 electoral reforms.[41] As a result, the candidate-centered individual district electoral system was replaced with a mixed system based mainly on proportional representation, while retaining an unspecified number of individual districts. Given the constitutional ban on the

Table 7.3 Legislative Elections in Egypt, 1984–2010

Electoral system	1984 List proportional representation	1987 List proportional representation	1990 Single candidate	1995 Single candidate	2000 Single candidate	2005 Single candidate	2010 Single candidate
National Democratic Party	390	348	360	417	388	311	420
Muslim Brotherhood	8	30	Boycott	1	17	88	1
New Wafd	50	35	Boycott	6	7	6	6
Socialist Labor		27	Boycott				1
Liberals		3	Boycott				
Progressive Unionists			5	5	6	2	5
Arab Democrats					2		2
Nasserists					5		
el-Ghad						1	1
Independents			79	13	16	24	68
Total	448	443	444	442	441	432	504

Sources: International Foundation for Electoral Systems (IFES), "IFES Election Guide—Country Profile: Egypt"; Daniel Brumberg, "Liberalization Versus Democracy: Understanding Arab Political Reform," Carnegie Endowment for International Peace, May 2003, http://carnegieendowment.org/files/wp37.pdf.

formation of religious parties, the amendments favored parties that could form lists, thus targeting the Muslim Brotherhood's ability to field independent candidates and its performance during the 2005 elections. At the same time, the amendments sought to counter the manner in which judicial supervision of elections had made the 2005 elections more competitive and transparent, namely by creating a new electoral commission, one whose autonomy from government intervention was dubious. The new stipulation requiring elections to be held nationwide and on a single day also constrained the ability of judges and civil society activists to monitor elections.

One Arab newspaper described the 28 November 2010 election and its 5 December runoff as akin to "parliamentary appointments."[42] A combination of institutional measures, organized violence, blatant corruption, and unabashed interference in the workings of electoral commissions guaranteed the NDP a landslide victory in an election insulated from international monitoring (see Table 7.3). The legal opposition was consequently decimated, and later opted to withdraw from parliament. The elections signaled the determination of the regime's younger elements, gathered around Gamal Mubarak in the NDP's Higher Policy Council, to use the electoral process as a vehicle for Gamal's hoped-for ascension to the presidency.

The regime had overplayed its hand, however. The violence and rigging of the 2010 elections exacerbated anti-regime sentiments to the breaking point. This was reflected in rather low voter turnout rates, around 20 percent in the first round and less than 10 percent in the runoff stage.[43] Writing after the first round of elections was over, Wael Abdul Fattah described Egyptians as hostages of a long and difficult election day, "charged by events with rage and anger coupled with a feeling of incapacity, and nobody knows where all this anger will lead!"[44] Less than two months later, all this anger was directed at the regime that had orchestrated the 2010 sham elections, ultimately forcing its leader and main figures out of office. Far from contributing to authoritarian maintenance and facilitating Gamal's presidential ambitions, Egypt's 2010 elections in fact expedited regime change.

The Electoral Engineering of Authoritarianism

In the decades preceding the 2010–2011 Arab uprisings, authoritarian regimes organized elections to co-opt the opposition and expand political participation, but to avoid democratization. These elections served to absorb opposition activity into the regime's institutional framework, according to the rules established by the regime.[45] The opposition tolerated regime dominance in return for indispensable yet limited and easily reversed legal and material privileges. Furthermore, by limiting the arena of political competition to parliament, Arab regimes walled-off "the executive branch in such a way that no act of legislature can transform the system."[46] For example, in Morocco's September 2007 elections, King Mohammed VI demonstrated his skills in "distorting the link between the ballot box and the parliament chamber, making each new government look much the same as the one before."[47] Not surprisingly, then, the struggle to make the executive answerable to a popularly elected legislative assembly has emerged as one of the most important demands following the uprisings of the Arab Spring.

Legislative elections were also used by authoritarian Arab regimes as sites of regime-orchestrated "competitions over access to state resources," or "competitive clientalism," which precludes rather than promotes democratization.[48] Both voters and candidates recognized the clientalistic dynamics involved in these elections. This explains why voters often voted for candidates connected to the ruling party—who can deliver services and material resources because of those connections—rather than according to ideological considerations. Moreover, candidates entered the electoral race to reserve for themselves a place in the regime's clientalistic network or even to help gain parliamentary immunity, often a prerequisite for business success.[49] Finally, regimes deployed the clientalistic dynamics of elections to settle intraelite struggles away from the real locus of power, thereby avoiding jeopardizing regime cohesion and stability.[50] In turn, these clientalistic dynamics distorted the incentive structures of voters, unleashing political dynamics that "undermine[d] public support for institutions and individuals associated with democracy."[51]

Arab regimes also designed electoral laws to predetermine election results. As Table 7.4 shows, hegemonic authoritarian Arab regimes preferred plurality-based, winner-takes-all electoral systems—where an absolute majority (50 percent plus one vote) is not required to win a legislative seat—because these systems favor the ruling parties.[52] Alternatively, where the objective was to ensure that no single opposition party gained a majority of seats in parliament (and particularly not an Islamist party), then a proportional representation (PR) system was preferred. Morocco's PR electoral system was designed to deny any party, but especially the Islamist Parti de la Justice et du Développement (PJD, Justice and Development Party), a majority of seats in parliament.[53] A party-list PR electoral system produced a fractured parliament in Algeria after the 17 May 2007 elections. Those elections saw 24 parties field 12,229 candidates on 1,144 party lists, with an additional 102 candidates running as independents. The result was a weak parliament controlled by the executive through a presidential alliance that gathered together the legislature's three largest parties: the Front de Libération Nationale (FLN, National Liberation Front), the president's Rassemblement National Démocratique (RND, National Rally for Democracy), and the Mouvement de la Societé pour la Paix (MSP, Movement of Society for Peace).[54] The open-list PR system used in the 2010 Iraqi elections produced similar results, with parliament divided among at least three major coalitions—Iyad Allawi's Iraqi National Movement(al-'Iraqiya), Nuri al-Maliki's State of Law coalition, and a Shiite coalition called the Iraqi National Council, led by 'Ammar al-Hakim's Islamic Supreme Council of Iraq (ISCI). The law created a fragmented political landscape, one that exposed Iraq to greater external intervention and delayed the formation of a new government for nine months.

Not that regimes were always able to control election results by manipulating electoral laws, however. The most famous example is Hamas's surprise victory over Fatah during the 2006 Palestinian parliamentary elections, which was largely a consequence of a change in the electoral system. In the 1996 elections, the single-member, district-based plurality block-vote electoral system worked in the Palestinian National Authority's favor, producing a Fatah-dominated parliament.[55] But in March 2005, a new mixed electoral law was promulgated. According to the new law, half of parliament's 132 seats would be filled through a closed national-list PR system using a mini-

Table 7.4 Electoral Systems in the Arab World, 2010

	Electoral System for National Legislature	Type	Tiers
Algeria	List proportional representation	Proportional representation	1
Bahrain	Two-round system	Plurality/majority	1
Egypt	Two-round system	Plurality/majority	1
Iraq	Open-list proportional representation	Proportional representation	1
Jordan	Single nontransferable vote	Other	1
Kuwait	Multiple nontransferable vote	Plurality/majority	1
Lebanon	Block vote	Plurality/majority	1
Libya	None	—	—
Morocco	List proportional representation	Proportional representation	2
Oman	First-past-the-post (FPTP)	Plurality/majority	1
Palestinian Authority	Parallel	Plurality/majority	2
Qatar	None	—	—
Saudi Arabia	None	—	—
Sudan	FPTP	Plurality/majority	1
Syria	Block vote	Plurality/majority	1
Tunisia	Parallel	Mixed	2
United Arab Emirates	None	—	—
Yemen	FPTP	Plurality/majority	1

Sources: International Institute for Democracy and Electoral Assistance (IDEA), "Electoral Systems Worldwide," 2012, http://www.idea.int/esd/world.cfm.

mum threshold of 2 percent of the total valid votes, with the balance of the seats filled through a multimember, district-based majoritarian block-vote system.[56] In the subsequent 25 January 2006 legislative elections, Hamas won 74 out of 132 seats while Fatah secured 45 seats, though the popular-vote margin of difference between the two was much closer: 44 percent for Hamas versus 41 percent for Fatah. This mixed (or parallel) electoral system thus worked to Hamas's advantage. Pro-Hamas districts had 43 seats while the pro-Fatah districts had only 23 seats; moreover, Hamas fielded only one candidate per seat while the Fatah vote was often split among official and independent Fatah candidates.[57] Following the election, Palestinian Authority president Mahmoud Abbas promulgated a new electoral law aimed at eliminating Hamas's electoral advantage and favoring his own party in future elections. The new law replaced the existing mixed electoral system with a party-list PR system and eliminated district-level voting altogether. It also required candidates to recognize the Palestine Liberation Organization as the "sole, legitimate representative" of the Palestinian people and to subscribe to the Declaration of Independence. Though it was marketed as an instrument of national reconciliation through PR legislative elections, the new law in fact amounted to a legal coup aimed at reversing the results of the 2006 elections.[58]

Beyond manipulating electoral laws, authoritarian Arab regimes used districting and malapportionment to shape elections in their favor. Electoral districts were designed to favor pro-regime candidates and to underrepresent opposition candidates. For instance, Jordan's Hashemite regime has long overrepresented rural and southern areas and ethnoreligious minorities, and underrepresented the urban centers, where Palestinians and Islamists are heavily concentrated. In the 1989 legislative elections, Jordan's three main urban centers of Amman, Zarqa, and Irbid were allocated only 45 percent of the eighty seats, despite the fact that they account for roughly 65 percent of the population. Similarly, the populous Second District in Amman, with 73,435 registered voters, was allocated only three seats, whereas Maan, with only 25,535 registered voters, was allocated five seats.[59]

A new redistricting law was promulgated in Jordan before the 2003 elections. It raised the number of electoral districts from 20 to 45, increased the number of parliamentary seats from 80 to 110, and allocated new seats to the urban centers of Amman and Zarqa. However, it did not rebalance past malapportionment.[60] Yet another electoral law was promulgated in June 2010 in preparation for the November elections. Although it raised the number of seats allocated to Amman, Zarqa, and Irbid by four, and doubled the quota for women's representation from six to twelve seats, the new law retained the much despised SNTV electoral system and avoided any movement toward a PR system. Moreover, electoral districts were replaced by contrived "electoral zones," which are subdivided into smaller single-seat subdistricts, a change ostensibly undertaken to curb voting along tribal lines, but which in reality encourages tribal and clientalistic voting given the small size of the subdistricts.[61] Consequently, the Islamic Action Front, Jordan's main opposition party, opted to boycott the November 2010 parliamentary elections. As Table 7.2 (on page 153) shows, the 2010 elections produced another comfortable pro-regime parliamentary majority.

Similar districting and malapportionment practices have been used by the Sunni-minority regime in Bahrain to underrepresent the kingdom's Shiite majority. The Shiite opposition accuses the government of a host of gerrymandering tactics aimed at diluting the Shiite vote and favoring Sunni and progovernment Shiite candidates. It points to the fact that the number of voters in each of the kingdom's forty electoral districts varies substantially, with many districts designed to follow sectarian lines.[62] For example, one district in the Shiite-dominated Northern Governorate has 14,000 voters but is represented by a single member of parliament, while a district in the underpopulated Sunni Southern Governorate has 400 voters and is also represented by a single member of parliament.[63] The Shiite opposition accuses the royal family of trying to balance the numerical voting power of the Shiite majority by adding some 65,000–100,000 Sunnis to voter lists over the past decade through the naturalization of tens of thousands of Sunni Arabs and Asians, in an act of sectarian gerrymandering.[64]

In Lebanon, where sectarian considerations are paramount, electoral districts have been redesigned prior to every postwar parliamentary election. During the long Syrian era (1990–2005), districting served to manufacture pliant, pro-Syrian political figures. In the post-Syrian era, electoral engineering has served the interests of the sectarian elite at the expense of democratic representation and accountability. Moreover, some heavyweight members of the sectarian elite—namely the Sunni Future Movement, and the Druze Walid Jumblatt—resist attempts to introduce some variation on a PR electoral system, a prerequisite for the emergence of durable, national, cross-sectarian political coalitions.[65]

The Pandora's Box of Elections

The popular uprisings that shocked the Arab world from December 2010 onward proved that using elections to reproduce political power, depoliticize societies, and maintain authoritarianism was a failed regime strategy. In fact, carefully controlled elections may have further fueled resentment against already unpopular hegemonic authoritarian regimes. Voters had already started to express their disenchantment with managed elections well before 2010. Voter turnout in past parliamentary elections was not impressive—17 percent (according to independent sources) and 23 percent (according to government sources) in Egypt's 2005 elections, 36 percent in Algeria's 2007 elections, and 37 percent in Morocco's 2007 elections.[66] More revealing was the increase in the proportion of spoiled ballots—15 percent in Algeria's 2007 parliamentary elections and around 20 percent in Morocco's 2007 elections—as voters balanced their desire to practice their right to vote with their distaste for the kind of predetermined elections organized by authoritarian Arab regimes.[67] Unperturbed, Arab regimes pushed through even more managed elections, thus contributing to the deluge of mass resentment that ultimately exploded in their faces.

Elections and electoral laws have reemerged as central sites of contestation in Arab politics. Authoritarian regimes bent on containing the aftereffects of popular uprisings on regime stability found in elections a welcome diversion. Reacting to the Arab uprisings, but also to restrained local calls for reform,[68] the UAE government decided in July 2011 to expand the number of eligible voters to 129,274. On 24 September 2011, elections were held to contest half of the Federal National Council's seats. Voter turnout was rather small, however, only 28 percent, reflecting voter disenchantment with the council's insignificant prerogatives.[69] Worried by similar transregional pressures but also domestic demands, Saudi authorities announced in March 2011 that municipal elections, postponed since 2009, would be held in September 2011. The only exciting feature of the 28 September 2011 elections was the king's declaration a few days prior, on 25 September, that women would be granted the right to vote and run in the 2015 municipal elections, and that they would also be appointed to the toothless Shura Council. The timing of both decisions aimed to defuse domestic demands for reform following the Arab uprisings.[70]

In Morocco, King Mohammed VI submitted a package of constitutional reforms for a popular referendum to contain calls by the February 20 Movement for democratic changes. In his 17 June 2011 televised speech on a proposed new constitution, the king promised that henceforth the prime minister "will be appointed from the party which wins the general elections, thereby confirming that the government will result from direct universal suffrage."[71] A novelty in Moroccan politics, this new stipulation is nevertheless checked by the king's constitutional prerogative to name the prime minister and approve his cabinet. In Jordan, the Hashemite regime reacted to popular protests by signaling its willingness to alter the much-loathed SNTV electoral law. A regime-established National Dialogue Committee proposed a new two-tier electoral law whereby fifteen seats would be elected by PR voting at the national level, with the balance of the seats elected by the 1989 unlimited-vote system. Opposition groups favored a different law, however: a dual-list law whereby half of the seats would be elected by PR voting at the national level, with the balance elected by the unlimited-vote system at the governorate level.[72]

Popular uprisings also touched off debates throughout the Arab world over the proper timing of parliamentary elections, the sequence that should be followed between elections and the drafting of new constitutions, and the types of electoral laws that best represent the will of the people and guarantee limited rule and government accountability. In Tunisia, for example, the transitional authority decided that an elected 217-member National Constituent Assembly had one year to draft a new constitution. By contrast, the transition from authoritarianism in Egypt was marred by debates over the timing of elections for a prospective foundational constitutional assembly and the sequence to follow in the drafting of a new constitution. During the 19 March 2011 Egyptian referendum, Islamist groups, but especially the Muslim Brotherhood, voted in support of a package of constitutional amendments that called for the election of a new parliament from which 100 MPs would be elected to form a constituent assembly responsible for drafting a new constitution no later than six months after the elections. Liberal and secular groups voted against this proposal, preferring instead a "constitution first" approach whereby a new constitution would be drafted prior to parliamentary elections. As noted in Chapter 2, the latter groups fear that a new parliament dominated by the Muslim Brotherhood would result in "an Islamist-leaning constitution."[73] Determined to overhaul the country's authoritarian edifice and build new democratic institutions, Egypt's revolutionary groups have had to confront their own illiberal inclinations. Moreover, their suspicion that Islamists will use the democratic process to hijack the postauthoritarian political order is shared by secular groups across the Arab world.

The choice of electoral laws is another bone of contention as new political orders are being organized in the Arab world. In Tunisia, the High Commission for the Fulfillment of Revolutionary Goals, Political Reform, and Democratic Transition opted for a largest-remainder closed-list PR electoral law. Moreover, and in a groundbreaking feat in the Arab world, a parity principle stipulated that half the list must be composed of women candidates and that the order of names on the list must be predetermined and alternate between male and female candidates. The new law also contained an age principle prescribing that each list must contain at least one candidate who is younger than thirty years old and setting the minimum age of suffrage at eighteen years and the minimum age for candidates at twenty-three years. Furthermore, elections were managed by the Instance Supérieure Indépendante pour les Élections (ISIE, Higher Independent Authority for the Elections), a body packed with independents. Finally, the law prohibited a number of former government officials who were also members of the former ruling RCD from running for office, as well as those who had appealed to Zine el-Abidine Ben Ali to run for another presidential term in 2014.[74]

By contrast, the promulgation of a post-Mubarak electoral law in Egypt was marred by complications. The new law first established a parallel voting system in which half of parliament's seats were to be selected through a closed-list largest-remainder PR system, with the balance decided by the older system of district-level, individual candidacy in majoritarian two-member, two-round contests. Moreover, although it lowered the voting age from thirty to twenty-five, the new law abandoned the women's quota (associated with Suzanne Mubarak, wife of the deposed president), banned international monitors, and retained an anachronistic proviso requiring that half of parliament's seats go to workers and farmers.[75]

Critics quickly suggested that by insulating the two votes from each other, and given the tendency of winner-takes-all systems to encourage vote-buying, neopatrimonial practices, and intimidation, the proposed law favored already organized parties and groups, namely the Muslim Brotherhood, former members of the long-ruling NDP, and businessmen. Under pressure from an array of political and youth groups, the Egyptian cabinet amended the law on 25 September 2011, reducing the number of seats elected by individual-candidacy majoritarian contests to only a third, but prohibiting party candidates from running for these seats. However, this fell short of opposition demands to hold the elections for all parliamentary seats based on a closed-list PR system, and some political parties, namely the Muslim Brotherhood, threatened street protests if the law was not amended. The Supreme Council of the Armed Forces (SCAF) consequently intervened, organizing a meeting on 30 September 2011 with a group of political parties, including the Muslim Brotherhood, but excluding the revolutionary youth groups, to defuse the crisis. Most significant, the SCAF allowed political parties to run candidates in seats reserved for individual-candidacy winner-takes-all contests, reduced the duration of the transition to civilian rule by six months, accepted international election observers, and promised to study an election ban against an unspecified number of former NDP high-ranking officials.[76] In so doing, the SCAF managed to engineer an electoral law that favored some parties, but especially the Muslim Brotherhood, while limiting the electoral prospects of others, namely the liberals, the leftists, and the Revolutionary Youth Coalition.

The Islamist Tsunami

The most recent wave of elections held on the morrow of the Arab uprisings unleashed a veritable Islamist electoral tsunami. Islamist parties, once banned or besieged by authoritarian regimes, achieved stunning electoral victories (see Table 7.5). In Tunisia's 23 October 2011 elections, the Islamist Ennahda Movement captured 89 of the National Constituent Assembly's 217 seats (41 percent), leaving the centrist Congrès pour la République to trail behind it with only 29 seats (13 percent).[77] More important, Ennahda captured some 37 percent of the popular vote, demonstrating not only that it is Tunisia's strongest party but also that it possesses "deeper support, more evenly spread across the country, than any other party, having won at least 30 percent of seats in all districts but two, and more than one seat in every single domestic district."[78] Similarly, in Egypt's November 2011–January 2012 legislative elections, the Muslim Brotherhood's Freedom and Justice Party captured 216 (43 percent) of the People's Assembly's 498 elected seats. Islamist and Salafi parties scooped some 70 percent of legislative seats, a harsh defeat to the liberal and revolutionary groups that led the uprising against Mubarak's regime.[79] In Morocco, the Islamist Justice and Development Party garnered 107 of parliament's 395 seats. Finally, in Kuwait, Islamist groups captured 22 out of 34 opposition seats in the country's February 2012 parliamentary elections.[80]

These Islamist victories were rooted in a number of complex factors. They were partly a sympathy vote in reaction to decades of regime persecution against Islamist groups. Electoral laws also played their role in these victories, however. Tunisia's closed-list PR electoral system fragmented the political landscape—around 1,600 lists competed for 217 seats—resulting in a substantial percentage of wasted votes—some 28.5 percent at the national level. "The biggest bloc of votes in most districts, usually after En-

Table 7.5 Islamist Parties and Legislative Elections After the 2011 Arab Uprisings

	Percentage Share of Parliamentary Seats
Egypt (Freedom and Justice Party and Salafis)	70.2
Tunisia (Ennahda)	41.0
Morocco (Justice and Development Party)	27.1
Kuwait (Muslim Brotherhood, Salafis, and independent Islamists)	44.0

Sources: al-Safir, 15 November 2011; Issandr el-Amrani and Ursula Lindsey, "Tunisia Moves to the Next Stage," *Middle East Report Online*, 8 November 2011; and *al-Hayat*, 4 February 2012.

nahda, tended to be dispersed among parties and lists that did not obtain any seats." Moreover, in "at least 13 districts, these 'wasted votes' collectively amounted to a larger proportion of the vote than what any one party took."[81] In Egypt, the closed-list PR system worked in favor of already established and organized political groups, namely Islamist ones.[82] New secular parties lacked the organizational capabilities, social networks, and national breadth required to mobilize sizable votes behind their lists. Moreover, the large size of the individual-candidate districts worked against new contestants who lacked the support of well-organized political parties. The timing of the elections also operated in favor of the Muslim Brotherhood, which presented itself as the real custodian of democracy, insisting that elections be held before the promulgation of a new constitution, a tactic aimed at depriving nascent political groups the requisite time to organize.

Grassroots campaigning and direct interaction with voters, a hallmark of Islamist election strategies, played a decisive role in Islamist electoral victories. Islamist parties campaigned against corruption, hijacked the otherwise leftist discourse on social justice, and promised to improve socioeconomic conditions.[83] In Tunisia, campaigns by secular parties portraying Ennahda as a party bent on turning the country into an Islamic state backfired. Ennahda successfully presented itself as a victim of both Ben Ali's authoritarian regime and the secular parties' demonizing attacks.[84] In Morocco the Justice and Development Party's electoral platform was based on a promise of 7 percent economic growth, a 40 percent income increase, and a staggering 50 percent reduction in poverty levels. Similarly, Egypt's Muslim Brotherhood eschewed religious debates, focusing its electoral campaign on social justice promises and the fight against corruption, themes originally voiced by the revolutionary youth groups. Egypt's Salafi groups, however, turned to more nefarious tactics, using religious decrees to proscribe voting for Christian candidates.

Secular and leftist groups are understandably alarmed by the extent of this Islamist comeback. Religious clashes in Egypt, secular-Salafi confrontations in Tunisia and Morocco, the role played by Salafi armed militants in Libya's and Syria's uprisings, and sectarian tensions throughout the region have exacerbated apprehensions of Islamist electoral victories. The fear that Islamist groups will use democracy to assume control of government institutions and implement undemocratic visions of the social order is cause for much concern. Calls for the restoration of the Islamic caliphate and the histrionic acts of Salafi deputies—such as adding a religious proviso to their parliamentary oaths or interrupting proceedings to call for prayers—have raised many eyebrows in Egypt. The Freedom and Justice Party's control of the speakership and fifteen of the People's Assembly's nineteen committees has led some to suggest that it is increasingly behaving like a neo-

NDP.[85] This has undermined the credibility of the party's guarantees that the drafting of the new constitution will be a conciliatory process rather than one dominated by the Islamist parliamentary majority.

The return of competitive elections to the Arab world is a moment of opportunity but also trepidation. Finding the right electoral law in different national contexts may require multiple election cycles and a balancing act between different political groups possessing different socioeconomic and political agendas and visions of their country. Nevertheless, the return of competitive elections to many Arab states has restored a sense of political contestation and debate long denied by authoritarian regimes. These contests and debates will determine whether or not the new political orders organized in many parts of the Arab world will represent the will of the peoples who sacrificed all for democracy or, alternatively, negotiated pacts between elements of the ancien régime and some of the political forces unleashed by the popular uprisings that are determined to frustrate this will.

Notes

1. Uncontested presidential elections offer little added utility when examining the uses of elections in authoritarian contexts, and the era of contested presidential elections is at a nascent stage.

2. See Jason Brownlee, *Authoritarianism in an Age of Democratization* (Cambridge: Cambridge University Press, 2007); Jennifer Gandhi and Ellen Lust-Okar, "Elections Under Authoritarianism," *Annual Review of Political Science* 12 (2009).

3. See Lisa Wedeen, "Seeing like a Citizen, Acting like a State: Exemplary Events in Unified Yemen," *Comparative Studies in Society and History* 45, 4 (October 2003); Lisa Wedeen, *Peripheral Visions: Publics, Power, and Performance in Yemen* (Chicago: University of Chicago Press, 2008).

4. See Daniel Brumberg, "Authoritarian Legacies and Reform Strategies in the Arab World," in Rex Brynen, Bahgat Korany, and Paul Noble, eds., *Political Liberalization and Democratization in the Arab World,* vol. 1, *Theoretical Perspectives* (Boulder: Lynne Rienner, 1995).

5. See Bob Woodward, *Plan of Attack* (New York: Simon and Schuster, 2004), pp. 88, 284.

6. See Staffan I. Lindberg, ed., *Democratization by Elections: A New Mode of Transition* (Baltimore: Johns Hopkins University Press, 2009).

7. See Iliya Harik and Denis J. Sullivan, eds., *Privatization and Liberalization in the Middle East* (Bloomington: Indiana University Press, 1992); Bahgat Korany, Rex Brynen, and Paul Noble, *Political Liberalization and Democratization in the Arab World,* vol. 2, *Comparative Experiences* (Boulder: Lynne Rienner, 1998); Eberhard Kienle, "More Than a Response to Islamism: The Political Deliberalization of Egypt in the 1990s," *Middle East Journal* 52, 2 (Spring 1998); Laurie A. Brand, "The Effects of the Peace Process on Political Liberalization in Jordan," *Journal of Palestine Studies* 28, 2 (Winter 1999).

8. See Steven Heydemann, *Upgrading Authoritarianism in the Arab World* (Washington, DC: Brookings Institution, October 2007); Lisa Blaydes, *Elections*

and Distributive Politics in Mubarak's Egypt (Cambridge: Cambridge University Press, 2011).

9. See Philip G. Roessler and Marc M. Howard, "Post–Cold War Political Regimes," in Lindberg, *Democratization by Elections,* pp. 124–125.

10. Steven Heydemann, "Defending the Discipline," *Journal of Democracy* 13, 3 (July 2002), p. 105.

11. See Rex Brynen, "The Politics of Monarchical Liberalism: Jordan," in Korany, Brynen, and Noble, *Political Liberalization and Democratization in the Arab World,* vol. 2, *Comparative Experiences,* pp. 81–82.

12. For the 1989 parliamentary elections, see Kamel S. Abu Jaber and Schirin H. Fathi, "The 1989 Jordanian Parliamentary Elections," *Orient* 31, 1 (March 1990).

13. See Daniel Brumberg, "Islam, Elections, and Reform in Algeria," *Journal of Democracy* 2, 1 (Winter 1991), p. 59; Dirk Vandewalle, "Islam in Algeria: Religion, Culture, and Opposition in a Rentier State," in John Esposito, ed., *Political Islam: Revolution, Radicalism, or Reform?* (Boulder: Lynne Rienner, 1997).

14. See Larbi Sadiki, *Rethinking Arab Democratization: Elections Without Democracy* (Oxford: Oxford University Press, 2009), p. 115.

15. See Pradeep K. Chhibber, "State Policy, Rent Seeking, and the Electoral Success of a Religious Party in Algeria," *Journal of Politics* 58, 1 (February 1996).

16. See Kienle, "More Than a Response to Islamism."

17. See Abla M. Amawi, "The 1993 Elections in Jordan," *Arab Studies Quarterly* 16, 3 (Summer 1994).

18. See Bush's "Forward Strategy of Freedom" speech of 6 November 2003 at http://www.al-bab.com/arab/docs/reform/bush2003.htm.

19. George W. Bush, *Decision Points* (New York: Crown, 2010), p. 397; see also pp. 398, 437.

20. Bush's faith in the transforming power of elections is clear in his memoirs. See ibid., pp. 406–407, 436–438.

21. See, for example, Secretary of State Condoleezza Rice's comments to the *New York Post* editorial board, 25 September 2006, http://www.state.gov/secretary/rm/2006/73107.htm; Michele Dunne, "The Baby, the Bathwater, and the Freedom Agenda in the Middle East," *Washington Quarterly* 32, 1 (January 2009).

22. See Amr Hamzawi, "The Saudi Labyrinth: Evaluating the Current Political Opening," Carnegie Papers no. 68 (Washington, DC: Carnegie Endowment for International Peace, April 2006), p. 12.

23. See Nadia Abou el-Magd, "Voters Cast Ballots in UAE Elections," *Washington Post,* 20 December 2006, http://www.washingtonpost.com/wp-dyn/content/article/2006/12/20/AR2006122002179.html.

24. See Sadiki, *Rethinking Arab Democratization,* p. 68.

25. Michael Herb, "Princes and Parliaments in the Arab World," *Middle East Journal* 58, 3 (Summer 2004), p. 378.

26. Dunne, "The Baby, the Bathwater, and the Freedom Agenda in the Middle East," pp. 134–136.

27. See Herb, "Princes and Parliaments in the Arab World," pp. 376–378.

28. See Abd al-Nabi al-Ekry, "Al-Wefaq and the Challenges of Participation in Bahrain," Carnegie Endowment for International Peace, 19 May 2007, http://www.carnegieendowment.org/arb/?fa=show&article=20932.

29. See Elie Shalhoub, "Al-Bahrain: Inqilab Malaki," *al-Akhbar,* 9 September 2010.

30. See *al-Sharq al-Awsat,* 1 November 2010.

31. See "Bahrain By-Elections: 1 in 5 Vote," News24, 25 September 2011, http://www.news24.com/World/News/Bahrain-by-elections-1-in-5-vote-201109252011.

32. See *al-Hayat,* 4 February 2012.

33. Nathan J. Brown, "What Is at Stake in Kuwait's Parliamentary Elections?" p. 2, Carnegie Endowment for International Peace, May 2008, http://carnegieendowment.org/files/brown_kuwait_elections_FAQ_final.pdf.

34. Sadiki, *Rethinking Arab Democratization,* p. 71.

35. See Kevin Koehler, "Authoritarian Elections in Egypt: Formal Institutions and Informal Mechanisms of Rule," *Democratization* 15, 5 (December 2008), pp. 982–983.

36. See Vickie Langohr, "Cracks in Egypt's Electoral Engineering: The 2000 Vote," *Middle East Report Online,* 7 November 2000, http://www.merip.org/mero/mero110700.html.

37. For an overview, see Michele Dunne and Amr Hamzawy, "The Ups and Downs of Political Reform in Egypt," in Marina Ottaway and Julia Choucair-Vizoso, eds., *Beyond the Façade: Political Reform in the Arab World* (Washington, DC: Carnegie Endowment for International Peace, 2008), pp. 17–43.

38. Mona el-Ghobashy, "Egypt's Paradoxical Elections," *Middle East Report* 238 (Spring 2006), http://www.merip.org/mer/mer238/elghobashy.html.

39. See Issandr el-Amrani, "Controlled Reform in Egypt: Neither Reformist Nor Controlled," *Middle East Report Online,* 15 December 2005, http://merip.org/mero/mero121505.html.

40. See David Rose, "The Gaza Bombshell," *Vanity Fair,* April 2008, http://www.vanityfair.com/politics/features/2008/04/gaza200804.

41. See Dunne and Hamzawy, "The Ups and Downs of Political Reform in Egypt," pp. 27–28, 41–42.

42. See *al-Safir,* 6 December 2010.

43. See Michele Dunne and Amr Hamzawy, "From Too Much Egyptian Opposition to Too Little—and Legal Worries Besides," Carnegie Endowment for International Peace, 13 December 2010, http://www.carnegieendowment.org/2010/12/13/from-too-much-egyptian-opposition-to-too-little-and-legal-worries-besides/chf.

44. Wael Abdul Fattah, "Intikhabat al-Tazwir 'Eini 'Einak," *al-Akhbar,* 29 November 2010.

45. See Jennifer Gandhi and Adam Przeworski, "Authoritarian Institutions and the Survival of Autocrats," *Comparative Political Studies* 40, 11 (November 2007).

46. Michael McFaul and Tamara Cofman Wittes, "The Limits of Limited Reforms," *Journal of Democracy* 19, 1 (January 2008), p. 20.

47. Ibid., p. 30.

48. Ellen Lust-Okar, "Legislative Elections in Hegemonic Authoritarian Regimes: Competitive Clientalism and Resistance to Democratization," in Lindberg, *Democratization by Elections,* p. 231.

49. See Koehler, "Authoritarian Elections in Egypt," p. 980.

50. See Blaydes, *Elections and Distributive Politics in Mubarak's Egypt.*

51. Lust-Okar, "Legislative Elections in Hegemonic Authoritarian Regimes," p. 242.

52. See Marsha Pripstein Posusney, "Multi-Party Elections in the Arab World:

Institutional Engineering and Oppositional Strategies," *Studies in Comparative International Development* 36, 4 (Winter 2002), p. 40.

53. See McFaul and Cofman Wittes, "The Limits of Limited Reforms," p. 20.

54. See Louisa Dris-Ait-Hamadouche, "The 2007 Legislative Elections in Algeria: Political Reckonings," *Mediterranean Politics* 13, 1 (March 2008).

55. See As'ad Ghanem, "Founding Elections in a Transitional Period: The First Palestinian General Elections," *Middle East Journal* 50, 4 (Autumn 1996).

56. See National Democratic Institute, "Final Report on the Palestinian Legislative Council Elections," 25 January 2006, http://www.cartercenter.org /resources/pdfs/news/peace_publications/election_reports/Palestine2006-NDI-final.pdf.

57. See Khalil Shiqaqi, "Sweeping Victory, Uncertain Mandate," *Journal of Democracy* 17, 3 (July 2006), p. 120.

58. See Mu'tasem Hemadé, "Marhaban bi-Qanun al-Intikhabat—al-Fadiha" [Welcome Scandalous Electoral Law], *al-Nahar,* 13 September 2007.

59. See *Intikhabat 1989: Haqa'ik wa Arqam* [The 1989 Elections: Facts and Numbers] (Amman: Markaz al-Urdun al-Jadid lil-Dirasaat, 1993).

60. Ellen Lust-Okar, "Competitive Clientalism in Jordanian Elections," in Ellen Lust-Okar and Saloua Zerhouni, eds., *Political Participation in the Middle East* (Boulder: Lynne Rienner, 2008), p. 89.

61. See Curtis R. Ryan, "Jordan's New Electoral Law: Reform, Reaction, or Status Quo?" Middle East Channel, *Foreign Policy Magazine,* 24 May 2010, http://mideast.foreignpolicy.com/posts/2010/05/24/jordan_s_new_electoral_law_ reform_reaction_or_status_quo.

62. See Mazen Mahdi, "Bahrain Split by Electoral Boundaries," *The National,* 2 June 2010, http://www.thenational.ae/apps /pbcs.dll/article?AID=/20100603/FOREIGN706029865/1002/LIFE.

63. See Abdellah al-Derazi, "Old Players and New in the Bahraini Elections," *Arab Reform Bulletin,* 2 June 2010, http://carnegieendowment.org /arb/?fa=show&article=40903.

64. See Thanassis Cambanis, "Crackdown in Bahrain Hints of End to Reforms," *New York Times,* 26 August 2010, http://www.nytimes.com /2010/08/27/world/middleeast/27bahrain.html?_r=1.

65. See Bassel F. Salloukh, "The Limits of Electoral Engineering in Divided Societies: Elections in Postwar Lebanon," *Canadian Journal of Political Science* 39, 3 (September 2006); and 'Abdo Sa'd, *Al-Intikhabat al-Niyabiya li-'Am 2009: Qira'aat wa Nata'ej* [The 2009 Parliamentary Elections: Reflections and Results] (Beirut: CIEL, 2009).

66. For Algeria and Morocco, see the International IDEA voter turnout results at http://www.idea.int/uid/fieldview.cfm?id=221; for Egypt, see Amira Huwaidi, "'An Misr al-lati Satantakheb . . . wa Misr al-lati la Taktareth" [About Egypt that Will Vote... and Egypt that Does Not Care], *al-Safir,* 26 November 2010.

67. See Dris-Ait-Hamadouche, "The 2007 Legislative Elections in Algeria," p. 89; McFaul and Cofman Wittes, "The Limits of Limited Reforms," p. 21.

68. See Anna Louie Sussman, "Repression in the United Arab Emirates," *The Nation,* 1 June 2011, http://www.thenation.com/article/161058/repression-united-arab-emirates.

69. See *al-Safir,* 26 September 2011.

70. See Neil MacFarquhar, "Saudi Monarch Grants Women Right to Vote,"

New York Times, 25 September 2011, http://www.nytimes.com/2011 /09/26/world/middleeast/women-to-vote-in-saudi-arabia-king-says.html.

71. "Text of King Mohammed VI's Speech on Proposed Constitution," Moroccans for Change, http://moroccansforchange.com/2011/06/17/king-mohamed-vi-speech-on-proposed-constitution-61711-full-text-feb20-khitab.

72. See International Crisis Group, "Popular Protest in North Africa and the Middle East (IX): Dallying with Reform in a Divided Jordan," 12 March 2012, http://www.crisisgroup.org/en/regions/middle-east-north-africa/iraq-iran-gulf/jordan/118-popular-protest-in-north-africa-and-the-middle-east-ix-dallying-with-reform-in-a-divided-jordan.aspx.

73. See Omar Ashour, "Egypt Secularists and Liberals Afraid of Democracy?" *BBC News,* 13 July 2011, http://www.bbc.co.uk/news/world-middle-east-14112032.

74. See International Foundation for Electoral Systems, "Elections in Tunisia: The 2011 Constituent Assembly," http://www.ifes.org/~/media/Files/Publications /White%20PaperReport/2011/Tunisia_FAQs_072011.pdf.

75. See International Foundation for Electoral Systems, "Elections in Egypt: Analysis of the 2011 Parliamentary Electoral System," http://www.ifes.org /Content/Publications/White-Papers/2011/~/media/Files/Publications /White%20PaperReport/2011/Analysis_of_Egypts_2011_Parliamentary_Electoral_ System.pdf.

76. See *al-Safir,* 3 October 2011; Marc Lynch, "Saving Egypt's Elections," 2 October 2011, http://lynch.foreignpolicy.com/posts/2011/10/02/egypt_struggles_to _change_course.

77. See *al-Safir,* 15 November 2011.

78. Issandr el-Amrani and Ursula Lindsey, "Tunisia Moves to the Next Stage," *Middle East Report Online,* 8 November 2011, http://www.merip.org/ mero/mero110811.

79. See "Results of Egypt's People's Assembly Election," Carnegie Endowment for International Peace, http://egyptelections.carnegieendowment.org/ 2012/01/25/results-of-egypt%E2%80%99s-people%E2%80%99s-assembly-elections.

80. See *al-Hayat,* 4 February 2012.

81. el-Amrani and Lindsey, "Tunisia Moves to the Next Stage."

82. See Mazen Hassan, "The Effects of Egypt's Election Law," Middle East Channel, *Foreign Policy Magazine,* 1 November 2011, http://mideast.foreignpolicy.com/posts/2011/11/01/egypts_electoral_cunundrum.

83. See Erik Churchill, "Tunisia's Electoral Lesson: The Importance of Campaign Strategy," Carnegie Endowment for International Peace, 27 October 2011, http://carnegieendowment.org/2011/10/27/tunisia-s-electoral-lesson-importance-of-campaign-strategy/6b7g; Amira Howaidi, "Misr Taseer fi Itijahayn" [Egypt Moves in Two Directions], *al-Safir,* 28 November 2011; Imad Istitu, "Islamiyu al-Maghreb Amam Imtihan al-Sulta" [Morocco's Islamists and the Challenge of Power], *al-Akhbar,* 30 November 2011.

84. See Asma Nouira, "Tunisia: Elections . . . and Then What?" p. 4, Arab Reform Initiative, 15 January 2012, http://www.arab-reform.net/spip.php?article5124.

85. See Wisam Mata, "Al-Islamiyoun fi-l-Parluman: Hizb Watani Jadid?!" [Islamists in Parliament: A New National Democratic Party], *al-Safir,* 26 January 2012.

8

The Politics of
Monarchical Liberalization

Out of the nineteen Arab states in the Middle East and North Africa, no fewer than eight—Kuwait, Bahrain, Qatar, the United Arab Emirates (UAE), Oman, Saudi Arabia, Jordan, and Morocco—are monarchies. These are not monarchies of the contemporary European type, in which royalty has a largely ceremonial role. On the contrary, the Arab monarchies all involve the king or emir ruling and reigning, even in the countries where they are slightly constrained by a written constitution. In no other region of the developing world have so many postcolonial monarchies survived to the present day, and in those that have, the monarch's power is far more circumscribed. Indeed, among African and Asian monarchs, only the king of Swaziland and the sultan of Brunei enjoy domestic authority that is comparable to that of their Arab counterparts.

Today, the puzzle of monarchical survival in the Middle East has been joined by the question of whether the monarchies will be more resistant to the pressures of the Arab Spring than their republican counterparts. Certainly Bahrain was rocked by widespread protests, prompting a brutal crackdown that was supported by other Gulf monarchies. Protests were also seen in Jordan, Morocco, Oman, and elsewhere. However, by the summer of 2012 none of the monarchies had experienced regime change or civil war—unlike Tunisia, Egypt, Yemen, Libya, and Syria. This led some to suggest that many monarchies were better able to undertake limited liberalization and modest reforms so as to divide oppositions and lessen domestic pressures.[1]

Both sets of questions—why monarchies have endured in the past and whether they will prove more enduring in the future—hinge on the question of regime type. Are the Arab monarchies essentially different from the Arab republics in important ways? Or are they simply minor variants of autocracy?

Noting the parallels between the two—including the inclination of authoritarian presidents to groom their sons for succession—Egyptian sociologist Saad Eddin Ibrahim famously coined the Arabic term *gumlukiya* (republicomonarchy) to highlight their apparent convergence. He was subsequently thrown into an Egyptian prison by the Mubarak regime, an act that underscored similarities between the regime types at least in terms of their openness to criticism.[2] On the other hand, authoritarian monarchs—unlike the authoritarian republics—do not try to maintain the fiction of holding elective office. Instead they typically promote the notion that they are above daily politics, serving as guardians of the national interest and national unity—even as they are intimately involved in the running of "their" kingdoms.

The differences between and among the various Arab monarchies are substantial, as shown in Table 8.1. In 2010, gross domestic product (GDP) per capita (adjusted for purchasing power parity) ranged from $4,800 in Morocco and $5,400 in Jordan to $40,000 or more in most of the other monarchies (and over $179,000 in Qatar).[3] Six of the cases—that is, the Gulf monarchies—are clearly rentier states, in which the majority of both the economy and state revenues are linked to the oil sector. Jordan can make some claim to having been a semi-rentier state at various times in its history, with foreign aid making up a significant portion of its budget in the 1950s through to the 1970s.[4] By contrast, Morocco is very much a "production state," with state resources extracted from the domestic economy.

The monarchies diverge significantly in size and social makeup. With the exception of Morocco (population of 32 million) and Saudi Arabia (population of 26 million), most have relatively small numbers of citizens: a little over 6 million in Jordan, less than 3 million in Oman, under 2 million in Kuwait, around 1 million in the UAE, and even less than this in Bahrain and Qatar. The social cleavages and fragmentations within each society differ as well. Tribalism has long been an important influence in all of the Gulf states, among East Bank Jordanians, and among some segments of the Moroccan population. In Jordan, East Bank–Palestinian tensions have often been important, to the point of civil war in 1970–1971. In Bahrain, the tensions between the Sunni royal family and the Shiite majority were a major factor in shaping the popular protests of 2011–2012, as well as much of the country's politics since independence.

The degree of constitutional constraint and parliamentary tradition varies markedly too. Morocco, Jordan, Kuwait, and Bahrain all have written constitutions that call for an elected parliament, which in theory limits the monarch's power. By contrast, Saudi Arabia, Qatar, and Oman (until 2011) all have semiappointed or appointed consultative bodies with little influence, while the UAE is itself a complex federation of absolute monarchies coupled with a partly elected, partly appointed consultative council.

In practice, of course, monarchs in the "constitutional monarchies" have a deep reservoir of constitutional and informal powers to call upon. They have often manipulated electoral processes to ensure victory by loyalists; ig-

Table 8.1 The Arab Monarchies, 2010

	Legal Structure	Royal Family	GDP per Capita (adjusted for purchasing power parity)	Freedom House Score
Bahrain	Constitutional monarchy with bicameral (elected and appointed) legislature	Dynastic	$40,300 (rentier)	6 (political) 5 (civil) "not free"
Jordan	Constitutional monarchy with bicameral (elected and appointed) legislature	Non-dynastic	$5,400 (semi-rentier)	6 (political) 5 (civil) "partly free"
Kuwait	Constitutional monarchy with elected legislature	Dynastic	$48,900 (rentier)	4 (political) 4 (civil) "partly free"
Morocco	Constitutional monarchy with bicameral (directly and indirectly elected) legislature	Non-dynastic	$4,800 (nonrentier)	5 (political) 4 (civil) "partly free"
Oman	Semi-constitutional monarchy with elected advisory council	Semi-dynastic	$25,600 (rentier)	6 (political) 5 (civil) "not free"
Qatar	Semi-constitutional monarchy with appointed consultative assembly	Dynastic	$179,000 (rentier)	6 (political) 5 (civil) "not free"
Saudi Arabia	Absolute monarchy with appointed advisory council	Dynastic	$24,200 (rentier)	7 (political) 6 (civil) "not free"
United Arab Emirates	Federation of absolute monarchies with mixed indirectly elected and appointed advisory council	Dynastic	$49,600 (rentier)	6 (political) 5 (civil) "not free"

Sources: Michael Herb, *All in the Family: Absolutism, Revolution, and Democracy in the Middle Eastern Monarchies* (Albany: State University of New York Press, 1999); Central Intelligence Agency, *CIA World Factbook*; Freedom House, *Freedom in the World 2010*.

nored, dissolved, or suspended parliament; and ruled by decree when need be.[5] Certainly the 2011–2012 crackdown in Bahrain has shown how brutal monarchical regimes can be in suppressing popular protests and preserving royal power. Still, in Kuwait, and at times in Morocco and Jordan too, electoral politics has not been entirely insignificant. In Kuwait in particular, as well as in all three countries in earlier periods, real tensions have erupted over such issues as the limitations on free speech and the degree of accountability of the cabinet. As discussed later, both the Jordanian and Moroccan monarchies responded to increasing pressures for reform in 2011 by announcing a series of changes that would somewhat weaken their constitutional power.

Middle Eastern Monarchies: An Overview

In addition to contemporary differences, the various Arab monarchies also arise from very different political histories. As the region passed from colonialism to full independence in the twentieth century, no fewer than thirteen of the new Arab states—that is, a majority of them—featured some form of monarchy. In Morocco, the Alawi dynasty had ruled since the seventeenth century, and had even been permitted to continue to rule during the period of French colonial domination, despite the short-lived exile of King Mohammed V. In Tunisia, Muhammad VIII al-Amin declared himself king of the newly independent state in March 1956. Libya gained its independence in 1951 under King Idris, who had been recognized by the British as the local ruler of the area prior to the Italian occupation. In Egypt, the dynasty that had been established by Muhammad Ali in the early nineteenth century had been permitted to remain in place under British colonialism, and the country became a constitutional monarchy when it gained formal independence in 1922. After World War I and the establishment of League of Nations mandates over several former Ottoman territories, the British installed two of their Hashemite allies, Faisal and Abdullah, as the monarchs of Iraq and Transjordan respectively.

In the Arabian Peninsula, political systems gradually evolved into increasingly monarchical forms over the course of the nineteenth and twentieth centuries. Prior to this, leading tribal families and family leaders had governed in a rather more fluid manner, their authority contingent on a complex combination of tribal power and alliances that changed over time. This, coupled with a degree of traditional accountability within tribes and families, made their power less than absolute. In many cases, such as the al-Sabah family, who first emerged as rulers of Kuwait in the mid–eighteenth century, their power was also dependent on the resources provided by the merchant community.[6]

This latter factor was muted by the impact of British colonialism, sedentary settlement of once-nomadic tribes, and the development of the oil industry.[7] Britain established a series of protectorates in the Gulf, providing them with advice, resources, and protection against both external and, in many cases, internal foes. With this also came increasing demarcation of what had previously been much more ambiguous territories, culminating in the emergence of Kuwait, Qatar, Bahrain, the UAE, and Oman as fully recognized and independent states in the 1960s and 1970s. After World War II, the rulers of these states also enjoyed rapidly growing oil revenues, which greatly enhanced their power while simultaneously ending any financial dependence on merchant families.

North Yemen was a partial exception to this pattern. There, as with the Alawi dynasty in Morocco, the Zaydi imamate had a long tradition of religious-political authority, though with historically fluctuating territorial boundaries and power. With the final collapse of Ottoman administration in coastal Yemen by 1918, the country emerged as an independent, monarchical state.

Saudi Arabia was another partial exception to this pattern. It was never a colonial protectorate. Instead, the modern Saudi state was carved out of the Arabian Peninsula between 1904 and 1932, through alliance and conquest by the Saudi family and their tribal supporters, as well as by the Islamist zeal of the Sunni Wahhabi movement. Its territorial limits were for the most part determined by where it came into contact with the edges of British-controlled or British-protected territory, and its subsequent evolution was deeply shaped by its interaction with the West.

Finally, across the Gulf in non-Arab Iran, the Qajar dynasty had ruled since 1794. When it was removed from power in 1925, the military leader who had overthrown it, Reza Khan, declared himself Shah and established a new Pahlavi dynasty.

Not all of these political systems survived the tumultuous era of the 1950s and 1960s, when the postcolonial instability that affected most newly independent countries in Africa and Asia was compounded by the effects of new Arab nationalisms, tensions with the West, and the Arab-Israeli conflict. In Egypt, King Farouk was overthrown by Gamal Abdul Nasser and the Free Officers in 1952, three decades after Egypt had gained its independence. In Tunisia, the "king" never ruled effectively; he was placed under house arrest and the monarchy was abolished by the new Tunisian parliament in 1957. In Iraq, the Hashemite monarchy was overthrown in 1958, and King Faisal II was killed. In Yemen, republican forces and subsequent Egyptian intervention overthrew the monarchy in 1962. In southern Yemen, British plans to establish a federation of tribal entities were swept aside by violence and the 1967 victory of the leftist National Front. In Libya, King Idris was toppled in the September 1969 military coup that brought Muammar Qaddafi to power. On the other side of the Arabian Gulf, the Shah Mohammed Reza Pahlavi was overthrown in a popular Islamist revolution in 1979.

Other monarchies that did survive often did so narrowly. In Jordan, King Hussein was the target of coup attempts in the 1950s and also fought a full-scale civil war against the Palestinian nationalist movement in 1970–1971. In Oman, the country faced serious challenges from the Dhofar rebellion in the 1960s and 1970s, which was eventually defeated not just with British, Jordanian, and Iranian support, but also due to the modernizing reforms undertaken by Sultan Qabus bin Said following his overthrow of his much more conservative father, Sultan Said bin Taymur in 1970. Perhaps luckiest of all was King Hassan II of Morocco, who—as noted in Chapter 2—faced multiple coup attempts, barely escaping alive from two of them.

The 1970s, 1980s, and 1990s were in general a time of remarkable stability for all of the surviving Arab monarchies, and indeed for most of the Arab republics. This stability, however, did not mean that they were unchanging. Some faced internal "palace coups" from within the royal family (including Oman in 1970, Sharjah/UAE in 1972, and Qatar in 1995), although none of these imperiled monarchical survival. Indeed, in some cases (notably in Jordan in 1952, Saudi Arabia in 1964, and Kuwait in 2006), monarchs were removed by their fellow royals precisely with the aim of enhancing their dynasty's collective prospects by selecting a more suitable ruler.[8]

Given that state policy can change substantially from monarch to monarch, any changes in royal leadership can have broader implications. In several cases, the introduction of reforms followed the accession to power of new monarchs intent on distinguishing their rule as being more modern or liberal than that of their fathers, as for instance with Mohammed VI of Morocco. Reform can also be a way of sweeping aside old elites associated with a previous ruler, or even of reshaping politics within the royal family. In the Qatari case, for example, Shaikh Hamad's initial period of apparent enthusiasm for reform was driven in large part by such calculations, and the later fading of reform prospects seems to be associated with the emir's consolidated hold on royal power.[9]

In the 1980s and 1990s, a number of monarchical regimes embarked on limited processes of political liberalization, generally in response to a confluence of both internal and external forces. In Jordan, for example, external pressures as a result of the country's declining foreign aid and remittances, as well as growing foreign debt in the late 1980s, resulted in the adoption of structural economic adjustments that in turn provoked a wave of protests in 1989. King Hussein responded by opening up the political system, both as a quid pro quo for popular acceptance of necessary economic measures and as a way of avoiding being solely blamed for future hard decisions. Parliamentary elections took place in November, and the legalization of political parties followed later. As part of this process, Jordan adopted in 1991 a national charter that was written by a royal commission made up of leading notables from across the political spectrum who had been charged with delineating "general guidelines on the exercise of political pluralism." The first principle of the charter, not surprisingly, was that "the system of government in the Hashemite Kingdom of Jordan is parliamentary, monarchic and hereditary."[10] Rather tellingly, the official website of the late King Hussein described the charter as demarking the limits of reform rather than as a blueprint for continuing change: "Perhaps most importantly, the Charter has given Jordanian leaders a sense of direction, an insurance policy against outbidding by unrestrained groups, and a degree of predictability in political affairs. It has also eased concerns about the consequences of unbridled freedom of expression. The National Charter, along with the Jordanian Constitution, provides a compass for the national debate on fundamental issues."[11]

In other words, post-1989 reforms in Jordan were far more a limited process of political liberalization than a thoroughgoing democratization. Indeed, such liberalization was very much intended by the regime as an alternative to, rather than a step toward, democratization. As discussed in greater detail in Chapters 3 and 7, Jordan's electoral law was modified in the 1990s to prevent the opposition Islamic Action Front from winning a large share of seats, while the monarchy continued to wield preeminent constitutional power, and with patronage and other forms of political control used to variously co-opt and discourage certain types of political activism or discourse.[12] As a result, after a few initial years of substantial reform, the Jordanian political system under both King Hussein (1953–1999) and his son and successor King Abdullah II (1999–) reverted to a state of stasis, with effective public participation (and enthusiasm for participation) slowly eroded over time.

In Kuwait, demands for reactivation of the National Assembly (dissolved in 1986) were strengthened by the effects of Iraq's 1990–1991 occupation of the country. In October 1990, Kuwaiti opposition leaders met with the emir in exile in Saudi Arabia, and won explicit promises for a return to constitutional rule and parliamentary elections. These elections were held in October 1992, a year and a half after the liberation of the country.[13]

In contrast with Jordan, parliaments in Kuwait have not only seen a higher proportion of liberal, nationalist, and independent opposition figures elected, but have also seen the National Assembly willing to challenge some royal prerogatives. In particular, the assembly has demanded the right to subject members of the cabinet, including royal-family members, to questioning and a parliamentary vote of confidence. This has led to periodic showdowns with the emir, during the reign of both Shaikh Jabir (1977–2006) and that of Shaikh Sabah (2006–). In 2006, 2008, and again in 2009, elections were held after the emir had dissolved the National Assembly early due to tensions over political accountability and other issues. In 2010, Prime Minister Nasser Mohammed al-Sabah—a member of the royal family—was subject to a parliamentary vote of confidence for the first time.

In Bahrain, the partially elected National Assembly called for under the 1973 constitution was suspended in 1975 by Shaikh Isa ibn Salman al-Khalifa, after parliamentarians objected to a harsh new state security law. But following Shaikh Isa's death in 1999, his son and successor Shaikh Hamad bin Isa al-Khalifa introduced a national charter and a new constitution in 2001 and 2002, respectively, leading to parliamentary elections in October 2002. Although members of the Shiite opposition party al-Wifaq did well in the 2006 and 2010 elections despite government harassment, parliament had little substantial effect on public policymaking. As a consequence, the Shiite majority in the country continued to feel marginalized, which would ultimately lead to the explosion of tensions between the regime and the Shiites in 2011.

In Qatar, Shaikh Hamad bin Khalifa al-Thani promised significant reforms after deposing his father as emir in 1995. A new constitution was drawn up and approved by referendum in 2003, local government elections were instituted, and parliamentary elections were promised. Even in Saudi Arabia, a new basic law was introduced in 1992 that included an appointed Shura (consultative) Council, this despite the kingdom's sometimes overt disapproval of Kuwait's renewal of parliamentary life.[14] In 2005, the kingdom also held limited local council elections, as discussed in Chapter 7.

Further afield, in Morocco, parliamentary elections took place throughout the reign of King Hassan II, though these were punctuated by a state of emergency as well as by substantial degrees of repression, bribery, and manipulation by the palace. While controls were relatively relaxed toward the end of the king's reign, it was not until his death in 1999 and the accession of his son Mohammed VI to the throne that a more substantial era of political liberalization began, marked by greater freedoms for the press and civil society, as well as by a more active (if still constrained) role for the legislature.

Such developments through the 1990s and into the new millennium led some analysts to predict that monarchical systems had greater prospects for political reform than did the Arab republics. Some argued that the very stability of the monarchies showed that they were better able to ensure "stability and security, [which are] important prerequisites for the development of democratic practices."[15]

Certainly monarchies had some potential advantages in managing reform, especially to the extent that they were able to position themselves to establish the rules governing political openings while simultaneously acting as both interested players and far-from-impartial umpires in the reform process itself.[16] Moreover, unlike the nominally elected presidents of the Arab republics, they could do so without any hint that they were placing their own positions in question. Liberalizing monarchs also tended to maintain their power through fragmentation of the opposition, patronage, and divide-and-rule tactics, thereby creating a situation in which royal favor can tilt political balances and many individuals and parties are anxious to receive royal support. As Ellen Lust and Amaney Jamal found in their comparative study of Arab electoral systems, this results in monarchical regimes being significantly more likely to put in place rules that lead to highly fragmented parliaments (with weaker parties and significant numbers of independents), which are more amenable to these forms of influence and control. By contrast, authoritarian republics are likely to engineer overwhelming majorities for a pro-regime party or set of parties, as a form of "democratic" endorsement for the president.[17]

Limited political liberalization is not, of course, an inevitable step toward democratization. On the contrary, these reforms were adjustments by regimes intended to preserve the long-term foundations of monarchical power in the face of changing circumstances. Monarchs also retained the ability to delay, reverse, or undercut reforms.[18] In Jordan, there was no democratization after the initial period of liberalizing reform in the 1990s—rather, elections, parties, and parliament became less significant. In Morocco, the initial reforms instituted by Mohammed VI left the power of the palace (and those close to it) intact. In Qatar, promulgation of the new constitution and the holding of elections were repeatedly delayed, while Saudi Arabia initially chose to postpone its nascent experiment with limited local elections. Commenting in 2009 on the notion of an elected Shura Council, Prince Nayef bin Abd al-Aziz al-Saud argued that "appointing the members always ensures that the best are selected. . . . If it was to happen through elections, the members would not [be] this competent."[19] In Bahrain, the run-up to the 2010 elections saw a fresh crackdown against Shiite political activists.

Explaining Monarchical Survival

The adaptive behavior of Arab monarchies is particularly interesting in light of the rigidity that social scientists have often attributed to monarchical regimes. Samuel Huntington's statement of the "King's Dilemma" is one classic example of this.[20] Monarchies, Huntington famously argued, must centralize power in order to undertake necessary social and economic reforms. In doing so, however, they not only face resistance from traditional aristocrats, but also have difficulty in accommodating the participation of the new middle class and other groups that emerge from modernization.[21] He went on to suggest several possible strategies for monarchical survival: transformation to a more electoral regime, including possible institutionalization of a pro-monarchy political party; co-optation within the bureaucracy; greater ideological legitimation of the monarchy itself, whether through traditionalist or nationalist appeals; external support; or even greater reliance on repression and the security forces. None of these approaches would be very successful in the long term, he suggested. Indeed, according to Huntington, monarchy as a system of governance would prove an increasingly hard sell to the middle class and other newly emergent groups with aspirations of political participation. The bureaucracy would not be able to co-opt potential opponents fast or fully enough. Moreover, traditionalist appeals were outmoded, insular, and at odds with the demands of modernization, and monarchs would have a difficult time portraying themselves as avatars of the national interest. External support could be corrosive to domestic legitimacy, while repression risked making the monarch a prisoner of his own security forces and in the end was antithetical to the need to broaden political participation. Huntington concluded:

> The future of the existing traditional monarchies is bleak. Their leaders have little choice but to promote social and economic reform, and to achieve this they must centralize power. This process of centralization under traditional auspices has reached the point where the peaceful adaptation of any of them . . . to broader political participation seems most unlikely. The key question concerns simply the scope of the violence of their demise and who wields the violence.[22]

In many ways, Huntington's analysis seems to foreshadow the challenges that finally overwhelmed the Shah of Iran and set in motion the Iranian revolution: centralized, dislocating modernization from above that ultimately isolated a monarch who became dependent on the military and security establishment, until it too failed him in the face of overwhelming revolutionary demands for change. It also speaks to some of the challenges that overwhelmed other failed Middle Eastern monarchies, or the threats that nearly toppled King Hussein of Jordan in the 1950s through 1970, or King Hassan II of Morocco in the 1970s. Huntington's predictions, however, clearly run counter to the experience of Arab monarchies over the past several decades. Not only were more than half of all Arab regimes monarchies at the time of independence, but also more than half of those have endured until the present.

The easiest way to explain such monarchical survival and recent regime stability in the region is to attribute it to Arab traditions, Islam, and other deep-seated political-culture factors. After all, elements of traditional hereditary and dynastic power have long been found in the region—as, for that matter, elsewhere around the world. Within the Islamic caliphate, the principle of consultation that shaped the selection of the first successors to the prophet Muhammad soon gave way to the entrenchment of hereditary succession. The sultans of the Ottoman Empire generally acceded to power the same way.[23]

It would be a mistake, however, to see Middle Eastern monarchies as simply traditional forms of kinship-based rule surviving into the modern age, let alone to accept that political-culture explanations can completely account for their survival.[24] As already noted, many of the supposedly "traditional" monarchies of the Arab world function quite differently than did their tribally and family based antecedents, having been very much transformed in the modern era by colonialism, oil wealth, and the resources and machinery of the modern state. Moreover, while some of the surviving monarchies can claim deep historical roots, others are demonstrably recent inventions. In Jordan, for example, the Hashemites were transplanted from the Hejaz (in present-day Saudi Arabia) and installed in Transjordan by the British after World War I as a reward to their wartime ally, Abdullah bin al-Hussein. Certainly the Hashemites had a long history of tribal leadership (and leadership of tribal coalitions), as well as the legitimacy that derived from descent from the prophet Muhammad. However, modern Jordan was built on very different foundations, with the armed forces assigned a key role as a mechanism of national integration and coercion, and state- and aid-financed neopatrimonialism used to knit together sufficient support from key social constituencies. In short, the societal and historical lineages of successful Arab monarchies are not any stronger (and are often rather weaker) than other, less successful monarchies elsewhere in the world. One needs to look somewhere other than essentialist notions of political culture for explanations of their comparatively high rate of survival.

Lisa Anderson, in suggesting an alternative explanation for monarchical survival, takes a very different approach than Huntington by suggesting that such regimes have proven particularly suited to the task of modernization and statebuilding due to their "institutional flexibility and inclusiveness."[25] She also notes their ability to legitimize themselves through the invention or manipulation of history and traditions that serve regime interests.[26] This does not explain, however, why other monarchies elsewhere in the world were so much less successful in their statebuilding efforts.

A complementary explanation for monarchical survival would focus on the role that oil and other rents have played in strengthening these regimes—

an aspect that is unique to the Arab oil monarchies, plus (perhaps tellingly) the sultanate of Brunei. As noted in Chapter 9, explanations of stable authoritarianism that hinge on the rentier characteristics of the state have been much contested in recent years. Certainly several of the failed monarchies (Pahlavi Iran, Hashemite Iraq, and Sanusi Libya) have had rentier-state characteristics, underscoring that exogenous resources are no guarantee of political stability. Indeed, Huntington would likely have suggested that the rapid social change engendered by oil-fueled growth would be especially destabilizing in societies where political power is organized along traditionalist lines (even if those monarchical "traditions" are relatively recent ones). On the other hand, with state resources comes an enhanced capacity to both co-opt (through state patronage) and coerce (through the repressive apparatus of the state), perhaps allowing royals to offset some of the challenges of inclusion associated with "the King's Dilemma."

In the case of the Middle East, oil has had the secondary effect of increasing the strategic salience of both the region and the pro-Western monarchies within it. As F. Gregory Gause has suggested, external support has therefore been another element in monarchical survival, since Western countries have sought to promote regional stability to ensure their access to the resource. This is in contrast with other, less strategically important regions of the world.[27]

Michael Herb has suggested that the impact of petroleum wealth is best understood as an intervening variable rather than an independent one, influencing preexisting political structures but not, in and of itself, accounting for political stability.[28] For him, what is far more important is the presence of large dynasties where members of the royal family serve in a variety of critical roles within the political, security, and administrative apparatus. Examples of such countries would include most of the Gulf states (other than, in some regards, Oman). The most extreme case is of course Saudi Arabia, where there are approximately 7,000 members of the current royal family, including approximately 200 direct descendants of the founder of the modern state, Abd al-Aziz ibn Saud. Herb also suggests that in dynastic monarchies, the presence of princes in important posts makes coup-making more difficult, since they will tend to support the existing regime whether out of familial loyalty or a self-interested desire to preserve their positions. These large royal families also act in a way that enhances information networks, facilitates succession, and creates a degree of accountability (within the royal family).[29]

Herb's analysis offers great insight into how the specific institutional characteristics of certain types of monarchical rule may affect regime stability. It also provides the springboard for several other interesting analytical questions. First, how do we determine the relative contribution of rents and internal regime structure? If Jordan is counted as at least a semi-rentier state (based on the very large role that external aid has played during critical periods in its political evolution), only one of the surviving monarchies (Morocco) is a nonrentier state. Moreover, it is no coincidence that all of the dynastic monarchies are petrostates: while large dynasties may in large part be rooted in patterns of royal marriage and reproduction, the ability of the ruler to keep scores, hundreds, or even thousands of royal-family members happy is undoubtedly facilitated by state wealth.

Second, does having a small population matter, whether by facilitating the royal family's ability to monitor and control society or by facilitating the neopatrimonial political management?[30] Of the successful Middle Eastern monarchies, most have small or very small populations—indeed, the combined citizen population of the six smallest monarchies is less than the population of the city of Cairo. In other words, these are political systems in which it is possible for the monarch to have personal knowledge of virtually every member of the country's social, economic, and political elite.

Third, and closely related to the second point, to what extent does social differentiation matter? Of the failed Middle Eastern monarchies, Egypt, Iraq, and Iran were all very large, complex, and highly cosmopolitan societies. By contrast, of the surviving monarchical systems, only Morocco approaches these countries' level of social complexity—and social complexity, understood here to refer to ethnic, socioeconomic, regional, linguistic, and other relevant social groupings and cleavages, presumably also complicates political control. It would also tend to exacerbate the problems of social mobilization and political inclusion raised by Huntington. Conversely, the existence of certain social formations amenable to patrimonial and neopatrimonial mechanisms (such as the tribalism found in the Gulf states, among East Bank Jordanians, and in parts of Morocco) would make it easier for a regime to manage social forces.

What this discussion is pointing toward is the notion that monarchical survival has been the product of a mixture of factors—none of them sufficiently important on their own—that increase the capacity to govern, contain, repress, and respond to external shocks. Having access to oil wealth (or other external rents) helps, especially in the context of a dynastic monarchy able to marshal those resources through a network of numerous family members to spin an effective web of political control over the key levers of political power. The neopatrimonial political management at which all these monarchies excel is easier to accomplish in smaller and less complex societies, as well as in preexisting social formations (such as tribalism) that may be receptive to this form of political management.

Key to the success of the monarchies has been the ability of most of them to instill a widespread notion of their permanence, such that even reformers rarely challenge the existence of the monarchy, only some of its powers and privileges. Monarchical regimes have sought to characterize themselves as providing an island of stability in an otherwise chaotic region. Consequently, they devote considerable resources not only to emphasizing—or even inventing—their traditional and historical credentials, but also to portraying themselves as enduring, beneficent bedrocks of social and political stability. It is perhaps noteworthy that while a central slogan of the Arab Spring was that "the people want to topple the regime" *(al-sha'b yurid isqat al-nizam)*, in most of the monarchies—Bahrain excepted—the 2011 protests saw more limited demands for constitutional reform or change in government.

Royal Responses to the Arab Spring

Monarchical responses to the Arab Spring were unsurprising, given the foundations of their prior stability. Part of the answer was, of course, repression. Saudi Arabia clamped down on even the smallest signs of protest, especially in Shiite areas of its Eastern province. In Jordan, pro-monarchy thugs attacked protesters in March 2011 while police looked on. By far the most repressive response was in Bahrain, where a state of emergency was announced, security forces used live ammunition to break up demonstrations, and there were mass arrests of regime opponents.

The petromonarchies were also quick to offer new spending programs in the hopes of attenuating social discontent. In January 2011, Kuwait announced new payments of $3,500 per citizen. Saudi Arabia unveiled $36 billion in new social spending in February and a further $67 billion just one month later. In April, Oman announced $2.6 billion in additional expenditures, on top of new payments to the unemployed. The UAE raised retirement wages for military personnel, subsidized bread and rice prices, promised to spend $1.6 billion to develop the infrastructure of the underdeveloped northern emirates, and in July announced that some 1,235 land plots had been distributed to citizens in the country's western emirates.[31] However, the deployment of oil rents was not an infallible response to demands for reform: in Bahrain, the offer of $2,600 per family proved no more successful at averting protests than similar offers of cash in republican Libya.[32]

In the nonoil monarchies, by contrast, greater emphasis was placed on the promise of constitutional reform. As noted in Chapter 3, Jordan's King Abdullah II offered revisions to the electoral law and "the formation of governments based on parliamentary majority" in a June 2011 speech, suggesting that election outcomes rather than royal prerogative might determine who held the position of prime minister in future. However, a series of constitutional amendments proposed in August did little to limit royal powers.[33] As noted in Chapter 2, more than 98 percent of Moroccan voters approved constitutional amendments in July 2011 that included recognition of the Tamazight (Berber) language, greater gender equality, and greater powers for the prime minister. Moreover, the prime minister would in the future be chosen from the largest party in parliament, and not wholly at the king's discretion. Again, however, the proposed reforms left the essential elements of the king's power intact.

Several monarchies also held limited elections for previously established consultative or local government bodies: Oman (where Sultan Qabus promised that the Consultative Council would enjoy somewhat expanded powers), the UAE (where the limited electorate for the Federal National Council was expanded, although half the seats remained appointed), and Saudi Arabia (where local municipal elections were held, with the promise of extending the vote to women in the future). In Bahrain, carefully stage-managed by-elections were held to replace those opposition members of parliament who had resigned in protest over government repression.

In virtually all of the monarchies, close relations with the West constrained Western calls for change. This was especially true in the strategically important and oil-rich Gulf states, and particularly so in Bahrain (headquarters of the US Fifth Fleet). While Washington and others emphasized the need for reform, they did not impose the kinds of sanctions imposed on Libya or Syria. The unlikely possibility that protests would overturn regimes in the immediate future meant that Western governments were reluctant to antagonize allied regimes too much.

Finally, Arab monarchies undertook a series of important collective actions to preserve their positions. Gulf Cooperation Council (GCC) countries, for example, provided aid to Oman, Morocco, and Jordan to help finance new spending. The GCC also sought to manage a transition in Yemen that would reduce the destabilizing effects of regime change there. As noted in Chapter 11, Qatari-owned Al Jazeera and Saudi-owned Al Arabiya toned down their televised coverage of the situation in Bahrain, certainly compared to Al Jazeera's coverage of Tunisia, Egypt, Yemen, and Syria. Perhaps a more obvious example of the collective defense of authoritarianism, however, was military intervention by over a thousand "Peninsula Shield" troops from the GCC in Bahrain in March 2011 to shore up the regime. The GCC thus confirmed itself as a "club of kings" concerned with acting to protect monarchical regimes across the Middle East. As one member of the Saudi royal family told the *New York Times,* "We're sending a message that monarchies are not where this is happening."[34] The consolidation of even stronger webs of transnational authoritarianism has important implications for the study of both reform and international relations in the region, with antipathy to internal democracy emerging as an important element of external political and military alliance.

In Spain in the 1970s and 1980s, King Juan Carlos won considerable public support for the monarchy because of his role in navigating the country from the legacies of the Franco dictatorship to a full-fledged democracy. To date, no Arab monarch has decided to similarly position himself as a transitional figure. Instead, all have made marginal modifications to the political system intended to protect the status quo.[35] Nonetheless, in some countries (Kuwait, possibly Morocco) those changes could yet prove significant. Monarchical reform in these countries might resemble not so much the rapid political transformations that brought about so-called third wave democratization in Latin America, Eastern Europe, and elsewhere, but something rather more incremental, akin to the gradual evolution of European constitutional monarchies. In Europe, of course, a host of issues related to parliamentary and democratic rights versus royal prerogative—in terms of control over cabinet appointments and parliamentary confidence, taxation and expenditures, the expansion of public freedoms, and increasing limitations on the powers of appointed upper parliamentary chambers—marked the gradual change in political accountability, at least for those monarchies that survived bouts of revolutionary turmoil. This is not to say that Arab monarchies are destined to take the roughly seven centuries that it took Britain to become a democracy (from the Magna Carta in 1215 to the Parliament Act of 1911 or perhaps the enfranchisement of women after World War I). It is to suggest that constitutional struggles such as that in Kuwait between the emir and the National Assembly over the responsibility of (royal) cabinet ministers to parliament may one day be regarded as a significant element in a process of gradual evolution. Moreover, to the extent that these struggles remain within constitutional bounds, this might—as Nathan Brown has argued—facilitate a gradual evolution toward a more rules-based political system.[36]

Notes

1. See, for example, Russell Lucas, "Is the King's Dilemma only for Presidents?" *Arab Reform Bulletin,* 6 April 2011, http://www.carnegieendowment.org/2011/04/06/is%2Dking%2Ds%2Ddilemma%2Donly%2Dfor%2Dpresidents/1uz0; Anne Allmeling, "Are Monarchs More Prone to Reform?" *al-Arabiyya News,* 13 June 2011, http://english.alarabiya.net/articles/2011/06/13/153165.html.

2. The term is a sardonic amalgam of the Arabic words for "republic" *(jumhuriyya)* and "monarchy" *(mamlukiyya).* Mona el-Ghobashy, "Antinomies of the Saad Eddin Ibrahim Case," *Middle East Report Online,* 15 August 2002, http://www.merip.org/mero/mero081502.html.

3. Central Intelligence Agency, *The World Factbook,* https://www.cia.gov/library/publications/the-world-factbook.

4. On this, see Rex Brynen, "Economic Crisis and Post-Rentier Democratization in the Arab World: The Case of Jordan," *Canadian Journal of Political Science* 35, 1 (1992).

5. For a rare discussion of constitutionalism in the Arab monarchies, see Nathan J. Brown, *Constitutions in a Nonconstitutional World: Arab Basic Laws and the Prospects for Accountable Government* (Albany: State University of New York Press, 2002), pp. 35–66.

6. Pete Moore, *Doing Business in the Middle East: Politics and Economic Crisis in Jordan and Kuwait* (Cambridge: Cambridge University Press, 2004), pp. 30–32. See also Jill Crystal, *Oil and Politics in the Gulf: Rulers and Merchants in Kuwait and Qatar* (Cambridge: Cambridge University Press, 1995).

7. For an overview of how the "traditional" pillars of tribalism and Islam have changed, see F. Gregory Gause III, *Oil Monarchies: Domestic and Security Challenges in the Arab Gulf States* (New York: Council on Foreign Relations Press, 1994), pp. 10–77.

8. For a much more detailed discussion of these and other succession issues, see the extensive discussion in Joseph A. Kéchichian, *Power and Succession in Arab Monarchies: A Reference Guide* (Boulder: Lynne Rienner, 2008).

9. Mehran Kamrava, "Royal Factionalism and Political Liberalization in Qatar," *Middle East Journal* 63, 3 (Summer 2009).

10. "The Jordanian National Charter," chap. 1, http://www.kinghussein.gov.jo/charter-national.html.

11. See the website of the late King Hussein, http://www.kinghussein.gov.jo/charter-national.html.

12. Brynen, "Economic Crisis and Post-Rentier Democratization in the Arab World"; Rex Brynen, "The Politics of Monarchical Liberalism: Jordan," in Bahgat Korany, Rex Brynen, and Paul Noble, eds, *Political Liberalization and Democratization in the Arab World,* vol. 2, *Comparative Experiences* (Boulder: Lynne Rienner, 1998).

13. Jill Crystal and Abdallah al-Shayeji, "The Pro-Democratic Agenda in Kuwait: Structures and Context," in Korany, Brynen, and Noble, *Political Liberalization and Democratization in the Arab World,* vol. 2, *Comparative Experiences,* pp. 104–108.

14. Then-king Fahd famously commented to a Kuwait newspaper in 1992 that "the democratic system prevalent in the world is not appropriate for us in this region . . . our peoples in their makeup and characteristics differ from that . . . world. The elections system has no place in the Islamic creed, which calls for a government of advice and consultation and for the shepherd's openness to his flock, and holds the ruler fully responsible before his people." Timothy D. Sisk, *Religion, Politics, and Power in the Middle* East (Washington, DC: US Institute of Peace Press, 1992), p. 50.

15. Owen H. Kirby, "Want Democracy? Get a King," *Middle East Forum* 7, 4 (December 2000), http://www.meforum.org/52/want-democracy-get-a-king. For a more cautious interpretation, see Anoushiravan Ehteshami, "The Politics of Participation in the Oil Monarchies," in Tom Pierre Najem and Martin Hetherington, eds., *Good Governance in the Middle East Oil Monarchies* (London: RoutledgeCurzon, 2003), p. 81.

16. For an earlier discussion of this, see Rex Brynen, Bahgat Korany, and Paul

Noble, eds., "Conclusion: Liberalization, Democratization, and Arab Experiences," in Korany, Brynen, and Noble, *Political Liberalization and Democratization in the Arab World,* vol. 2, *Comparative Experiences,* p. 276.

17. Ellen Lust-Okar and Amaney Jamal, "Rulers and Ruled: Reassessing the Influence of Regime Type on Electoral Law Formation," *Comparative Political Studies* 35, 3 (April 2002).

18. Michael Herb, "Princes, Parliaments, and the Prospects for Democracy in the Gulf," in Marsha Pripstein Posusney and Michele Penner Angrist, eds., *Authoritarianism in the Middle East: Regimes and Resistance* (Boulder: Lynne Rienner, 2005). Herb devotes particular attention to the potential reform-retarding role of weak parliamentary powers, government electoral fraud, electoral malapportionment, the threat of parliamentary suspension, weak public support for parliamentarianism, and weak parliamentary parties.

19. "Women MPs and Elections Not Needed—Saudi Prince," Reuters, 25 March 2009. Prince Nayef also remarked that he did not "see the need" for female members of the council.

20. See, for example, Michael Hudson, *Arab Politics: The Search for Legitimacy* (New Haven: Yale University Press, 1977), p. 166; Michael Herb, *All in the Family: Absolutism, Revolution, and Democracy in the Middle Eastern Monarchies* (Albany: State University of New York Press, 1999), p. 14; Joseph Kostiner, ed., *Middle East Monarchies: the Challenge of Modernity* (Boulder: Lynne Rienner, 2000), p. 7; Marina Ottaway and Michelle Dunne, "Incumbent Regimes and the 'King's Dilemma' in the Arab World: Promise and Threat of Managed Reform," Carnegie Papers no. 88 (Washington, DC: Carnegie Endowment for International Peace, December 2007).

21. Samuel Huntington, *Political Order in Changing Societies* (New Haven: Yale University Press, 1969), pp. 177–191.

22. Ibid., p. 191.

23. For this sort of argument regarding dynastic rule as being historically, even culturally, entrenched, see Bernard Lewis, "Monarchy in the Middle East," in Kostiner, *Middle East Monarchies,* p. 19–21.

24. Lisa Anderson, "Absolutism and the Resilience of Monarchy in the Middle East," *Political Science Quarterly* 106, 1 (Spring 1991).

25. Lisa Anderson, "Dynasts and Nationalists: Why Monarchies Survive," in Kostiner, *Middle East Monarchies,* p. 55.

26. Ibid., p. 65. On strategies for monarchical legitimation in the "modernizing monarchies," see also Hudson, *Arab Politics,* pp. 165–229.

27. F. Gregory Gause III, "The Persistence of Monarchy in the Arabian Peninsula: A Comparative Analysis," in Kostiner, *Middle East Monarchies,* pp. 177–181. Close ties to the West did not save Egypt's Hosni Mubarak, however—and it is difficult to imagine a scenario today where (unlike British intervention in Jordan in 1958, or support for Oman in the 1960–1970s) the West acted with force to save a monarchical regime.

28. Herb, *All in the Family,* pp. 241–243.

29. Ibid., pp. 236–228.

30. This point has also been made by Russell E. Lucas in his useful review essay "Monarchical Authoritarianism: Survival and Political Liberalization in a Middle Eastern Regime Type," *International Journal of Middle East Studies* 36, 1 (February 2004), p. 111.

31. *al-Safir,* 5 July 2011.

32. "Saudi Arabia's King Abdullah Promises $36 Billion in Benefits," *Christian Science Monitor,* 23 February 2011; "Bahrain's Promised Spending Fails to Quell Dissent," *New York Times,* 6 March 2011; "Saudi King Boosts Spending As Protests Sweep Arab World," *Business Week,* 18 March 2011; "Oman to Spend $2.6 Billion to Satisfy Protest Demands," Reuters, 17 April 2011.

33. English text of the speech by King Abdullah II in *Jordan Times,* 13 June 2011, http://www.jordantimes.com/?news=38420.

34. "Saudi Arabia Scrambles to Limit Region's Upheaval," *New York Times,* 27 May 2011, http://www.nytimes.com/2011/05/28/world/middleeast/28saudi.html.

35. Marina Ottaway and Marwan Muasher, "Arab Monarchies: Chance for Reform, Yet Unmet," Carnegie Papers, December 2011, http://carnegieendowment.org /files/arab_monarchies1.pdf.

36. Brown, *Constitutions in a Nonconstitutional World,* pp. 198–200.

9

Rentierism and Resource Politics

Until the 1980s, it was common among Western scholars and popular commentators to associate lack of democracy in the Middle East with the region's culture or religion. What became known as rentier-state theory provided the first serious blow to these culturally determinist conceptions of "oriental despotism." This cluster of arguments claimed that the character of a state's revenue rather than its culture or religion determines its basic politics. Among the Gulf states, as well as in some other developing-world states, the predominant form of revenue is either oil or some other similar source of easy external revenue (mineral commodities and foreign aid, for example). The simple insight that economic factors like this shape politics was expanded upon through a number of comparative studies and articles by scholars of the Middle East. The most enduring argument became the claim that oil impedes democracy and limits political liberalization. Indeed, leading up to the 2011 Arab Spring uprisings, it was common to link nearly all Middle Eastern and even many African problems (including authoritarianism, civil war, terrorism, and so on) to oil.[1] However, a curious twist has taken place on the way to this theory becoming a "law."[2] In the past decade, and aside from a few other regional specialists,[3] a new generation of scholars of the Middle East have come to critique and reject some of the basic elements of rentier-state theory, ironically at nearly the same time that scholars focused on other regions of the world have increasingly come to appropriate elements of the theory.[4]

The 2011 uprisings in Libya and Bahrain, as well as smaller though still important demonstrations in other oil-producing countries, will surely prompt investigations into the roles of oil wealth and the link between external rents and democratization. Indeed, this is the central theme of this chapter. What are we to make of the link between rent revenue, the tenacity of authoritarianism, and the weakness of political liberalization in the Arab Middle East? Do external rents and political authoritarianism correlate, or is there a stronger relationship there? And how politically similar are rentier states? In addition to surveying the diverse scholarly arguments, our

193

analysis is able to take advantage of the fact that Middle Eastern oil states have gone through two oil boom periods (1970s and 2000s), two bust periods (1980s and post-2008), and now the most significant political uprisings in the region's modern history. These events offer us a rich context within which to consider the chapter theme, particularly as many of the original ideas about rentier politics were derived from the experiences of the oil boom of the 1970s, and predicted that with declines in oil price such as were seen in the 1980s, political participation would expand and democratization would proceed. In fact, while there was certainly political change during the bust decades, meaningful liberalization remained elusive. Now with the 2011 uprisings, we again have outcomes that challenge the conception of oil as a uniform factor in generating political outcomes. How are we to explain large-scale uprisings and popular mobilization in Bahrain and Libya but much smaller-scale occurrences in Algeria and Kuwait? At the same time, the emerging roles of Saudi Arabia and the United Arab Emirates (UAE) in leading a regional counterrevolution through the pursuit of common rentier strategies (revenue and repression) suggest that regime oil wealth figures in more than just domestic political economies and is in fact constitutive of regional and international political economies as well.

Stepping back from the events of 2011, the purpose of this chapter is to take stock of the debate around rentier theory and to highlight areas of promising future research. The basic argument is that while there are a number of holes in the "oil impedes democracy" argument, the significance of oil to relations between political rulers and their societies cannot be discounted. Authoritarianism in the Middle East has thus been connected to significant state rents, but not in simple ways. To move the debate forward, three investigations are offered to combine a domestic analysis of rentier politics with an appreciation of the transnational aspects of resource wealth. How are the sociopolitical relations and institutions that prevailed before the arrival of oil rents important to what transpired politically afterward? How do persistent regional conflict and security issues interact with the availability and impact of rents? And how do other forms of rent besides oil shape regimes' survival strategies and regional dynamics? The chapter begins with a review of the development of rentier-state theory, then assesses the critiques and limits of the theory, and finally presents a revised rentier-state theory.

Rise of the Oil States and Development of Rentier Politics

In beginning a discussion of rentier politics, it is first important to distinguish rentier-state theory from what are termed "resource curse" arguments. Both sets of arguments agree that easy money is bad, but each focuses on different outcomes. Resource-curse theories try to explain why commodity reliance tends to create economies that lack diversity and are essentially prone to crises once prices decline. Rentier-state theory assumes that the basis of a state's revenue influences its politics; thus it focuses on the sociopolitical impact of oil rents. Rentier states are states that rely extensively (although measurements vary, as will be discussed) on revenue external to the country, with these flows controlled exclusively by the state, and with the revenue requiring few people to produce it. Rent therefore has a character of being unearned or easy to produce. The basic contrast is with states deriving revenue from earned domestic sources and taxation. The concern with deriving one's income from easily obtained external revenue is not a new one; in fact, Ibn Khaldun, like Adam Smith, chastised "weak minded persons" who seek to "discover property under the surface of the earth and make some profit from it. . . . When such a person cannot earn enough in a natural way, his only way out is to wish that in one stroke, without any effort, he might find sufficient money to pay for the (luxury) habits in which he has become caught."[5] In the modern oil-dependent world, those "weak minded" persons are states with exclusive access to, or control over, profitable commodities like oil. But unlike buried treasure, oil resources promise high profit margins for states over long periods. Moreover, this kind of buried treasure attracts friends and allies. By 1973, many countries had nationalized their domestic oil companies so that oil profits flowed directly to governments.

This rise of the oil producers created a problem for analysts of the developing world. By the 1970s, a number of Middle Eastern oil exporters had become, in terms of per capita gross domestic product (GDP), as rich as the developed industrialized democracies. According to the dominant theories of the day, particularly dependency theory and modernization theory, this was not supposed to happen. So-called peripheral states like Kuwait and the UAE, those that were late in achieving political independence and were dependent on commodity export, should not, theoretically speaking, have been able to accumulate the levels of capital and wealth one expected only in the core capitalist countries. Furthermore, because modernization theory held that greater wealth should lead to urbanization, education, political decentralization, and ultimately political democracy, explaining the lack of democracy (or even of significant democratizing measures) in such wealthy countries was a problem.

One of the more influential early attempts to establish rentier-state theory argued that the Arab oil producers were essentially "distributive states,"[6] a new category of peripheral states. The approach called for a return to what sociologist Joseph Schumpeter termed "a fiscal sociology of the state"— that is, to the idea that how a state derives its resources influences its rela-

tions with society and the economy.[7] It was reasoned that the resource structure of the Middle Eastern oil states shifted the organizational bases of society away from class conflict (given there was little domestic taxation) and
toward more traditional forms or new "political hybrids." Oil-rich states
distributed oil proceeds throughout their society, thereby hindering capitalist development and fostering instead a nation of citizens bereft of class interests or identities. In most oil exporters, the vast majority of the native
labor force would come to work for the state. Without an autonomous middle class and with muted class conflict, there would be little political pressure to decentralize economic resources. Thus, the first rentier-state
argument linking oil to a lack of democracy was class-based, and seemed
to answer the dependency problem of peripheral states moving out of the periphery (but at a social cost) and the modernization problem of wealth without democracy (but with the preservation of tradition).

By the late 1980s and 1990s, a number of scholars began applying this
basic analytical framework directly to the issue of democracy and political
liberalization. Two economists, Hazem Beblawi and Giacomo Luciani, dras-
tically increased the profile of rentier-state arguments through a series of
journal articles and an influential edited volume.[8] One of their contributions
was a better elaboration of rents and their measurement. Recalling that classic conceptions of rent equated it with reward, they said that modern rents
had three properties: they were revenue that came from outside the country,
the revenue flowed directly to the state, and few people were involved in the
generation of the wealth, meaning the money was less earned than granted
(making it like Ibn Kahldun's ground treasure). Beblawi and Luciani proposed measuring whether a particular state is a rent state based on the percentage of its budget that is composed of rents. So states with a percentage
of generally 50 percent and above were considered rentier states, though it
should be noted that Beblawi and Luciani gave no explanation for why they
set the threshold at this level and not another. Also, this definition seemed
to include other rents aside from oil, such as mineral exports (potash and
phosphates in Jordan and Morocco, for instance), foreign aid, and transit
fees (such as from Egypt's Suez Canal). While measurement issues are to
be discussed later, this definition of rentier states ignores the size of a country's population relative to the amount of rents, a ratio that could condition
proposed links between rents and political outcomes. It also means that a
complete set of Middle Eastern rentier states could include not just the major
oil exporters, but in certain periods other states as well. In addition to offering a measurement standard, Beblawi and Luciani also connected rents to
lack of democracy by arguing that state access to rents broke the taxation-
representation linkage that was crucial to the development of democracy in
the West. In this way, rentier-state theory linked to a larger literature on the

Table 9.1 Selected Oil and Other Rentier States of the Middle East

	Major Source of External Revenue (ordered by significance)
Bahrain	Oil, gas, foreign aid
Egypt	Suez Canal, oil, foreign aid
Jordan	Potash, phosphates, foreign aid
Kuwait	Oil
Libya	Oil
Saudi Arabia	Oil
Yemen	Foreign aid, oil

political economy of state formation and representative democracy. Table 9.1 shows the various sources of external rent historically available to Arab governments.

The most well known of these linkages was to Charles Tilly's work on states and war.[9] In Tilly's analysis, West European rulers locked in violent competition with one another from the fourteen to nineteenth centuries were ultimately compelled to develop extensive domestic taxation institutions to fund those conquests. Extracting domestic funds requires significant information about one's society and thus such states grew deep roots into their societies. Eventually, according to Tilly, the citizens who were being taxed began to demand more involvement in the decisionmaking about distribution of services. Scholars focused on the developing world later extended Tilly's findings to note that because rulers in rentier states do not need to extract domestic revenue, the institutions and capacities of the state focus on distributing money rather than on responding to social demands or enhancing the ability of society to generate revenue on its own. Hence the argument became that with no taxation, there would be no demands for political representation.

Following from the taxation and representation argument, other scholars began focusing on how societies were connected to and affected by their oil-rich states. Simply put, rent profits allowed states to buy off and co-opt important social groups and individuals. Typically, in Gulf societies prior to the arrival of oil rents, local rulers were compelled to consider and at times acquiesce to the interests of merchants and tribal leaders. Merchants occasionally funded the ruler's court while tribes provided manpower for defense. Once significant oil revenue appeared in the 1950s and 1960s, however, this relationship changed. A new social contract took hold whereby oil-fueled patronage could be used to purchase political acquiescence.[10] Since rulers controlled vast sums of revenue, it was rather easy to create countless means of buying off or co-opting political rivals, for example through service on the ruler court, directorship of large public companies, or the awarding of lucrative public works. In fast-expanding urban areas like Kuwait City and Riyadh, state land could be transferred at very low prices to political clients, who later often leased or sold the land at higher prices back to the state. Religious leaders were absorbed into government ministries and religious trusts, or were directly employed by the state to serve local mosques. Saudi Arabia provides the most large-scale example of the co-optation of religious elites, but the other, smaller Gulf states followed similar routes. Tribal leaders were likewise made state clients either through direct state employment or by the awarding of lucrative state land for development.[11]

Finally, the expansion of the state and public sector also included a significant expansion of the military and security services. Measured in numerous ways, defense budgets in the Middle East in general and the Gulf in particular have been consistently ranked among the highest in the world over the past three decades. These expansive security organizations provide not just for external defense, but can and have been used against domestic oppositions as well.

Taking all three arguments together—oil has impeded class development, oil has broken the taxation-representation linkage, and oil has eased the purchase and security of political loyalty—we get a very specific picture of the typical rentier state. On the one hand, the rentier state appears massive in terms of its functional and symbolic presence and in terms of the size of the public sector (among Gulf states, over 80 percent of the labor force is directly or indirectly employed by state agencies). On the other hand, such a state is "flabby" and cannot do much in terms of, say, gathering economic information or implementing many policies apart from revenue distribution. The overall impression therefore is of state and society in stable equilibrium and comfortably nondemocratic. But this was all expected to change with the steady decline of oil prices in the 1980s and 1990s. After all, if high oil revenues allowed obstacles to political participation, then lower prices would presumably do the opposite.

Expectations, Problems, and Revisions

As the argument went, reduced state revenue should result in a turn toward domestic taxation and ultimately to demands for representation. More particularly, the private sector should gain a greater voice, the middle class should be able to expand, and fewer resources would be available to buy off social elites, all of which should strengthen political opposition. In the heyday of Eastern European and Latin American democratizations in the 1980s and 1990s, optimism that this phenomenon might spread to the Arab Middle East was rampant.[12] For some the language was quite deterministic: "A clear trend was discernible, particularly in countries whose access to reliable sources of external funding was declining . . . with great trepidation, governments were being forced to face the unpleasant prospect of holding themselves accountable to taxpayers."[13] Even scholars not focused on the Middle East got into the act: "Only prolonged fiscal crisis is likely to provoke change, and adjustment, when it comes, will be especially abrupt and severe." For the oil exporters of the Middle East, the expectation was that there would be a "deleterious combination of economic deterioration and political decay."[14] But by the late 1990s, it was clear that no outright democratization had taken place in any of the rentier states and that political openings when they occurred were modest at best. So what happened?

Certainly rentier states, like many developing states, faced financial crisis in these decades. By the mid-1980s, Kuwait was running a deficit for the first time in its history. In Saudi Arabia, declining oil reserves and a growing population cut in half that country's per capita GDP by the late 1990s. And to be sure, there were political reactions to these pressures. Declining oil revenue has been singled out as one factor in the rise of Algeria's Islamist opposition and the eight years of brutal civil war in the 1990s. Saudi officials announced the creation of appointed consultative councils, the emirate of Dubai in the UAE launched its experiment with liberal economic expansion, and Kuwait restored its elected parliament in the early 1990s. But in all cases, these fell far short of true democratization and moreover were not necessarily linked to oil. For example, Kuwait's reinstituted parliament of 1992 was no more powerful than previous iterations dating back to the 1960s. And Saudi promises of a consultative council actually predated the oil bust. Thus, based on the important empirical testing ground of actual financial crisis, rentier-state theory missed a lot. Consequently, three types of critiques have developed.

First, oil exporters in the Middle East are not uniform in their entrenchment of authoritarianism or in their limitation of liberalism. States with similar dependencies on rent income (like Libya, Yemen, Qatar, Kuwait, and Saudi Arabia) have exhibited quite different levels of political opposition and reaction to fiscal crisis. In other words, Middle Eastern rentier states may be undemocratic and authoritarian, but they exhibit these characteristics in different ways, and are moreover perhaps not as autonomous as has been portrayed. Indeed, upon closer examination—and particularly in light of the events of 2011—societies in rentier states do not appear to be as static or bereft of political opposition as had once been theorized. And while revenue extraction may be low, political conflict and opposition can be generated around distinctions in who benefits from oil rents,[15] or on issues not directly tied to economic rents, such as identity or ruling-family cohesion.[16]

Second, the link between taxation and representation may not be as simple as was first thought.[17] While rentier states found a number of ways to avoid increased domestic extraction during the bust years (like running deficits and increasing borrowing),[18] private sector actors in a number of countries did gain a greater political voice in how austerity measures would be carried out, but this participation did not expand to other social actors.[19] Rather, the evidence suggested that as long as private sector actors had some voice in economic policy, most would be willing to acquiesce to various forms of nondemocratic rule.

Third, if one more broadly compares Middle Eastern oil rentier states with the rest of the world's oil exporters, the effects on political democracy become more complicated. Mexico, Norway, the United Kingdom, Canada, and Indonesia are all democracies, yet are also major oil producers and exporters. One could even include some mineral exporters that have bucked the trend of Middle Eastern rentier states. For example, Botswana, which is highly dependent on diamond rents, has nevertheless remained one of Africa's most stable democracies. Or if we make the comparison with other developing states, many of the unique features ascribed to the rentier state, such as having a bloated state sector and weak state capacities, can also be found in nonrentier developing states. In other words, oil does not seem to have unique causal properties and is not the only factor influencing the type of regime that takes hold in a given country.[20]

By the new century, most Middle East scholars had come to agree that more than simply oil rents were at play in the region's resistance to deeper liberalization. Against this trend, quantitative tests of the theory began confirming its original three hypotheses, and thus reinforced the conclusion that oil impedes democracy.[21] Yet as with many statistical studies, altering the measurement assumptions can lead to different conclusions.[22] Outside these academic debates, journalists seized upon the simplicity of rentier-state theory to posit "a law of petro politics," that as oil prices increase, freedom suffers. This of course implies the opposite law as well, that as prices decrease, states should become more free. So we seemed to be back where we started.

One way forward was to start with a group of empirically rich, structured case studies that moved past the original framework of rentier-state theory.[23] These studies integrated the barebones economic aspects of rentier-state theory, but also considered sociopolitical relations before the onset of large oil revenue, coalition formation pressures, and institutional structures. Thus they presented an approach that acknowledged empirical similarities among rent-dependent states (such as weak administrative and institutional capacities) yet still explained important variations among those same regimes and societies. Varieties of and variance in political participation short of outright democratization thereby emerged as important to understanding the endurance of authoritarian regimes. Perhaps then it may be better to ask not if oil impedes democracy, but how rulers with access to international rents have more generally built enduring authoritarian regimes. How have rents intersected with other factors such as regional conflict? And does the type of rent affect regime survival strategies?

In the next sections, revisions to rentier-state theory are discussed in three areas: the importance of pre-rent sociopolitical relations and institutions, regional patterns of conflict and security, and disaggregation of rent types and variation in how and when they decline in volume or value. The first two areas require integrating a state's access to exogenous rents with considerations regarding timing, context, and transnational security politics. The latter area involves a deeper understanding of what can be considered state rents and how we measure them.

The Importance of What Came Before to What Comes After

A primary direction of revision has been that what prevailed prior to the impact of oil revenues—such as colonial legacies and relations between rulers and other sociopolitical elites—shaped how rulers met the political challenges of building coalitions to ensure political rule.[24] Lisa Anderson termed this the "raw materials" of statebuilding. In her influential study about state formation, *The State and Social Transformation in Tunisia and Libya,* she argued that the Middle Eastern bureaucratic state was largely a product of its encounter with the international system. Yet in Anderson's cases of Tunisia and Libya, rulers constructed regime coalitions in different ways owing to different center-periphery relations within their territories before and after colonial rule (the first through a mass-based civilian party and the other through military rule). Hence for Anderson, the arrival of oil to newly independent Libya is an important historical variable in conjunction with preceding patterns. Rents emerge as important variables insofar as they expand political and economic strategies for rulers and arrive at specific junctures in ongoing sociopolitical development. Moreover, just as pre-rent conditions can breed political inertia, so too can decades of dependence on easy exogenous revenue.

In a number of cases, the arrival of exogenous rents, through either colonial grants or early mineral concessions, fostered change in established political arrangements, though did not completely alter them. Thus the timing of the arrival of rents interacts with the pre-rent administrative and institutional settings and existing sociopolitical arrangements. Historians of the Middle East have shown that Ottoman rule in the region varied administratively and substantively across and within political districts, and that these differences increased as European powers sought to lure Arab parts of the empire away from central Ottoman control.[25] It has also been well documented that there were important political and administrative variations in the transition from Ottoman domination of the Middle East to European domination. For instance, Anderson demonstrated varying levels of military, tax, and commercial reform by Ottoman and later European authorities in Tunisia and Libya. The result was that while Tunisia entered the postcolonial period with the semblance of a bureaucratic state, Libya faced independence with few centralized institutions. New scholarship on Saudi Arabia, particularly focusing on the formative period of the 1940s and 1950s, suggests a much more consequential role for US oil engineers and advisers in the creation of the Saudi state than was previously realized.[26] By taking such starting points seriously, it becomes clear that the arrival of rents does not take place upon a blank sociopolitical slate.

One can also conceive of pre-rent relations between political authorities and important social groups such as merchants and tribes as important factors affecting the evolution of political opposition after the arrival of rents. To take one example, on the eve of the arrival of oil rents to Libya, "clientalistic ties of the Ottoman period had crumbled and been replaced by a resurgence of kinship networks during the Italian occupation."[27] Access to exogenous rents at the onset of statebuilding thus unfolded under conditions in which political authority had achieved little penetration of rural areas and in which kinship ties predominated. One result of these conditions has been the comparative lack of a well-developed political opposition in Libya, a weakness that plagued the Libyan protesters in 2011 and contributed (along with intervention by the North Atlantic Treaty Organization) to the uprisings developing into open warfare.

In the pre-rent Gulf of the late nineteenth and early twentieth centuries, the ability of merchants to exit a ruler's domain provided an important check on political power. Consider Kuwait and Saudi Arabia in this regard. In pre-oil Kuwait, merchant leaders and the ruling al-Sabah family shared common sociohistorical origins as well as mutual political and economic dependence. In what would become modern Saudi Arabia, the largest elite merchants of the Arabian Peninsula, located in the Hejaz (the western portion of Saudi Arabia), never consistently enjoyed such relations of equality with the future rulers of the area, the al-Saud family.[28] Thus, once massive oil monies arrived to Kuwait and Saudi Arabia in the 1940s and 1950s, the al-Sauds used their greater financial independence to marginalize and replace Hejazi merchants with more politically loyal merchant groups, while the al-Sabahs of Kuwait sought to co-opt their existing merchant elites. The result was that both merchant groups were removed from political participation (and exit was barred) in a specific time period due to the financial autonomy afforded by the arrival of oil revenues, but the means employed by political authorities were different. Consequently, co-opted Kuwaiti merchants could and would compose a powerful political opposition in the future, while Hejazi merchants never achieved comparable political organization.

Finally, an aspect of rentier theory that is more developed regarding economic liberalization but less so regarding other dependent variables is the legacy of inertia arising from rent dependence. If pre-rent sociopolitical and institutional patterns matter after the arrival of rents, then decades of dependence on rents may have similarly significant effects after such exogenous sources of revenue decline or other external shocks impact a ruler's strategies. In a number of Middle Eastern states, rents allowed the construction of "preindustrial welfare states"[29] ranging from Jordan's very minimal provisions to the more robust provisions of housing, education, and full employment in Kuwait and the United Arab Emirates. The experience of these social contracts,[30] accompanied as they were by few extractions from society, contributed to the development of strongly held social expectations about governance and state-society relations. Of course one could locate this commitment to distribution not in rents per se but in regional and local moral economies.[31] In either case, rents are part of the narrative but are not the entire story.

Regional Conflict and Security

Though rentier-state theory did not explicitly deal with issues of regional conflict and security, it did take seriously how newly independent states interacted with the world and regional subsystems. In other words, rentier-state theory is one of the earliest approaches that took transnational links seriously. As discussed in Chapter 12, various forms of regional conflict, war, and intervention have accompanied statebuilding in the Middle East. While there are arguments tying the effects of interstate war to political liberalization or greater pluralism (that of Charles Tilly being the most prominent), violent conflict in the developing world unfolded under different conditions. Therefore, how has the combination of chronic violent conflict in a region with widespread access to rents influenced authoritarian durability and the weakness of liberalization? Two general effects come to mind: the entrenchment of regional networks of political patronage and the role of the military in domestic politics.

The nature of conflict in the developing world points toward two starting points for our analysis. First, issues of security and conflict in the Middle East blur the standard international versus domestic distinction,[32] such that regimes are often oriented against perceived internal threats as much or more than external ones—something the 2011 uprisings highlighted. And second, interstate war, when prosecuted, occurs under circumstances in which international norms and external powers constrain border changes or sovereign extinction.[33] Consequently, the social and political effects of such conflict do not follow the Tilly narrative of war fostering advanced state-building and instead may act to entrench various authoritarian power structures and norms. The most observable link between interstate war and rents in the region is that intrastate war or perceived threats to state security, particularly during the Cold War, sparked increases in exogenous aid to antagonists. The United States, the former Soviet Union, and the oil-rich Gulf states all directed aid and military assistance to their allies (Egypt, Syria, and Jordan) throughout the 1960s and 1970s. Thus geostrategic and regional position can be seen to act like mineral wealth as a national endowment bringing external rents.[34]

Military and security–driven assistance once simply meant weapons, but since the 1970s has grown to include long-term assistance for military industries, state-owned enterprises, and advanced surveillance technologies. In the 1960s and 1970s, for instance, the Soviet Union undertook significant infrastructure projects in Syria, Yemen, and Egypt, while early US assistance to Saudi Arabia involved similar nonmilitary investments to build that country's National Guard,[35] ironically the very same Saudi units that were sent to Bahrain in March 2011 to crush the uprising there. After the Cold War, US and European aid to allied regimes have increased with each bout of instability. For example, from 2000 to 2008, official US military assistance to the Middle East jumped by 36 percent.[36] This link between rents and conflict engenders a structural impediment to greater political participation and decentralization. Rulers not threatened by outside invasion or potential territorial loss have less need for national unity and can focus their attention upon domestic rivals, thereby limiting civil openings to participation. The rise of Saudi Arabia as counterrevolution headquarters in 2011, a role in which it has directly aided other leaderships in battling their own citizens, suggests the maturation of a new kind of rentier superpower. One country's domestic insecurity is another's external threat, and so the way to address that threat is through a regional extension of strategies honed domestically to distribute revenue and deploy repression.

Regional conflict and rents have also contributed to the evolution of new roles for domestic military and security institutions, roles that require deep transnational connections and that provide further incentives for repressing political opposition. Security aid and subsidized government-to-government arms purchases indirectly contribute to general domestic patronage, because all forms of aid, even military, are fungible.[37] But security rents also directly enhance forces of centralization and political repression.[38] Given that national security organizations in the Middle East are often oriented toward perceived internal threats, security aid for external threats may be so in name only, especially for regimes closely tied to Washington. In the past decade, a great deal of US security assistance has awarded such allied regimes with enhanced "dual use" surveillance and tracking capacities. And the same tools that allow them to meet "terrorist threats" can also be used to track, monitor, and punish professional associations, dissidents, and legal opposition movements. In this regard, then, rents do not cause regime-opposition dynamics; rather, external funding and technologies allow Arab militaries and security organizations to greatly expand their domestic political and economic roles.

More broadly, military and security institutions across the region have evolved into important rent seekers and socioeconomic players. The much commented upon domestic economic roles of Iran's Revolutionary Guard (running construction and trade companies, for example) are comparable to the evolution of "militarized welfare states" in Egypt, Syria, and Jordan.[39] Among the Gulf states, the patterns change slightly. Instead of external military aid, Gulf regimes have channeled their own oil rents to military and security organs through the "offset programs." These involve some percentage of a contract to purchase weapons or technology from a Western defense firm being set aside for investment in a domestic enterprise.[40] Some of these enterprises have become profitable public-private conglomerates in which former military and security officials predominate. By transforming state security institutions into essentially rent-seeking conglomerates that employ key regime personnel, new constituents with interests in avoiding and even in preventing the kind of political participation that could impede such arrangements may be evolving.

The Disaggregation and Decline of Rents

Political scientists using rentier theory have tended to view variation in rents as dichotomous; that is, rents go up, "boom," or rents go down, "bust." The previous section has already examined how boom periods and their timing are not uniform given preexisting variables. With the rent declines of the 1980s and 1990s across the Middle East and Africa producing divergent political-economic outcomes, attention must be focused upon differences in the bust period in particular countries and why sustained liberalization did not follow from crisis. Two lines of inquiry seem promising: examining how different types of rent affect a ruler's strategies and how differences in rentier economic crises shape potential political liberalization. Related to each line of inquiry is the need to develop more accurate measures of what constitutes rents.

To understand how different types of external rents may have different political and institutional effects, we can examine the cases of oil rents in Saudi Arabia and labor remittances in the case of Yemen.[41] Both states experienced rapid capital inflows (a boom period) at roughly the same time. Yemen's remittance income filtered into the domestic economy through a complex informal banking system that was structurally distinct from that of the Yemeni state. Thus in both political and institutional terms, Yemen's private sector evolved beyond state management. Conversely, oil receipts to Saudi Arabia flowed into the domestic economy through the state as a result of its ownership of the oil industry and its control of the distribution mechanisms (primarily government ministries). Private sector elites were thus wed even more tightly to state largess. Given its institutional and political distance from merchant elites, the Yemeni state found it easier to pursue austerity measures in the late 1980s that hurt private sector interests, while a more tightly bound Saudi state could not pursue such policies. There are a number of avenues for expanding this logic. For instance, how does foreign aid as rent affect domestic arrangements around political participation?[42] This is important because a number of Middle Eastern countries— not to mention African and some Asian countries—rely on foreign aid for significant portions of their public budget.

Distinctions in rent types are tied to differences in how rents decline. An inherent difficulty of the type of paired case studies that drove the revisions of rentier-state theory in the 1980s was the assumption that inflows and declines in rent were similar across cases. The idea is that economic crisis periods provide the best window into what matters in domestic politics. The problem is that rentier fiscal crises are rarely identical. Quantitative tests of oil busts encounter the same problem in trying to establish a starting point for regional economic crises. We saw this phenomenon in the 1980s when specialists on the Middle East assumed that the 1982 world decline in oil prices would translate into similar fiscal pressures on all oil states, when in fact the crisis began in the late 1970s for some and not until the early 1990s for others. Differences in rentier fiscal crises are important not merely due to variation in the pressures on a state to respond but also because of issues of public perception, the ability to craft policy responses, and the ability to implement reform. In part, differences in crises can be traced to differences in rent types, as discussed earlier. For instance, the biggest oil exporter with the largest reserves, Saudi Arabia, can by itself push the oil market in directions that affect world price and therefore the fate of its own public revenue. More broadly, we can see important differences in crisis types according to the timing, depth, and longevity of a crisis.

Abrupt and massive crises can spark emergency responses, whereas a "slow burn" may delay reform efforts and impede necessary public-private coordination. Kuwait's decades of debt and fiscal crisis were sparked not by a decline in oil prices but by the crash of an illegal stock market in 1981. The crisis deepened with Iraq's invasion nearly a decade later. In this case, early and intense business-state coordination evolved to meet the emergency and lay the groundwork for future resolution efforts. By contrast, Bahrain's fiscal crisis was more gradual but became acute in the 1990s due to growing unrest among the country's poor majority-Shiite population, who became increasingly resentful of Sunni political and economic dominance. That the 2011 uprisings came to Bahrain in the absence of acute and immediate economic dislocation suggests that these factors can build over time and overlap with other grievances.

Finally, regardless of whether one is focused upon types of rent or their decline, developing greater care in measurement is warranted. Two methods have traditionally been employed: one involves measuring rent dependency as a percentage of GDP, while the other measures dependency as a percentage of state revenue. The first measure has been employed largely in quantitative studies,[43] as the ratio of oil (or mineral) exports to GDP over time. This calculation provides a more comprehensive measure of a country's economic dependence on oil, and moreover the sources of data are more standardized and widely available. But this measure does not capture other forms of state rent that are not usually reported in the international datasets (aid, military assistance, and debt forgiveness), and for the purely oil-exporting states, this measure does not capture revenue earned from previous investments of oil concessions, known as sovereign wealth funds.[44] Recent critiques also fault this measurement, rent dependency as a percentage of GDP, for selection bias, since measuring rent dependency according to GDP is an indicator (of underdevelopment, for example) rather than a cause of something else.[45]

The second measure, rent dependency as a percentage of state revenue, has been employed by specialists on the Middle East to distinguish rentier and nonrentier states by measuring the difference between domestically and externally derived revenue. It has the advantage of being a more specific measure of a state's dependence on external revenue. Of course, governments that report such data are aware of this fact, and thus this measure is suspect for uneven reporting and omitted sources. Given these strengths and weaknesses in the measurements, choosing one measurement over another can influence the set of cases one studies. In short, political rents are clearly more than just oil, but to move forward in our analysis of them we need to understand the differences among types and how their measurement and comparison may influence conclusions.

Conclusion

In scholarly debates on the issue of the rentier state, no one claims that oil or state-controlled rents are unimportant to outcomes like political liberalization. Yet rents alone can explain very little, which is why the trend of linking so much to oil has led to an analytical dead end. In the sociopolitical world, oil or similar physical resources do not cause anything on their own. Incorporating pre-rent sociopolitical variables, transnational linkages, and different rent types offers a number of ways to expand the rentier/resource-curse debate in promising directions. Three further points are relevant in regard to doing so.

One conclusion highlighted in this review is the critique that rentier-state theory hangs all its explanatory power on oil or similar exogenous resources at the expense of political, institutional, or social factors. As has been shown, social scientists studying the Middle East have rarely treated economic rents as undifferentiated, nonhistorical variables; rather they have taken access to rents as an important component of a broader and more substantive approach to political economy. That important pre-rent variables were missed or that there was a tendency to imbue the rentier state with autonomy and agency it may have lacked are important critiques and should not be ignored.

The second conclusion is methodological and emphasizes the value of intra–Middle Eastern comparisons and case studies as complements to large–sample size and cross-regional studies. A common critique of the evolution of rentier-state theory is the claim that since there is little variation among Arab cases, case comparison of rentier states is methodologically underdeveloped.[46] Recent large–sample size tests in which the Arab countries of the Middle East constitute a single dependent variable help to isolate and test specific mechanisms and thus to generate more research questions. But placing such diverse regimes as found in say Syria, Kuwait, and Yemen (not to mention a number of African countries) into blanket authoritarian/nondemocratic categories raises doubts about how such ordering contributes to our understanding of these countries.[47] Indeed, there are important differences between Syria's institutionalized populist authoritarian rule through a mass-based political party, Kuwait's crafting of a preindustrial welfare state through a patrimonial monarchy, and the Yemeni regime's formation of an alliance with powerful social groups through violent social conflict. Methodologically, this means "paying attention to the diverse ways a common outcome can be reached."[48] Returning to the 2011 uprisings, divergences among the oil exporters—in that some experienced mass uprisings while others did not, or only did to a much smaller extent—drives this point home.

Finally, though the finite quality of mineral resources and the fickleness of foreign aid leave the impression that rentier states will eventually disappear, the rentier literature actually enjoys the advantage of being tested against the (re)creation of new rentier states. Already-discovered oil reserves among the Southern Caucasus countries are currently creating rentierlike states there, while in Africa, significant domestic changes have occurred in the wake of massive oil discoveries in Equatorial Guinea and Angola. And beyond these new players, the grand dames of the oil patch, the Gulf rulers and their Western allies, face an uncertain future in which the use of revenue and repression may not be enough to protect the privileges of rent wealth.

Notes

1. John Judis, "Blood for Oil?" *New Republic,* 31 March 2003; Daphne Eviatar, "Petrol Peril: Why Iraq's Oil Wealth May Do More Harm Than Good," *Boston Globe,* 13 April 2003; Nancy Birdsall and Arvind Subramanian, "Saving Iraq from Its Oil," *Foreign Affairs* 83, 4 (July–August 2004).

2. Thomas Friedman, "The First Law of PetroPolitics," *Foreign Policy,* 25 April 2006.

3. Among critical Middle East specialists, see Steven Heydemann, "The Political Logic of Economic Rationality: Selective Stabilization in Syria," in Henri Barkey, ed., *The Politics of Economic Reform in the Middle East* (New York: St. Martin's, 1992); David Waldner, "States, Markets, and Development: What We Know—and Do Not Know—About the Political Economy of the Modern Middle East," paper for the ESF/SCSS Exploratory Workshop, May 2003; John Waterbury, "Democracy Without Democrats? The Potential for Political Liberalization in the Middle East," in Ghassan Salamé, ed., *Democracy Without Democrats? The Renewal of Politics in the Muslim World* (London: Tauris, 1994); Eva Bellin, "The Politics of Profit in Tunisia: Utility of the Rentier Paradigm?" *World Development* 22, 3 (1994); Gwenn Okruhlik, "Rentier Wealth, Unruly Law, and the Rise of the Opposition: The Political Economy of Oil States," *Comparative Politics* 31, 3 (April 1999); Michael Herb, "No Representation Without Taxation? Rents, Development, and Democracy," *Comparative Politics* 37, 3 (April 2005); Timothy Mitchell, "Carbon Democracy," *Economy and Society* 38, 3 (August 2009); Anne Peters and Pete Moore, "Beyond Boom and Bust: External Rents, Durable Authoritarianism, and Institutional Adaptation in the Hashemite Kingdom of Jordan," *Studies in Comparative International Development* 44, 2 (2009). Among non–Middle East specialists, see Marcus Kurtz, "The Social Foundations of Institutional Order: Reconsidering War and the 'Resource Curse' in Third World State Building," *Politics and Society* 37, 4 (2009); Andrew Shrank, "Reconsidering the Resource Curse: Selection Bias, Measurement Error, and Omitted Variables," unpublished manuscript, Yale University, New Haven, 2003.

4. Terry Lynn Karl, *The Paradox of Plenty: Oil Booms and Petro-States* (Berkeley: University of California Press, 1997); Richard F. Doner, Bryan K. Ritchie, and Dan Slater, "Systemic Vulnerability and the Origins of Developmental States: Northeast and Southeast Asia in Comparative Perspective," *International Organization* 59, 2 (2005); Daron Acemoglu and James A. Robinson, "Economic Backwardness in Political Perspective," *American Political Science Review* 100, 1 (February 2006); Michael Ross, *The Oil Curse: How Petroleum Wealth Shapes the Development of Nations* (Princeton: Princeton University Press, 2012).

5. Ibn Khaldun, *The Muqaddimah: An Introduction to History,* vol. 2, translated by Franz Rosenthal (New York: Pantheon, 1958), pp. 319–321.

6. Jean Delacroix, "The Distributive State in the World System," *Studies in International Comparative Development* 15, 3 (1980).

7. Joseph Schumpeter, "The Crisis of the Tax State," in Alan T. Peacock, ed., *International Economic Papers* no. 4 (London: Macmillan, 1954), p. 17.

8. Hazem Beblawi, *The Arab Gulf Economy in a Turbulent Age* (London: Croom Helm, 1984); Hazem Beblawi and Giacomo Luciani, eds., *The Arab State* (New York: Croom Helm, 1987); Giacomo Luciani, "Economic Foundations of Democracy and Authoritarianism: The Arab World in Comparative Perspective," *Arab Studies Quarterly* 10, 4 (1988).

9. Charles Tilly, *Coercion, Capital, and European States, AD 990–1990* (Cambridge: Blackwell, 1990).

10. Jill Crystal, *Oil and Politics in the Gulf: Rulers and Merchants in Kuwait and Qatar* (Cambridge: Cambridge University Press, 1995).

11. F. Gregory Gause III, *Oil Monarchies: Domestic and Security Challenges in the Arab Gulf States* (New York: Council on Foreign Relations Press, 1994), p. 8.

12. Luciani, "Economic Foundations of Democracy and Authoritarianism."

13. Lisa Anderson, "Remaking the Middle East: The Prospects for Democracy and Stability," *Ethics & International Affairs* 6, 1 (March 1992), p. 172.

14. Karl, *The Paradox of Plenty,* p. 241.

15. Gwenn Okruhlik, "Rentier Wealth, Unruly Law, and the Rise of Opposition: The Political Economy of Oil States," *Comparative Politics* 31, 3 (April 1999).

16. Herb, "No Representation Without Taxation?" and Michael Herb, *All in the Family: Absolutism, Revolution, and Democracy in the Middle Eastern Monarchies* (Albany: State University of New York Press, 1999).

17. Heydemann, "The Political Logic of Economic Rationality: Selective Stabilization in Syria"; Waterbury, "Democracy Without Democrats?"; Herb, "No Representation Without Taxation?"

18. This suggests that perhaps the full weight of crisis was not transmitted to publics and therefore the original mechanisms are still at work. While general forms of austerity can be observed in the 1980s and 1990s, we lack good case studies on Gulf austerity and retrenchment.

19. Eva Bellin, *Stalled Democracy: Capital, Labor, and the Paradox of State Sponsored Development* (Ithaca: Cornell University Press, 2002); Pete Moore, "Rentier Fiscal Crisis and Regime Stability in the Middle East: Business and State in the Gulf," *Studies in Comparative International Development* 37, 1 (Spring 2002).

20. Kurtz, "The Social Foundations of Institutional Order." See also Benjamin Smith, "Oil Wealth and Regime Survival in the Developing World, 1960–1999," *American Journal of Political Science* 48, 2 (April 2004).

21. Ross, "Does Oil Hinder Democracy?"

22. Herb, "No Representation Without Taxation?"

23. Lisa Anderson, *The State and Social Transformation in Tunisia and Libya, 1830–1980* (Princeton: Princeton University Press, 1986); Kiren Aziz Chaudhry, *The Price of Wealth: Economies and Institutions in the Middle East* (Ithaca: Cornell University Press, 1997); Dirk Vandewalle, *Libya Since Independence: Oil and State-Building* (Ithaca: Cornell University Press, 1998); Laurie Brand, "Economic and Political Liberalization in a Rentier Economy: The Case of the Hashemite Kingdom of Jordan," in Iliya Harik and Denis J. Sullivan, eds., *Privatization and Liberalization in the Middle East* (Bloomington: Indiana University Press, 1992); Crystal, *Oil and Politics in the Gulf.*

24. Smith, "Oil Wealth and Regime Survival in the Developing World."

25. Frederick Anscombe, *The Ottoman Gulf: The Creation of Kuwait, Saudi Arabia, and Qatar* (New York: Columbia University Press, 1997).

26. Robert Vitalis, *America's Kingdom: Mythmaking on the Saudi Oil Frontier* (London: Verso, 2009); Toby Jones, *Desert Kingdom: How Oil and Water Forged Modern Saudi Arabia* (Cambridge: Harvard University Press, 2010).

27. Vandewalle, *Libya Since Independence*, p. 32.

28. Crystal, *Oil and Politics in the Gulf;* Chaudhry, *The Price of Wealth,* pp. 48–50.

29. Lisa Anderson, "Prospects for Liberalism in North Africa: Identities and Interests in Preindustrial Welfare States," in John Entelis, ed., *Islam, Democracy, and the State in North Africa* (Bloomington: Indiana University Press, 1997), pp. 127–140.

30. Steven Heydemann, "Toward a New Social Contract in the Middle East and North Africa," *Arab Reform Bulletin* (Washington, DC: Carnegie Endowment for International Peace, January 2004), http://carnegieendowment.org/2008/08/20/toward-new-social-contract-in-middle-east-and-north-africa/7k6.

31. Charles Tripp, *Islam and the Moral Economy: The Challenges of Capitalism* (Cambridge: Cambridge University Press, 2006).

32. Baghat Korany, Rex Brynen, and Paul Noble, eds., *The Many Faces of National Security in the Arab World* (New York: St. Martin's, 1993).

33. Ian Lustick, "The Absence of Middle Eastern Great Powers: Political 'Backwardness' in Historical Perspective," *International Organization* 51, 4 (1997).

34. One could add elections as a reason for rent inflows. In particular, recent elections in Iraq and Lebanon have seen significant flows of money from states trying to influence the vote.

35. Nadav Safran, *Saudi Arabia: The Ceaseless Quest for Security* (Cambridge: Harvard University Press, 1985); Peter Mangold, *Super Power Intervention in the Middle East* (New York: St Martin's, 1978).

36. USAID, "US Overseas Loans and Grants," http://gbk.eads.usaidallnet.gov/.

37. Howard Pack and Janet Rothenberg Pack, "Foreign Aid: The Question of Fungibility," *Review of Economics and Statistics* 75, 2 (May 1993).

38. Eva Bellin, "Coercive Institutions and Coercive Leaders," and Jason Brownlee, "Political Crisis and Restabilization: Iraq, Libya, Syria, Tunisia," both in Marsha Pripstein Posusney and Michele Penner Angrist, eds., *Authoritarianism in the Middle East: Regimes and Resistance* (Boulder: Lynne Rienner, 2005).

39. Anne Marie Baylouny, "Militarizing Welfare: Neoliberalism and Jordanian Policy," *Middle East Journal* 62, 2 (Spring 2008).

40. Shana Marshall, "Money for Nothing? Offsets in the U.S.–Middle East Defense Trade," *International Journal of Middle East Studies* 41, 4 (November 2009).

41. Though there is debate on this, remittance income from expatriate workers can be considered a rent insofar as the person receiving the transfer did not earn it and the rapid inflow of remittances tends to have similar economic effects (liquidity induced inflation, for instance).

42. Karen L. Remmer, "Does Foreign Aid Promote the Expansion of Government?" *American Journal of Political Science* 48, 1 (January 2004).

43. Ross, "Does Oil Hinder Democracy?"; Smith, "Oil Wealth and Regime Survival in the Developing World."

44. Today almost all oil exporters have some sort of "fund for future generations" in which a portion of annual oil revenue is invested overseas. Kuwait was the first to do this and by the late 1980s was earning more from its overseas investments than from its annual sales of oil.

45. Shrank, "Reconsidering the Resource Curse"; Herb, "No Representation Without Taxation?"; Kurtz, "The Social Foundations of Institutional Order."

46. Ross, "Does Oil Hinder Democracy?"

47. See, Thomas Carothers, "The End of the Transition Paradigm," *Journal of Democracy* 13, 3 (January 2002).

48. Charles Ragin, "Turning the Tables: How Case-Oriented Research Challenges Variable-Oriented Research," *Comparative Social Research* 16 (1997), p. 32.

10

Economic Liberalization

There are few ideas from Western liberal thought as powerful as the assertion that "free markets make free politics." In recent decades, that idea has been institutionalized and expressed through a set of international policies, often termed "neoliberalism." Dissenters from this tradition have argued that greater political participation flows from curtailment of market forces rather than from abdication to unfettered market rule. This position has informed arguments that the global spread of market forces would lead not to greater political participation but rather to exclusion and inequality.

In the Arab world, these arguments have played out over several decades. Since the 1970s, nearly all Arab states have at some time initiated economic liberalization programs that have differed in content and effect. By the 1980s, international organizations like the World Bank and the International Monetary Fund (IMF) as well as private banks came to play more active roles in shaping the trajectory of economic reform through adjustment loans and attached neoliberal policy conditions. A consensus ultimately emerged that although the Arab countries have experienced periods of economic growth (meaning expansion and increase in gross domestic product [GDP]), economic development (meaning more productive investment and increasing worker skills) has stagnated or even reversed in some cases. The fact that the very regimes implementing policies of economic reform were, until 2011 at least, durably authoritarian was not lost on observers and citizens of the region alike. Indeed, in at least one respect there was a strong trend in 2011 among protesters: that there was a link between the privilege and wealth of their unaccountable leaders and their society's lack of opportunity and development.

Among the more pointed chants and protest signs held up during the 2011 Egyptian uprising were "Hosni Mubarak, you agent, you sold the gas and only the Nile is left to be sold!" and "I am an Egyptian laborer. Where's the money the companies are making, sons of bitches!" These kinds of basic political economy concerns are of course found in all countries, but it was startling and unprecedented how they burst forth across the Arab World in 2011 after roiling below the surface for decades previous. And while these were not the only claims made by protesters concerned with justice and fairness, they nonetheless prompted some commentators to reopen and rehash some old debates by crediting neoliberal reforms or advancements in economic development more generally as being responsible for the uprisings.[1] Other commentators have countered by claiming that neoliberalism made Arab societies worse-off and more unequal; thus it was the failure of reform that ignited protests.[2] Combining elements of both approaches, it may be that long-held public expectations for higher living standards failed and this fed the protests.

It will be some time before a more complete understanding of how socioeconomic factors figured into the 2011 uprisings is possible. Thus this chapter concentrates on the broader issue of how economic liberalization may or may not be connected to political liberalization. It considers such ancillary questions as what has constituted economic liberalization in the Middle East, what have been its effects, and what such liberalization might mean for the political and economic transitions that ultimately emerge from the 2011 uprisings.

Economic to Political Liberalization?

The concept of economic liberalization and how it may connect to political liberalization originates in the liberal tradition linking economic development to democracy in the West. More specifically, political development scholars in the 1950s and 1960s contended that democracy develops slowly in response to particular socioeconomic preconditions. They argued that economic changes such as industrialization, urbanization, and increased personal income would foster change toward political democracy through empowerment of political opposition or perhaps by helping to engender mass attitudinal shifts that would lead to an embrace of values associated with democracy. In other words, material interests translate into political outcomes, with economic decentralization pushing political decentralization. It is upon these assumptions that the neoliberal policy consensus of the 1980s and 1990s was built.

Generally, links between economic and political liberalization have been analyzed at the societal level, envisioning change as a bottom-up process.[3] The most enduring societal accounts focus on organized interests and classes, especially the middle class. Defined in income terms, the middle class has been the consensus actor pushing political liberalization and ultimately democratization.[4] As economic assets or more economic wealth spread throughout a society, an independent and growing middle class should result. Such a dynamic middle class has greater access to information and education, and thus its members should be more sociopolitically active. This active middle class is then expected to provide the counterweight to centralized state power by making demands for public services and representation.

Other societal accounts have stressed broader civil society as the principal agent of change rather than emphasizing just the middle class. Definitions of civil society vary, but the traditional approach stresses that organized groups located below the level of the state and above that of the family can play vital political roles in deepening political liberalization and achieving democratization.[5] Thus, as economic wealth and opportunity expand through liberalization, organized professionals, workers, and concerned citizens are better able to mobilize to demand greater participation in political decisionmaking. Organized labor in particular looms large in accounts linking economic development to democracy. Here, industrialization and its social ramifications (urbanization and education) empower labor in two ways: (1) more workers means better chances for unionization and organization and (2) industrialized development fosters shared material interests among workers to seek a political voice.[6] Effective organizing and shared interests together are powerful forces for bottom-up change.

Finally, societal accounts also embrace a role for the private sector, or for capitalists more generally.[7] According to this view, liberalization of economic resources away from the state and toward society empowers an autonomous capitalist class that is beyond state control. And as with labor, there are interests and organizational issues at play. Though capitalists may clash among themselves on some economic interests, when it comes to the issue of how a state extracts domestic resources and spends them, business is expected to have a unified interest so as to be able to influence those decisions. Indeed, holding rulers accountable for revenue collection and spending is deemed a hallmark of political liberalization and democratization. It should be noted that these societal accounts envision economic development as a slow and fitful process, and thus expect political change to also be slow and fitful.

During what was known as the third wave of democratization in the 1980s and 1990s, this bottom-up approach to change was linked with top-down considerations through an increased focus on the state. It is argued that the usual spark to change at the state level involves some economic or fiscal crisis, which complicates easy responses.[8] Economic or financial crisis, for example a sudden currency devaluation or a decline in commodity prices, catalyzes social groups into action. In such a circumstance, nondemocratic leaders face the choice of either repressing these social groups in order to maintain power or granting them greater political voice. Eventually, elites within the state may split over what to do, thereby giving social actors a means to influence state policies. To stave off deeper economic crisis or to avoid being blamed, leaders may opt to decentralize (liberalize) economic power to social groups. Political liberalization may then follow.

By looking at ideas linking economic changes to the political, one can see how neoliberalism came to be linked with democracy. Neoliberalism's argument for the kind of economic development that would evolve toward democracy is tidy: limit state controls on economic activity, lower barriers to trade, privatize state-owned assets, and generally ensure the free flow of capital. But there is an equally large literature that is at odds with these pro-market arguments and that asserts that a free market does not mean decentralized economic power or that social actors are empowered by the market. Instead, it says that a free market simply means freedom for the most powerful to secure exclusive access to economic assets. These critiques offer a different historical perspective on the rise of democracy and markets, one in which links between the two are not as harmonious as has often been assumed.[9] The free market, or what Karl Polanyi termed "that satanic mill," required changes in human society that would lead to unsustainable inequality.[10] Left unrestricted, markets limited and punished social freedom and action,[11] a situation that is anathema to democratic principles. In this view, modern social democracy began with a rejection of the unfettered market that emerged in the nineteenth century as European societies exercised governance through the political action of unions, class actors, and social associations demanding political participation. Seen from this vantage, neoliberal calls to free the market from political interference emerge as being at odds with the advancement of political participation, and ultimately of democracy. Thus instead of a tidy argument linking economic change to the political, the more critical argument sees a role for political and social action to change the economic, for both positive and less positive ends.

This cursory review of opposing views on economic and political liberalization does not even touch upon the more heterodox approaches that may combine elements of both. Ultimately, most positions in this debate acknowledge the interconnectedness of political and economic dynamics, but this only leads to more questions rather than helping to answer existing ones. For example, arguments connecting economic to political liberalization tend to be structural. Nothing about these theories means that political liberalization is axiomatic, just that certain socioeconomic conditions appear to be more conducive to political participation than others.

From 1970s Infitah to 2000s Burj Khalifa

In economic terms, one cannot really speak of a single Arab region today. Consider that only about 800 miles separates the highest skyscrapers in the world in Dubai, in the United Arab Emirates (UAE), from the oldest in Shibam, in Yemen. This points to the significant socioeconomic differences that exist between countries, and increasingly within them. Nevertheless, there are regional and historical similarities in how states have built their economies and integrated themselves into the global capitalist system. This section reviews three phases to economic development and liberalization in the Middle East leading up to the 2011 uprisings: an early statist phase, the *infitah* (economic opening) phase, and the structural adjustment, or neoliberal, phase. Each phase has been accompanied by leaders calling for reform with new policies following, yet only uneven progress has been realized in terms of productive economic growth and—at least until 2011— very little political liberalization.

In the decades after political independence, political leaders in the Arab world were faced with the need to construct national economies from the remnants of colonial rule. In most cases, the economic policies of the European colonial powers had stressed the central role of political authority in managing domestic as well as regional economies.[12] In the political economic sense, transition to independence dovetailed with the consensus among development economists of the 1950s that successful economic development required strong state leadership to "kick-start" advancement. Across the Middle East, socialist-oriented countries (such as Iraq and Egypt) as well as countries that were professed adherents of the free market (such as Jordan) implemented what can be termed "statist economic policies," such as encouraging the growth of the public sector, nationalizing private firms or creating state-owned enterprises, implementing price and trade controls, and making some attempts at rural land reform. Two aspects of this period are particularly important for understanding later efforts at economic liberalization.

First, it is important to recognize that these ambitious policies and rapid changes did not take a place in a vacuum; rather there were a variety of political constraints and opportunities that were also affecting events. This is because newly independent regimes had to construct national economies while simultaneously under pressure to secure their political rule. As the great social historian Ibn Khaldun once remarked, no king is powerful alone; he requires people to support his rule. Economic policies can then be seen as a principal means of securing that political support by rewarding allies and punishing rivals. Second, while this first phase did not deliver sustainable economic development, growth and social advancements did take place. In terms of real GDP growth per capita, the Middle East outperformed all other parts of the developing world other than East Asia until 1979.[13] Most interesting for a region that is not considered to be economically productive, the Middle East even performed much better than the United States in terms of the growth rate of GDP per worker until the 1970s (see Table 10.1).

State policies in these decades led to the construction of urban infra-structure, expanded road networks, new power grids, and the modernization of port facilities. Expansion of public education succeeded in boosting lit-eracy levels, and increasing public employment allowed women to enter the work force in large numbers for the first time. Unfortunately, however, because these gains were tentative and built upon the necessity of securing political rule, they would also prove to be susceptible to stagnation and hard to reform. It is also important to keep in mind the future expectations that these periods of growth would instill in the region's peoples, who were keen to ensure a better standard of living for their posterity.

After the boom in oil prices in the early 1970s, a number of Arab coun-tries began to experience mounting public debt and declining rates of growth. In response, some Arab countries undertook economic opening, in what is known as the infitah phase. Egypt and Tunisia are acknowledged to have launched the first infitah policies, in the early 1970s, while other coun-tries, Algeria and Iraq, followed suit in the 1980s (see Table 10.2). Though the specific policies pursued varied, infitah generally sought to increase re-liance on market forces through the implementation of policies aimed at en-couraging greater private sector investment, more openness to international markets, and reform of the public sector. In Egypt, for example, a series of laws were introduced beginning in 1974 that made it easier for foreign in-vestors to establish joint ventures with local enterprises; in Tunisia, a 1972 law provided incentives for firms to export to international markets; the Moroccan government launched its infitah reforms in 1978; in Algeria, start-ing in 1982, the government dismantled and reorganized sixty-six of its largest state-owned companies;[14] and even Baathist Iraq, in the midst of war with Iran, launched a rather expansive privatization program of its own.

Several features of these early liberalization programs are noteworthy. First, with some exceptions, the programs were domestically conceived and

Table 10.1   Regional Economic Performance, 1960–1994
(Annual percentage growth rate in GDP per worker)

	1960–1973	1973–1984	1984–1994
Africa	1.9	–0.6	–0.6
East Asia	4.2	4.0	4.4
Latin America	3.4	0.4	0.1
Middle East	4.7	0.5	–1.1
South Asia	1.8	2.5	2.7
United States	1.9	0.2	0.9

Source: Dani Rodrik, "Where Did All the Growth Go? External Shocks, Social Conflict, and Growth Collapses," *Journal of Economic Growth* 4 (December 1999), p. 389.

implemented, in contrast to the more widespread involvement of international lending agencies a decade later. Second, in many cases the programs were not solely concerned with economic goals but were shaped by political calculations of the regimes that were implementing them. Thus, for example, Anwar Sadat's policy of infitah was as much a tactical effort to secure political support from the country's private sector as it was an effort to stimulate national economic development.[15] And Saddam Hussein's policies of liberalization in Iraq in the 1980s were concerned with both the economic and the political survival of his regime. Additionally, because these policies were adopted in the wake of economic dislocations, ensuing austerity measures posed new political problems. In all cases, austerity measures were met with labor strikes and mass protests that prompted crackdowns by security forces (Egypt in 1977, Tunisia in 1977, Morocco in 1979, and Algeria in 1988).[16] Third, these policies did little to address lagging development and little to decentralize political power. For example, Egypt's impressive growth in the latter half of the 1970s owed more to increasing commodity prices and domestic consumption than to the country's reform policies.[17] Likewise, while old-guard capitalists enjoyed greater participation in the policymaking process, broader political inclusion or decentralization did not take place.

As oil prices began their decline in the early 1980s, oil exporters curbed bilateral aid to other Arab states and there was a decline in labor remittances. Egypt, Yemen, Jordan, Syria, and Morocco all experienced declines in GDP growth and increases in public debt, which culminated in acute economic crisis for some (such as Jordan's currency devaluation in 1988–1989). At first, leaders simply muddled through, not wanting to suffer the political costs of austerity measures and hoping that global conditions would change. Eventually, some were forced to implement austerity measures as a result of acute economic dislocations. Like the earlier liberalization experiments,

Table 10.2 Major Economic Liberalization Phases in the Middle East

	Initiation	External Actor
Tunisia	1972	International Monetary Fund, 1986
Egypt	1974	International Monetary Fund, 1976
Morocco	1981	International Monetary Fund, 1983
Algeria	1982	International Monetary Fund, 1989
Kuwait	1982	None
Saudi Arabia	1984	None
Iraq	1984	None
Jordan	1985	International Monetary Fund, 1989
United Arab Emirates	2000	None

these austerity measures sparked mobilized public resistance, as occurred in parts of southern Jordan in 1989, for example.

Along with these economic constraints, the ascendancy of US financial power propelled a revival of classical liberal thought, leading to a new consensus on the best economic order. Past commitments to state-led economic growth were replaced with core neoliberal emphases on liberalization, privatization, and deregulation. What would become known as the Washington Consensus embraced a broad array of these policies and became institutionalized within the two principal international lending agencies, the International Monetary Fund and World Bank. In return for loan assistance, countries would have to enter into agreements termed structural adjustment programs, requiring policies that on paper at least went far beyond infitah efforts. They involved removing distortions in market exchanges so as to "get the price right"—that is, to allow markets to set prices rather than having states do so through subsidies and price controls. Additional policies called for reductions in the size of the public sector, the sale of state-owned enterprises, reductions in barriers to external trade, and devaluation of currencies.

With the exception of the oil exporters, many Arab states turned to the international lending agencies and embraced the new development ideologies to help stabilize their economies. Regardless of the exact policy mix, states such as Algeria, Egypt, Jordan, Morocco, and Tunisia signed structural adjustment programs with the IMF and the World Bank. And even for Arab states that did not officially sign on to the Washington Consensus, the international environment was such that if they faced economic dislocation in the 1980s or 1990s, structural adjustment policies were the currency of the realm. So, for example, Kuwait elected to launch its own privatization program in the late 1980s as a result of facing the crash of a semilegal stock market at a time of declining oil prices. Baathist Syria, facing similar financial constraints in the 1990s, opted to loosen investment and import laws to encourage greater private sector activity. Even Iran and Iraq initiated their own liberalization programs in the aftermath of their devastating war.

In return for liberalized trade reform, eleven Arab countries joined the World Trade Organization by 2000. Other states have signed free trade agreements with the European Union and the United States. In line with Washington Consensus ideas, all of these agreements require elements of trade and financial liberalization. Among the Gulf oil exporters, external conditionality is not in play, but other forms of economic liberalization have taken hold. In Bahrain, the United Arab Emirates, and Qatar, liberalization of finance and investment have paved the way for significant expansion in the real estate, transportation, and service sectors. Dubai in the UAE has epitomized this trend by allowing nonlocals to own land and businesses, changes that have opened up channels of international financing and led to the success of Jebel Ali port and high-end tourist projects such as Burj al-Arab, reportedly the most expensive hotel in the world, as well as Burj Khalifa, the world's tallest building to date.

So what have these persistent and varied efforts at economic liberalization wrought? In terms of economic development, not much. But there is a caveat to this response, one that also relates to economic questions surrounding the 2011 uprisings: the available socioeconomic data from the Arab world are uneven and incomplete. As well, it is important to acknowledge that a great deal of significant economic activity (e.g., domestic black and gray markets, transnational trade, property rights, foreign assistance, and so on) is not fully captured by reported statistics. With these limits in mind, there have certainly been increases in aggregate growth in the Middle East since the dawn of the neoliberal era, but much of that has been of the boom-and-bust, easy-come-easy-go variety. In parts of every Arab capital, there are enclaves of high-end consumption, Internet access has spread, and literacy rates have increased. But the kind of growth promised by neoliberalism has not materialized. Referring back to Table 10.1 (on page 218), we can see that the Middle East was already lagging behind Africa in terms of GDP growth per worker by the mid-1990s. Another way to understand this lag is to examine manufactured exports from the region as a percentage of GDP. The underlying logic here is that as economic development takes hold, a given country should be able to manufacture products that are competitive in external markets. This is because higher-value production, increased worker skills, and increased domestic investment should show up in increases in manufactured exports. By contrast, exports of primary commodities like oil do not contribute to this type of export-led productive development. So in Table 10.3, we can see an intraregional comparison over time of this percentage.

Table 10.3 Manufactured Exports in the Middle East as Percentage of GDP, 1970–1999

	1970–1979	1980–1989	1990–1999
Algeria	0.6	0.3	0.8
Egypt	3.1	1.5	2.4
Jordan	1.9	5.4	9.5
Morocco	2.1	6.0	7.5
Tunisia	4.6	11.7	21.2

Source: Mustafa Kamel Nabil and Marie-Ange Veganzones-Varoudakis, "Exchange Rate Regime and Competitiveness of Manufactured Exports: The Case of the MENA Countries," Working Paper no. 27 (Washington, DC: World Bank, August 2002), p. 8.

Table 10.4 Manufactured Versus Fuel Exports by Region, 2006
(percentage of total exports)

	Fuel	Manufactured
East Asia	8	80
Europe and Central Asia	32	46
Latin America	21	53
Middle East	76	15
South Asia	9	72
Sub-Saharan Africa	—	28

Source: World Bank, *World Development Indicators* (Washington, DC, 2008), p. 212.

Oil-exporting Algeria exhibits patterns similar to all regional oil exporters, large and small: a lack of manufactured exports and little change over time. Egypt, Jordan, and Morocco show some progress over time, but these gains are weak in comparison to those of Tunisia, the Arab world's most industrialized economy by 2000. It is also important to keep in mind that manufactured exports in the Jordanian case are inflated significantly by US duty-free garment exports from Asian–owned and operated factories in the country's "qualified industrial zones," so Jordan is hardly a case of productive development.[18] When comparing the Middle East against other regions (see Table 10.4), we can see a general lack of progress.

The unavoidable conclusion from this data is that after decades of various neoliberal reforms, little developmental progress has been made in the Middle East. In some cases, "islands of reform" have resulted in the development of successful business sectors (private and public) in certain countries that are competitive regionally and internationally.[19] The Tunisian garment industry, the Saudi Basic Industries Corporation (SABIC), and Dubai's Emirates Airlines are examples of such successful players. And there are certainly pockets of high wealth and consumption in the Gulf states and in urban centers in the region; but broader development has proven elusive, as many of these achievements tend to remain in enclaves that are not deeply connected to the domestic economy.

The question thus remains, how is the failure of economic reform linked to the fact of limited political reform?

The Political Economies of Brittle Authoritarianism

There are several approaches to explain how economic liberalization and authoritarian endurance went together so smoothly for so long in the Arab world. One approach stresses institutions and political decisions taken long before reform efforts began, which then conditioned or limited the extent of the liberalization that followed. Other analyses focus on the conditions and pressures present when states embarked on economic liberalization. Both perspectives agree that economic liberalization policies were harnessed to maintain centralized political power, a finding that goes some way to explaining why economic development has stagnated in the region. Of course the 2011 uprisings challenge a conclusion that lack of genuine reform in those decades signaled the strength of a system in which economic advancement was unequal and slowing while political participation was narrowing. In some ways, economic liberalization contributed to "an upgrading of authoritarianism," but clearly it also contributed to citizens' growing opposition to policies that were not lifting all boats.

Distant or more historical accounts of the failure of reform move us back to the ideas of development scholars in the 1950s. Across the region, economic liberalization programs generally failed to generate the kind of sustainable and productive economic development assumed to herald political liberalization. Why?

Since Alexander Gerschenkron's famous essay on late economic development,[20] the political conditions of economic development have been taken seriously in trying to understand a particular country's trajectory. The story of development in the West, unfolding as it did over hundreds of years in relative isolation from external actors and allowing for the gradual evolution of social actors able to oppose centralized political power, appears unique. By contrast, under conditions of late political development in the twentieth century, achieving the political institutions required to support successful transition to market economies proved much more difficult.[21] For newly independent Arab, Asian, and African countries in the twentieth century, the demand was to build states and national economies at the same time and under conditions of significant domestic and international competition. Additionally, preexisting sociopolitical divisions or institutional arrangements in a given country could shape the outcome of those efforts.[22] In much of Africa and the Middle East, what emerged were nondemocratic political coalitions built on state patronage and state-directed distribution. Labor and business were less independent actors and more creatures of the state.[23] Such arrangements preserved the centralization of political power, and for a short while delivered some socioeconomic advancement. But overall, these political economies would prove resistant to long-term development and reform. By contrast, some of the more economically successful Asian states, such as South Korea and Taiwan, enjoyed different sociopolitical conditions that allowed them to pursue long-term economic policies that eventually yielded productive economic development and ultimately democracy.[24]

Such explanations for the lack of development thus locate the so-called original developmental sin prior to the 1980s and 1990s. That is, decisions surrounding liberalization as well as its actual implementation in those decades were fundamentally constrained by the political calculus and institutions of decades past. Among more proximate accounts for the failure of reform, the focus is not upon a rejection of distant accounts but rather on more immediate conditions and pressures. These include adaptation to economic crisis, the role of external actors, the role of the middle class and business, and the effects of persistent regional conflict. Finally, and notwithstanding events in 2011, the remarkable cohesion of Arab regime elites through periods of economic crisis appears to be a key factor in why these political economies remained impervious to liberalization and why political participation remained exclusionary for so long.

In the wake of the 2011 uprisings, it is quite obvious that economic crisis is not the only trigger for political change, as some previous analysis expected. Periods of economic crisis in the late 1970s and 1980s yielded little sustained political uprising, while the 2011 uprisings did not follow any acute economic crisis. What is less obvious is how regimes that in 2011 looked politically brittle were for decades so adept at weathering economic crisis. In considering this question, we can see that the oil-exporting Gulf states had some natural advantages. While price downturns did spark some public budget cutbacks in the 1980s and 1990s, on the whole these states simply went further into debt, thereby avoiding tough political decisions and waiting out the downturn. Major oil exporters thus had a longer time horizon to manage crisis before they would be forced to undertake political reforms. Among the non–oil exporters, the crisis periods were more painful and involved bouts of public unrest, but here again states were not powerless to respond. For one thing, rulers with external patrons could benefit from timely support and assistance, thereby weathering crisis without political restructuring.

Given the geostrategic importance of the Middle East to the West and the importance of domestic lobbies with interests in the Middle East, Western powers have long favored the status quo, particularly the survival of some of the region's nondemocratic regimes. This is hardly a radical statement, since even former US president George W. Bush admitted as much in justifying his own policies in the region. Washington's funneling of budgetary and military aid to Egypt, Jordan, Lebanon, Yemen, and Morocco throughout the decades of economic crisis reveals a preference for political stability above a pursuit of economic development. And international organizations like the IMF and World Bank were hardly at odds with Western governments in this respect. For instance, the timing and maintenance of IMF and World Bank loans to Algeria, Egypt, Tunisia, and Jordan had little to do with factors arising from economic crisis or performance. Even when these states failed to live up to program requirements, loans and aid continued.[25] Free trade treaties have not fared any better in compelling rulers to fulfill the terms of agreements. Despite a US free trade agreement in 1994 that committed Jordan to trade-union and associative freedom, Washington barely reacted as Jordan's leaders steadily rolled back associative freedoms in the 1990s and 2000s.[26] One conclusion is that Western lenders, like regime elites, are unwilling to impose the kind of conditionality that would politically weaken regional allies. Another conclusion, tied to earlier critiques, is that neoliberal policies are neither growth-inducing nor favorable to engendering greater political participation. It was little surprise, then, that prior to the 2011 uprisings, IMF officials lauded Egypt, Libya, Bahrain, and other countries in the region for their reform agendas and macroeconomic progress.[27]

Even without powerful external patrons, regimes were able to pursue aspects of economic opening while bracketing the political. Iraq in the 1980s and 1990s, Syria in the 1990s, and the UAE in the 2000s each selectively implemented privatization and investment reform with no political adjustment. Indeed, today, according to some measures of economic freedom, and turning the "free markets, free politics" dictum on its head, the countries in the region with the so-called freest economies (Bahrain and the UAE) are among the most politically closed.[28] It may also be the case that regime leaders have learned over time how to navigate economic crises in ways that bolster centralized rule. Crises and the requirements of reform that follow may in theory be a threat to centralized rule, but they may also be opportunities. Rulers, particularly in Jordan, Syria, and Egypt, proved adept throughout the 1980s, 1990s, and 2000s at using crisis and reform to divide the political opposition. Inclusion of some groups and not others, favoritism in redistribution of state resources, and the awarding of monopolies can present tangible obstacles to a unified opposition. Tactically, regimes have also learned from the crises of the 1970s and 1980s to avoid quick and surprising policy turns. For example, Jordan's 1989 austerity protests came in the wake of a sudden government decision to lift subsidies on basic staples. Today, Amman floats such ideas informally, gauges the public reaction, recalibrates, and then ultimately implements change piecemeal.

It is also significant that a number of regimes have gone through hereditary leadership successions without splits or defection. In monarchies as well as republics (Syria, Jordan, and Morocco), sons of previous leaders smoothly transitioned into power, bringing with them newer and younger public-private business elites.[29] While older elites might have been pushed out, their fall or exile was not drastic enough to encourage opposition among the political elite. Regimes have also enhanced intraelite cohesion through the growing role of the military and security institutions in the private econ-

omy. Whereas in the 1970s public sector involvement in the private economy took place through public-private shareholding or state-owned companies, today that involvement is more personal and less transparent.
Military-owned factories in Egypt, retired generals turned real estate developers in Amman, and international firms in the Gulf owned by rulers and
their families constitute new forms of engagement in the region's economies
by public sector and military actors. These new economic conglomerates,
or "militarized welfare states,"[30] straddle domestic and regional markets
and have institutionalized status quo political interests. Following their military or security service, individuals and groups have new access to social
advancement, access that reinforces their loyalty to centralized political
power. Such backroom deals, involving public resources but shielded from
public scrutiny, are anathema to genuine political participation.

It may also be the case that social groups are not manipulated but simply resist aspects of economic liberalization or political decentralization to
protect their own interests. For instance, public sector employees or organized labor may not wish to see changes that would adversely impact their
own financial security. Likewise, private sector elites in the region have
hardly adopted the liberalizing role envisioned by some advocates of neoliberalism. Where private sector actors have gained greater voice in policymaking or come into policy positions as a result of economic reform,
those gains have remained narrow and alliances with other social actors limited. Instead, a reassertion of the private sector has bolstered rather than
weakened authoritarian rule, particularly in the Gulf.[31] While economic reform in theory seeks to reduce webs of patronage and monopoly rents that
ostensibly weigh on economic development and make authoritarian rule
harder, the reality has been quite different. In fact, political patronage networks have been characterized by redesign, adaptation, and selective cap-
turing in the wake of most economic reform. Rather than posing a threat to
politically mediated profits on such things as import licensing, public works
projects, or special subsidies, reform has allowed private sector elites new
rent access and has given them privileges that constrain, not expand, market access for others.[32] Nor have these private actors been simply passive recipients. In the Gulf as well as in the Levant, new groups of private
businesses have expanded through new linkages to state elites and regional
opportunities driven by globalization. These business groups, often based on
family ties or ruling-elite connections, tend to concentrate in the construction, transportation, and services sectors—thus these are not industrialized
or export-oriented private actors. In most cases, these actors have acquiesced or supported limits to political liberalization in their home countries
at the same time that they were benefiting from economic liberalization.
Labor and the middle class all too often paid the price for the narrow gains

arising from the reform. It is likely no coincidence that in addition to the 2011 slogans mentioned at the start of this chapter, large chunks of popular opinion across Tunisia, Egypt, Syria, and Yemen singled out the wealthy cronies of embattled leaders as powerful symbols of what was wrong with their societies.

Whereas income inequality in the Arab world was comparatively low through the 1970s, and increased in the 1980s, there has been relatively little overall change in the decades since. Figure 10.1 measures inequality based on household consumption and does not capture other forms of income and wealth inequality. Some case-study research suggests growing inequality in other facets, within and across countries, in the past two decades.[33] Instead of expanding dynamically and becoming capable of pushing for political participation, the Arab middle class has taken a beating of late. This is due to a number of economic factors, as well as the fact that the middle class is enjoying fewer and fewer opportunities for socioeconomic advancement, upgrading of employment skills, and access to better education. Youth unemployment in the region has been among the highest in the world for decades.[34] Not only has aggregate job creation not kept up with demographic growth, but the quality of those jobs and the labor skills of the youth have not improved much. While population growth is now leveling off, decades of youth frustration with the lack of employment likely fig-

Figure 10.1 Inequality in the Arab World, 1981–2011

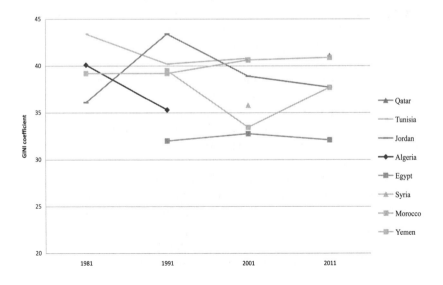

ured in 2011's popular uprisings. Poverty, especially in urban areas, has hardly improved in most countries, and in some has worsened.

Therefore, if we combine the hard-data portrait of stagnation with the more detailed case studies of the decline appearing in every society in the region, there is a perception of increasing levels of inequality—and such a perception may become even more politically significant over time. It was common across the region in the years leading up to the 2011 uprisings to hear complaints about rising prices, especially urban property values and the prices of fuel and of food. As well, global food-price increases in 2010 had a particularly marked effect in some Arab countries, especially Egypt.

Also of consequence has been the weakening and containment of social associations, unions, and other actors who give voice to the demands of the middle and lower working classes for greater participation in economic reform. Another trend that is found regionwide, one that is particularly noticeable in the Gulf, is the use of foreigners rather than domestic citizens for labor in the new private sectors and enterprises. Indeed, aside from garment production in North African countries, Arab labor continues to skew toward nonmanufacturing sectors or the public sector. Even prior to 2011 when facing mobilization against reform policies, regimes were able to contain the protests through legal maneuvers or through outright intimidation by security forces. The failure of regimes to stymie the broad-based public opposition that arose in 2011 will require some future explanation.

The least-understood of the adverse conditions that accompany economic reform are informal markets within and between countries and the effects of persistent violent conflict. While measurement of informal sectors is difficult,[35] most indicators suggest that they have expanded and deepened in the past several decades. And whether they take the form of capital flight, black market labor, smuggling, or systematic public sector corruption, unregulated economies are present to varying degrees throughout the region. The exact causes of this expansion are unclear, though persistent regional conflict, globalization, and even aspects of economic reform may play a role. Clearly some state elites benefit politically and monetarily from these markets. And the presence of large swaths of exchange and employment outside more inclusive sociopolitical institutions can hardly be a positive for linking economic and political reform. For one thing, such informal institutional arrangements can resemble organized criminal networks and persist over decades.[36] In other words, individual actors in these networks see no advantage to change, though the outcomes harm society as a whole. On the other hand, corruption alone may not be an impediment to development, as most scholars acknowledge that development success in South Korea and Taiwan was not corruption-free. As well, there is an argument that informal markets contribute to economic stability and help to raise household incomes where formal employment or state support are lacking. What might be agreed upon is that where informal or corrupt networks enforce exclusivity and contribute to increasing obscurity, political change toward greater inclusion and transparency may be more difficult.

Linked to informal markets are the conditioning effects of persistent regional conflict in the Middle East. The liberalization policies from the 1980s to the 2000s took place within a wide range of intraregional and international conflicts, and such persistent violent conflict has conditioned economic reform and the growth of informal markets in ways that, beyond quantitative observations,[37] we are only beginning to understand. Not only have the political economies of the antagonists been reshaped—as happened to communities in Iraq, Iran, Lebanon, and Palestine—but also the fates of regional bystanders to these conflicts that may or may not have been completely innocent, such as Jordan, Turkey, and the UAE, have been affected. Violent conflict brutalizes communities, scattering those with the means to leave and punishing those who must stay. Particularly in cases of civil or substate violence, development in any sense regresses as local violent control of particular areas of the country overlaps with control of markets. Economic or political reform means little under such conditions, and "postwar" economies and societies seem unable to completely shake off the antidevelopmental legacies.[38] Consequently, networks of certain types of corruption that are reinforced over decades of enduring conflict, even ones that have ceased being violent, can carry long-term detrimental effects.

In light of the uprisings of 2011, it seems clear that the story of failed economic liberalization in the Middle East is not one of continuity or lack of change. Rather, the same factors and dynamics that were blocking liberalization of economic resources were also likely contributing to popular declines in regime support. And while initial levels of reform were compatible with authoritarian rule, that situation might now have changed.

Conclusion

Within the context of authoritarian rule, economic liberalization in the Arab world has not led to greater political participation. Indeed, while recognizing that in some cases political exclusion predated reform, it nevertheless seems clear that weakened political opposition capacities have generally followed economic openings, in varied ways. Yet momentous political events like those in late 2010 and 2011 usually have economic repercussions. In the short term, these have included losses in investment and in the tourism sector in a number of countries. Still, for many there is great optimism that important political change has begun. For that change to lead to more productive and equitable economic development, two issues connected to economic and political reform will have to be addressed. First, international lenders based in Washington continue to extol the virtues of liberal economic reform, while for many in the Arab world this type of reform has largely failed. If political participation deepens in say Egypt and Tunisia, political leaders will likely find it more difficult to adopt whatever policies the IMF and World Bank prescribe. Conversely, given the continued global financial downturn and lack of alternatives, international lenders will be able to punish national leaders who stray from accepted visions of economic reform.[39] Second, many of the political constraints and interests that informed economic development and liberalization efforts in the past remain in place. Political economic change will likely be slow, perhaps much slower than publics are willing to endure. How organized labor and professional associations respond after decades of political acquiescence will be critical. Also consequential will be the response from a private sector accustomed to privileged political access. The experiences of other regions struggling with participatory governance and economic development, Latin America for example, suggest the beginning of a lengthy post–Arab Spring period involving difficult economic adjustments and political setbacks.[40]

Notes

1. Dani Rodrik, "The Poverty of Dictatorship," Al Jazeera English, 10 February 2011; Martin Wolf, "Egypt Has History on Its Side," *Financial Times,* 15 February 2011; Robert B. Zoellick, "The Middle East and North Africa: A New Social Contract for Development," speech at the Peterson Institute for International Economics, Washington, DC, 6 April 2011.

2. Walter Armbrust, "The Revolution Against Neoliberalism," *Jadaliyya,* 23 February 2011, http://www.jadaliyya.com/pages/index/717/the-revolution-against-neoliberalism-; Austin Mackell, "The IMF Versus the Arab Spring," *The Guardian,* 25 May 2011.

3. Seymour Martin Lipset, "Some Social Requisites of Democracy: Economic Development and Political Legitimacy" *American Political Science Review* 53 (March 1959), pp. 69–105.

4. Barrington Moore Jr., *Social Origins of Dictatorship and Democracy: Lord and Peasant in the Making of the Modern World* (Boston: Beacon, 1966).

5. For an application to the Middle East, see Richard Augustus Norton, *Civil Society in the Middle East* (Leiden: Brill, 1996).

6. Dietrich Rueschemeyer, Evelyne Huber Stephens, and John D. Stephens, *Capitalist Development and Democracy* (Chicago: University of Chicago Press, 1992).

7. Charles Tilly, ed., *The Formation of Nation States in Western Europe* (Princeton: Princeton University Press, 1975).

8. Guillermo O'Donnell and Philippe C. Schmitter, *Transitions from Authoritarian Rule: Tentative Conclusions About Uncertain Democracies* (Baltimore: Johns Hopkins University Press, 1986).

9. Ha-Joon Chang, *Bad Samaritans: The Myth of Free Trade and the Secret History of Capitalism* (London: Bloomsbury, 2008).

10. Karl Polanyi, *The Great Transformation: The Political and Economic Origins of Our Time* (Boston: Beacon, 2001).

11. Charles Lindblom, "The Market as Prison," *Journal of Politics* 44, 2 (May 1982).

12. Clement Henry and Robert Springborg, *Globalization and the Politics of Development in the Middle East* (Cambridge: Cambridge University Press, 2001); Robert Vitalis and Steven Heydemann, "War, Keynesianism, and Colonialism: Explaining State-Market Relations in the Postwar Middle East," in Steven Heydemann, ed., *War, Institutions, and Social Change in the Middle East* (Berkeley: University of California Press, 2000).

13. International Monetary Fund, *World Economic Outlook* (Washington, DC, 2003).

14. Alan Richards and John Waterbury, *A Political Economy of the Middle East* (Boulder: Westview, 1990), pp. 238–253.

15. John Waterbury, *Egypt: Burdens of the Past, Options for the Future* (Bloomington: Indiana University Press, 1978).

16. David Seddon, "Austerity Protests in Response to Economic Liberalization in the Middle East," in Tim Niblock and Emma Murphy, eds., *Economic and Political Liberalization in the Middle East* (London: Tauris, 1993).

17. Richards and Waterbury, *A Political Economy of the Middle East,* pp. 240–244.

18. Marwan A. Kardoosh and Riad al-Khouri, *Qualifying Industrial Zones and Sustainable Development in Jordan* (Amman: Jordan Center for Public Policy Research and Dialogue, September 2004).

19. For such success among state-owned enterprises, see Steffen Hertog, "Defying the Resource Curse: Explaining Successful State-Owned Enterprises in Rentier States," *World Politics* 62, 2 (April 2010).

20. Alexander Gerschenkron, *Economic Backwardness in Historical Perspective* (Cambridge MA: Belknap, 1962).

21. Kiren Chaudhry, "The Myths of Market and the Common History of Late Developers," *Politics and Society* 21, 3 (September 1993).

22. David Waldner, *State Building and Late Development* (Ithaca: Cornell University Press, 1999).

23. Eva Bellin, *Stalled Democracy: Capital, Labor, and the Paradox of State-Sponsored Development* (Ithaca: Cornell University Press, 2002).

24. Richard F. Doner, Bryan K. Ritchie, and Dan Slater, "Systemic Vulnerability and the Origins of Developmental States: Northeast and Southeast Asia in Comparative Perspective," *International Organization* 59, 2 (2005).

25. Jane Harrigan and Hamed el-Said, *Aid and Power in the Arab World: World Bank and IMF Policy-Based Lending in the Middle East and North Africa* (Basingstoke: Palgrave Macmillan, 2009).

26. "Justice for All: The Struggle for Workers Rights in Jordan" (Washington, DC: American Center for International Labor Solidarity, 2005), pp. 48–50.

27. Pierre Briancon and John Foley, "IMF Reviews Praise Libya, Egypt, and

Other Nations," *New York Times,* 22 February 2011.

28. Clement Henry and Robert Springborg, *Globalization and the Politics of Development in the Middle East* (Cambridge: Cambridge University Press, 2001), p. 196.

29. Michael Herb, *All in the Family: Absolutism, Revolution, and Democracy in the Middle Eastern Monarchies* (Albany: State University of New York Press, 1999).

30. Anne Marie Baylouny, "Militarizing Welfare: Neo-liberalism and Jordanian Policy," *Middle East Journal* 62, 2 (Spring 2008).

31. Pete Moore, "Rentier Fiscal Crisis and Regime Stability in the Middle East: Business and State in the Gulf," *Studies in Comparative International Development* 31, 1 (Spring 2002).

32. Steven Heydemann, ed., *Networks of Privilege in the Middle East: The Politics of Economic Reform Revisited* (Basingstoke: Palgrave Macmillan, 2004).

33. For examples, see Timothy Mitchell, "Dreamland: The Neoliberalism of Your Desires," *Middle East Report* 210 (Spring 1999); Henry and Springborg, *Globalization and the Politics of Development in the Middle East.*

34. International Labour Office, *Global Employment Trends for Youth* (Geneva, August 2010), http://www.ilo.org/public/english/region/afpro/addisababa/pdf/getforyouth.pdf.

35. Edgard L. Feige and Katarina Ott, eds., *Underground Economies in Transition: Unrecorded Activity, Tax Evasion, Corruption, and Organized Crime* (Aldershot: Ashgate, 1999); Serdar Sayan, ed., *Economic Performance in the Middle East and North Africa: Institutions, Corruption, and Reform* (London: Routledge, 2009).

36. Diego Gambetta, "Mafia: The Price of Distrust," in Diego Gambetta, ed., *Trust: Making and Breaking Cooperative Relations* (London: Blackwell, 1990).

37. Paul Collier et al., *Breaking the Conflict Trap: Civil War and Development Policy* (Washington, DC: World Bank, 2003); Dani Rodrik, "Where Did All the Growth Go? External Shocks, Social Conflict, and Growth Collapses," *Journal of Economic Growth* 4, 4 (December 1999).

38. Reinoud Leenders, "Public Means to Private Ends: State Building and Power in Post-War Lebanon," in Eberhard Kienle, ed., *Politics from Above, Politics from Below: The Middle East in the Age of Economic Reform* (London: Saqi, 2003).

39. Missy Ryan, "Changes May Spur Middle East Growth If Populism Set Aside," Reuters, 16 April 2011.

40. See, Marcus Kurtz, "The Dilemmas of Democracy in the Open Economy: Lessons from Latin America," *World Politics* 56, 2 (January 2004); Moises Arce and Paul T. Bellinger, "Low Intensity Democracy Revisited: The Effects of Economic Liberalization on Political Activity in Latin America," *World Politics* 60, 1 (October 2007).

11

The New Arab Media

Who would have thought that a picture of a burning Mohamed Bouazizi, captured by a mobile phone camera and relayed through the Internet, would spark anti-regime upheavals throughout much of the Arab world? That bloggers and Al Jazeera's televised coverage of the Tunisian uprising would help propel Zine el-Abidine Ben Ali's humiliating exit from the country? That a Facebook invitation to an anti-regime demonstration in Egypt on 25 January 2011 would contribute to mass protests that ultimately forced Hosni Mubarak out of office? Or that images of regime brutality against protesters in Syria taken by mobile phone cameras would embolden demonstrators to confront a brutal security machine? Such is the change that has transpired in the new Arab media environment.

The mushrooming of terrestrial and satellite channels, Internet sites, Twitter users, Facebook groups, and bloggers has created a veritable revolution in communications technology in the Arab world. Gone are the days when Arab regimes monopolized access to information and determined what their publics saw on television and read in print. The new communications technology offers Arab audiences different sources of information and has created virtual space for deliberation and anti-regime organization. Arab regimes that sought to discipline their citizens by projecting the image of an omniscient and omnipresent leader have been exposed as less than all-powerful by civil society activists.[1] Officials who assumed immunity from public sarcasm have become the subject of text-message jokes.[2]

Studies of the new Arab media have tended to debate its democratization potential and the extent to which it has produced a novel Arab identity. Some have suggested that the new Arab media, with its emphasis on debating taboo topics, is creating a new, critical, and articulate Arab public sphere. This, in turn, is "building the underpinnings of a more liberal, pluralistic politics."[3] According to this optimistic view, the new Arab media is producing a new kind of Arabism held together by a feeling of a common Arab destiny that transcends state frontiers,[4] and a new Arab public mobilized not on the basis of rigid ideological platforms but rather around specific policy issues—such as the Arab-Israeli conflict, US policies in the Middle

East, and socioeconomic and political demands.[5] Others have taken a more skeptical view of the democratizing effects of the telecommunication and media revolution in the Arab world. Although they have acknowledged the greater pluralism engendered by the new Arab media, they have warned that authoritarian Arab regimes have assimilated the new Arab media into a larger set of "authoritarian strategies of governance" aimed at "upgrading authoritarianism in the Arab world."[6] According to this view, the new Arab media has served to impede rather than promote genuine political reforms and democratization.

Such binary positions fail to capture the very different impacts the new media has had on politics in the Arab world, however. It is more useful to disaggregate the new Arab media environment, distinguishing between its diverse components and their varied impact on politics in different parts of the Arab world. Though not a cause of the recent uprisings and regime changes in the Arab world, major segments of the new Arab media have played an enabling role in this process. In Tunisia and Egypt, Facebook groups and bloggers served as virtual spaces for deliberation, organization, and mobilization before the outbreak of popular uprisings. Twitter and Facebook supplied avenues of information and communication despite regime censorship once the uprisings began. YouTube exposed the brutality of authoritarian regimes against unarmed demonstrators. When these regimes pulled the plug on cellular phones and Internet technology in a bid to cut off communications between protesters, and between them and the outside world, many—but not all—satellite stations doubled as communication channels between protesters in different parts of the country, and as platforms to the outside world.

This chapter traces the origins of the new Arab media and its breadth and varied permutations. It examines the media's role in recent popular upheavals, underscoring the arguments made about demonstration effects and regional permeability in Chapter 5. On the other hand, it also highlights the limitations of the media and its potentially detrimental impact on sectarian relations in the region. The chapter then surveys the different legal and extralegal techniques that authoritarian Arab regimes have used to monitor and control the new media environment. It closes with an evaluation of the new Arab media's effects on democratization and the making of a different kind of regional permeability.

Channels of a New Permeability

Arab satellite broadcasting is a product of regional wars. It began with the launch of the Egyptian Satellite Channel (ESC) on 12 December 1990, in the immediate aftermath of Iraq's August 1990 invasion of Kuwait. The Egyptian government opted to align with Kuwait against Iraq, and dispatched Egyptian troops to the Gulf. The ESC was established to "boost the morale of Egyptian troops in the Gulf" and offer them an alternative media message to that disseminated by Iraq.[7] The ESC was followed by the London-based, Saudi-owned Middle East Broadcasting Centre (MBC) in 1991. While the 1990–1991 Gulf War was the catalyst for the launch of these two stations, it also had the larger effect of underscoring the need for a new kind of news coverage, one that was both regionally indigenous and based on the twenty-four-hour news format, in large measure a result of CNN's successful real-time coverage of the war. This led to the birth of the Al Jazeera satellite news channel on 1 November 1996 and the concomitant transformation of the Arab media environment.

Al Jazeera's origins can be traced to two overlapping developments: the rise to power in Qatar of a young, modernizing ruler, Shaikh Hamad bin Khalifa, and the collapse of BBC Arabic TV following editorial disagreements with its financial sponsor, Saudi Arabia. Al Jazeera inherited the latter's staff and served as springboard for Qatar's new domestic and regional ambitions.[8] The satellite station went on to set new standards for news reporting and talk shows in the region. Its reporters were ideologically involved and covered the news with emotional engagement, a far cry from the existing Soviet-style, state-controlled Arab media in which anchorwomen and anchormen read out bland, government-censored statements. Al Jazeera current affairs host Faysal al-Qasem's histrionics aside, programs such as *al-Ittijah al-Mu'akes* (The Opposite Direction) and *al-Ra'y al-Akhar* (The Other Opinion) introduced a new, combative spirit to political talk shows, where opponents defended their viewpoints passionately and often polemically, without the usual niceties associated with state-owned stations. Opposition figures and, to the Arab public's initial shock, Israeli officials, once banned from Arab television stations, now became part of the guest roster for the new satellite media.

Al Jazeera's reporting style has not come without costs, however. It was banned in public places for airing interviews with Arab opposition figures and incurred the wrath of Arab regimes when the station's local bureaus uncovered domestic government abuse. In January 2011, Palestinian Authority (PA) president Mahmoud Abbas accused the station of sabotaging his political career when it posted leaked documents exposing concessions made by PA negotiators to their Israeli counterparts concerning Jerusalem and the Palestinian refugees.[9] Perhaps the deadliest attack against the station took place in Libya as Al Jazeera covered the popular uprising against the regime. On 12 March 2011, pro-regime gunmen ambushed Al Jazeera's news crew, killing its chief cameraman and wounding another journalist.

With an estimated audience of 50 million viewers for some shows, Al Jazeera towered over other satellite stations, such as MBC, the Arab News Network (ANN), the Lebanese Broadcasting Corporation (LBC), the Saudi-owned Arab Radio and Television network (ART) and Orbit, and Abu Dhabi TV. It rose to prominence in the Arab world with its coverage of the US sanctions against Iraq and the second Palestinian intifada in late 2000. Its debut on the international stage was a function of its coverage of the 11 September 2001 terrorist attacks and the subsequent US-led military campaign against Taliban-controlled Afghanistan.[10] Its unorthodox reporting, but especially its exclusive airing of Osama bin Laden's taped speeches, led some commentators to charge that Al Jazeera was anti-American and that it "deliberately fans the flames of Muslim outrage."[11] The station's coverage of the US invasion and subsequent occupation of Iraq prompted a storm of protest from Washington.[12] The network was not intimidated, however, and continued to cover news in a new kind of way, free from the taboos that bedeviled the Arab media of past decades. This is especially true of the station's opposition to the US invasion and occupation of Iraq in 2003, the pro-Hezbollah coverage of Israel's July 2006 war against Lebanon, its coverage of Israel's war against the Gaza Strip in 2008–2009, and the airtime it dedicated to covering the colonial practices of Israeli settlers in the West Bank and East Jerusalem.

Nothing compares to Al Jazeera's coverage of the popular uprisings that swept across the Arab world in 2011, however. Its moving reporting of anti-regime protests and its airing of demonstration footage that was otherwise banned on national television galvanized popular sentiment and accelerated regime change in Tunisia. Little wonder that Tunisians celebrated Ben Ali's departure with "Shukran lil-Jazeera" (Thank You Al Jazeera) placards.[13] A similar dynamic transpired in Egypt, from which Al Jazeera ran a continuous, often live, reporting cycle. Egyptian authorities responded by closing down the station's Cairo office and suspending its transmission on the Nilesat satellite network. The station switched to an alternative bandwidth and resumed its riveting coverage, at a time when Egyptian government terrestrial and satellite channels were describing the protests as the work of foreign actors bent on destabilizing the country.[14] By the time Mubarak stepped down on 11 February 2011, Al Jazeera had amplified the Arab regional demonstration effect that triggered popular protests and reformist demands from Morocco to Oman. Protesters celebrating Mubarak's departure in Tahrir Square raised placards that read "Shukran Tunis, Shukran al-Jazeera" (Thank You Tunisia, Thank You Al Jazeera).

New social media played an enabling role in these popular uprisings. Internet use in the Arab world was rising steadily well before the Arab Spring,

Table 11.1   Internet Use in the Arab World, 2010

	Number of Internet Users per 100 Inhabitants
Bahrain	55.0
Egypt	26.7
Iraq	2.5
Jordan	38.0
Kuwait	38.3
Lebanon	31.0
Libya	14.0
Morocco	49.0
Oman	62.0
Palestinian Authority	37.4
Saudi Arabia	41.0
Syria	20.7
Tunisia	36.8
United Arab Emirates	78.0
Yemen	12.4

Source: International Telecommunication Union (ITU), "Information and Communication Technologies (ICT) Statistics Database," 2010, http://www.itu.int/ITUD/ICTEYE/ Indicators/Indicators.aspx#.

whether for political, social, religious, or personal purposes (see Table 11.1).[15] Its utility varied, however. While the late Sayyed Muhammad Husayn Fadlallah's website Bayyanat expounded a modern interpretation of Islam and preached Sunni-Shiite coexistence,[16] radical Salafi groups use the Internet to spread anti-US and anti-Western ideas, and to counter what they describe as an Iranian-orchestrated invasion by the "Rafida" (a pejorative Wahhabi label for the Shiites) of Muslim societies.[17] Terrorism manuals and graphic videos of terrorist attacks and executions are posted on jihadist Internet sites as part of an al-Qaeda strategy to lure new recruits.[18] Facebook is also deployed in Sunni-Shiite sectarian battles in Lebanon, Iraq, Kuwait, and Bahrain, with devastating effects on national unity.[19]

Internet sites, blogs, Twitter, and Facebook are most effective as sources of alternative information, social mobilization, and political protest. The Internet is a virtual space rallying otherwise unaffiliated opposition groups around specific events and objectives. As the political activity of the Kefaya movement during Egypt's 2005 elections demonstrated, the alliance of activists and bloggers coalescing and communicating via the Internet proved an effective tool for political mobilization and contestation.[20] Bloggers have exposed police brutality and regime abuses against opposition figures or ethnic and sectarian minorities;[21] they have redefined everyday engagements with politics and demystified social taboos, making it difficult for Arab regimes to silence dissident voices.[22]

Table 11.2 Type and Degree of Internet Filtering in the Arab World, 2010

	Political	Social	Conflict/Security	Internet Tools
Algeria	No evidence	No evidence	No evidence	No evidence
Bahrain	Substantial	Selective	No evidence	Selective
Egypt	No evidence	No evidence	No evidence	No evidence
Iraq	No evidence	No evidence	No evidence	No evidence
Jordan	Selective	No evidence	No evidence	No evidence
Libya	Substantial	No evidence	No evidence	No evidence
Morocco	No evidence	No evidence	Selective	Selective
Oman	No evidence	Pervasive	No evidence	Substantial
Saudi Arabia	Substantial	Pervasive	Selective	Substantial
Syria	Pervasive	Selective	Selective	Substantial
Tunisia	Pervasive	Pervasive	Selective	Substantial
United Arab Emirates	Selective	Pervasive	Selective	Substantial
Yemen	Selective	Pervasive	Selective	Substantial

Source: Source: OpenNet Initiative, "Country Profiles," http://opennet.net/research/profiles.
Note: Spectrum of filtering: no evidence, suspected, selective, substantial, pervasive.

Unsurprisingly, Arab regimes invested substantial resources in censorship technologies. Table 11.2 shows the type and scope of Internet filtering in the Arab world before the 2011 uprisings. Governments and Internet service providers censored a range of material considered by Arab governments to be politically sensitive—especially criticism of leaders and regime members that was deemed morally offensive or socially impermissible. Political filtering has been most pervasive in Syria, Saudi Arabia, and Ben Ali's Tunisia, targeting opposition voices and websites publicizing human rights violations. Social filtering, on the other hand, is widespread in the Gulf countries and targets pornography and lesbian, gay, bisexual, and transgender sites.

Arab governments introduced Internet-specific laws and cybercrime laws to regulate and monitor Internet traffic. In 2007, the United Arab Emirates (UAE) promulgated a national Internet law that criminalized hacking and any Internet activity that involves breaches of privacy, accessing sensitive government information, and threats to public order.[23] In January 2008, Saudi Arabia introduced new legal provisions criminalizing the use of the Internet in support of terrorism and in breach of the kingdom's social mores and public order. The Algerian government introduced new measures in 2008 requiring Internet providers to obtain new licenses and store Internet correspondence for at least one year.[24] Owners of Internet cafes in a number of Arab states are required to register with the government, install stealth censorship cameras inside cyber cafes, and maintain registries of the personal information of cafe users along with details of their online activities.[25]

Bloggers in the Arab world are harassed by the state's coercive agencies. In 2009 the New York City–based Committee to Protect Journalists placed Syria, Saudi Arabia, Ben Ali's Tunisia, and Mubarak's Egypt on its list of "10 worst countries to be a blogger," ranking them third, fifth, seventh, and tenth respectively.[26] This trend continues after the Arab uprisings. Many bloggers are incarcerated or physically assaulted because of their critical writings. Even tweets have incurred upon some the wrath of state authorities.[27] Independent Web-based newspapers are blocked by government authorities when they cross regime-delineated red lines. Criticism by the London-based Saudi e-newspaper Elaph.com of the kingdom's opaque religious rulings, and the daring insinuation that not even the kingdom's founder should be immune from criticism, incurred a two-year ban against its Internet site.[28] The ban was later lifted in February 2009 by order of the Saudi royal court.

These censorship techniques ultimately failed to prevent the new social media from playing a mobilizing, triggering, and momentum-maintaining role in the 2011 popular uprisings. New social media served to connect protesters and motivate them against authoritarian regimes.[29] In Tunisia, Facebook groups and Internet blogs were the primary organizers of anti-regime demonstrations, because the regime controlled almost all other media outlets in the country. Once popular demonstrations commenced on 17 December 2010, Facebook groups such as Tunisie[30] and Takriz[31] displayed images of the regime's thuggish tactics and the resilience of the demonstrators; they also served as a means of information-sharing and coordination among the protesters.[32] Twitter and mobile phones turned every protester into a roaming reporter, allowing information-sharing and uploading of images to the Internet in real time. Al Jazeera then beamed these Facebook and Twitter posts to captivated audiences across the Arab world. The daily *La Presse* best captured this Facebook effect in Tunisia. Commenting on Beji Caid Essebsi's appointment as prime minister in March 2011, a cartoon declared: "In my opinion, our real prime minister is called Facebook!"[33]

Egypt's Facebook-based groups, such as Harakat 6 April (6 April Youth Movement)[34] and Kulena Khaled Sa'eed (We Are All Khalid Said),[35] inspired by nonviolent struggles, had spent years mobilizing followers on behalf of peaceful democratic change in Egypt using daily blogs and online democratic participation exercises.[36] Galvanized by the success of the Tunisian uprising, and borrowing its slogans, they called through their Facebook walls for an anti-regime demonstration on Police Day on 25 January 2011. To the regime's shock, the Facebook invitation avalanched into a popular uprising that overthrew Mubarak, set Egypt on a new course, and boomeranged throughout the Arab world. Moreover, all subsequent "Day of

Rage" (Yawm al-Ghadab) calls throughout the Arab world were announced via Facebook.

To be sure, the new social media may not have caused these upheavals. Nevertheless, it provided the "connective muscle," the networking, organization, and information-sharing that promotes self-empowerment in the face of seemingly omnipotent authoritarian regimes, thus triggering the kind of collective action that overwhelmed regime security agencies.[37] As Wael Ghonim, founder of the "We Are All Khalid Said" Facebook group, later commented: "If there [were] no social networks," Egypt's revolution "would have never been sparked. . . . Without Facebook, without Twitter, without Google, without YouTube, this would have never happened."[38]

Politics of the New Arab Media

The new Arab media is not a monolithic body, nor is it immune from direct or indirect political influence. As Table 11.3 shows, almost all major Arab satellite stations are either directly or indirectly affiliated with Arab regimes or with individuals connected to those regimes, with Saudi Arabia enjoying substantial influence over many stations. This has led to self-imposed, and in some cases regime-imposed, limits on their coverage. It has also generated proxy interstate and intrastate political battles camouflaged as media contests. This nexus of political and media battles is best expressed in the tug-of-war between Al Jazeera and Al Arabiya.

Al Jazeera's launch and content expressed the new Qatari regime's determination to legitimize its geopolitical choices and balance Islamic cultural influences from Saudi Arabia and Iran.[39] It was founded by a Qatari royal decree with a startup budget of $137 million and continues to be subsidized by the royal court at a cost of about $300 million annually. The Qatari regime uses religious preaching on Al Jazeera, namely Mufti of Qatar Shaikh Yusuf al-Qaradawi's program *al-Shari'a wa-l-Hayat* (Islamic Law and Life), to shore up its Islamic credentials and insulate the emirate from Salafi criticism. Airing reporting critical of the United States aims to cover up Qatar's special military relationship with Washington. Moreover, the station's choice of themes and guests is heavily influenced by Doha's foreign policy choices. For example, when Qatari-Saudi relations were at a nadir, Saudi dissidents were regular guests on Al Jazeera talk shows, and the station aired documentaries critical of the Saudi royal family. In 2002, Saudi Arabia recalled its ambassador from Doha to protest Al Jazeera's broadcast of a debate pertaining to Saudi Arabia's position on the Palestinian question that contained criticism of the Saudi royal family. But when amicable relations between the two states were restored, criticism of Saudi domestic and foreign policies ended on Al Jazeera, and Saudi Arabia returned its ambassador to Doha in March 2008.[40]

Al Arabiya, which was launched from Dubai Media City in 2003 with Saudi backing, to counter Al Jazeera's media war against Riyadh and legitimize the latter's geopolitical policies, is deployed for similar political ends. By the time Abdel Rahman al-Rahsed, a veteran Saudi journalist close to Saudi king Abdullah bin Abdulaziz and having staunchly pro-US ideological predilections,[41] assumed the helm at Al Arabiya, the station had taken a blatantly anti-Iranian, anti-Hezbollah, anti-Hamas, and, after the assassination of Lebanese prime minister Rafiq al-Hariri on 14 February 2005,

Table 11.3 Arab Satellite Television Stations and Their Political Orientation

	Political Orientation	Political Sponsor
Abu Dhabi TV (United Arab Emirates)	Abu Dhabi	Abu Dhabi
Arabic News Broadcast (ANB) (Lebanon/United Kingdom)	Semi-independent	Nazmi Aouchi and Boutros Khoury
Al Aqsa (Palestine)	Hamas	Hamas
Arab Radio and Television (ART)	Saudi Arabia	Shaikh Saleh Kamel
Al Arabiya (United Arab Emirates)	Saudi Arabia	al-Walid al-Ibrahim and Prince 'Abdel Aziz bin Fahd
Egyptian Satellite Channel (ESC)	Egypt	Egyptian government
Future News (Lebanon)	Saudi Arabia	Saad al-Hariri
Future TV (Lebanon)	Saudi Arabia	Saad al-Hariri
Al Hurrah (Free)	United States	US administration
Al Jadeed (New TV) (Lebanon)	Independent	Shaikh Hamad bin Jassim bin Jabr al-Thani
Al Jazeera (Qatar)	Qatar	Shaikh Hamad bin Jassim bin Jabr al-Thani
Lebanese Broadcasting Corporation-SAT (LBC-SAT)	Saudi Arabia	Prince al-Walid bin Talal
Al Manar (Lebanon)	Iran/Syria	Hezbollah
Middle East Broadcasting Centre (MBC)	Saudi Arabia	al-Walid al-Ibrahim and Prince 'Abdel Aziz bin Fahd
National Broadcasting Network (NBN) (Amal Movement, Lebanon)	Syria	Nabih Berri
Nile Television Network (NTN)	Egypt	Egyptian government
Orbit[a]	Saudi Arabia	Prince Khaled bin Abdallah bin Abdel Rahman
Orange TV (OTV) (Lebanon)	Free Patriotic Movement	Michel 'Awn
Al Quds (Palestine)	Hamas	Hamas
Al Ra'i (Kuwait)	Semi-independent	Semi-independent

Source: Author interviews with Lebanese and Arab journalists, Beirut, 2011; Mamoun Fandy, *(Un)Civil War of Words: Media and Politics in the Arab World* (London: Praeger Security International, 2007), pp. 16–18.

Note: a. Orbit Group and the Dubai-based, Kuwaiti-owned Showtime Arabia announced their merger on 12 July 2009, thus consolidating the region's pay-television satellite industry.

anti-Syrian position. Al Arabiya responded in kind to Al Jazeera's campaign against Saudi Arabia, reporting on Qatar's secret liaisons with Israel, its special military relationship with the United States, and the scandals of the Qatari royal family. It has also played a key role in justifying US policies in the Middle East to Arab audiences. It was the first station to broadcast the death of Abu Musab al-Zarqawi on 7 June 2006, and its coverage of post-Saddam Iraq has earned it the wrath of militant Sunni groups.[42] Al Arabiya's critical coverage of Tehran's domestic and regional politics put it on a collision course with Iranian authorities.[43] Its more than provocative reporting of Hezbollah's takeover of predominantly Sunni West Beirut caused the pro-Shiite NBN television station to label Al Arabiya as "al-'Ibriya" (the Hebrew one).

Qatar's and Saudi Arabia's use of media wars to wage proxy political battles is demonstrated in the manner that Al Jazeera and Al Arabiya report upon and interpret news stories.[44] Whether it is covering domestic politics in Lebanon, Israel's July 2006 war against Lebanon, intra-Palestinian squabbles, terrorist attacks against US and other coalition troops in Iraq and Afghanistan, or the Israeli invasion of Gaza in December 2008–January 2009, Al Arabiya and Al Jazeera color their reporting with the political interests and agendas of their financial and political sponsors—Saudi Arabia and Qatar respectively.

This politicized coverage was displayed live during the 2011 popular uprisings. As mentioned earlier, Al Jazeera's emotional coverage of events in Tunisia fueled the momentum of the anti–Ben Ali crowds and generated a demonstration effect across the Arab world. On the other hand, Al Arabiya reacted coldly and belatedly to the Tunisian upheavals. The contrast between the two satellite stations was exposed patently in their coverage of Egypt's popular demonstrations.

Beaming a round-the-clock image of the demonstrators in Tahrir Square, Al Jazeera focused on people power, the number and steadfastness of the demonstrators, and the scope of the anti-Mubarak opposition throughout Egypt. The station also aired live reports and interviews from Tahrir Square in support of the demonstrators and showed Internet footage exposing the brutality of the security forces and pro-regime thugs. In contrast, when Al Jazeera was broadcasting night images of hundreds of thousands of demonstrators in Tahrir Square, Al Arabiya's camera zoomed in on an empty section of Cairo's Nile Boulevard. Randa Abul 'Azm, Al Arabiya's Cairo reporter, preferred to discuss acts of looting and civil disorder rather than the demands of the protesters, and urged people to clear the square and return to their homes in a bid to project a pro-regime air of normalcy in the country. While Al Jazeera hosted opposition figures and granted Yusuf al-Qaradawi ample time to denounce Mubarak, Al Arabiya's guests were almost all regime apologists who tried to downplay the effects of the "crisis."[45] When Hafiz al-Mirazi, host of Al Arabiya's political show *Studio Cairo,* voiced his desire to dedicate an episode to discuss the implications of Egypt's upheavals on Saudi Arabia, his show was abruptly suspended.[46]

This contrast in coverage was a function of regime calculations in Riyadh and Doha. Saudi Arabia feared the domino effect that a repeat of the Tunisian scenario in Egypt might have, while Qatar wanted to polish its Arab nationalist credentials, settle old diplomatic scores with Cairo, and project itself as leader of a nascent Arab order. Nevertheless, when anti-regime demonstrations erupted in Bahrain on 14 February 2011, Al Jazeera's coverage was subdued. Furthermore, when Bahraini security forces committed a massacre against peaceful demonstrators in Pearl Square on 17 February 2011, Al Jazeera opted not to show footage uploaded on Facebook. Instead, it broadcast images of an orderly army deployment in Manama's empty streets. Nor did the station display its usual pro-people coverage when Gulf Cooperation Council (GCC), but mainly Saudi, troops intervened in Bahrain to prop up the kingdom's minority-Sunni monarchy. Covering popular upheavals in faraway Tunisia, Egypt, Libya, or Syria was one thing, but covering Shiite-led demonstrations against a Sunni minority regime in a GCC member state was an entirely different calculus. In this case, Al Jazeera opted to place Gulf regime security and solidarity above professional standards, thus undermining its credibility substantially. Similar calculations shaped Al Arabiya's coverage of anti-regime demonstrations in Syria, Bahrain, and Saudi Arabia. Although the satellite station spearheaded coverage of the uprising in Syria, and was even accused of editing some of its broadcast footage to exaggerate the regime's troubles,[47] it nevertheless was mute about Saudi troop deployments in the kingdom's Shiite-populated Eastern province and the Bahraini regime's bloody clampdown against the opposition. Al Arabiya's and Al Jazeera's coverage of the Syrian uprising reflect Riyadh's and Doha's geopolitical convergence in favor of regime change in Damascus.

Nor has satellite broadcasting been immune from government intervention and censorship. Although privately owned satellite stations ostensibly possess a wider margin of freedom than public ones, regimes have employed an array of legal and extralegal measures to "minimize citizens' exposure to competing constructions of political reality" through satellite stations.[48] Led by Mubarak's Egypt and Saudi Arabia, and under the guise of regulating satellite transmission, Arab governments—with the notable exception of Qatar and Lebanon—adopted on 12 February 2008 a charter outlining "principles for regulating satellite broadcasting transmission in the Arab world."[49] Despite affirming the freedom of satellite information and competition, the charter shields Arab regimes and heads of state from criticism; it also empowers Arab governments to suspend the transmission of satellite stations judged (by state authorities) to be in contravention of the charter's stipulations. For example, Article 4, Section 5, of the charter commits broadcasters "not to adversely affect social peace and national unity and the public order and general propriety." Similarly, Article 6, Section 9, calls upon satellite broadcasters to "commit to the religious and ethical values of Arab society." Most important, however, Article 7, Section 4, calls upon satellite stations and providers to respect the national sovereignty of every state and "to refrain from insulting its leaders and national and religious figures." Finally, Article 13 makes satellite broadcasting provisional on obtaining a license from the appropriate local authorities and empowers these authorities to suspend the license of any satellite station deemed by state authorities to be in contravention of the charter's regulations. Clearly the loose and open-ended terminology adopted in the charter places satellite stations and providers at the mercy of the state.

Arab regimes also employ extralegal measures to control the content of satellite stations. The privatization of satellite broadcasting is both partial and selective, serving regime interests in collaboration with dominant transnational media corporations.[50] Table 11.3 maps out the affinity between new media and financial and political power in the Arab world. The interlocking business and financial relations between satellite station owners, government bodies, and regime members allow the latter substantial veto power over the content of satellite broadcasting.

Pitfalls of the New Arab Media

The politicization of the new Arab media has had an especially pernicious impact on postwar Lebanon and postinvasion Iraq. A 1994 audiovisual law that organized broadcasting in postwar Lebanon followed clientalistic and neopatrimonial lines, dividing the media space into sectarian fiefdoms. As detailed in Tables 11.3 (on page 241) and 11.4, almost all postwar television stations in Lebanon are mouthpieces for local sectarian leaders and serve the geopolitical interests of their respective sect's external patron.

During the 1990–2005 Syrian era in Lebanon, most television stations avoided crossing Syrian red lines. Recalcitrant ones were either intimidated into submitting to the Syrian order or shut down. The Syrian army's withdrawal from Lebanon on 26 April 2005 following Hariri's assassination released television stations from the grip of Syrian and Lebanese security services. Yet in the subsequent domestic and regional struggle over Lebanon, television stations emerged as vehicles for sectarian incitement. They became mere extensions of sects, playing an instrumental role in "fan-

Table 11.4 Lebanese Satellite Television Stations and Their Sectarian and Political Orientations

	Sectarian Orientation	Political Orientation
Arabic News Broadcast (ANB)	Independent	None
Future TV	Sunni	Pro–Saudi Arabia and United States
Lebanese Broadcasting Corporation International (LBCI)	Maronite	Pro–Saudi Arabia and United States
Al Manar	Shiite	Pro–Iran and Syria
Murr TV (MTV)	Greek Orthodox	Pro–Saudi Arabia and United States
National Broadcasting Network (NBN)	Shiite	Pro-Syria
New TV	Independent	None
Orange TV (OTV)	Maronite	None
Télé Liban	State television	State television
Télé Lumiere	Christian	None

Source: Author interviews with Lebanese and Arab journalists, Beirut, 2011.

ning the flames of sectarianism"[51] and demonizing each group's sectarian or religious "other." Every station broadcasts programs and covers the news in a manner that reflects its own sectarian vision and definition of Lebanon and legitimizes the regional policies of its sect's external allies. During Hezbollah's violent military takeover of West Beirut in May 2008, it went as far as closing down the Sunni Future Movement's television and radio outlets. This exacerbated Sunni-Shiite tensions to the breaking point, but also underscored media power as a tool of sectarian and political agitation. Far from rallying the Lebanese around common national interests, the media have contributed to the "re-feudalization of the public sphere"[52] in the post-Syria phase. Lebanon's marketplace of ideas has thus failed to promote democratic citizenship norms and civic peace. This has hardened sectarian tensions, especially among Sunnis and Shiites, and exposed Lebanon to further external manipulation.

The media scene in post-Saddam Iraq has experienced similar dynamics. Satellite television stations in Iraq (see Table 11.5) have mushroomed since the collapse of Saddam's regime, reflecting the country's overlapping sectarian, ethnic, and political fault lines. These stations cover events selectively, and with a heavy dose of sectarian interpretation, rather than targeting national audiences. For example, on the day after the 22 February 2006 bombing of a Shiite shrine in Samarra, Shiite-affiliated television stations focused on the damage to the shrine caused by the attack and on Shiites suffering under Saddam's rule, while Sunni-affiliated stations covered retaliatory Shiite attacks against Sunnis. As in Lebanon, this type of sectarian broadcasting serves to harden sectarian fissures and mobilization.

Disseminating conservative religious views is another pitfall of the new Arab media. Salafi preaching on satellite television is increasing substantially, led by the popular Saudi-owned Al Nass (People) network of stations; the Al Rahma (Mercy) station, owned by the charismatic Salafi preacher Shaikh Mohammad Hassan; the Al Majd (Glory) station, which is the primary religious satellite channel in Saudi Arabia and is funded by Saudi businessman Abdul Rahman al-Hmaymri; in addition to the popular Islamist Iqraa (Read) station and the Al Resalah (Message) station.[53] In the ongoing battle of ideas in the Arab world, Salafi satellite television serves to defend a puritanical interpretation of Islam and insulate Sunni societies from purported Shiite proselytizing. Shiite satellite stations broadcasting in Arabic, such as Al Kawthar (Iran), Al Anwar (Kuwait), and Al Zahra (Lebanon), also cater to the sectarian tastes of their viewers.

The politicization of Arab satellite broadcasting has affected popular talk shows and Ramadan dramas. While the 2007 Ramadan drama *Al-Malek Farouq* (King Farouq) was made available on many satellite stations, the equally popular 2008 Ramadan drama *Nasser* was ignored by Gulf satellite stations as well as by Egypt's terrestrial stations—which is ironic given that these terrestrial stations were started during Gamal Abdul Nasser's presidency. It was provided to Egyptian audiences only on the encrypted Nile Drama satellite station, with many of the episodes aired in mute mode. This

Table 11.5 Iraqi Satellite Television Stations by Sectarian and Political Orientations

	Sectarian Orientation	Political Orientation
ATB	Kurdish	Kurdistan Communist Party
AhluBayt	Shiite	Ayatollah Hadi al-Modarresi
Ashur (Baghdad, California)	Assyrian	Assyrian Democratic Party
Babel	Sunni	Iraqi Front for National Dialogue
Baghdad	Sunni	Iraqi Islamic Party
Baghdadia	Sunni	Private
Al Forat	Shiite	Islamic Supreme Council of Iraq
Ghadeer	Shiite	Higher Council of the Islamic Revolution
Kurdistan	Kurdish	Kurdistan Democratic Party
Al Huriyya	Kurdish	Patriotic Union of Kurdistan
Al Iraqiyya	Shiite	Pro-government
Al Masar	Shiite	Islamic Da'wa Party
Patriotic Union of Kurdistan (PUK)	Kurdish	Patriotic Union of Kurdistan
Al Salam	Shiite	Pro–Muqtada al-Sadr
Turkmeneli	Turkoman	Iraqi Turkmen Front

Source: Paul Cochrane, "The 'Lebanonization' of the Iraqi Media: An Overview of Iraq's Television Landscape," *Transnational Broadcasting Studies* 16 (2006), http://www.tbsjournal.com/Cochrane.html.

is because the moderate Arab states were engaged in a geopolitical contest with their pro-resistance counterparts at the time and neither the Gulf monarchs nor the Mubarak regime wanted contemporary audiences to draw comparisons with Nasser's Arab nationalist era. They were willing to countenance a rosy interpretation of King Farouq's times, however. Another example of government interference with Arab satellite broadcasting is when Hamdi Qandil's popular show *Qalam Rasas* (Pencil) was pulled off Dubai TV in early 2009 after its host defended Hezbollah's resistance to Israel and lamented the defeatist attitude of Arab publics and regimes vis-à-vis Israel.[54] Qandil's pro-resistance and Arab nationalist stance clashed with the UAE's geopolitical membership in the moderate Arab camp.

The close connection between media and power was displayed in the way Egyptian satellite stations reacted to the charges leveled against regime-connected business tycoon Hisham Talaat Moustafa for the murder of Lebanese singer Susan Tameem. Apprehensive lest Talaat's business and regime connections affect them adversely, owners of Egyptian satellite stations instructed their staff to react dispassionately and without the usual media hype. Only Amr Adib's *al-Qahira al-Youm* (Cairo Today) of the Orbit network dared spotlight the crime.[55] Adib's program was later suspended as part of a regime-orchestrated crackdown aimed at silencing critical media and opposition voices in the lead-up to the November 2010 parliamentary elections.[56] And when Malik Maktabi's *Ahmar bil-Khat al-'Arid* (Thick Red Line), a controversial talk show on LBC preoccupied with topics deemed taboo in Arab societies, aired an interview with a Saudi man describing his sexual escapades, Saudi authorities closed the satellite station's Jeddah and Riyadh offices, noting that the show's subject contravened public morality and Islamic law.[57] In fact, Saudi Arabia's Salafi establishment has repeatedly condemned satellite stations for airing what it considers immoral material.[58]

State control over satellite channels is relaxed when satellite broadcasting serves regime interests or helps produce a depoliticized public. The Mubarak regime allowed satellite channels to broadcast chauvinistic statements about Algerians following a World Cup qualifying soccer match between the two national teams on 18 November 2009. The aim was to rally the people around the regime, portray the president and his sons, Gamal and Alaa Mubarak, as the guardians of Egyptian national interests, and divert attention from Egypt's domestic challenges.[59]

Reality television shows, with their competitive voting procedures, invaded Arab satellite channels with programs such as *Super Star* (Future TV), *Star Academy* (LBC), *Arabs Got Talent* (MBC), and *Arab Idol* (MBC). They were once described as "the best hope for democracy in the Arab world."[60] Yet far from promoting democratic participatory norms, reality television shows allowed Arab, but especially Gulf, regimes to mobilize their publics around parochial national sentiments and cloak their authoritarianism with a veneer of participation.[61] The entertainment produced by Saudi Prince al-Walid bin Talal's Rotana music company and television channels seeks similar objectives. Indeed, the Saudi-controlled media complex is so extensive that it saturates viewers and readers with information serving Riyadh's geopolitical interests and cultural preferences.[62]

Satellite broadcasting has served to invent a glorious Arab past as counterpoint and diversion from contemporary political and socioeconomic conditions.[63] Accordingly, satellite channels have been deployed in part to manufacture sociopolitical complacency and docile political cultures. For example, Ramadan serials preoccupy themselves with themes that invent idealized Bedouin, social, or historical traditions. The popular Syrian serial *Bab al-Hara* (Neighborhood Gates), first aired in 2006, has run through four consecutive seasons. It is an escape from the omnipresent intelligence-infested contemporary reality into an invented Damascene quarter of the interwar period. Other serials, such as *Nasser, King Farouq, Asmahan, Sira' 'ala al-Rimal* (Struggle over Sand), *Finjan al-Dam* (Blood Cup), and *Abu Ja'far al-Mansur*, have served similar purposes.

This urge for escapism from the present found its best expression in the hugely popular Turkish melodrama *Gümüs* (Silver), aired on MBC as *Noor* (Light) in colloquial Syrian dialect. Whereas *Bab al-Hara* emptied streets in many Arab capitals during the 2007 Ramadan season and *Noor* attracted the highest number of viewers in the history of Arab television, some 85 million for the final episode,[64] *al-Ijtiyah* (The Invasion), a serial that re-created the trauma caused by Israel's 2002 invasion and siege of Jenin, Ramallah, and Bethlehem and the resistance by the defenders of the Jenin refugee camp, was largely ignored during the 2007 Ramadan season after many satellite channels refused to air it.[65] Produced by Jordan's Arab Telemedia Productions (ATP) and aired only on LBC, *al-Ijtiyah* ironically went on to capture the 2008 Golden Emmy Award in the telenovela category. A similar situation transpired during the 2010 Ramadan season. *Ana al-Quds* (I Jerusalem), an intensely emotional television drama that gathered a bouquet of star Arab actors and actresses to recount dramatically the Palestinian tragedy from 1918 until the 1967 war, was aired only on Hezbollah's Al Manar station and on Syrian and Palestinian stations.[66]

The politicization of satellite stations has persisted even after popular uprisings forced authoritarian leaders out of office. In Egypt, for example, state-owned but also most private satellite stations joined the counterrevolutionary wave, branding anti–Supreme Council of the Armed Forces (SCAF) demonstrations and calls for civil disobedience as the actions of agents of foreign powers bent on destabilizing Egypt.[67] The Muslim Brotherhood's satellite channel Misr 25 (Egypt 25) and Salafi satellite stations ridiculed and delegitimized protesters who demanded a swift transition to civilian rule. Even opposition satellite stations that were created after the Egyptian uprising, such as 25 April and al-Tahrir (Liberation), were tamed and forced to toe the SCAF line. Only Naguib Sawiris's ONtv assumed an openly pro-revolutionary stance.[68] That so many anchormen and anchorwomen continue to use Mubarak-era tactics underscores just how slowly Egypt's media landscape has changed after his departure from power.

The Tragedy of the Print Media

Arab regimes pay special attention to the print media. As Table 11.6 shows, almost all major Arab newspapers are politicized, reflecting the views of the government or their financial and political backers; moreover, they are tied to regimes, either directly or indirectly. In most Arab states, the print media have been hitherto penetrated by intelligence agencies and controlled by repressive press and publication laws. Journalists are at the forefront of popular demands for greater freedoms and an end to censorship. A quick look at *al-Ahram*'s headlines before and after Mubarak's downfall exposes the damage done to the print media from years of state control. Little won-

Table 11.6 Arab Newspapers and Their Political Orientations

	Political Orientation
Al-Ahram (Egypt)	Government-owned
al-Akhbar (Lebanon)	Pro–March 8, Iran, and Syria
al-Anwar (Lebanon)	Pro–March 14
al-Diyar (Lebanon)	Pro–March 14 (as of Fall 2009)
al-Dustour (Jordan)	Government-owned
al-Ghad (Jordan)	Semi-independent
al-Hayat (United Kingdom)	Pro–Saudi Arabia
al-Intiqad; al-'Ahed weekly (Lebanon)	Hezbollah/Iran
al-Mustaqbal (Lebanon)	Future Movement
al-Nahar (Lebanon)	Pro–March 14 and Saudi Arabia
al-Qabas (Kuwait)	Merchant class
al-Quds (Palestinian Authority)	Fatah
al-Quds al-Arabi (United Kingdom)	Pro–Qatar
al-Ra'i (Jordan)	Government-owned
al-Ra'i (Kuwait)	Semi-independent
al-Safir (Lebanon)	Pro–March 8, Syria, and Qatar
al-Sharq al-Awsat (United Kingdom)	Pro–Saudi Arabia
Elaph (London-based, e-newspaper)	Pro–Saudi Arabia and Prince 'Abdel Aziz bin Fahd

Source: Author interviews with Lebanese and Arab journalists, Beirut, January 2010.

der that the post-Mubarak order replaced swiftly all the editors of government newspapers and news agencies.

As for the pan-national print media, they are either owned by or beholden to the financial largess of Gulf regimes. For example, *al-Hayat* is owned by Saudi prince Khaled bin Sultan and consequently publicizes Riyadh's political agenda. On the other hand, *al-Quds al-Arabi,* purchased recently by Qatar, presents an anti-Saudi perspective. Similarly, *al-Sharq al-Awsat,* ostensibly owned by Saudi Research and Marketing, is in fact the political mouthpiece of Saudi prince Salman bin Abdulaziz. It spearheads the anti-Iran, anti-Syria, and anti-Hezbollah propaganda campaign in the regional geopolitical contest. During Egypt's upheavals, the newspaper portrayed the popular protests as acts of vandalism, ignored the sociopolitical causes of the protests, and tried to deflect attention from Mubarak's regime by spotlighting opposition demands in Iran.[69]

Lebanese newspapers, traditionally far more critical and enjoying greater freedom than their Arab counterparts, have mutated into mouthpieces of sectarian leaders or cartels—as in the cases of *al-Mustaqbal* and *al-Akhbar*—or have succumbed to the lure of Gulf financial largess—as in the cases of *al-Nahar* and *al-Diyar.*[70] Even newspapers that try to maintain a semblance of independence and professionalism, such as *al-Safir,* neither refuse Gulf subsidies nor hide their local or regional biases. Financial and political considerations have consequently narrowed substantially the margin of liberties once enjoyed by Lebanese newspapers. Newspapers in Lebanon practice rigorous self-censorship and have abandoned the kind of investigative reporting that can expose the corrupt practices of the political and financial elite.

The print media are thus a primary casualty of ongoing domestic and regional contests in the Arab world; they are also beleaguered by a web of financial and institutional constraints. Many journalists have placed their pens at the service of ruling regimes, producing articles and editorials that are nothing more than invoices to be paid by their financial backers. Others, like the late Samir Kassir, paid a blood tax for their unwavering commitment to democracy and telling the truth.

New Media, New Identities, and Democratization in the Arab World

Powerless to prevent the spread of new information technologies and satellite channels, authoritarian Arab regimes used them as "outlets that mitigate social pressures that might otherwise become politicized."[71] They embedded the new media in complex regulatory and monitoring mechanisms, and besieged it with formal and informal modes of control. In fact, when it comes to the new media, old authoritarian habits seem to die hard. Although promulgated on the morrow of the 2011 uprisings in Tunisia and Egypt, and after the government had lifted a ban on Facebook and YouTube sites, Syria's long-anticipated Internet law fell far short of the aspirations of Internet users and bloggers, and was soon overshadowed by the slide to civil war.[72]

Satellite stations were used in proxy intra- and interstate conflicts, exacerbating parochial national loyalties and sectarian animosities. Saudi-controlled media outlets played an instrumental role in fomenting a new anti-Shiism in the region, while Qatar deployed Al Jazeera's reach to co-opt Islamist groups and audiences throughout the Arab world. Even US diplomats tried to influence Arab satellite broadcasting. The US ambassador in Cairo lobbied Egyptian officials on more than one occasion to remove Hezbollah's Al Manar satellite station from the Nilesat satellite network.[73]

Despite these efforts, however, the new Arab media played an enabling role in the popular upheavals that overwhelmed Arab regimes. New social media opened up greater space for public debate and criticism, as well as alternative avenues for political mobilization and contestation—necessary conditions for the emergence of the kind of viable collective action that can withstand the coercive capabilities of authoritarian regimes. Coverage by some satellite channels helped demonstrators maintain popular pressure on beleaguered regimes. To be sure, however, there are limits to this mobilizing potential.[74] A Facebook call for an 11 March 2011 "Hunayn Revolution" in Saudi Arabia failed to materialize, and coverage by Al Arabiya and Al Jazeera ultimately followed the regime security calculations of Saudi Arabia and Qatar, respectively. This suggests that, on its own, the new Arab media cannot explain the causes of the popular upheavals of 2011 in the Arab world, a topic we shall return to at the end of this volume.

Satellite stations and the new social media have emerged also as channels of a new permeability in the Arab world. Unlike the transnational permeability of the 1950s and 1960s, which was largely stimulated from above and served regime interests, the permeability shaped by the new Arab media is driven from below, and expresses a set of common political and socioeconomic demands, ranging from individual freedoms and freely elected and accountable governments, to a fairer distribution of national wealth and foreign policies that reflect public opinion rather than the idiosyncratic interests of regime members. In turn, this new permeability is shaping a novel Arab identity, one that is not trapped in old binary choices between pan-Arab *or* national interests. Instead, what seems to be developing is a new polyphonic and expansive Arab identity, one that takes pride in its national loyalties without dismissing pan-national affiliations.

Notes

1. See Kanan Makiya, *Republic of Fear: The Politics of Modern Iraq* (Berkeley: University of California Press, 1989); Lisa Wedeen, *Ambiguities of Domination: Politics, Rhetoric, and Symbols in Contemporary Syria* (Chicago: University of Chicago Press, 1999).

2. In December 2007, when Saudi Prince Mish'al bin Abdulaziz was appointed head of the newly formed Baya Council, a body responsible for confirming the king and crown prince after the tenure of King Abdullah bin Abdulaziz and Crown Prince Sultan bin Abdulaziz, Saudis exchanged a telling text-message joke: "Whose job starts when that of Azrael ends?"

3. See Marc Lynch, *Voices of the New Arab Public: Iraq, Al-Jazeera, and Middle East Politics Today* (New York: Columbia University Press, 2006), p. 3.

4. See Jon B. Alterman, "New Media, New Politics? From Satellite Television to the Internet in the Arab World," Policy Paper no. 48 (Washington, DC: Washington Institute of Near East Policy, 1998), p. 54.

5. See Edmund Ghareeb, "New Media and the Information Revolution in the Arab World: An Assessment," *Middle East Journal* 54, 3 (Summer 2000), pp. 398–399.

6. Steven Heydemann, *Upgrading Authoritarianism in the Arab World* (Washington, DC: Brookings Institution, October 2007), p. 23. See also Mohamed Zayani, *Arab Satellite Television and Politics in the Middle East,* Emirates Occasional Paper no. 54 (Abu Dhabi: Emirates Center for Strategic Studies and Research, 2004); Mamoun Fandy, *(Un)Civil War of Words: Media and Politics in the Arab World* (London: Praeger Security International, 2007); Lawrence Pintak, "Satellite TV News and Arab Democracy," *Journalism Practice* 2, 1 (February 2008).

7. Naomi Sakr, "Contested Blueprints for Egypt's Satellite Channels," *Gazette* 63, 2–3 (May 2001), p. 154.

8. See Ghareeb, "New Media and the Information Revolution in the Arab World," pp. 400–402.

9. See the Al Jazeera Palestinian Papers website, http://english.aljazeera.net/palestinepapers.

10. See Hugh Miles, *Al-Jazeera: How the Arab TV News Challenged the World* (London: Abacus, 2005).

11. Fouad Ajami, "What the Muslim World Is Watching," *New York Times Magazine,* 18 November 2001, p. 50.

12. In 2001 the station's Kabul office was destroyed by two smart bombs, and in 2003 Al Jazeera reporter Tareq Ayoub was killed in a US missile strike on the station's Baghdad office.

13. See Muwaffaq Harb, "Al-Internet wal-Telfizyon Yotihan Ra'isan" [Internet and Television Topple a President], *al-Hayat,* 17 January 2011.

14. Most bizarrely, the Egyptian private satellite station Al Mihwar aired an interview with a woman who claimed that she had received riot training in the United States, and that her Israeli trainers had instructed her to engage in sabotage activity should a social upheaval erupt in Egypt. See Muhammad Abdul Rahman, "Qanat al-Mihwar: Kul Hathihi al-Akazib" [Al Mihwar Channel: All These Lies], *al-Akhbar,* 8 February 2011.

15. See Albrecht Hofheinz, "The Internet in the Arab World: Playground for Political Liberalization," *Internationale Politik und Gesellschaft* 3 (2005).

16. See Fadlallah's website, http://www.bayynat.org.lb.

17. See Shabakat al-Difa' 'An al-Sunna [Network for the Defense of the Sunna], http://www.dd-sunnah.net.

18. See the essay "Terrorism Recruiting Manual Discovered by West Point Researchers Worries Authorities," on the National Terror Alert website, 23 March 2009, http://www.nationalterroralert.com/updates/2009/03/23/terrorism-recruiting-manual-discovered-by-west-point-researchers-worries-authorities. See also Thomas Hegghammer, *Jihad in Saudi Arabia: Violence and Pan-Islamism Since 1979* (Cambridge: Cambridge University Press, 2010), pp. 122–123.

19. See Muhammad Muhsin, "Harb Ahliya 'ala Facebook" [Civil War on Facebook], *al-Akhbar,* 12 March 2011; Paul Eedle, "Iraq: Civil War on the Internet," *The World Today,* March 2007, pp. 8–9, http://www.chathamhouse.org.uk/files/2963_wt030708.pdf; Bader Ibrahim, "Al-I'lam al-Kuwaiti Yanfukh fi Nar al-Fitna" [Kuwaiti Media Exacerbates the Fires of Sedition], *al-Akhbar,* 29 August 2009; and the footage http://www.youtube.com/watch?v=DK8X47q-tlY.

20. See Rania al-Malky, "Blogging for Reform: The Case of Egypt," *Arab Media and Society* 1 (Spring 2007), http://www.arabmediasociety.com/?article=12.

21. For example, Wael Abbas's blog *Al-Wa'i al-Misri* (Egyptian Conscience) exposed police brutality in Egypt and across the Arab world; see http://misrdigital.blogspirit.com and http://www.youtube.com/user/waelabbas. Nouwara Najem's blog *Jabhat al-Tahyees al-Sha'biya,* [The Popular Front of Pontificating] established in 2006, attracted 15,000–20,000 readers daily, a number that rose to 30,000 during the January 2011 uprisings; see http://tahyyes.blogspot.com.

22. See Marc Lynch, "Blogging the New Arab Public," *Arab Media and Society* 1 (Spring 2007), http://www.arabmediasociety.com/?article=10.

23. See *Gulf News,* 2 November 2007, http://archive.gulfnews.com/articles/06/02/13/10018507.html.

24. See 'Adlan Madi, "Al-Jaza'er wa Huriyat al-Ta'bir: Al-Internet Tahta al-Hisar" [Algeria and Freedom of Expression: The Internet Beseiged], *al-Akhbar,* 11 December 2008.

25. See "After Blocking Ten Thousand Sites in Saudi Arabia, New Security Measures Against Internet Cafes," 19 April 2009, http://www.openarab.net/en/node/902.

26. See special report of Committee to Protect Journalists, "10 Worst Countries to be a Blogger," 30 April 2009, http://cpj.org/reports/2009/04/10-worst-countries-to-be-a-blogger.php. Other states on the list include Burma (ranked first, or worst), Iran (second), Cuba (fourth), Vietnam (sixth), China (eighth), and Turkmenistan (ninth). The Initiative for an Open Arab Internet traces blogger harassment by Arab regimes; see http://www.openarab.net/en.

27. Saudi journalist Hamza Kashgari was repatriated from Malaysia and incarcerated because his tweets about the prophet Muhammad were considered blasphemous by the kingdom's political and religious authorities.

28. See Youssef Ibrahim, "Saudi Liberals Get the Lash," *New York Sun,* 18 April 2006, http://www.nysun.com/foreign/saudi-liberals-get-the-lash/31122.

29. See Christopher Wilson and Alexandra Dunn, "Digital Media in the Egyptian Revolution: Descriptive Analysis from the Tahrir Data Sets," *International Journal of Communication* 5 (2011).

30. See the Facebook page http://www.facebook.com/?ref=home#!/pages/Tunisie/182307965129841.

31. See the Facebook page http://www.facebook.com/ group.php?v=wall&viewas=0&gid=7928575635.

32. See Aidan Lewis, "Tunisia Protests: Cyber War Mirrors Unrest on Streets," *BBC News,* 14 January 2011, http://www.bbc.co.uk/news/world-africa-12180954.

33. Quoted in Robert Fisk, "The Tunisian Whose Jihad Was for the People, Not God," *The Independent,* 5 March 2011, http://www.independent.co.uk/ opinion/commentators/fisk/robert-fisk-the-tunisian-whose-ijihadi-was-for-the-peo- ple-not-god-2232981.html.

34. See the Facebook page http://www.facebook.com/shabab6april.

35. See the Facebook pagehttp://www.facebook.com/?ref=home#!/ElShaheeed.

36. See David D. Kirkpatrick and David E. Singer, "A Tunisian-Egyptian Link That Shook Arab History," *New York Times,* 13 February 2011, http://www.nytimes.com/2011/02/14/world/middleeast/14egypt-tunisia- protests.html. Founded by Ahmad Maher, the 6 April Youth Movement emerged in support of the March 2008 labor protests in Mahalla, while "We Are All Khaled Said" was established by Wael Ghonim to spotlight policy brutality after the brutal killing of Said by the police.

37. Roger Cohen, "Revolutionary Arab Geeks," *New York Times,* 27 January 2011, http://www.nytimes.com/2011/01/28/opinion/28iht-edcohen28.html.

38. See the interview with Ghonim on *60 Minutes,* 13 February 2011, http://www.cbsnews.com/stories/2011/02/13/60minutes/main20031701.shtml.

39. See the discussion in Fandy, *(Un)Civil War of Words,* pp. 39–65.

40. See Robert F. Worth, "Al Jazeera No Longer Nips at Saudis," *New York Times,* 4 January 2008.

41. See al-Rashed's editorials in *al-Sharq al-Awsat,* http:// www.aawsat.com/leader.asp?wrid=140. Al-Rashed's editorials were suspended dur- ing the summer of 2010 after Al Arabiya aired a documentary titled *Islam and the West* that was critical of Wahhabi thought. The Wahhabi establishment mobilized Prince Salman bin Abdulaziz, governor of the Riyadh province, against al-Rashed, who tendered his resignation from Al Arabiya on 14 September 2010 in protest. The resignation was rejected, however, and al-Rashed resumed his responsibilities at the station. This incident reflects the role of the media as a site in the struggle be- tween different wings of the Saudi royal family. See Layal Haddad, "Abdel Rahman al-Rashed: 'Libirali' fi Mahab al-Wahabiya" [Abdel Rahman al-Rashed: A Liberal Among Wahhabism], *al-Akhbar,* 17 September 2010.

42. Al Arabiya correspondent Atwar Bahjat was abducted on 22 February 2006 and murdered while covering the aftermath of the bombing of a mosque in Sam- mara. Bahjat's nonsectarian reporting antagonized the militant Sunni group Jaysh Muhammad (Muhammad's Army). A member of this group confessed in August 2009 to the rape and murder of Bahjat. See *al-Safir,* 5 August 2009.

43. In September 2008 the Iranian authorities revoked the license of Al Ara- biya's Tehran bureau chief, Hasan Fahs, after the station aired a documentary titled *The Road to the Revolution.*

44. See the comparative analysis in Fandy, *(Un)Civil War of Words,* pp. 58–64.

45. See Rana Hayek, "Al-Thawra lam Taqa' 'ala Al Arabiyya" [The Revolu- tion Did Not Happen on Al Arabiyya], *al-Akhbar,* 31 January 2011.

46. See Faten Qubaisi, "Al-Mirazi: Al Arabiyya man Khana al-Amana al-Sa- hafiya Laysa Ana" [Al-Mirazi: Al Arabiyya Betrayed Journalistic Ethics Not Me], *al-Safir,* 23 February 2011. See also Al-Mirazi's comments at http://www.youtube.com/watch?v=Q3oMCjg6PlI.

47. See Ghassan Sa'ud, "Suriya Tashku Tadakhul Lubnan fi Shu'uniha" [Syria Complains About Lebanese Interference in Its Own Affairs], *al-Akhbar,* 1 April 2011.

48. Andreas Schedler, "Authoritarianism's Last Line of Defense," *Journal of Democracy* 21, 1 (January 2010), p. 74.

49. "Mabadi' Tanzim al-Bath wa-l-Istiqbal al-Fada'i wa-l-Idha'i wa-l-Telefizyouni fi-l-Mantaqa al-'Arabiya." For the Arabic version of the charter, see *al-Safir,* 19 February 2008. For an unofficial English translation, see http://www.arabmediasociety.com/?article=648. All quotations are from the Arabic text.

50. See Sakr, "Contested Blueprints for Egypt's Satellite Channels."

51. See Paul Cochrane, "Are Lebanon's Media Fanning the Flames of Sectarianism?" *Arab Media and Society* 2 (Summer 2007), http://www.arabmediasociety.com/?article=206; Fandy, *(Un)Civil War of Words,* pp. 66–80.

52. Nabil Dajani, "The Re-Feudalization of the Public Sphere: Lebanese Television News Coverage and the Lebanese Political Process," *Transnational Broadcasting Studies* 16 (2006), http://www.tbsjournal.com/Dajani.html.

53. See Nathan Field and Ahmed Hamam, "Salafi Satellite TV in Egypt," *Arab Media and Society* 8 (Spring 2009), http://www.arabmediasociety.com/?article=712.

54. See Qandil's comments at http://www.youtube.com/watch?v=dAWQJjGOtV8. Qandil's very popular show *Ra'is al-Tahrir* (Editor-in-Chief) on Dream TV was also suspended in 2003 after he criticized Arab regimes for failing to prevent the invasion of Iraq.

55. See Muhammad Abdul Rahman, "Al-Fada'iyat al-Misriya Takhaf 'ala Hisham Tal'at" [Egyptian Satellite Channels Worry About Hisham Talaat], *al-Akhbar,* 12 September 2009.

56. Ibrahim 'Isa, editor-in-chief of the independent *al-Dustur* newspaper, and staunch critic of the Mubarak regime, was also dismissed from his position, on 4 October 2010, as part of the same crackdown. In this case, however, the regime used an indirect approach to silence 'Isa: the newspaper was first purchased by two businessmen close to the regime, Rida Edward and Sayyed Badawi, the latter being the chairman of the New Wafd party, who later dismissed 'Isa. See Muhammad Abdul Rahman, "Wa Oqila Ibrahim 'Isa . . . Ahlan bi-l-Sahfa al-Mudajana" [Ibrahim Isa was Removed: Welcome to the Tamed Press], *al-Akhbar,* 6 October 2010.

57. An alternative explanation suggests that the decision was part of an ongoing struggle between the Salafi wing of the kingdom, supported by Prince Khaled bin Talal, and the more liberal wing, represented by Prince al-Walid bin Talal, owner of Rotana and majority shares in LBC-SAT. See Bader Ibrahim, "Rotana wa-l-Walid . . . wa-l-Ahmar Thalithuhuma: Hurras al-Fadila Yuharibun al-Fikr al-Haddam" [Rotana and al-Walid and Red is their Third: The Custodians of Virtue Combat Destructive Thought], *al-Akhbar,* 10 August 2009. Yet others suggest that the decision was meant to punish LBCI chief executive officer Pierre al-Daher, who had received financial rewards from Saudi Arabia to enlist LBCI in the pro-Saudi 14 March alliance's 2009 parliamentary campaign, but later reneged on his promise. Author interviews with Lebanese and Arab journalists, Beirut, September 2009.

58. As in the bizarre case of former chief justice of Saudi Arabia's Supreme Judicial Council, Shaikh Salah bin Muhammad al Luhaydan, who announced that it was permissible to kill owners of satellite stations broadcasting immoral material during the holy month of Ramadan. See Robert F. Worth, "Arab TV Tests Societies'

Limits with Depictions of Sex and Equality," *New York Times,* 26 September 2008, http://www.nytimes.com/2008/09/27/world/middleeast/27beirut.html.

59. See Wael Abdel-Fattah, "Daraweesh al-Shashat" [The Dervishes of the Screens], *al-Akhbar,* 21 November 2009.

60. Tyler MacKenzie, "The Best Hope for Democracy in the Arab World: A Crooning TV 'Idol'?" *Transnational Broadcasting Studies* 13 (Fall 2004), http://www.tbsjournal.com/Archives/Fall04/mackenzie.html.

61. Marc Lynch, "'Reality Is Not Enough': The Politics of Arab Reality TV," *Transnational Broadcasting Studies* 15 (Fall 2005), http://www.tbsjournal.com/Archives/Fall05/Lynch.html.

62. See Andrew Hammond, "Saudi Arabia's Media Empire: Keeping the Masses at Home," *Arab Media and Society* 3 (Fall 2007), http://www.arabmediasociety.com/countries/index.php?c_article=121.

63. See Shawqi Najem, "Faragh al-Thaqafa" [The Hollowness of Culture], *al-Nahar,* 3 October 2008.

64. See Worth, "Arab TV Tests Societies' Limits with Depictions of Sex and Equality."

65. See Maher Mansour, "Abbas Nouri: Ba'd al-Muqata'a Fakarna bi-'Ardehi 'ala Al Jazeera!" [Abbas Nouri: We Thought of Screening It on Al Jazeera After the Boycott], *al-Safir,* 26 November 2008.

66. See Wisam Kan'an, "'Ana al-Quds': Al-Musalsal al-Lathi Az'aja al-Jami'" [I Jerusalem: The Serial that Irritated Everybody], *al-Akhbar,* 28 September 2010.

67. Bassem Youssef's comedy show el-Bernameg on ONtv has brilliantly demystified these media tactics. See especially his 30 December 2011 episode http://www.youtube.com/watch?v=eAOPmlwymns.

68. See Muhammad Khair, "Wa-Ifranqa' al-Fada' al-Misri 'an al-Thawra . . . Ila ONtv" [Egypt's Satellite Media Abandons the Revolution... Except ONtv], *al-Akhbar,* 28 February 2012.

69. See Bader al-Ibrahim, "Al-Sa'udiya: Inaha Intifadat al-Haramiya" [Saudi Arabia: Is It the Thieves' Uprising], *al-Akhbar,* 31 January 2011.

70. *Al-Diyar*'s saga is telling in this respect. Traditionally a pro-Syrian newspaper owned by Charles Ayoob, it switched sides in the autumn of 2009 and became staunchly pro-Saudi after the Saudi embassy in Lebanon allegedly pledged to pay its owner's debts at the Casino du Liban. Author interview with Lebanese journalists, Beirut, January 2010.

71. Heydemann, *Upgrading Authoritarianism in the Arab World,* p. 21.

72. See Wisam Kan'an, "Suriya Tu'amem al-Shabaka al-'Ankabutiya" [Syria Nationalizes the Web], *al-Akhbar,* 1 March 2011.

73. See the 22 August 2006 cable to the US embassy in Cairo titled "Al Manar Next Steps," http://www.al-akhbar.com/node/6648.

74. See Marc Lynch, "After Egypt: The Limits and Promise of Online Challenges to the Authoritarian Arab State," *Perspectives on Politics* 9, 2 (June 2011).

12

Impact of the Regional and International Environment

The 2011 antiauthoritarian uprisings that swept the Arab world contained relatively few references to the regional security issues that have historically mobilized Arabs, such as the Arab-Israeli conflict. As they poured into the streets of their respective countries, Tunisians, Egyptians, Libyans, Yemenis, Bahrainis, and Syrians did not much use the issue of Palestine or opposition to the US invasion of Iraq to press their claims or to criticize the performance of their governments.

This lack of reference to regional and international issues in the 2011 uprisings is all the more interesting because of the continued salience of such issues for understanding so much of politics in the region. Several factors have contributed to the unequalled cross-border reverberation of ideologies, events, and political movements in the Middle East.[1] Middle Eastern countries have common historical legacies; they also have similar though not identical patterns of state formation; a majority of their people share a Muslim religiocultural background; and they are united by a common language, Arabic. Arab nationalism and a strong inter-Arab connectedness among both states and societies made the Arab world into "a vast sound-chamber in which currents of thought, as well as information, circulated and enjoyed considerable resonance across state frontiers," as Paul Noble famously put it.[2]

Not only is the region characterized by high permeability, but it is also afflicted with considerable levels of regional conflict. Indeed, hopes that the end of the Cold War would usher in an era of peace were dashed relatively quickly. In the past decade, both the Arab-Israeli and the Gulf arenas have experienced sustained outbursts of violence. And while regimes elsewhere lost their foreign patrons with the end of the Cold War, strategic considerations, including the security of the state of Israel and the oil factor, have ensured that the Middle East remains of considerable interest to the rest of the world, especially the United States.

What role have the regional and international environments played in the persistence of authoritarian regimes in the past decade? What part, if any, have they played in their fall? What role are they likely to play following the 2011 uprisings? This chapter steps back from current events to discuss three principal ways in which external factors have influenced regimes in the Middle East since the end of the Cold War: conflict dynamics, transnational Islamist appeals, and Western efforts at democracy promotion. For each, we provide a brief overview of the empirical context, outline both how and the extent to which it has affected regime security, and assess the ways in which regimes developed (or failed to develop) policies to react to challenges and to take advantage of opportunities to survive. In conclusion, the chapter considers the continued efficacy beyond 2011 of the main instruments that regimes have used to respond to the challenges and to take advantage of the opportunities provided by the regional and international environments. We pinpoint issues likely to affect the nature of linkages between domestic politics and foreign policy in the years ahead, and we suggest avenues of analytical inquiry to help us to get a better grasp on those issues.

Domestic and Foreign Policy Linkages

In the Middle East as elsewhere, the relationship between domestic politics and foreign policy has been the subject of much debate. Neorealist scholars argue that foreign policy decisions are primarily influenced by factors outside state boundaries. States craft their foreign policies to balance against one another. Some believe that weaker states bandwagon with more powerful ones; others, like Stephen Walt, argue that they balance against "the states that pose the greatest threat."[3] Critics argue that domestic politics and foreign policy are linked.[4] The direction in which the arrow of causality runs has also been the subject of much debate. So have the extent and depth of linkages, the factors that account for these linkages, as well as their consequences both for domestic politics and for international relations.

Scholars have argued both sides of the issue when it comes to identifying the direction of causality between domestic politics and foreign policy. Focusing on the impact of war-making on state-making, analysts of the Middle East have argued that high levels of regional conflict have provided continued justification for military development, and that war has historically contributed to the centralization of state authority in the hands of mostly nondemocratic regimes.[5] Others have focused on the role of foreign policy as an instrument of domestic politics that states use to balance against internal threats, "appeasing other states . . . in order to counter the more immediate and dangerous domestic threats."[6] Michael Barnett and Jack Levy, for example, make the point that regimes in weak states must balance domestic political stability, economic considerations, and external security threats.[7]

A second set of arguments discusses the extent and depth of the linkages between domestic and foreign policy. One perspective highlights the permeability of the Arab world and the consequent vulnerability of Arab regimes to the ripple effects of events beyond their borders. Another stresses the growing maturity of Arab states, and their ability to control and insulate their societies.

As with all things analytical, the pendulum has swung back and forth between these two sets of arguments. From the 1950s to the 1970s, the Arab state system was highly unstable. This was a time when regional developments, such as the rise of Gamal Abdul Nasser in Egypt, and international dynamics, such as the US attempt to draw the region into the Baghdad Pact, had a profound impact on domestic politics across the Middle East. It thus made sense to study Arab states not as sovereign, independent units, but as "a set of interconnected organisms separated only by porous membranes, or alternatively, a large-scale domestic system divided into compartments of varying degrees of permeability."[8] With the 1967 Arab *naksa* (setback), Arab nationalism was declared dead.[9] This opened the way to a maturing, Westphalian Middle Eastern system where state capacity to control and insulate society from transnational ideologies was deemed to be on the rise.[10] For instance, despite societal empathy for and sympathy with the plight of Palestinians, the first intifada, while it might have mobilized the "Arab street," did not pose significant challenges to Arab regimes.[11] Nor were many Arab regimes hamstrung by widespread domestic support for the rhetoric of Saddam Hussein in siding with the US-led coalition following Iraq's 1990 invasion of Kuwait. While some scholars have sought to identify historical periods of greater permeability or autonomy and to unearth the reasons for this variation,[12] others have argued that the variation depends on the nature of state-society relations and that these can vary across states in any given time period.[13]

A third set of debates revolves around the relative importance of power, interests, and identity in shaping foreign policies as well as domestic politics. There are those who argue that conventional power politics provides a compelling explanation for the behavior of Arab leaders. Shibley Telhami, for example, argued that shifting regional and international power considerations caused the Egyptian leadership to reconsider what policies would be most likely to allow it to meet its long-standing security interests, thus leading President Anwar Sadat to sign the Camp David Accords.[14] Others, like Michael Barnett, have sought to highlight the role of ideas, specifically the changing notions of Arabism, in shaping the nature of interactions between Arab states and thus in determining the type of regional order that these interactions produce.[15] The linkages between domestic politics and foreign policy have been explored to understand a range of outcomes. In the Middle East, two outcomes have historically stood out as privileged domains of inquiry: regional (dis)order and the persistence of authoritarianism.

Although authoritarianism has been causally linked to the protractedness of regional conflict in the Middle East and elsewhere, researchers have concluded that regime type is not determinative in explaining the prevalence of war in the Middle East.[16] A variant of the democratic peace argument contends that stalled transitions from autocracy, not authoritarian states, are more likely to precipitate the onset of conflict. According to this account, conflict is the unintended result of the inability of leaders to escape the belligerent politics that they unleash in their search for domestic support. In many ways, this is the story commonly told of Yasser Arafat's decisionmaking prior to the unleashing of the second intifada, of a domestically embattled leader who used nationalist rhetoric to bolster his legitimacy and who stoked nationalist fires among his supporters, but ultimately failed to assert control over their actions.

Belligerent behavior is also believed to be a strategy that leaders pursue to divert attention from the problems in their society.[17] Facing impending challenges at home, they trigger external crises and generate rally-around-the-flag effects. Iran's economic difficulties and its political woes related to the reelection of President Mahmoud Ahmadinejad in summer 2009 are said to have provided "considerable domestic political incentives to foster hostile relations with the United States to distract attention from the ongoing economic difficulties."[18] This led some analysts to suggest that Iran has used the nuclear question as a diversion that could bolster support for the regime and shift attention away from its domestic problems.[19] Others, however, have not been able to find support for this hypothesis.[20] Recent research has also made the related point that regime insecurity is a key driver of interstate conflict. Gregory Gause, for example, has proposed that this might be one way of thinking about Iraq's decisions to go to war in the 1980s and 1990s, as evidence suggests that Saddam Hussein launched the wars to quell direct threats to his regime's survival.[21]

Whereas research has linked the prevalence of war to the authoritarian nature of regimes, other research has reversed the argument, linking the persistence of authoritarianism to the existence of conflict in a country's immediate or extended environment. Gregory Gause contends that war poses "two disincentives [to leaders] taking the risks of opening up their political systems."[22] First, transitions are messy and may send a message of vulnerability to enemies. Second, nondemocratic leaders who believe they can suppress oppositions are less interested in co-opting them or reaching some sort of compromise. However, the attitude of nondemocratic leaders has varied in the absence of regional conflict as well. In Morocco, King Mohammed VI proposed a new constitution that would transfer executive powers to the prime minister. In nearby Tunisia, not only did Zine el-Abidine Ben Ali unleash police onto protesters, but he also threatened to bring the full force of the law to bear in the prosecution of those he described as a minority of extremists and mercenaries who resort to violence and disorder.

Inter- and Intrastate Conflict

The end of the Cold War did not result in dramatically lower levels of conflict in the Middle East—instead, the region continues to rank among the most conflict-ridden in the world. Nor were the recent regional episodes of violence contained; rather, each spilled across international borders. Following the second intifada and in spite of Israel's withdrawal from Lebanon, incidents involving Hezbollah and the Israel Defense Forces were increasingly reported at the Lebanon-Israel border, culminating in the 2006 Israel-Hezbollah war. The first decade of the twenty-first century saw multiple instances of Israeli military operations in the occupied Palestinian territories, most prominently Operation Cast Lead against Gaza in 2009. Since 2004, the activities of the Kurdistan Workers Party (PKK) in Turkey and Iraqi Kurdistan have led to repeated Turkish military incursions into Iraq. Iran's development of its nuclear capabilities in the face of massive opposition from the major powers has increased threat perceptions in Israel as well as in Arab Gulf countries. Saudi engagement in Yemen's internal conflicts reawakened memories of the "Arab Cold War." Pointing to the heightened level of regional tension and the potential interconnectedness of the various theaters of instability, the International Crisis Group warned in August 2010 that the drums of regional war were sounding loudly.[23]

Middle Eastern regimes have also had to deal with violent internal challenges. The Saudi monarchy was faced with a spate of terrorist bombings from 2003 to 2007, while Iran was shaken by the strong reaction to the reelection of Ahmadinejad in summer 2009. But the extent of the violence and the outcome of these challenges have varied widely, as the 2011 uprisings show. Presidents have been deposed in Egypt and Tunisia; fierce fighting has broken out in Syria; the regime has fallen in Libya; protesters have been repressed in Bahrain; and Saudi Arabia has reintroduced generous benefit packages to quell dissent in the kingdom. An important factor accounting for this variation is the ability of regimes to use interstate and internal conflict to maintain themselves in power.

Little needs to be said about the ways in which both external and internal conflict can and often do challenge regime stability. During the heyday of Arab nationalism, the permeability of societies resulted in the so-called Arab Cold War, "a contest between purportedly secular-revolutionary and conservative regimes, anchored in domestic exigencies and the quest for regional hegemony, but camouflaged by ideology."[24] This contest was often expressed by way of proxy wars, such as Saudi Arabia's conflict with Egypt in the Yemeni civil war that followed the establishment of the Yemen Arab Republic, in which the Saudis backed the deposed Yemeni ruler while the Egyptians backed the revolutionary forces.[25] Regional conflict also contributed to the shift from civilian to military regimes, particularly as officers in the armed forces of Arab states held civilian rulers responsible for the defeats that beset Arab frontline states against Israel, defeats that precipitated the coups d'état in Egypt and Syria. Likewise, security threats—both internal and external—have been a constant theme of the international politics of Gulf states. Since the end of the Cold War, the Gulf region has been the site of two major wars, the Gulf War of 1990–1991 and the 2003–2011 US intervention in Iraq. In both instances, not only did the conflicts threaten the immediate protagonists, but their ripple effects also had profound impacts on the sense of insecurity and threat felt across the region.[26]

Armed conflict creates not just threats to state and regime security; it also creates conditions that increase the state's capacity to maintain a monopoly on the means of coercion and survival, even in the face of growing popular illegitimacy and discontent. The armed forces remain the cornerstone for authoritarian regimes seeking to maintain themselves in power. Thus while many—though not all—Middle Eastern states achieved independence with mostly small constabulary forces, the trend since has been toward "relatively massive military establishments."[27] The 1948 and 1956 wars were instrumental in the expansion of the Egyptian, Jordanian, and Syrian armies.[28] Incorporation into the "global security order" also played a part, as the United States and the Soviet Union developed military-security relationships with various Middle Eastern states, providing regimes with "massive amounts of arms and military assistance . . . either at low cost, or via privileged access."[29] Eva Bellin identified this—that the region is exceptionally well-endowed with conditions that foster robust authoritarianism—as the true source of the Middle East's exceptionalism.[30] Middle Eastern states are "world leaders in the proportion of [gross national product] spent on security. . . . They are also among the biggest spenders in terms of arms purchased. . . . The percentage of the population engaged in various branches of the security apparatus is high by world standards"[31] (see Table 12.1). Moreover, security-related rents have not only strengthened the coercive apparatus of Arab states, but also potentially influenced the institutional balance of power within the state itself.

Yet other observers have demonstrated that the correlation between military expenditures and democratization is path-dependent,[32] a point that was empirically driven home by the fact that the size of militaries was not the only variable at play in the 2011 uprisings. Indeed, the militaries in Tunisia and Egypt ultimately proved reluctant to repress on behalf of embattled leaders, which suggests the importance of paying attention to civil-military relations. Historically speaking, traditional security threats have justified large militaries and high military expenditures in the Middle East, a trend that continues to this day. Since 2005, defense expenditures in the Middle East have remained steadily higher as a percentage of gross domestic product (GDP) than defense expenditures in all other regions of the world. In 2008, according to the International Institute for Strategic Studies, four of the ten leading recipients of arms deliveries to developing nations, as well as six of the ten leading recipients of arms transfer agreements with developing nations, were Middle Eastern states.[33] As in years past,[34] there is a stark difference in levels of defense expenditures between Arab Maghreb and Mashreq states, with

Table 12.1 Defense Expenditures and Military Personnel in the Middle East

	Defense Expenditures as Percentage of GDP		Number of Personnel in Armed Forces (thousands)	Estimated Number of Reservists (thousands)	Number of Paramilitary Personnel (thousands)
	2006	2008	2010	2010	2010
Algeria	2.64	3.03	147	150	187
Bahrain	3.42	2.76	8	0	11
Egypt	4.01	2.90	469	479	397
Iran	3.98	2.84	523	350	40
Iraq	—	—	578	0	0
Israel	8.05	7.41	177	565	8
Jordan	7.54	10.63	101	65	10
Kuwait	4.92	4.38	16	24	7
Lebanon	2.60	2.71	59	0	20
Libya	1.13	1.22	76	40	0
Mauritania	0.69	0.69	16	0	5
Morocco	3.78	3.48	196	150	50
Oman	10.99	8.53	43	0	4
Palestinian Authority	—	—	0	0	56
Qatar	1.89	1.75	12	0	0
Saudi Arabia	8.30	8.15	234	0	16
Syria	4.09	3.78	325	314	108
Tunisia	1.61	1.28	36	0	12
United Arab Emirates	5.58	5.09	51	0	0
Yemen	6.11	6.35	67	0	71
Total	5.29	4.71	3,134	2,137	1,002

Source: Adapted from International Institute for Strategic Studies, *The Military Balance 2010* (London, 2010), tab. 39, "International Comparisons of Defence Expenditure and Military Manpower," pp. 441–472.

the Maghreb states closer to non-Arab comparative cases. That being said, there is no clear correlation between the degree of militarization and repression. Bahrain's and Egypt's defense expenditures as a percentage of GDP are similar, but whereas the Egyptian army stood on the sidelines in the 2011 uprisings, Bahrain's armed forces severely repressed protesters.

Whether armed forces stand by the regime or whether they decide to throw their weight behind protesters can be essential to the outcome of any struggle for democracy. In the Middle East, analysts widely assumed that the armed forces would always be at one with the regimes. As Gregory Gause argues, this was not an unreasonable assumption,[35] since many Arab leaders came from the ranks of the military, among them Hosni Mubarak of Egypt and Zine el-Abidine Ben Ali of Tunisia. Moreover, regimes invested heavily in the expansion of the armed forces. And last but not least, militaries benefited disproportionately from the public purse, not only in the form of generous work conditions but also in terms of access to economic opportunities, as the case of the Egyptian military amply demonstrates. Yet the empirical record does not unanimously support this assumption about armed forces' loyalty to regimes. In Egypt and Tunisia, armed forces dissociated themselves from the political leadership; in Libya, Yemen, and to a certain extent Syria, the armed forces imploded, with loyal units continuing to defend the regime while others defected to the opposition and others simply went home; and in Bahrain, the army carried out the repression of protesters on behalf of the regime. Two explanations seem to account for this variation: the nature of societal cleavages and the degree to which these are reflected in the composition of the armed forces, as well as the degree of professionalism of the military.

On this score, the Egyptian armed forces might have provided the best-case scenario for continued regime loyalty—not only are the country and its military relatively homogeneous, but the Egyptian armed forces have also been the recipient of substantial US aid that has contributed to its professionalization. In 2010, $1.3 billion of Washington's $2 billion annual aid package to Egypt went to strengthening the Egyptian armed forces, while another $1.9 million was directed toward training meant to bolster long-term US-Egyptian military cooperation.

Aside from large militaries and defense expenditures, regimes historically resorted to alliances as the primary strategy to dampen the impact of regional insecurity. This held true whether the threats emanated from outside the state's borders, as with Gulf states' concerns with Iranian nuclear capabilities and regional ambitions, or from within, as in the fight against jihadi terrorists. In true realist fashion, Middle Eastern leaders were adept at maintaining a favorable balance of power, carefully crafting both domestic and international alliances.

In their search for outside allies, Middle Eastern states have been particularly helped by their geostrategic and regional position. In the 1960s and 1970s, the superpowers provided aid, political support, and military assistance to their allies. This included not only weapons but also long-term assistance for military industries, state-owned enterprises, and advanced surveillance technologies. Unlike Africa, where the end of the Cold War ushered in an era of great-power disinterest, the Middle East has continued to attract the attention of major powers, from the US-led coalition's efforts to restore Kuwait's sovereignty to the North Atlantic Treaty Organization's (NATO) 2011 Operation Unified Protector in Libya. While some alliances have ended—for instance, the one that existed between Iraq and the various Western and Gulf states that supported it in its war against Iran—others have endured despite serious crises.

An example of such an enduring relationship is the US-Saudi alliance, which weathered the severe crisis triggered by the events of 11 September 2001. To date,[36] and despite bumps along the road, the strategic partnership between Saudi Arabia and the United States has been sustained by common interests and a shared perception of threats, particularly (but not only) emanating from Iran.[37] A long series of US arms transfers to Saudi Arabia has built up critical Saudi mission capabilities, and developed the interoperability capabilities of Saudi forces.[38] These transfers "are steadily improving [the Saudi] capability to deter and defend against Iran in all forms of intimidation and warfare, as well as give Saudi Arabia and other local forces the capability to deal with any terrorist or low-level threats like the tribal attacks from Yemen into Saudi Arabia [in 2009]."[39] Such external support also strengthens the regime against potential domestic challenges. Nor was this game played only with Saudis. Rather, US arms transfers to Saudi Arabia "are part of a broader pattern . . . that not only build[s] up Saudi capabilities but also those of other Gulf Cooperation Council (GCC) states."[40] Similarly, the US-Egyptian alliance was instrumental in making it possible for the Mubarak regime to maintain itself in power despite its limited commitment to reform and democratization. As Vincent Durac has argued, international support—or international indifference—allowed the Egyptian regime to craft and maintain a favorable balance of internal power, and to maintain its grip on an increasingly restless society.[41]

Another important set of alliances are those domestic alliances that regimes forge to ward off internal and external threats. This internal balancing act is as important to regime survival as the search for external allies. Yet the two are also related, in that alliances with outside powers can be instrumental in providing the resources necessary for the patronage that is at the heart of the internal balancing act.

The 2011 uprisings affected the ability of regimes to craft and maintain internal and external alliances. With regard to the latter, outside powers have been increasingly constrained in their ability to back authoritarian rulers in the name of regional stability, especially where regimes use widespread repression against their people. In Libya, Muammar Qaddafi's use of repression brought NATO intervention. In Syria, similar repression brought more limited sanctions and a failed United Nations peace plan. In other cases, however, outside powers have been more reluctant to destabilize long-standing allies: Washington has tread carefully with regard to the authoritarian clampdown in Bahrain, while Russia and China signaled their unwillingness to authorize strong measures against Syria in the United Nations Security Council.

Within the region, states threatened by the Arab Spring have also found both allies and opponents. The Arab League supported measures against Libya and Syria, and some Arab states actively backed rebels in both countries with arms and financing. In Bahrain, by contrast, the Gulf Cooperation Council (GCC) provided military forces to buttress the Khalifa monarchy, and the wealthier Gulf states also provided aid and encouragement to Oman, Morocco, and Jordan to buttress those monarchies against domestic reformist protests. Saudi Arabia and the GCC also played a key role in mediating Ali Abdullah Saleh's departure from power in Yemen. Riyadh in particular has often seen regime change through the prism of its strategic rivalry with Iran—hence its support for the Bahraini regime and its opposition to Iranian ally Bashar al-Asad in Syria. The Arab Spring has thus underscored the salience of regional alliances and foreign policies, while presenting both new sources of threat and opportunity for regional leaders.

Transnational Threats and Appeals

The purported death of Arab nationalism did not spell the end of transnational influences in the Middle East. Since the late 1970s, Arab regimes and Western governments have placed much emphasis on the key role played by Islam in regional security dynamics. What role have Islamist transnational appeals played in shaping the domestic politics and foreign policies of Middle Eastern states? And to what extent, if any, do they contribute to determining the nature of regimes? To answer these questions, we trace the growth of transnational Islamist appeals. We then proceed to document the manner in which these appeals were perceived as threats to regime and regional security. Finally, we explore the manner in which regimes skillfully used (or built up) these threats to maintain themselves in power, quash domestic opponents, and deal with troublesome neighbors in the name of security.

In the first decade of the twenty-first century, pan-Islamic appeals managed to undo some of the gains Arab states had made in terms of their capacity to insulate their societies. These transnational influences had domestic and regional dimensions. Domestically, they encouraged regimes to maintain an authoritarian grip on their "dangerously restless" societies, while regionally they contributed to what has been described as a new Arab Cold War. Taken together, these two dynamics contributed to maintaining a sense of shared pan-Arab identity, an identity that some recognize as a contributing factor to the 2011 uprisings.[42]

Following the 11 September 2001 terrorist attacks in the United States, the "radical edge of political Islam began to present itself as a new international security challenge for the dominant state actors."[43] Yet political Islam had already established itself as one of the most sustained and serious *domestic* threats to the survival of authoritarian regimes in the 1970s as Islamist movements, unlike their liberal, nationalist, or leftist counterparts, managed to maintain an autonomous power base and to mobilize substantial grassroots support.[44]

In the post-9/11 environment, many (Western) media reports and policy debates focused on the transnational dimension of Islamist struggles, neglecting their national dimension and the domestic use of political Islam as an instrument to oppose authoritarianism. While radical Islamist groups mounted violent challenges to governments in various parts of the Arab world, stretching from Yemen to Algeria, these were increasingly being carried out by organizations more or less loosely claiming connections to al-Qaeda. Al-Qaeda in the Arabian Peninsula (AQAP) claimed responsibility for the wave of terrorist bombings that shook Saudi Arabia from 2003 to 2007; further afield, violence in Algeria and attacks against foreigners in North Africa—reaching as far afield as Mali—were increasingly claimed by al-Qaeda in the Islamic Maghreb (AQIM). In other words, there seemed to be a higher degree of organizational cooperation and coordination among Islamist groups as compared to in the 1980s and 1990s. Scholars who study these new al-Qaeda "franchises" highlight the role played by recent wars in Bosnia, Afghanistan, and Iraq in the transnational mobilization of Islamists.[45] For example, Thomas Hegghammer argues that AQAP is not a sociorevolutionary group bent on regime change, but first and foremost a pan-Islamist group concerned with defending the umma in a context where it might be more urgent to attack "non-Muslims who kill Muslims and occupy Muslim territory" than to worry about the threat posed by Lady Gaga or other vectors of cultural Westernization.[46] However, it is important to underline that mainstream nonviolent Islamist parties have stood to gain from the sense that Islam was under global attack. Indeed, following the events of 9/11, many scored considerable successes in national elections in Morocco, Algeria, Bahrain, and Turkey, among others.[47]

The presence and the activities of Islamist jihadists, coupled with the renewed strength of Islamist parties in many Arab and majority-Muslim countries, forced regimes to take greater stock of a revitalized pan-regional popular sentiment, which is often linked with the emergence of the media revolution ushered in by Al Jazeera. The reawakening of the "Arab street" was not spurred by events in Afghanistan; rather, Arabs first poured onto the streets in outrage at the Israeli military offensive in the West Bank in 2002. "For a short while, states lost their tight control and publicly vocal opposition groups proliferated, even among the 'Westernized' and 'apolitical' students of the American University in Cairo."[48] As the United States prepared to forcibly remove the regime of Saddam Hussein, 1 million Yemenis marched in Sanaa, over 10,000 protested in Khartoum, thousands took to the streets in Damascus and Rabat, and hundreds followed suit in Bahrain.[49] Thus the 2011 uprisings have only confirmed the extent to which events resonate across borders in the region.

Regimes have had to contend with this renewed permeability. This is visible in that while many Arab and Islamic countries sympathized with the victims of 9/11, not all governments were equally prompt to provide all-out material support to the subsequent US war effort in Afghanistan, as they were worried about the potential domestic backlash.[50] Thus Kuwait, Bahrain, Qatar, and Jordan provided total support, with Jordan being the only country to offer to contribute peacekeeping troops to a force in Afghanistan. Several other Middle Eastern states agreed to share intelligence, freeze financial flows, and provide diplomatic support to the US effort. Egypt and Saudi Arabia, which had previously contended with Islamist-inspired violence, were more reserved. While they backed the United States in principle, they criticized certain aspects of the US response, including the suffering of Afghan civilians. This equivocal stance was later reflected in the responses to the 2006 Israel-Hezbollah war, with Arab regimes—particularly Jordan, Egypt, and Saudi Arabia—initially reacting to the Hezbollah operation that sparked the conflict by describing it as "harming 'the Arab interest.'" But as civilian casualties rose, these regimes "began distancing themselves—at least rhetorically—from the US and Israel, and instead tried to raise their Arab profiles by sending humanitarian aid and reintroducing the Arab Peace Initiative."[51] Reactions to the 2011 uprisings also underscore the extent to which regimes worry about permeability. A number of regimes, including Saudi Arabia, used their media to warn about the public disorder related to the uprisings rather than highlight the struggle against authoritarianism.

Increased permeability to transnational pan-Islamic appeals also translated into what some authors dubbed the new Arab Cold War.[52] This refers to the growing challenge that Islamist actors within society pose to the regional status quo and the concomitant efforts by regimes to quell these challenges. Much as was the case in the 1950s, this challenge highlights the vulnerability of states to foreign influences, particularly in the "warmest" theaters of this new Cold War, Lebanon, Yemen, and now Syria.

The two camps of the new Arab Cold War could be described as pro– and anti–status quo, the status quo in this case being post-2003 US ascendancy in the Middle East. Where the Arab Cold War of the 1950s pitted conservative regimes against revolutionary regimes, the more recent confrontation pitted regimes close to the United States—such as the Jordanian and Saudi monarchies, the Mubarak regime, and the post-2005 Fouad al-Siniora government in Lebanon—against "societal actors led by Islamists with considerable popular support and subscribing to a popular driven Islamic Political Arabism."[53] The lead actors of this latter group, much like their revolutionary predecessors, have sought to discredit their adversaries domestically, by exposing the rift between the ruling elites and society, and externally by discrediting the claim of status quo regimes that they have the best interests of the Arab world at heart.

The summer 2006 conflict between Hezbollah and Israel was a stark illustration of the new Arab Cold War. Prior to the war, Hezbollah had pledged not to stand idly by in the face of what it considered to be a grave injustice being meted out by Israel on fellow Arabs and Muslims in the Palestinian territories. By taking on the most powerful state in the region and the key ally of the United States, Hezbollah came to embody Arab feelings about Palestine while also indirectly condemning the inability and unwillingness of Arab states to act decisively in order to alter the status quo. This was particularly significant given that Palestine remains much more than a political question for many Arabs, as has been demonstrated time and time again by international polls.[54] Across the Arab world, popular support for Hezbollah expressed itself in ways reminiscent of the heyday of the first Arab Cold War, as demonstrators explicitly linked Hezbollah leader Hassan Nasrallah with the nationalist hero, former Egyptian president Nasser.[55] Although they initially accused Nasrallah and his party of hurting the Arab interest by entering into an open confrontation with Israel, Arab regimes subsequently backed down and sought to play the pan-Arabism card by sending humanitarian aid to Lebanon.

This new Arab Cold War not only produced regional tensions between pro– and anti–status quo actors, but also spilled over into the domestic politics of the most vulnerable Arab states, triggering domestic crises that have at times threatened regime stability. The clearest illustration of the spillover of this new Arab Cold War into domestic politics was the 2006–2008 crisis between the Hezbollah-led March 8 coalition and the Saad Hariri–led March 14 coalition in Lebanon. In ways reminiscent of the 1958 Lebanese civil war, the conflict fused domestic grievances with disagreements over the foreign policy orientations of the regime. The situation was further complicated by the external actors involved, with the March 14 group being backed by the Western powers (particularly the United States and France) and Saudi Arabia, and the March 8 group drawing its support from Syria and Iran. These differences continue to periodically convulse Lebanese politics.

The reemergence of transnational ideologies and the concomitant increased permeability of Arab states to external influences did not simply create liabilities for Arab regimes. They have also been used by several authoritarian regimes to reclaim their grip on society. This has involved two types of strategies: quelling dissent in the name of the fight against terror and attempting to reclaim the mantle of legitimacy.

Jihadist activity has provided authoritarian regimes with arguments to delay reform and quash opposition forces in the name of state security. In Egypt, the regime deployed a "state of emergency" rationale to repress violent as well as nonviolent opposition actors, and indeed did so even before the events of 9/11.[56] Considerations of regime security are key to understanding the attitude of the Mubarak regime toward the opposition, including but not limited to the Islamists. In the early 1990s, the Egyptian regime seemed to fear an Algerian-style scenario whereby the Muslim Brotherhood would come to power through elections.[57] This fear was further deepened by the successes of the Muslim Brothers in seizing control of the lawyers syndicate in 1992,[58] and by the increase in Islamist violence against the regime in the 1990s. In fact, from 1990 until 1997, "Egypt witnessed a low-level war of attrition between the authorities and revolutionary Islamists, like al-Jama'a al-Islamiya (Islamic Group) and Jihad, resulting in about 1,300 casualties, billions of dollars in damage to the tourist industry, and considerable costs to relations between state and society."[59]

The regime's response was sweeping. It launched a full onslaught on civil society and professional associations, linking Islamist violence in Egypt to foreign attempts at destabilizing the country.[60] President Mubarak "tried to portray the internal struggle for power in Egypt as part of an international campaign orchestrated and financed by Islamic Iran and Sudan: 'We are confronting foreign plots and attempted intervention.'"[61] As Fawaz Gerges demonstrated convincingly, the Bill Clinton administration accepted the regime's argument, with the result that "Mubarak felt empowered to emasculate all opposition, Islamist and secular, thus prolonging Egypt's crisis of political governance."[62]

The second part of the Egyptian regime's strategy involved attempts at reclaiming the mantle of legitimacy. Much like its strategy of quashing the opposition, this was an old and practiced art form. In the 1970s, President Anwar Sadat used Islamic symbols to assuage the opposition and thus to strengthen his rule. In the 1990s, Egypt regained membership in the Arab League—it had been suspended after making peace with Israel—and sought to use its privileged relations with Israel and the United States to become one of the engines of the Arab-Israeli peace process. Nonetheless, the regime continued to shore up its Islamic and Arab credentials. For example, in the fall of 2000, the culture minister banned the novel *A Banquet for Seaweed* for

> dangerously depart[ing] from "accepted religious understanding" and threaten[ing] "the solidarity of the nation." Having thus defended the faith, the government then shut down the very opposition newspaper that had exposed the offending book! However cynical, the move made perfect sense. The political party that published the paper had close ties to the mainstream Muslim Brotherhood, and the state was out to underscore its own role as the supreme arbiter of matters Islamic (for good measure, the authorities had two hundred Muslim Brothers arrested).[63]

Two years later, the same regime was once again attempting to don the mantle of Arab legitimacy, by portraying itself as a defender of the human security of Palestinians and of the sovereign decisions of Arab states. Much like its counterparts in Jordan, Sudan, or Yemen, it tacitly approved the massive popular demonstrations in support of Palestinians, in part because these were directed primarily against outside adversaries.[64] And while the regime clearly sought to contain the Egyptian protesters when the latter demonstrated against the US war on Iraq,[65] it nevertheless attempted to take on "the role of defender of national sovereignty in setting limits to 'foreign' intervention in domestic affairs."[66]

The new Arab Cold War ultimately contributed to the persistence of authoritarianism as regimes used the threat of potential domestic spillover from regional conflicts to delay reform. King Abdallah II of Jordan highlighted his country's special situation as a "neighbor" of three civil wars—in Palestine, Lebanon, and Iraq—to ward off calls for the implementation of reforms.[67] Egypt used similar arguments to justify its lack of progress on political reform. In Yemen, President Saleh accused the Houthi rebellion of serving as an instrument of Iran's foreign policy agenda "and used this as a justification (among others) for his scorched earth policy and his refusal to address the grievances of the Houthi rebels regarding the manner in which the country was being ruled."[68] Last but not least, in Lebanon, the Siniora government drew strength and support from its Western allies in refusing to engage with Hezbollah on the issue of Shiite representation in the political system.[69]

In an essay titled "Why Middle East Studies Missed the Arab Spring," Gregory Gause draws attention to the pan-Arab dimension of the 2011 uprisings. Gause correctly points out that it is no coincidence that Arabs took to the streets in 2011 after Mohamed Bouazizi set himself on fire in Tunisia rather than in 2009 when mass demonstrations against the reelection of President Ahmadinejad of Iran were severely repressed by the regime.[70] This demonstration effect underscores the existence of a pan-Arab dynamic that can only be ignored by regimes and outside actors at their own peril. Transnational Islamist appeals, Islamist threats both domestic and transnational, and the reactions of Arab (and Western) powers seeking to deal with these challenges have contributed to the rekindling of this pan-Arab dynamic.

Democracy Promotion

The third wave of democracy, following the collapse of authoritarian regimes at the end of the Cold War, led analysts and practitioners to assume the existence of a "'natural sequence' whereby a loosening of authoritarian controls is followed by breakthrough elections and a transfer of power to liberal-democratic forces."[71] Initially, the pattern seemed to hold in the Middle East, where political liberalization unfolded in several countries as illustrated by electoral processes in Algeria, Jordan, and Yemen, limited democratization in Egypt and Morocco, and peaceful leadership change coupled with political opening in Tunisia. Much as they did in Latin America in the mid-1980s, US and other policymakers stepped in to support these changes. At the same time, brokers of democracy, mostly US and European actors, focused on liberal civil society in their efforts to promote democratic values.

The events of 11 September 2001 gave a new impetus to US democracy promotion efforts, by tying them to the war against terror. "Whether, where, and how the United States should promote democracy around the world [became] central questions in U.S. policy debates with regards to a host of countries,"[72] including Egypt, Iran, Iraq, and Saudi Arabia. In the words of the George W. Bush administration's Freedom Agenda, this was supposed to be a "generational challenge to instill democracy in the Arab world" and thus improve US security.[73]

The 2011 uprisings offer a fortuitous historical conjuncture for assessing the impact of Western efforts to promote democracy in the Middle East and the extent to which this was a genuine objective or a convenient instrument that Western governments deployed to other ends.[74] That different storylines can be told in this regard is both empirically significant and analytically telling. One could, for example, propose three different readings of democracy promotion's contribution to the Egyptian uprising. According to one perspective, it had no impact; in fact, it could be argued that beyond the rhetoric, democracy promotion always took a backseat to considerations of regional stability. Thus Egyptian protesters toppled the Mubarak regime *in spite of* Western, particularly US, support of the regime. In another view, democracy promotion had at best a limited and indirect impact, with programs aimed at civil society having imbued some activists with democratic norms and ideals. But this account fails to explain the timing of the uprisings, as well as the widespread participation of swaths of Egyptian society who had been left out of democracy promotion programs, including the supporters of the Muslim Brotherhood. A third and final account suggests that democracy promotion had a significant and direct—though maybe unconventional[75]—impact on the course of events.[76] Indeed, US military assistance might be credited with the professionalization of the Egyptian army, which in turn contributed to the critical decision of the armed forces not to use violence against the people or to side with the Mubarak regime.

Before the global "war on terror," the bulk of US democracy promotion programs were concentrated at the US Agency for International Development (USAID), the National Endowment for Democracy, the National Democratic Institute, the International Republican Institute, and the Ford Foundation. For their part, Europeans established the Euro-Mediterranean Initiative and the MEDA Democracy Initiative. As Sheila Carapico documents extensively,[77] in the 1990s most grants went to nonprofit institutions. Among other things, these grants sought to improve democratic representation, to strengthen the rule of law, and to empower civil society. For their part, UN agencies focused on institutional capacity building, notably in the area of electoral assistance.

Notwithstanding the use of force to bring about change in places such as Iraq, and despite the fact that the global "war on terror" might have put Western democracy promotion into the limelight, little has changed since the 1990s when it comes to the nature of democracy promotion programming. Western countries continue to operate with top-down approaches: "They have focused on political elites, giving preference to secular, Western-style opposition movements with very limited popular appeal."[78] The focus on civil society organizations has also suffered from similar drawbacks, as these elite groups are often unrepresentative of wider societal concerns.[79] Further, US and European Union democracy promotion efforts have systematically marginalized Islamist political and civil society organizations.[80] The United States engaged in public diplomacy, with officials emphasizing the importance of democratic reform as a core objective of US policy; it also sought to promote reform by establishing mass media outlets such as Radio Sawa (Together) and the Al Hurrah (Free) television network. But on the whole, post 9/11 programs such as the Middle East Partnership Initiative, the Broader Middle East and North Africa Initiative, and the European Neighbourhood Project consisted of "limited initiatives" that emphasized civil society organizations and particularly human rights nongovernmental organizations, as well as technical assistance to legislatures and judiciaries. Such initiatives, Katerina Dalacoura and others argue, are limited in that they cannot curb the executive.[81] Speaking more particularly about programs for women's rights, Marina Ottaway has maintained that although these efforts might change the lives of the participants involved, they are a distraction that steers resources away from weakening executive power.[82] Indeed, by polishing some of the "rough edges" of authoritarianism, they might have even contributed to its persistence.

Western efforts to promote democracy can be partially credited with the adoption of a democratic discourse by regimes in the Middle East, though these regimes often have done so narrowly and instrumentally.[83] Across the region, meetings of intellectuals and activists have also produced pro-reform statements. In 2004, the establishment in Yemen of the Arab Democratic Dialogue Forum, the Alexandria conference on "Arab reform," and the Doha Declaration for Democracy and Reform attested to the renewed mobilization of elites and political activists.[84] This spurred reactions from governments and from the Arab League, which in its Tunis Declaration of May 2004 made mention of political reform. And although they cannot be fully credited to Western democracy promotion, substantial popular mobilizations occurred before the 2011 uprisings in the context of Lebanon's Cedar Revolution, of the Kefaya movement in Egypt, and of the contestation of President Ahmadinejad's 2009 reelection in Iran. However, it is accurate to say that during the global war on terror, the extent to which Western democracy promotion efforts have threatened regimes in the Middle East has depended in great part on whether the latter were perceived as friends or foes by the United States and their Western allies.

Unlike in Africa or Latin America,[85] the Middle East has not seen a decline in foreign interest and intervention since the end of the Cold War. For a number of reasons—many of which have to do with the security of world oil supplies, US and European commitments to the security of the state of Israel,[86] and concerns about the rise of global jihadism—Western economic and security interests continue to be directly tied to developments in the Middle East. As Laura Guazzone and Daniela Pioppi argue, the enduring link between regional and global conflicts resides in the fact that "it has been through conflicts originating in the Arab Middle East—the Egyptian-

Saudi roots of Sunni jihadism in Afghanistan, the renewal of the Israeli-Palestinian conflict since 2000 and the insurgency in Iraq since 2004—that the new patterns of international security have come to be perceived as a global phenomenon, namely with regard to al-Qaeda style global terrorism."[87] This growing entanglement of regional and international security dimensions has had important consequences for the manner in which Western powers pursue democracy promotion.

Where Western security concerns have coincided with the agendas of authoritarian regimes, the latter have been given a relatively wide margin of maneuver in skirting pressure to reform. Where the United States has been dealing with foes, it has pursued democratic reform "in tandem with security objectives such as containing the threats of terrorism and [weapons of mass destruction] and protecting Israel."[88] From the US military invasion that ousted the regime of Saddam Hussein in 2003 to Operation Unified Protector in Libya, attempts were made to rein in "rogue" regimes. The extent to which these attempts have threatened regime stability has varied. In Iraq and Libya, US democracy promotion was key; less so in Syria, where US democracy promotion may have contributed to emboldening opposition activists but where, prior to 2011, the West's focus on securing Syrian withdrawal from Lebanon diverted the Western powers' attention from, and lessened their interest in, domestic democratic reform. Following the withdrawal of Syrian troops from Lebanon, the Syrian authorities' crackdown on opposition forces elicited little if any outside reaction.[89] Similar variation in the earnestness with which Western powers support democratic transformation where broader regional and international security considerations are also at play is evident in reactions to the 2011 uprisings. In Syria, the regime of Bashar al-Assad initially managed to gain some breathing space in part because its fall would have had regional implications with direct bearing on Israel and Iran. Outside pressure for political reform, though it might have opened or widened a window of opportunity for regime opponents, did not automatically result in the weakening of authoritarianism and the concomitant strengthening of democrats within.

Whereas the United States and its allies went so far as to use force to help dislodge autocrats in Iraq in 2003 and Libya in 2011, most regimes that are allied with the United States and with the West more generally have managed to ward off the threats to their continued authoritarian rule. In so doing, autocrats in the Middle East have skillfully "securitized" the issue of Islamist political movements, painting them as a threat to regime and Western interests alike. They have also been able to break promises of reform without endangering the political and material support that they receive from the West. Some have even gone so far as to reject aspects of democracy promotion as foreign interference in domestic politics.

Relatedly, Middle Eastern regimes skillfully and successfully took advantage of the opportunity provided by the post-9/11 global war on terror. In many "friendly" countries, including Saudi Arabia, Egypt, Jordan, Tunisia, Algeria, and Yemen, regimes have been further strengthened by the generous support that they have received "lest undemocratic Islamic extremism [become] empowered."[90] And despite post-9/11 calls for a recalibration of US-Saudi relations—and to borrow from the title of a 2003 report on the state of these relations—the Saudi connection to the 9/11 terrorist attacks ultimately proved to be more "a bump in the road" than "the end of the road."[91] In Tunisia, where President Ben Ali particularly succeeded in fostering the securitization of Islamists and in discrediting his main political opponent, the Nahda party, the regime justified its policies to European partners by appealing to their own concerns regarding Islamist radicalization and terrorism.[92] In Yemen, the United States perceived the government of Ali Abdullah Saleh as struggling against a common enemy, AQAP, and extended offers of military support.[93]

The global war on terror also helped Middle Eastern regimes fight political reform in another important way, in that they were able to use foreign alliances as sources of external rents in their efforts to build and maintain armies. This assistance provides allied regimes with dual-use domestic surveillance and security capacities that could equally be used to meet domestic terrorist threats as well as to track, monitor, and punish domestic opponents. Unlike European states, where the civilianization of government and domestic politics has prompted militaries to "shed [their] internal security functions to concentrate on what grew to be considered as 'traditional' external threats to national security,"[94] in the Middle East, armies continue to be used to deal with internal threats to regime survival, including from prodemocracy forces, as was illustrated when the Bahraini armed forces were deployed to suppress protests in 2011.

It must be said that the United States did put pressure on friendly regimes to undertake reforms, and that Bahrain, Qatar, Kuwait, Yemen, Saudi Arabia, Egypt, Jordan, Algeria, and Morocco to varying degrees took minor steps to improve civil rights and to allow greater political participation.[95] But as Ellen Lust has convincingly argued, even as regimes allowed political participation, this was structured in ways that prevent the genuine contestation of power.[96] Moreover, regimes also rolled back reform without triggering much reaction from their Western allies. This was the case, for example, when President Mubarak of Egypt introduced constitutional amendments in 2007 that not only infringed on the protection of human rights but also closed off avenues for the peaceful participation of the Muslim Brotherhood in the political process. Prior to the 2011 uprisings, and in spite of changes to the structure of its aid to Egypt—historically the second largest recipient of US bilateral aid—Washington had not decreased its support for the Mubarak regime. Instead, civil society bore the brunt of budgetary cuts in spite of an internal USAID audit that identified direct grants to civil society initiatives as the most successful US democracy promotion programs in Egypt, and that held the Egyptian government responsible for the lack of cooperation with US efforts.[97]

The tension between the West's democracy promotion discourse and Western governments' security imperatives has, in some instances, been skillfully used by Western allies to cast doubt on the entire democracy promotion enterprise, in the name of national sovereignty and as part of their attempt to don the mantle of legitimacy. For example, the Mubarak regime strongly opposed the George W. Bush administration's Greater Middle East Initiative, which was disclosed at the 2004 summit meeting of the Group of Eight (G8), the largest industrialized countries. An angry Mubarak, irked by the fact that no Middle Eastern state had been consulted, was quoted as responding that "we hear about these initiatives as if the region and its states did not exist, as if they had no sovereignty over their land."[98] In a replay of the manner in which the fight against terrorism was used to quell non-Islamists, the Mubarak regime proceeded to politicize foreign support for civil society and human rights organizations. "The case of Saad Eddin Ibrahim, who was arrested in 2000 and subsequently jailed for seven years on charges of 'accepting international funding without government permission' in addition to 'tarnishing Egypt's reputation abroad,' sent a clear message to civil society activists that the regime was willing to play this card even in relation to one of the most [respected] civil society activists, both nationally and internationally."[99] The White House's decision not to honor a $130 million Egyptian request for supplemental aid did very little to sway the regime. In Egypt, as elsewhere in the region, Western support potentially delegitimized political movements clamoring for change, in the eyes of their own constituencies as well as in the eyes of competitors.[100]

Regarding the ability of Western powers to press for democratic change while also pursuing their security objectives, the 2011 uprisings complicated matters. That is, while they were initially inclined to stand by their allies in the name of regional stability, they have had to tread carefully. It took over four months for President Barack Obama to articulate the US position on the uprisings, and when this came, he tried to uphold US commitments to universal rights and freedoms while simultaneously reiterating US support for allies and partners. But that tightrope became increasingly difficult to walk, in light of NATO's intervention in Libya, ostensibly to protect civilians but in reality also to effect regime change, and in light of the difficulties encountered in articulating a strong and clear position on the crisis in Syria.

Looking Ahead

As was the case before the end of the Cold War, the regional and international environments have been an omnipresent factor in the decisionmaking of Middle Eastern regimes. Since the early 1990s, there have been three primary ways that external forces have come into play: through conflicts, transnational Islamist threats, and Western democracy promotion efforts. Although treated separately, these are intimately connected. And while each could and did create threats for regimes, whether these threats have translated into vulnerabilities or opportunities seems to depend on a set of factors: alliances, rents, and coercive apparatuses.

This chapter has already touched upon alliances and coercive apparatuses; it has said less about rents, although they are a core element of authoritarian regimes' survival strategies.[101] Financial resources can be used as a source of patronage (as discussed in Chapter 9), but also as a tool of foreign policy intended to deal with threats emanating from the regional environment. The ability of the Saudis and others to use their oil wealth to shape the regional environment has waxed and waned depending on the price of oil. But while oil booms have provided authoritarian regimes with a potent tool of foreign policy, oil busts have not necessarily increased their vulnerability at home. Rentier states have found a number of ways to avoid increased domestic extraction. Further, differences in rent types, in state-society relations, and in the nature of crisis can affect the ability of regimes to craft responses and maintain themselves in power.

Where alliances, rents, and coercive apparatuses have been available, rulers have enjoyed "systemic invulnerability"; where one or more have been wanting, they have faced challenges. According to this reading, the fall of Saddam Hussein's regime can be described as the result of a shift from the pre-1990 situation, when his regime enjoyed Western support, oil rents, and a strong military, to the 2003 situation, when it was embattled as a result of having lost most of its external allies, its unhampered access to rent, and the ability to maintain the quality of its coercive apparatus. Likewise, in Libya, Egypt, and Tunisia, where the 2011 uprisings have resulted in the fall of the previous leaders, the authorities found that they could not count on allies, rents, or the armed forces to come to their rescue. By contrast, in Bahrain, Saudi support has bolstered the regime, while in Syria the loyalty of key units in the armed forces helped prolong the regime of Bashar al-Assad.

The linkages between domestic politics and foreign policy will continue to shape the decisions of regimes in the aftermath of the Arab Spring. But there are indications that, in the new environment of the post-2011 uprisings, both authoritarian and transitional regimes are likely to face a number of challenges in developing policies to deal with these linkages in ways that do not increase their vulnerability. First, whereas Arab rulers could historically argue that their internal opponents were being "manipulated" from outside (and could thus justify the use of repression against them), the leaderless quality of the uprisings in Egypt and Tunisia made such accusations increasingly difficult to sustain. Second, Western powers may experience limits to their margin of maneuver as they endorse the democratic aspirations of people in Egypt, Tunisia, or Libya yet remain relatively silent on other Arab authoritarianisms. How will these new constraints combine with the availability (or lack) of rents, and what impact will the combination have on the systemic invulnerability that most Arab regimes had seemingly enjoyed to date? Will these new conditions be sufficient to "chart paths away from the pathological relationships that have characterized the region's political life"?[102] Potentially fruitful avenues of research for answering these questions include analyses of the impact of systemic influences on military development, as well as a fine-grained understanding of the impact of the 2011 uprisings on civil-military relations in the region.

Notes

1. See Bassel F. Salloukh and Rex Brynen, eds., *Persistent Permeability? Regionalism, Localism, and Globalization in the Middle East* (Aldershot: Ashgate, 2004), p. 1.

2. Paul Noble, "The Arab System: Pressures, Constraints, and Opportunities," in Bahgat Korany and Ali E. Hillal Dessouki, eds., *The Foreign Policies of Arab States,* 2nd ed. (Boulder: Westview, 1991), p. 56.

3. Stephen Walt, *The Origins of Alliances* (Ithaca: Cornell University Press, 1987), p. 236.

4. See, for example, Steven David, "Explaining Third World Alignment," *World Politics* 43, 2 (1991); Michael Barnett and Jack Levy, "Domestic Sources of Alliances and Alignments: The Case of Egypt, 1962–73," *International Organization* 45, 3 (1991); Bahgat Korany, Paul Noble, and Rex Brynen, eds., *The Many Faces of National Security in the Arab World* (London: Macmillan, 1993).

5. F. Gregory Gause III, "Regional Influences on Experiments in Political Liberalization in the Arab World," in Rex Brynen, Bahgat Korany, and Paul Noble, eds., *Political Liberalization and Democratization in the Arab World,* vol. 1, *Theoretical Perspectives* (Boulder: Lynne Rienner, 1995), p. 285.

6. David, "Explaining Third World Alignment," p. 236.

7. Barnett and Levy, "Domestic Sources of Alliances and Alignments," p. 23.

8. Noble, "The Arab System," p. 57.

9. Fouad Ajami, "The End of Pan-Arabism," *Foreign Affairs* 57, 2 (Winter 1978).

10. Rex Brynen, "Palestine and the Arab State System: Permeability, State Consolidation, and the Intifada," *Canadian Journal of Political Science* 24, 3 (September 1991); Lisa Anderson, "The State in the Middle East and North Africa,"

Comparative Politics 20, 1 (1987); Michael N. Barnett, "Sovereignty, Nationalism, and Regional Order in the Arab States System," *International Organization* 49, 3 (Summer 1995).

11. Brynen, "Palestine and the Arab State System."

12. See Michael N. Barnett, "Regional Security After the Gulf War," *Political Science Quarterly* 111, 4 (Winter 1996–1997).

13. See Bassel F. Salloukh, "Regime Autonomy and Regional Foreign Policy Choices in the Middle East: A Theoretical Exploration," in Salloukh and Brynen, *Persistent Permeability,* pp. 81–104.

14. Shibley Telhami, *Power and Leadership in International Bargaining* (New York: Columbia University Press, 1990).

15. Michael N. Barnett, *Dialogues in Arab Politics: Negotiations in Regional Order* (New York: Columbia University Press, 1998).

16. David Garnham and Mark Tessler, eds., *Democracy, War, and Peace in the Middle East* (Indiana: Indiana University Press, 1995), especially chapters by James Lee Ray, Mark Tessler, and Marilyn Grobschmidt.

17. Jack Levy, "The Diversionary Theory of War: A Critique," in Manus I. Midlarsky, ed., *Handbook of War Studies* (London: Unwin Hyman, 1989).

18. Graeme A. Davies, "Inside Out or Outside In? Domestic and International Factors Affecting Iranian Foreign Policy Towards the United States, 1990–2004," *Foreign Policy Analysis* 4, 3 (July 2008), p. 210.

19. Wade L. Huntley, "Rebels Without a Cause: North Korea, Iran, and the NPT," *International Affairs* 82, 4 (2006).

20. Davies, "Inside Out or Outside In?"

21. F. Gregory Gause III, "Iraq's Decisions to Go to War, 1980 and 1990," *Middle East Journal* 56, 1 (Winter 2002).

22. Gause, "Regional Influences," p. 287.

23. International Crisis Group, "Drums of War: Israel and the 'Axis of Resistance,'" Middle East Report no. 97 (Brussels, 2 August 2010).

24. Salloukh and Brynen, *Persistent Permeability,* p. 4. The term "Arab Cold War" was coined by Malcolm Kerr in *The Arab Cold War, 1958–1964: A Study of Ideology in Politics* (London: Oxford University Press, 1965).

25. See Malcolm Kerr, *The Arab Cold War: Gamal Abdal Nasir and His Rivals, 1952–1970* (London: Oxford University Press, 1971).

26. See F. Gregory Gause III, *The International Relations of the Persian Gulf* (Cambridge: Cambridge University Press, 2010).

27. Keith Krause, "Insecurity and State Formation in the Global Military Order: The Middle Eastern Case," *European Journal of International Relations* 2, 3 (1996), p. 332.

28. J. C. Hurewitz, *Middle East Politics: The Military Dimension* (New York: Praeger, 1969), p. 450, cited in Krause, "Insecurity and State Formation," p. 333.

29. Krause, "Insecurity and State Formation," p. 333.

30. Eva Bellin, "The Robustness of Authoritarianism in the Middle East: Exceptionalism in Comparative Perspective," *Comparative Politics* 36, 2 (January 2004), p. 143.

31. Bellin, "The Robustness of Authoritarianism," p. 147.

32. See Richard F. Doner, Bryan K. Ritchie, and Dan Slater, "Systemic Vulnerability and the Origins of Developmental States: Northeast and Southeast Asia in Comparative Perspective," *International Organization* 59, 2 (Spring 2005).

33. Leading recipients of arms deliveries include Saudi Arabia (ranked first), Israel (fifth), Egypt (sixth), and Iraq (ninth). Leading recipients of arms transfer agreements include the United Arab Emirates (ranked first), Saudi Arabia (second), Morocco (third), Iraq (fifth), Egypt (sixth), and Israel (ninth). International Institute for Strategic Studies, *The Military Balance 2010* (London, 2010).

34. Gause, "Regional Influences," p. 285.

35. Gause, "Why Middle East Studies Missed the Arab Spring," pp. 87–88.

36. The United States is increasingly prompted to reconsider the assumption that playing balancer has contributed to containing Iran. See Toby Jones, "Counter-revolution in the Gulf," Peace Brief no. 89 (Washington, DC: US Institute of Peace, 15 April 2011).

37. Anthony Cordesman, *Saudi Arabia: National Security in a Troubled Region* (New York: Praeger, 2009), particularly chaps. 1, 2, 11.

38. Anthony Cordesman, *The Saudi Arms Sale: Reinforcing a Strategic Partnership in the Gulf,* Burke Chair in Strategy Report (Washington, DC: Center for Strategic and International Studies, 3 November 2010).

39. Ibid., p. 5.

40. Cordesman, *The Saudi Arms Sale,* p. 6.

41. Vincent Durac, "The Impact of External Actors on the Distribution of Power in the Middle East: The Case of Egypt," *Journal of North African Studies* 14, 1 (March 2009). See also Jason Brownlee, "The Decline of Pluralism in Mubarak's Egypt," *Journal of Democracy* 13, 4 (October 2002); Peter Burnell, "The Domestic Political Impact of Foreign Aid: Recalibrating the Research Agenda," *European Journal of Development Research* 16, 2 (2004); Eberhard Kienle, "More Than a Response to Islamism: The Political Deliberalization of Egypt in the 1990s," *Middle East Journal* 52, 2 (1998).

42. F. Gregory Gause III, "Why Middle East Studies Missed the Arab Spring," *Foreign Affairs* 90, 4 (July–August 2011), pp. 92–94.

43. Frédéric Volpi, "Political Islam in the Mediterranean: The View from Democratization Studies," *Democratization* 16, 1 (2009), p. 21.

44. See Volker Perthes, ed., *Arab Elites: Negotiating the Politics of Change* (Boulder: Lynne Rienner, 2004). See also Marsha Pripstein Posusney and Michele Penner Angrist, eds., *Authoritarianism in the Middle East: Regimes and Resistance* (Boulder: Lynne Rienner, 2005).

45. See Quintan Wiktorowicz, "The New Global Threat: Transnational Salafis and Jihad," *Middle East Policy* 8, 4 (December 2001); Jean-Pierre Filiu, "The Local and Global Jihad of al-Qa'ida in the Islamic Maghrib," *Middle East Journal* 63, 2 (2009).

46. Thomas Hegghammer, "Islamist Violence and Regime Stability in Saudi Arabia," *International Affairs* 84, 4 (2008), p. 705. See also Thomas Hegghammer, "Lady Gaga vs. the Occupation," *Foreign Policy,* 31 March 2010.

47. Asef Bayat, "The 'Street' and the Politics of Dissent in the Arab World," *Middle East Report* 226 (Spring 2003), pp. 6–7.

48. Bayat, "The 'Street' and the Politics of Dissent," p. 7.

49. Ibid.

50. See Mustafa al-Sayyid, "Mixed Message: The Arab and Muslim Response to 'Terrorism,'" *Washington Quarterly* 25, 2 (Spring 2002).

51. André Bank and Morten Valbjørn, "Bringing the Arab Regional Level Back In: Jordan in the New Arab Cold War," *Middle East Critique* 19, 3 (2010), p. 312.

52. Ibid. See also Morten Valbjørn and André Bank, "Signs of a New Arab Cold War: The 2006 Lebanon War and the Sunni-Shi'i Divide," *Middle East Report* 242 (Spring 2007), pp. 6–11.

53. Bank and Valbjørn, "Bringing the Arab Regional Level Back In," p. 312.

54. James Zogby, *Arab Voices: What They Are Saying to US and Why It Matters* (New York: Palgrave Macmillan, 2010), pp. 157–173.

55. The Egyptian magazine *al-Arabi* published an entire supplement titled "Nasrallah 2006–Nasser 1956." See Giles Whittell, "To Arabs He Is the New Nasser but to the West He Has Become the New Bin Laden," *Sunday Times,* 29 July 2006.

56. Brownlee, "The Decline of Pluralism in Mubarak's Egypt," p. 7.

57. Hesham al-Awadi, "Mubarak and the Islamists: Why Did the 'Honeymoon' End?" *Middle East Journal* 59, 1 (Winter, 2005), p. 76. See also Fawaz A. Gerges, "The End of the Islamist Insurgency in Egypt? Costs and Prospects," *Middle East Journal* 54, 4 (Autumn 2000), p. 609.

58. al-Awadi, "Mubarak and the Islamists," p. 77.

59. Gerges, "The End of the Islamist Insurgency in Egypt?" p. 592.

60. "The Egyptian Organization for Human Rights documented more than 17,000 arrests between 1989 and 1997. The Arab Strategic Report estimated the number of political prisoners [as] between 15,000 and 30,000." Gerges, "The End of the Islamist Insurgency in Egypt?" p. 607.

61. Gerges, "The End of the Islamist Insurgency in Egypt?" p. 604.

62. Ibid., p. 606.

63. Daniel Brumberg, "The Trap of Liberalized Autocracy," *Journal of Democracy* 13, 4 (October 2002), p. 62.

64. Only in Egypt did demonstrators also target their government's policies. Bayat, "The 'Street' and the Politics of Dissent," p. 11, n. 20.

65. Bayat, "The 'Street' and the Politics of Dissent," p. 8.

66. Durac, "The Impact of External Actors," p. 86.

67. Bank and Valbjørn, "Bringing the Arab Regional Level Back In," p. 313.

68. See Elena Aoun and Marie-Joëlle Zahar, "Le Moyen-Orient en équilibre précaire au bord du gouffre," in Gérard Hervouet and Michel Fortmann, eds., *Les conflits dans le monde 2010* (Laval: Presses de l'Université Laval, 2010), p. 188.

69. See Marie-Joëlle Zahar, "Liberal Interventions, Illiberal Outcomes: The United Nations, Western Powers, and Lebanon," in Edward Newman, Roland Paris, and Oliver P. Richmond, eds., *New Perspectives on Liberal Peacebuilding* (Tokyo: United Nations University Press, 2009), pp. 292–314.

70. Gause, "Why Middle East Studies Missed the Arab Spring."

71. Sheila Carapico, "Foreign Aid for Promoting Democracy in the Arab World," *Middle East Journal* 56, 3 (Summer 2002), p. 380.

72. Thomas Carothers, "Promoting Democracy and Fighting Terror," *Foreign Affairs* 82, 1 (January–February 2003).

73. F. Gregory Gause III, "Can Democracy Stop Terrorism?" *Foreign Affairs* 84, 5 (September–October 2005), p. 62.

74. See Robert Vitalis, "The Democratization Industry and the Limits of the New Intervention," *Middle East Report* 187–188: *Intervention and North-South Politics in the 90's* (March–June 1994), pp. 46–50.

75. The professionalization of militaries is not an obvious example of democracy promotion. But one of its key consequences is the acceptation by militaries of civilian control. And because civilian control of the military is a core principle of

democracy, the professionalization of militaries has consequences for democracy promotion.

76. Steven E. Finkel, Aníbal S. Pérez Liñan, and Mitchell A. Seligson, "The Effects of U.S. Foreign Assistance on Democracy Building, 1990–2003," *World Politics* 59, 3 (April 2007).

77. Carapico, "Foreign Aid for Promoting Democracy."

78. Steven Heydemann, "The Uncertain Future of Democracy Promotion," p. 6, 30 August 2010, http://www.hivos.net/Hivos-Knowledge-Programme/Themes/Civil-Society-in-West-Asia/News/The-Uncertain-Future-of-Democracy-Promotion-by-Steven-Heydemann.

79. Katerina Dalacoura, "US Democracy Promotion in the Arab Middle East Since 11 September 2001: A Critique," *International Affairs* 81, 5 (2005), p. 976. Dalacoura, "US Democracy Promotion in the Arab Middle East," p. 976.

80. See Brieg Tomos Powel, "A Clash of Norms: Normative Power and EU Democracy Promotion in Tunisia," *Democratization* 16, 1 (February 2009), pp. 202–203. See also Amy Hawthorne, "Can the United States Promote Democracy in the Middle East?" *Current History,* January 2003; Dalacoura, "US Democracy Promotion in the Arab Middle East"; Heydemann, "The Uncertain Future of Democracy Promotion."

81. Dalacoura, "US Democracy Promotion in the Arab Middle East," p. 976. See also Heydemann, "The Uncertain Future of Democracy Promotion."

82. Marina Ottaway, "Women's Rights and Democracy in the Arab World," Carnegie Papers no. 42, February 2004, http://carnegieendowment.org/files/CarnegiePaper42.pdf.

83. It is important to note that leaders in the Arab world advocated elections and more participation even before Western democracy promotion was in vogue. See, for example, Lisa Wedeen, "The Politics of Deliberation: *Qat* Chews as Public Spheres in Yemen," *Public Culture* 19, 1 (Winter 2007).

84. Dalacoura, "US Democracy Promotion in the Arab Middle East," p. 967.

85. Paul F. Diehl, "New Roles for Regional Organizations," in Chester A. Crocker, Fen Osler Hampson, and Pamela Aall, eds., *Leashing the Dogs of War: Conflict-Management in a Divided World* (Washington, DC: US Institute of Peace, 2007), p. 540.

86. Many see this as an interest of the United States (and to a lesser extent of European powers) that has strengthened as Israel and the West have developed a kinship born out of the perception that they are similarly entangled in efforts to fight terror and safeguard democracy. See Pew Global Attitudes Project, *What the World Thinks in 2002: How Global Publics View Their Lives, Their Countries, the World, America* (Washington, DC: Pew Research Center for the People and the Press, 2002).

87. Laura Guazzone and Daniela Pioppi, "Globalisation and the Restructuring of State Power in the Arab World," *International Spectator* 42, 4 (December 2007), p. 519.

88. Dalacoura, "US Democracy Promotion in the Arab Middle East," p. 969.

89. Ibid., p. 970.

90. Roberto Aliboni and Laura Guazzone, "Democracy in the Arab Countries and the West," *Mediterranean Politics* 9, 1 (Spring 2004), p. 89.

91. Clifford Chanin and F. Gregory Gause III, "U.S.-Saudi Relations: Bump in the Road or End of the Road?" *Middle East Policy* 10, 4 (Winter 2003).

92. Powel, "A Clash of Norms."

93. See Steven Erlanger, "In Yemen, US Faces Leader Who Puts Family First," *New York Times,* 5 January 2010, p. A1. See also Aoun and Zahar, "Le Moyen-Orient en équilibre précaire au bord du gouffre."

94. Charles Tilly, *Coercion, Capital, and European States, AD 990–1990* (Oxford: Blackwell, 1990), p. 206, cited in Krause, "Insecurity and State Formation," p. 340.

95. Dalacoura, "US Democracy Promotion in the Arab Middle East," p. 968.

96. Ellen Lust-Okar, *Structuring Conflict in the Arab World: Incumbents, Opponents, and Institutions* (Cambridge: Cambridge University Press, 2005).

97. Stephen McInerney, "Shifts in U.S. Assistance to Egypt Alarm Democracy Advocates," *Arab Reform Bulletin,* 7 April 2010, http://carnegieendowment.org/arb/?fa=downloadArticlePDF&article=40530.

98. Durac, "The Impact of External Actors," p. 86.

99. Ibid., p. 86.

100. Guazzone and Pioppi, "Globalization and State Power in the Arab World," p. 513.

101. Benjamin Smith, "Oil Wealth and Regime Survival in the Developing World, 1960–1999," *American Journal of Political Science* 48 (2004); Russell E. Lucas, "Monarchical Authoritarianism: Survival and Political Liberalization in a Middle Eastern Regime Type," *International Journal of Middle East Studies* 36, 1 (February 2004); Jay Ulfeder, "Natural Resource–Wealth and the Survival of Autocracy," *Comparative Political Studies* 40, 8 (August 2007).

102. Krause, "Insecurity and State Formation," p. 347.

PART 3

Conclusion

13

From Fear to Hope?

Al-sha'b yurid isqat al-nizam—people want to overthrow the regime—has been the popular anthem of the Arab Spring. The uprisings of 2011 have so far toppled some authoritarian regimes, pitted others in bloody conflicts with their societies, forced some to accommodate or co-opt popular demands, and in the process sent tremors throughout the theoretical edifice that students of Arab politics assembled to explain authoritarian persistence. Although the democratization literature of the 1990s held some hopes for the kind of political liberalization then under way, no one predicted the sea changes unleashed by Bouazizi's flames. In fact, the intervening decade and a half since the publication of the 1995 and 1998 volumes of *Political Liberalization and Democratization in the Arab World,*[1] this book's ideational primogenitor, witnessed a substantial narrowing of democratic spaces, giving rise in the 2000s to a sophisticated "authoritarian upgrading" narrative of Arab politics. The academic community was then busy explaining not a counterfactual—the Arab world's democracy deficit in comparison to others parts of the globe—but rather the here and now of authoritarianism. In fact, "the academic literature missed the 2011 eruption because it was focused (and in many ways rightly so) on explaining the anomalous regime stability that characterized the Arab world in the 40 years leading up to these events."[2] Moreover, and in all fairness, it did so in part to debunk culturalist and Orientalist explanations of the authoritarian-proneness of the region and its peoples at a time when policymakers were preoccupied with al-Qaeda terrorism and the threat from Islamist movements. The 2011 uprisings further undermined such reductionist claims, but they also invited a fresh revision of past explanations of authoritarian persistence and how they missed possibilities for regime change. Explaining decades of authoritarian adaptation is thus a necessary undertaking to make sense of the causes behind the 2011 Arab uprisings, but also to evaluate their impact on the future of authoritarianism and democracy in the Arab world.

To be sure, the Arab uprisings have not ushered the long-awaited democratic age, not yet at least. As this book goes to print, the region is in flux. Some states (Egypt and Tunisia) find themselves in complex transitions, while others (Libya) are experiencing strong centripetal forces on the morrow of violent regime overthrow. Syria slipped into violence that tore its national unity apart. In less than a year the country was transformed from a major player in regional politics to a geopolitical playground. On the other hand, monarchies outside the Gulf region were proactive in containing popular protests. The kings of Morocco and Jordan offered packages of constitutional reforms—although neither offered to turn his kingdom into a democratic constitutional monarchy. Finally, in the Arabian Peninsula, the Bahraini regime crushed a peaceful protest movement, its Saudi counterpart dealt violently with demonstrations in the Eastern province, Oman swiftly quelled social unrest, a Saudi-US initiative defused Yemen's popular uprising while securing an alternative to Saleh, while the remaining oil-rich Gulf states managed to insulate themselves from mass protests. Here, but also in Algeria and Sudan, authoritarianism appeared to remain resilient. Thus both the past and the present of authoritarian endurance require explanation.

This volume has resisted embracing a unicausal explanation of the Arab world's authoritarian experience. We have also avoided relying on explanations that privilege a single variable among a catalog of coercive, institutional, structural, state-society, or symbolic ones. Nor have we privileged the domestic level of analysis at the expense of regional and international factors. We have opted instead for a *multicausal* and *multilevel* explanation, one that stresses the *catalytic* and *synergistic* effects different variables and levels have on each other.[3] According to this view, decades of authoritarian persistence in the Arab world are best explained by unpacking what Laurence Whitehead labels the "interlocking impediments" to democratization in the region.[4] These include a set of institutional and symbolic strategies that sustained authoritarianism, though not indefinitely; the political economy of state formation under late development; and the effects of the Arab world's regional environment and international geostrategic location. Unpacking the interactions between these variables and levels helps explain decades of authoritarian endurance. It also helps show how a sudden shift in the balance of these variables ended up opening possibilities for regime change in some states but not in others.

The balance of this final chapter is divided into two sections. The first synthesizes this book's argument and unpacks the causes of the 2011 uprisings. The second section examines the impact of the 2011 upheavals on the future of authoritarianism and democracy in the Arab world.

Explaining the Persistence and Breakdown of Authoritarianism in the Arab World

Many years of authoritarian persistence in the Arab world are best explained as the result of the catalytic and synergistic interactions among a set of variables operating at different levels. At the domestic level, Arab regimes deployed a set of formal and informal strategies aimed at maintaining their hold over the distribution of power and, concomitantly, impeding the emergence of viable alternatives to their rule.[5] Undoubtedly, the coercive agencies of the state were omnipresent, but their violence and intimidation reveals only part of an otherwise complex texture of authoritarian practices.

A number of chapters in this volume have examined the formal institutional mechanisms—such as elections, parliamentary procedures, political-party and associational laws, hereditary succession, and monarchical liberalization—that Arab regimes manipulated to avoid the kind of real political reforms that would have undermined authoritarian control. Moreover, and alongside these formal institutional strategies, Arab regimes organized informal, adaptive, and flexible national-populist social pacts aimed at the "patterned disorganization of political life."[6] At the heart of these social pacts were neopatrimonial networks and strategies that sought to reward and sanction regime supporters and opponents, narrow the scope of civil society collective action, and disrupt opposition organization.

Arab regimes also sought a monopoly over the institutions of cultural and symbolic production. We have argued that what was euphemistically termed "political culture" in the debate on the persistence of Arab authoritarianism is better conceived contingently rather than primordially, as a set of attitudes and sentiments that are dynamic, constantly negotiated and invented, and more closely affiliated with regional demonstration effects than with a presumed and unchanging Arab culture, mind, or essence. Basic to this process is the way in which Arab regimes employed fear, violence, spectacle, rhetoric, symbols, bureaucratic malaise, everyday practices of subjugation and humiliation, and the purposeful and callous disregard of human dignity and the rule of law to manufacture docile citizens and a concomitant depoliticized political culture.[7] Arab regimes deployed the new Arab media either to depoliticize their publics through heavy doses of entertainment and sports programs or to deflect criticism away from them and redirect it toward Israel and the United States.

Similarly, Arab regimes sponsored the creative arts, but only to subdue them as agents of critical thinking and opposition. A plethora of public and private institutions and awards were created to domesticate large swaths of the intellectual class. Many succumbed to the pleasures and rewards of proximity to power, permanent employment, or financial incentives. Inevitably, however, this effort was never complete. Many members of the intelligentsia in different Arab states resisted regime attempts at co-optation,[8] and a younger generation of writers and poets placed Arab regimes and societies at the center of their critical intellectual interrogations.[9]

We now know that these institutional and cultural strategies failed to protect many regimes from the popular uprisings that swept across the Arab world starting in December 2010. Managed elections, neopatrimonial strategies to co-opt strategic social sectors, the production of loyal opposition parties, the heavy-handedness of the state's security apparatus, and the new media may have contributed to rather than prevented the eruption of long-gestating resentment.

Managed elections proved especially fatal to authoritarian regime durability when used to orchestrate hereditary transitions in republican regimes. The desire to arrange father-to-son successions was long an open secret in Egypt, Libya, and Yemen. In Algeria there were signs that President Abdelaziz Bouteflika was preparing his younger brother, Said, to succeed him. In Tunisia the president's second wife, Leila Trabelsi, had accumulated enormous economic power and shuffled relatives to strategic state positions in an attempt to inherit the presidency after her husband; alternatively, her son-in-law, Saker el-Materi, was also waiting in the wings. As the 2010 Egyptian elections demonstrated, managed elections to secure family successions exacerbated public anger to the tipping point. Even in Syria, where the 2000 succession from Hafez to Bashar al-Assad went smoothly, anger at the hereditary nature of the republican regime reappeared once popular protests commenced on 15 May 2011.

Neopatrimonial strategies of co-optation and the coercive agencies' physical and symbolic power failed to prevent the emergence of the kind of collective action that overwhelmed the state's ability to control it. Exaggerating the coercive capabilities of the state and the role of civil society and nongovernmental organizations as democratizing agents deflected attention from everyday popular struggles for political and socioeconomic rights. To be sure, new social media played an instrumental role in triggering and organizing these protests, and satellite channels ensured that once the protests commenced, they retained their momentum. But it would be wrong to caricature these uprisings as the work of Facebook groups and Twitter alone. Prior popular protests against the regime's socioeconomic policies and coercive practices created the kind of collective-action precedents that later avalanched into popular uprisings once a trigger was available, in this case Mohamed Bouazizi's self-immolation and the permeability effect engendered by the fall of Zine el-Abidine Ben Ali. Whether worker strikes or sporadic Kefaya-movement protests in Egypt, everyday forms of urban and rural collective street dissent by those Asef Bayat labels the "middle-class poor," or the kind of perennial associational mobilization undertaken by regime-penetrated labor unions and professional syndicates, such as the Union Générale de Travailleurs Tunisiens (UGTT, Tunisian General Labor Union), these activities formed a genealogy of protests for the Arab uprisings.[10] They altered people's perceptions of the utility of collective action and the efficacy of police repression and, in hindsight, eroded steadily the deterrent effect of the state's coercive institutions, ultimately tearing down the wall of fear that regimes had built through decades of surveillance and repression. Egypt's popular uprising "telescoped the daily encounters between people and police that had played out for more than ten years."[11] This, in turn, made it possible for citizens to reimagine the parameters of the possible.

Many decades in the making, attempts by Arab regimes to deny their citizens agency by manufacturing subservient political cultures and docile subjects suddenly collapsed as citizens discovered their own capabilities. Nothing reflects more the shock that regimes experienced when popular uprisings exploded in their face than the bizarre speeches delivered by Ben Ali, Mubarak, Qaddafi, Saleh, and Assad. Such regime strategies did not crumble throughout the Arab world, however. Regime-engineered quiescent political cultures proved durable in the oil-rich Gulf states. Despite growing signs of open dissent, a combination of rents, repression, and religious dogma continue to sustain authoritarianism.

Nevertheless, Bouazizi's fire swept across the Arab world, redefining the region's permeability. The old regional permeability that had militated for authoritarian persistence was now replaced by a new one, from below, expressing a newfound belief in peoples' ability to remake their futures in a democratic way. The authoritarian bargains of past decades that skirted democracy for Arab national causes, industrialization, and social welfare gave way to new demands: *khubz, 'amal, huriyya, wa karama* (bread, jobs, freedom, and dignity). Democracy was now linked inextricably to national pride and the pursuit of social justice. The old binaries created by Arab regimes—democracy *or* social security, freedoms *or* economic development, national *or* pan-national causes—were renegotiated in a new peaceful accommodation. Moreover, anti-US foreign policy choices were no longer adequate to protect authoritarian regimes from popular demands for democratization. Embracing the Palestinian cause is no longer the litmus test for domestic popularity. The Syrian regime, which interpreted the fall of the Ben Ali and Mubarak regimes as vindication of its objectionist *(mumana'a)* foreign policy vis-à-vis US plans to dominate the geopolitics of the region,[12] was soon overwhelmed by popular protests. Replacing the one erected after the 1948 war, a new Arab order is being built on a synergy between hitherto regime-separated principles: democracy *and* Arab solidarity. The novel message emanating from the Arab uprisings is that regimes are pan-national as long as they are democratic.[13] And in the ledger of priorities, democracy, national dignity, and social justice precede and are a sine qua non for solidarity with the Palestinian cause.

The Arab uprisings have also invited a reappraisal of the role military institutions play in sustaining authoritarianism. In both our regional and our thematic chapters, we have demonstrated how the nature of civil-military relations played a determining role in regime survival or, alternatively, collapse, and if so, then in what ways. We have also stressed the different roles played by the military and security establishments in sustaining regime survival, and the perils that come with anchoring the latter on the loyalty of internal security and the intelligence services.

Military institutions in many Arab states have mutated into important rent seekers and socioeconomic players. In many cases, regimes maintained the welfare benefits that military institutions enjoyed despite the neoliberal turn and concomitant spending cuts. Nevertheless, the claim that military institutions that are heavily invested in their country's political economic systems make transitions away from authoritarianism impossible was debunked by the Egyptian military's instrumental role in regime change.[14] Nor is the attitude of the military establishment to regime change monolithic across the Arab world. Rather, a much more disaggregated picture of regime-military relations has emerged on the morrow of the Arab uprisings. Gregory Gause suggests a useful typology of this relation:

> 1) militaries whose officer corps share a minority sectarian and geographic status with the ruling elite will stand by the regimes in times of trouble (Saddam's Iraq, Syria, Bahrain, Saudi Arabia); 2) militaries in uninstitutionalized regimes, where personal and family ties determine promotion and leadership of units (Libya, Yemen), will fragment under pressure into loyalist units (headed by relatives of the leader) and those willing to go over to the opposition; and 3) highly institutionalized militaries in relatively homogenous societies are most likely to assume the arbiter role in political crisis, even if they are tied to the regime (Egypt, Tunisia).[15]

Ben Ali alienated the military establishment, kept it outside his ruling coalition, and relied instead on an oversized security apparatus—some 120,000–150,000 members compared to the army's 35,000.[16] Consequently, when he ordered the army to crack down against the demonstrators, the latter refused. By contrast, Egypt's military establishment possessed substantial political economic entitlements. It was connected indirectly to the 2-million-strong police state organized during Hosni Mubarak's long tenure. Though it was growing increasingly disillusioned with Mubarak's determination to hand over power to his son Jamal,[17] and equally so with the young business elite gathered around the latter in the National Democratic Party, it was the sudden collapse of this police state that convinced the army to support regime change, but only in an attempt to hijack the popular uprising and reestablish itself as umpire in Egyptian politics.

It is in Gause's first and second scenarios that the picture becomes bloodier and more complex. Syria epitomizes the difficult battle for change where the coercive agencies and praetorian units of the regime are recruited from minority groups. Saudi Arabia presents a somewhat comparable case. Recruited from the tribes of central and western Arabia and of nontribal recruits from central Arabia, the praetorian Saudi Arabian National Guard can handle domestic threats, especially in the Shiite Eastern province but also in Jeddah, Mecca, and Medina.[18] By contrast, the uninstitutionalized nature of the regime in Libya and Yemen expedited regime collapse—albeit in the former this entailed aerial and stealth ground support from the North Atlantic Treaty Organization—where army units disintegrated swiftly along regional and tribal lines.

Beyond these institutional and cultural strategies, this volume has traced how the logic of state formation under conditions of late development created social forces and classes that were economically dependent on authoritarian regimes, and gave rise to nondemocratic political coalitions organized around state patronage and distribution. Economic planning aimed at denying the private sector and the middle classes the institutional, organizational, and political autonomy they need to act as levers for democratic change. Regimes managed informal economies and implemented economic liberalization to divide the opposition, offset pressures for political liberalization, and retain the loyalty of strategic sectors of society. As our discussion of the logic of economic liberalization has shown, the result has been decades of economic liberalization with little developmental progress, a stark reality best exemplified by comparing the region's rates for manufactured and fuel exports with other parts of the world. Moreover, new private sector elites ended up exploiting economic liberalization to constrain rather than expand market access. The state remained central to economic development and distribution, but regimes used access to state contracts and resources to organize loyal socioeconomic coalitions and neopatrimonial networks to insulate themselves from democratization pressures.

None of these strategies proved a viable recipe for authoritarian endurance, however. Rather, the reorientation of the economy toward the nonindustrial and nonexport sectors (especially the service sectors, real estate, banking, and tourism), the lifting of subsidies on primary commodities, the urban development bias, extravagant consumption by a tiny elite, and the privatization policies that created a regime-cultivated crony capitalism best symbolized by the likes of Ahmed Ezz, Saker el-Materi, and Rami Makhlouf intensified popular resentment against regimes and their socioeconomic coalitions who behaved as if they owned rather than ruled the realm. Lebanon may be an extreme case, but is nevertheless symptomatic of a larger structural defect in the Arab world, where the political economic elite is preoccupied with the systematic theft of the country's natural endowments, and rent-making activities, at the expense of balanced and diversified national economic development strategies and sound fiscal policies. The Trabelsi clan's predatory economic practices even alienated the Tunisian bourgeoisie from the regime, contributing to its own downfall. In Syria, where the regime adopted the discourse of a social market economy while maintaining the modicum of populist practices, neoliberal policies introduced after 2005 impoverished the middle and lower classes, especially those in the rural areas, and contributed to the explosion of popular protests against the regime and its economic allies.

The popular uprisings thus signaled the collapse of a moral economy anchoring past authoritarian bargains and the consequent rise of new popular dyads: democracy *and* social justice, bread *and* freedom. They had less to do with objective trends in income inequality. What mattered more were "the feelings of injustice that the existing distribution of income had generated, and the perception that inequality was higher than it really was."[19] The uprisings are also a denunciation of the adverse economic and social impacts neoliberal policies have had on the peoples of the region. The placards of the uprisings said it all: "Khubz, Huriyya, 'Amal" (Bread, Freedom, Work) read one banner in Tunisia; "Khaskhasa is Laslasa" (Privatization is Theft) read another in Amman.

We have also argued in this volume that the relationship between rents and authoritarianism in the Arab world is neither simple nor similar across the rentier states. The theoretical tendency in the past to exaggerate the explanatory power of rents has led to an analytical dead end. It is thus important to combine a domestic analysis of rentier politics with an appreciation of the transnational aspects of resource wealth. Consequently, this book has examined the impacts of pre-rent sociopolitical relations and institutions, regional patterns of conflict and security, and different rent types—such as oil, labor remittances, and foreign aid—and crises on authoritarian persistence and prospects for political liberalization. The dynamics that emerge are far more complex, but also much more rewarding theoretically, than past attempts to explain everything by an undifferentiated and static notion of rents.

Oil alone tells us very little about authoritarian persistence or breakdown. How oil is spent—or not—to organize viable political and socioeconomic coalitions is another important distinction to draw among rentier states. The collapse of the Muammar Qaddafi regime proved that the availability of hydrocarbon wealth is an insufficient condition for regime survival. Instead of spending hydrocarbon wealth to organize an inclusive ruling coalition, Qaddafi ruled by withholding wealth from his population, thus underdeveloping the society, and by vivisecting the country along tribal and regional lines. A similar process was at the heart of the uprising in the not-strictly rentier Bahrain, albeit there socioeconomic dispossession overlapped with sectarian grievances.

Moreover, the relation between oil and authoritarianism in the Arab world is not causal but structural: "It has to do with the ways in which oil distorts the state, the market, the class structure, and the entire incentive structure."[20] Oil wealth permeates broad spaces of Arab economic, social, political, and cultural life. It created states with lopsided economies, with investments from oil revenues concentrated outside the real economy. It manufactured societies with materialistic cultures and excessively high consumption habits. It produced a parasitic and co-opted transregional Arab business class, one whose entrepreneurial success is a function of proximity to, or partnership with, regime members and access to state contracts. The political economies of oil-poor states are also distorted by the consumerist habits of returning immigrant communities, sharp income and intrastate regional disparities, remittances that produce artificial purchasing powers, and Gulf investments concentrated in mainly nonproductive sectors. Unsurprisingly, the spark of the popular uprisings came from the new middle and lower classes, who reaped none of the benefits associated with the regional recycling of petrodollars. Only where it was left out of the economic pie, as in Tunisia, did the bourgeoisie support regime change, albeit belatedly.

Oil rents affected the process of cultural and intellectual production in the Arab world. The entertainment industry, the media world, the arts, and religious education are increasingly financed by Gulf oil wealth.[21] This has had a widely distorting impact on everyday life, from aesthetic tastes, salary scales, advertisement criteria, music awards, and literary competitions, to the battle over religious interpretations. The grand mufti of al-Azhar, Ahmad al-Tayyeb, voiced concerns over al-Azhar losing its traditionally pragmatic leadership role in the Sunni Muslim world to the oil-financed Salafi Wahhabi interpretation of Islam—a process he labels *"fiqh al-badiya,"* or the jurisprudence of the desert—and the direct implications this has had on religious animosity and Sunni-Shiite sectarian tensions not just in the Middle East but also across the Muslim world.[22] Nourished by Saudi money and Wahhabi ideas, Salafi groups were rejuvenated by the popular uprisings and will undoubtedly make their mark on the regime transitions now under way.

Oil wealth is also an effective tool of regime security, geopolitical battles, and regional diplomacy. Riyadh spent billions of dollars buying security protection from the United States, but also in support of its geopolitical contests with Iran in Lebanon, Palestine, Iraq, and Yemen. It led the counterrevolutionary camp in an attempt to contain the regional contagion unleashed by Ben Ali's ouster. Riyadh emerged as the Mecca of political asylums, providing refuge for Tunisia's Ben Ali and Yemen's Saleh. It pressured the United States not to let go of Mubarak, flexed its financial power to shield him from a humiliating debacle, and when all else failed it switched to a co-optation strategy to buy influence in Egypt's new order. Similarly, it has scrambled to reorder the political deck in a manner that protects its political influence in a post-Saleh Yemen. Moreover, and in a move aimed at shielding nonoil monarchical regimes from the wave of popular uprisings, it led the drive to inject Bahrain and Oman with funds to buy political acquiescence.

Qatar also deployed its financial capabilities in its quest to assume a central role in Middle East diplomacy and, like Abu Dhabi and Dubai, to reserve a seat at the international stage. Intriguingly, Qatar opted to spend lavishly on sports as a vehicle to achieve global recognition, crowning its achievements with a successful bid to host the 2022 World Cup games. It used Al Jazeera as a tool for regional influence but also to co-opt Islamist and Arab nationalist public audiences alike as a new Arab order is being born.[23] Alongside the United Arab Emirates, Doha assumed a proactive role in Libya in support of the rebels, supplying them with financial aid and military assistance.[24] It did so to occupy the regional leadership role Saudi Arabia abandoned in Libya and to reserve for itself a privileged place in the good books of the United States. It also turned against Syria, once Qatar's doorway to regional diplomacy, for similar geopolitical objectives, condemning the regime's bloody clampdown against demonstrators and openly supporting the armed rebellion.

Regional dynamics also favored authoritarian endurance in the pre-Bouazizi Arab state system. Our discussion of the regional environment has shown how regional alliances, conflicts, insecurities, institutions, and interstate security cooperation all operated to hamper democratic openings. Like Arab nationalism in the past, transnational Islam and a new Arab Cold War were deployed by authoritarian regimes to reclaim their grip over society. Demonstration effects also operated against democratization. The failure of coercive regime change in Iraq, and the ensuing devastating civil war, militated against a change in the authoritarian status quo. The civil war following Algeria's derailed transition, civil war in Palestine after Hamas's 2006 electoral victory, Lebanon's perpetual instability despite Syria's exit, and the crackdown against reformers associated with the stillborn Damascus Spring, had similar negative regional demonstration effects. This effect was also operational at the level of inter-Arab regime cooperation and "authoritarian learning."[25] Arab regimes were at their best emulating each other's authoritarian practices, sharing information and strategies across security agencies, and appropriating the discourse and practices of democracy promoters but for the purposes of authoritarian persistence.

Once the wall of fear collapsed following Ben Ali's dramatic departure from Tunisia, regional dynamics began working in favor of regime change. A transformed regional permeability triggered a wave of popular uprisings in most Arab states. Arab regimes were no longer capable of offering themselves as a better alternative to the unpredictable instability that comes with regime change. Some regimes invoked the scarecrow of sectarian or tribal conflict, or that of an Islamist takeover, but the Arab Rubicon had been crossed. In some cases, however, regional geopolitical considerations disrupted the course of the popular uprisings.

Saudi Arabia's fear of Iran's growing geopolitical power played an instrumental role in the former's military intervention in Bahrain and the consequent annihilation of a genuinely cross-sectarian democratic movement demanding the establishment of a constitutional monarchy to replace minority Sunni rule. Its public support of the uprising in Syria is governed by similar geopolitical calculations, intended to force regime change in Damascus to compensate for Riyadh's loss of post-Saddam Iraq to Iran. This has complicated Syria's domestic situation, allowing the regime to invoke the pretext of foreign intervention and "conspiracies." On the other hand, Iran's geopolitical interests operate in favor of the Syrian regime's survival, as do Russia and China's. Israel, apprehensive lest its own security be exposed by radical Islamist forces capitalizing on newfound freedoms, lobbied Washington on behalf of allied authoritarian regimes, namely Egypt.[26]

Yet perhaps the Arab uprisings' most powerful effect has been to finally demystify the role external powers assumed in the past, and continue to do so selectively, as levers of authoritarianism. The Arab world's geostrategic location and its place in the global capitalist economy have long played in favor of authoritarian regimes. These regimes expected, and at different times received, rents and intervention from external actors to maintain them in, or restore them to, power. Even international organizations, such as the International Monetary Fund and the World Bank, structured their loans around strategic considerations rather than economic crisis and performance.

The international community, but especially the United States, was taken aback by the swiftness of Ben Ali's fall. The Obama administration was slow to react to the anti-Mubarak popular protests. Its original reaction was against regime change, and was governed by Mubarak's geopolitical value to US strategic interests rather than the democratic aspirations of the Egyptian people. Only when regime-orchestrated efforts to derail the uprising failed, and Mubarak's tenure became more a liability than an asset for US interests in Egypt and the region, did Obama come out publically in support of Mubarak's removal. But this was far from a return to idealism in US Middle East policy. Instead, it inaugurated a more selective approach, one based on maintaining the stability of Washington's strategic Arab allies while encouraging them to undertake some political reforms that could appease the opposition without amounting to democratization—a kind of "pluralism without democracy."[27] Open endorsement of regime change was reserved for, respectively, unpredictable and undervalued dictators such as Qaddafi or geopolitical opponents such as Syria. Oil-rich Saudi Arabia is the exception that proves the stability rule: its crackdown against domestic dissent and military intervention in neighboring Bahrain passed with only a US murmur.

Indeed, the brutal crackdown against the nonviolent popular uprising in Bahrain[28] exposed, once again, Washington's moral relativism in the Arab world—the same kind of relativism that in the past legitimized cooperation with authoritarian regimes under the pretext of fighting the "war on terror." Bahrain would prove to be the true litmus test of Obama's promise, delivered in his "A Moment of Opportunity" speech of 19 May 2011, at a time of great expectations in the Arab world, "to support transitions to democracy," "to work with all who embrace genuine and inclusive democracy," and "oppose . . . an attempt by any group to restrict the rights of others, and to hold on to power through coercion—not consent."[29] Home to the US Navy's Fifth Fleet, and an arm's length away from Saudi Arabia's oil-rich Shiite Eastern province, Bahrain's strategic value was too high to sacrifice for the sake of democracy. Nor was Washington willing to risk a confrontation with its Saudi ally over Bahrain. It consequently favored regime stability over the democratic aspirations of the Bahrainis. The contrast between Obama's rhetoric and the reality of US Middle East policy could not have been starker.

The Arab uprisings also exposed the hollowness of Western-designed democracy promotion programs. Like water in Samuel Taylor Coleridge's *The Rime of the Ancient Mariner,* democracy promotion programs sprouted everywhere after the terrorist attacks of 9/11, but produced not a single case of meaningful political change in the Arab world. Nor did they play an essential role in bringing about the Arab uprisings. Tunisia, the trigger of these uprisings, was not even on the radar of democracy promotion programs. The emphasis on well-funded but largely technical programs, especially electoral reform initiatives and capacity-building projects, created a cottage industry of well-paid foreign and local specialists, countless workshops, and a flood of reports and recommendations, but did little to affect the real organization and distribution of political power in Arab states. Instead, regimes channeled these programs to the kind of civil society promotional organizations that posed no real threat to their hold over power. No US, EU, or other Western-financed program to promote the rule of law, political-process strengthening, civic activism and advocacy, young Arab leaders, decentralization, or parliamentary, judicial, municipal, and electoral reforms proved a viable alternative to real economic and political pressures against regimes that abused their citizens' political and human rights. Only when Arab peoples braved their authoritarian regimes, and the wave of popular uprisings threatened regional stability, did Western governments scramble to apply real political and economic pressures, but only selectively, and in tandem with their own strategic interests.

The Long Arab Road Ahead

In a recent revisionist essay, Philippe C. Schmitter notes that "democratization has been easier than anticipated precisely because it has been less consequential than anticipated." Only when "the socially dominant and economically privileged" realized that "their interests would be better protected under democracy than they had been under authoritarianism" did they stop supporting autocracy.[30] The popular uprisings, and the often bloody regime responses they generated, suggest that the road to democracy in the Arab world will be long and hard, and far messier than Schmitter's quote implies. The brave young protesters who shook the authoritarian edifice in many Arab states find themselves in unequal contests with multiple counterrevolutionary forces—domestic old actors (the army and elements of the ancien régime) and the new (the Islamists), as well as regional and international parties—determined to deny them the democratic order they yearn for.[31] This combination of local, regional, and international factors has so far either shielded some regimes from democratization pressures or, alternatively, hijacked and complicated the post-uprising democratic transitions.

Tunisia may be the most optimistic candidate for a pacted transition to a parliamentary democracy protected by a professional, apolitical, military establishment. But this is because it is neither a regional pace-setter nor a strategic actor. It also fulfills Dankwart Rustow's precondition for a democracy: it boasts a substantial consensus on membership in its political community.[32] To be successful, however, this transition requires a peaceful reconciliation between the country's powerful secular and Islamist currents. Morocco is another candidate for a transition to a mongrel "constitutional parliamentary monarchy" that blends elements of a parliamentary democracy with a strong adjudicating role for the monarchy.[33] This is so because the February 20 Movement, the king, and Morocco's main political parties appear to have decided to manage incremental change in a largely cooperative rather than a confrontational manner.

On the other hand, Egypt's strategic weight and the political economic entitlements of its military establishment already impeded a smooth democratic transition. The hybrid coalition that brought down Mubarak has fractured. Egyptian youth and opposition groups were sidelined by what increasingly looks like an implicit pact between the Supreme Council of the Armed Forces (SCAF) and the Muslim Brotherhood, with US blessing. Consequently, Egypt may end up with a presidential political system based on pluralism but constrained by a military establishment possessing substantial influence over domestic and foreign policy. However, the present balance of political power between the SCAF and the Muslim Brotherhood is shifting with time in the latter's favor.[34] Egypt is also a laboratory for the dynamics opened up by Islamist political participation in postauthoritarian Arab states.

Long outlawed as legal political parties, and having joined the popular uprisings belatedly, Islamists swept the ballot boxes in most post-uprising elections. They have demonstrated the kind of tactical acumen on domestic and foreign policy that stunned their opponents. However, their newly assumed powers leave many questions unanswered. What is the true meaning of their slogan "a civil state with a religious source" *(dawla madaniya bi marja'iya diniya)*? What will be the role of (their version of) Islam in both public and private life? Will they permit the establishment of democratic, secular, civil states? And finally, who will be the source of legislation in the postauthoritarian political orders being organized: the peoples or the religious texts, and if the latter, then whose interpretation of those texts?[35] These are difficult but important questions for the future of democracy in the Arab world.

Democratic transitions in other parts of the Arab world may end up being much more difficult than the Tunisian, Moroccan, or Egyptian cases, especially where strategic calculations, namely oil and US security interests, are paramount. The Gulf states have so far confirmed the resilience of authoritarian rule in some parts of the Arab world. Yemen's strategic location has meant that its impressive popular uprising, one that assembled a collection of hitherto centrifugal forces and disparate groups, invited US and Saudi intervention to organize a transition of power from Saleh but not to democracy.

With the successful ouster of Qaddafi, Libya "confronts the complexity not of democratization but of state formation" and unification.[36] Decades of authoritarian rule via pulverizing society and underdeveloping some regions have created herculean statebuilding and socioeconomic challenges that may take precedence over democracy. The open embrace of federalism by the country's Eastern province suggests that the era of the unitary state in Libya may be over. Finally, Iraq's post-Saddam civil war and the sectarian overtones of Syria's violence suggest that in the Mashreq states, where segmental divisions are hard and mobilized easily, anything beyond new power-sharing pacts that institutionalize these divisions, à la postwar Lebanon and post-Saddam Iraq, may be a recipe for civil war or partition.

Be that as it may, the Arab world has entered a new phase in its political history. Many Arabs have suffered imprisonment, braved bullets, tank shells, and rockets, or died in pursuit of freedom and a dignified life. The main lesson of the events of 2011 is the one history teaches students of democracy everywhere: that political rights are never given, but rather gained as a result of protracted and sometimes bloody popular struggles. As one leader of Egypt's Revolutionary Youth Coalition mused on the eve of one of many *miluniyyat* (million-strong demonstrations) in Tahrir Square: "The SCAF heeds our demands only through popular pressure and *miluniyyat!*"[37] And "the people" have kept coming, whether in Egypt, Yemen, Syria, Bahrain, or many other Arab states. At stake in these ongoing struggles throughout the Arab world is ownership of the foundations upon which a new political order is being built. Will it be built on the popular will institutionalized in formal democratic political institutions, or will it be built on alliances between old and new actors aimed at constraining this will? It is these popular struggles and the responses they trigger from local, regional, and international actors that will determine the future of authoritarianism and the potential for democracy in the Arab world.

Notes

1. Rex Brynen, Bahgat Korany, and Paul Noble, eds., *Political Liberalization and Democratization in the Arab World,* vol. 1, *Theoretical Perspectives* (Boulder: Lynne Rienner, 1995); Bahgat Korany, Rex Brynen, and Paul Noble, eds. *Political Liberalization and Democratization in the Arab World,* vol. 2, *Comparative Experiences* (Boulder: Lynne Rienner, 1995).

2. F. Gregory Gause III, "The Middle East Academic Community and the 'Winter of Arab Discontent': Why Did We Miss It?" in Ellen Laipson, ed., *Seismic Shift: Understanding Change in the Middle East* (Washington, DC: Henry L. Stimson Center, 2011), p. 12.

3. A number of studies of authoritarian persistence in the Arab world made these assumptions implicitly without theorizing or disaggregating them, however. See, for example, Lisa Anderson, "Searching Where the Light Shines: Studying Democratization in the Middle East," *Annual Review of Political Science* 9 (2006); Larry Diamond, "Why Are There No Arab Democracies?" *Journal of Democracy* 21, 1 (January 2010).

4. Laurence Whitehead, "Losing 'the Force'? The 'Dark Side' of Democratization After Iraq," *Democratization* 16, 2 (April 2009), p. 231.

5. See Adam Przeworski, "Some Problems in the Study of the Transition to Democracy," in Guillermo O'Donnell, Philippe C. Schmitter, and Laurence Whitehead., eds., *Transitions from Authoritarian Rule: Comparative Perspectives* (Baltimore: Johns Hopkins University Press, 1986), p. 52.

6. Steven Heydemann, "Social Pacts and the Persistence of Authoritarianism in the Middle East," in Oliver Schlumberger, *Debating Arab Authoritarianism: Dynamics and Durability in Nondemocratic Regimes* (Stanford: Stanford University Press, 2007), p. 27.

7. See Kanan Makiya, *Republic of Fear: The Politics of Modern Iraq* (Berkeley: University of California Press, 1989); Lisa Wedeen, *Ambiguities of Domination: Politics, Rhetoric, and Symbols in Contemporary Syria* (Chicago: University of Chicago Press, 1999); Lisa Wedeen, *Peripheral Visions: Publics, Power, and Performance in Yemen* (Chicago: University of Chicago Press, 2008); and the literary representations of this process in 'Abdel Rahman Munif, *Al'an . . . Huna, Aw Sharq al-Mutawaset Mara Ukhra* [Now... Here, or East of the Mediterranean One More Time] (Beirut: al-Mu'assasa al-'Arabiya lil-Dirasat wa-l-Nasher, 1992); Khaled Khalifé, *Madih al-Karahiya* [In Praise of Hatred] (Beirut: Dar al-Adab, 2008); and Mustapha Khalifé, *Al-Qawqa'a* [The Shell] (Beirut: Dar al-Adab, 2008).

8. Most famously in the case of the Egyptian novelist Sonallah Ibrahim, who in November 2003 publicly rejected the Egyptian Ministry of Culture's annual Arab Novel Prize.

9. For a sample of their writings, see Samuel Shimon, ed., *Beirut 39: New Writing from the Arab World* (London: Bloomsbury, 2010).

10. See Joel Beinin and Hossam el-Hamalawy, "Egyptian Textile Workers Confront the New Economic Order," *Middle East Report Online*, 25 March 2007, http://www.merip.org/mero/mero032507.html; Asef Bayat, *Life as Politics: How Ordinary People Change the Middle East* (Stanford: Stanford University Press, 2010); Asef Bayat, "A New Arab Street in Post-Islamist Times," Middle East Channel, *Foreign Policy Magazine*, 26 January 2011, http://mideast.foreignpolicy.com/posts/2011/01/26/a_new_arab_street; Pete Moore and Bassel F. Salloukh, "Struggles Under Authoritarianism: Regimes, States, and Professional Associations in the Arab World," *International Journal of Middle East Studies* 39, 1 (February 2007); Laryssa Chomiak and John P. Entelis, "The Making of North Africa's Intifadas," *Middle East Report* 259 (Summer 2011).

11. Mona el-Ghobashy, "The Praxis of the Egyptian Revolution," *Middle East Report* 258 (Spring 2011), p. 12.

12. See the interview with Bashar al-Asad in the *Wall Street Journal*, 31 January2011,http://online.wsj.com/article/SB10001424052748703833204576114712441122894.html.

13. See Jihad al-Zayn, "Muqarana Bayna Shari'ayn 'Arabiyayn" [Comparing Two Arab Streets], *al-Nahar*, 23 March 2011.

14. See Steven Cook, *Ruling but Not Governing: The Military and Political Development in Egypt, Algeria, and Turkey* (Baltimore: Johns Hopkins University Press, 2007).

15. Gause, "The Middle East Academic Community and the 'Winter of Arab Discontent,'" p. 14.

16. See Maher Khalil, "Al-General 'Ammar al-Rajul al-Aqwa bi-Tunis" [General Ammar, the Strongest Man in Tunisia], 16 January 2011, http://www.aljazeera.net/NR/EXERES/31B3D757-CA71-4AD7-A067-78ABDA9CDA05.htm.

17. See Lally Weymouth's interview with Egypt's Supreme Council of the Armed Forces in *Slate,* 18 May 2011, http://www.slate.com/id/2294825.

18. See F. Gregory Gause III, "Rageless in Riyadh: Why the Al Saud Dynasty Will Remain," *Foreign Affairs,* 16 March 2011, http://www.foreignaffairs.com/articles/67660/f-gregory-gause-iii/rageless-in-riyadh.

19. Branko Milanovic, "Inequality and Its Discontents: Why So Many Feel Left Behind," *Foreign Affairs,* 12 August 2011, http://www.foreignaffairs.com/articles/68031/branko-milanovic/inequality-and-its-discontents.

20. Diamond, "Why Are There No Arab Democracies?" p. 98.

21. For example, among the literature prizes are the Emirates Foundation's al-Ja'iza al-'Alamiya lil-Riwaya al-'Arabiya-Booker [International Prize for the Arabic Novel—Booker], Ja'izat al-Sheikh Zayed lil-Kitab [Shaikh Zayed's Book Award], Ja'izat Sultan al-'Ouweiss al-Thaqafiya [Sultan Al Owais Cultural Award], Ja'izat al-Malek Feisal al-'Alamiya [King Faisal International Prize], and Ja'izat al-Ibda' al-'Arabi [Arab Creativity Award] by the Arab Thought Forum, whose patron is Prince Khaled al-Faisal. All these prizes are financed by Gulf money. In film there are the Doha Tribeca Film Festival, the Dubai International Film Festival, and the Abu Dhabi Film Festival. In journalism, prizes include the Ja'izat Dubai lil-Sahafa [Dubai Media Award] and Ja'izat al-Ibda' al-'Arabi [Arab Creativity Award].

22. See Jihad al-Zayn's interview with Grand Mufti Ahmad al-Tayyeb in *al-Nahar,* 15 October 2010; and Jihad al-Zayn, "Sahwat al-Azhar Bayna Fiqh al-Badiya wa-l-Tashayou' al-Amni" [Al Azhar's Revival between the Jurisprudence of the Desert and the Securitization of Shiite Conversion], *al-Nahar,* 19 October 2010.

23. See Rabie Barakat, "New Media in the Arab World: A Tool for Redesigning Geopolitical Realities," MA thesis, Lebanese American University, 2011.

24. For Qatar's role in Libya, see Samia Nakhoul, "Special Report: The Secret Plan to Take Tripoli," Reuters, 6 September 2011, http://www.reuters.com/article/2011/09/06/us-libya-endgame-idUSTRE7853C520110906.

25. See Steven Heydemann, "Authoritarian Learning and Current Trends in Arab Governance," in *Oil, Globalization, and Political Reform,* Doha Discussion Paper (Washington, DC: Brookings Institution, 2009), p. 35.

26. See Adam Entous and Julian E. Barnes, "U.S. Wavers on 'Regime Change,'" *Wall Street Journal,* 5 March 2011, http://online.wsj.com/article/SB10001424052748703580004576180522653787198.html.

27. See Ahmad Shokr and Anjali Kamat's interview with Fawwaz Traboulsi, "Escaping Mumana'a and the US-Saudi Counter-Revolution: Syria, Yemen, and Visions of Democracy," *Jadaliyya,* 2 September 2011, http://www.jadaliyya.com/pages/index/2544/escaping-mumanaa-and-the-us-saudi-counter-revoluti.

28. See the Al Jazeera English documentary *Bahrain: Shouting in the Dark,* http://www.youtube.com/watch?v=xaTKDMYOBOU.

29. Text of Obama's "A Moment of Opportunity" speech, http://www.whitehouse.gov/the-press-office/2011/05/19/remarks-president-barack-obama-prepared-delivery-moment-opportunity.

30. Philippe C. Schmitter, "Twenty-five Years, Fifteen Findings," *Journal of Democracy* 21, 1 (January 2010), p. 20, italics omitted.

31. See Hussein Agha and Robert Malley, "The Arab Counterrevolution," *New York Review of Books,* 29 September 2011, http://www.nybooks.com/articles/archives/2011/sep/29/arab-counterrevolution.

32. See Dankwart A. Rustow, "Transitions to Democracy: Toward a Dynamic Model," *Comparative Politics* 2, 3 (April 1970).

33. See Traboulsi, "Escaping Mumanaʻa and the US-Saudi Counter-Revolution."

34. See Robert Springborg, "Egypt's Cobra and Mongoose," Middle East Channel, *Foreign Policy Magazine,* 27 February 2012, http://mideast.foreignpolicy.com/posts/2012/02/27/egypt_s_cobra_and_mongoose.

35. See Fawwaz Traboulsi, "Al-Islamiyun fi-l-Qawl wal-Fiʻel" [Islamists in Discourse and Practice], *al-Safir,* 14 December 2011.

36. Anderson, "Demystifying the Arab Spring," p. 7.

37. See *al-Safir,* 7 September 2011.

Acronyms

ANN	Arab News Network
ART	Arab Radio and Television
AQAP	al-Qaeda in the Arabian Peninsula
AQIM	al-Qaeda in the Islamic Maghreb
ASU	Arab Socialist Union (Egypt)
ATP	Arab Telemedia Productions
CPA	Coalition Provisional Authority (Iraq)
CPR	Congrès pour la République (Congress for the Republic) (Tunisia)
ESC	Egyptian Satellite Channel
FIS	Front Islamique du Salut (Islamic Salvation Front) (Algeria)
FJP	Freedom and Justice Party (Egypt)
FLN	Front de Libération Nationale (National Liberation Front)(Algeria)
GCC	Gulf Cooperation Council
GDP	gross domestic product
G8	Group of Eight
ICAMES	Interuniversity Consortium for Arab and Middle Eastern Studies
IGC	Iraqi Governing Council
IFTU	Iraqi Federation of Trade Unions
IMF	International Monetary Fund
INM	Iraqi National Movement
ISCI	Islamic Supreme Council of Iraq
ISIE	Instance Supérieure Indépendante pour les Élections (Higher Independent Authority for the Elections) (Tunisia)
JMP	Joint Meeting Parties (Yemen)
KDP	Kurdistan Democratic Party
KRG	Kurdistan Regional Government
LBC	Lebanese Broadcasting Corporation
LIFG	Libyan Islamic Fighting Group
MBC	Middle East Broadcasting Centre
MSP	Mouvement de la Societé pour la Paix (Movement of Society for Peace) (Algeria)
NATO	North Atlantic Treaty Organization

NBN	National Broadcasting Network (Lebanon)
NDP	National Democratic Party (Egypt)
NGO	nongovernmental organization
NTC	National Transitional Council (Libya)
PA	Palestinian Authority
PJD	Parti de la Justice et du Développement (Justice and Development Party) (Morocco)
PLC	Palestinian Legislative Council
PLO	Palestine Liberation Organization
PR	proportional representation
PSD	Parti Socialiste Destourien (Socialist Destourian Party) (Tunisia)
PUK	Patriotic Union of Kurdistan
RCD	Rassemblement Constitutionnel Démocratique (Democratic Constitutional Rally) (Tunisia)
RND	Rassemblement National Démocratique (National Rally for Democracy) (Algeria)
SABIC	Saudi Basic Industries Corporation
SCAF	Supreme Council of the Armed Forces (Egypt)
SCIRI	Supreme Council of the Islamic Revolution in Iraq
SNC	Syrian National Council
SNTV	single nontransferable vote
TNA	Transitional National Assembly (Iraq)
UAE	United Arab Emirates
UGTT	Union Générale de Travailleurs Tunisiens (Tunisian General Labor Union)
USAID	US Agency for International Development
USFP	Union Socialiste des Forces Populaires (Social Union of Popular Forces) (Morocco)
WVS	World Values Survey (WVS)

Bibliography

Abd al-Jabbar, Falih. "Min Dawlat Hizb al-Wahid ila Dawlat al-Hizb/al-Usra" [From the One Party State to the Family-Party State]. *al-Thaqafa al-Jadida* 267 (December 1995–January/February 1996).

Abdelrahman, Maha. "'With the Islamists?—Sometimes; With the State?—Never!' Cooperation Between the Left and Islamists in Egypt." *British Journal of Middle Eastern Studies* 36, 1 (April 2009).

Abu Jaber, Kamel S., and Schirin H. Fathi. "The 1989 Jordanian Parliamentary Elections." *Orient* 31, 1 (March 1990).

Abu Rumman, Mohammad *The Muslim Brotherhood in the Jordanian Parliamentary Elections, 2007: A Passing "Political Setback" or Diminishing Popularity?* Amman: Friedrich Ebert Stiftung, 2008.

Acemoglu, Daron, and James A. Robinson. "Economic Backwardness in Political Perspective." *American Political Science Review* 100, 1 (February 2006).

Agha, Hussein, and Robert Malley. "The Arab Counterrevolution." *New York Review of Books,* 29 September 2011. http://www.nybooks.com/articles/archives/2011/sep/29/arab-counterrevolution.

Ajami, Fouad. *The Arab Predicament: Arab Political Thought and Practice Since 1967.* Updated ed. Cambridge: Cambridge University Press, 1993.

———. *The Dream Palace of the Arabs: A Generation's Odyssey.* New York: Random, 1999.

———. "Iraq and the Arab's Future." *Foreign Affairs* 82, 1 (January–February 2003).

———. "The Strange Survival of the Arab Autocracies." *Defining Ideas,* 13 December 2010. http://www.hoover.org/publications/defining-ideas/article/58836.

Albrecht, Holger, ed. *Contentious Politics in the Middle East: Political Opposition Under Authoritarianism.* Gainesville: University of Florida Press, 2010.

———. "How Can Opposition Support Authoritarianism? Lessons from Egypt." *Democratization* 12, 3 (June 2005).

Albrecht, Holger, and Eva Wegner. "Autocrats and Islamists: Contenders and Containment in Egypt and Morocco." *Journal of North African Studies* 11, 2 (June 2006).

Aliboni, Roberto, and Laura Guazzone. "Democracy in the Arab Countries and the West." *Mediterranean Politics* 9, 1 (Spring 2004).

Alterman, Jon B. "IT Comes of Age in the Middle East." *Foreign Service Journal* 82, 12 (December 2005).

———. "New Media, New Politics? From Satellite Television to the Internet in the Arab World." Policy Paper no. 48. Washington, DC: Washington Institute of Near East Policy, 1998.

Amawi, Abla M. "The 1993 Elections in Jordan." *Arab Studies Quarterly* 16, 3 (Summer 1994).

el-Amrani, Issandr. "Controlled Reform in Egypt: Neither Reformist Nor Controlled." *Middle East Report Online,* 15 December 2005. http://merip.org/mero/mero121505.html.

———. "Why Tunis, Why Cairo?" *London Review of Books,* 17 February 2011. http://www.lrb.co.uk/v33/n04/issandr-elamrani/why-tunis-why-cairo.

Anderson, Lisa. "Absolutism and the Resilience of the Monarchy in the Middle East." *Political Science Quarterly* 106, 1 (1991).

———. "Peace and Democracy in the Middle East: The Constraints of Soft Budgets." *Journal of International Affairs* 49, 1 (Summer 1995).

———. "Searching Where the Light Shines: Studying Democratization in the Middle East." *Annual Review of Political Science* 9 (2006).

———. *The State and Social Transformation in Tunisia and Libya, 1830–1980.* Princeton: Princeton University Press, 1986.

Andoni, Lamis. "The Palestinian Elections: Moving Toward Democracy or One-Party Rule?" *Journal of Palestine Studies* 25, 3 (Spring 1996).

Andoni, Lamis, and Jillian Schwedler. "Bread Riots in Jordan." *Middle East Report* 201 (October–December 1996).

Anscombe, Frederick. *The Ottoman Gulf: The Creation of Kuwait, Saudi Arabia, and Qatar.* New York: Columbia University Press, 1997.

Arce, Moises, and Paul T. Bellinger. "Low Intensity Democracy Revisited: The Effects of Economic Liberalization on Political Activity in Latin America." *World Politics* 60, 1 (October 2007).

Ashour, Omar. *The De-Radicalization of Jihadists: Transforming Armed Islamist Movements.* New York: Routledge, 2009.

———. "De-Radicalizing Jihadists the Libyan Way." Sada (Carnegie Endowment for International Peace), 7 April 2010. http://www.carnegieendowment.org/sada/2010/04/07/de-radicalizing-jihadists-libyan-way/6bak.

———. "Lions Tamed? An Inquiry into the Causes of De-Radicalization of Armed Islamist Movements: The Case of the Egyptian Islamic Group." *Middle East Journal* 61, 4 (Autumn 2007).

———. "Mubarak's Last Laugh." Project Syndicate, 5 August 2011. http://www.project-syndicate.org/commentary/ashour5/English.

al-Awadi, Hesham. "Mubarak and the Islamists: Why Did the 'Honeymoon' End?" *Middle East Journal* 59, 1 (Winter 2005).

Ayalon, Ami, and Haim Shaked, eds. *Middle East Contemporary Survey.* Vol. 12. Boulder: Westview, 1988.

Ayubi, Nazih. *Over-Stating the Arab State: Politics and Society in the Middle East.* London: Tauris, 1996.

Bank, André, and Morten Valbjørn. "Bringing the Arab Regional Level Back In: Jordan in the New Arab Cold War." *Middle East Critique* 19, 3 (2010).

Barakat, Rabie. "New Media in the Arab World: A Tool for Redesigning Geopolitical Realities." MA thesis, Lebanese American University, 2011.

Barany, Zoltan. "The Role of the Military." *Journal of Democracy* 22, 4 (October 2011).

Barkey, Henri, ed. *The Politics of Economic Reform in the Middle East.* New York: St. Martin's, 1992.

Barnett, Michael N. *Dialogues in Arab Politics: Negotiations in Regional Order.* New York: Columbia University Press, 1998.

———. "Regional Security After the Gulf War." *Political Science Quarterly* 111, 4 (Winter 1996–1997).

———. "Sovereignty, Nationalism, and Regional Order in the Arab States System." *International Organization* 49, 3 (Summer 1995).

Barnett, Michael, and Jack Levy. "Domestic Sources of Alliances and Alignments: The Case of Egypt, 1962–73." *International Organization* 45, 3 (1991).

Barwig, Andrew "Why New Electoral Rules Matter." Middle East Channel, *Foreign Policy Magazine,* 21 February 2011. http://mideast.foreignpolicy.com/posts/2011/02/18/why_new_electoral_rules_matter.

Bayat, Asef. *Life as Politics: How Ordinary People Change the Middle East.* Stanford: Stanford University Press, 2010.

———. *Making Islam Democratic: Social Movements and the Post-Islamist Turn.* Palo Alto: Stanford University Press, 2007.

———. "A New Arab Street in Post-Islamist Times." Middle East Channel, *Foreign Policy Magazine,* 26 January 2011. http://mideast.foreignpolicy.com/posts/2011/01/26/a_new_arab_street.

———. "The 'Street' and the Politics of Dissent in the Arab World." *Middle East Report* 226 (Spring 2003).

———. *Street Politics: Poor People's Movements in Iran.* New York: Columbia University Press, 1997.

Baylouny, Anne Marie. "Militarizing Welfare: Neo-Liberalism and Jordanian Policy." *Middle East Journal* 62, 2 (Spring 2008).

Beblawi, Hazem. *The Arab Gulf Economy in a Turbulent Age.* London: Croom Helm, 1984.

Beblawi, Hazem, and Giacomo Luciani, eds. *The Arab State.* New York: Croom Held, 1987.

Beinin, Joel, and Hossam el-Hamalawy. "Egyptian Textile Workers Confront the New Economic Order." *Middle East Report Online,* 25 March 2007. http://www.merip.org/mero/mero032507.html.

Beinin, Joel, and Frederic Vairel. *Social Movements, Mobilization, and Contestation in the Middle East and North Africa.* Stanford: Stanford University Press, 2011.

Bellin, Eva. "The Politics of Profit in Tunisia: Utility of the Rentier Paradigm?" *World Development* 22, 3 (1994).

———. "The Robustness of Authoritarianism in the Middle East: Exceptionalism in Comparative Perspective." *Comparative Politics* 36, 2 (January 2004).

———. *Stalled Democracy: Capital, Labor, and the Paradox of State Sponsored Development.* Ithaca: Cornell University Press, 2002.

Bennadji, Chérif. "Révision de la constitution: vers une présidence à vie pour Abdelaziz Bouteflika." L'Année du Maghreb 5 (2009).

Bensahel, Nora, and Daniel L. Byman, eds. *The Future Security Environment in the Middle East: Conflict, Stability, and Political Change.* Santa Monica: RAND, 2004.

Berman, Sheri. "Taming Extremist Parties: Lessons from Europe." *Journal of Democracy* 19, 1 (January 2008).

Bermeo, Nancy. "Democracy and the Lessons of Dictatorship." *Comparative Politics* 24, 3 (April 1992).

Berti, Benedetta. "Electoral Reform in Lebanon." *Mideast Monitor* 4, 1 (July–August 2009). http://www.mideastmonitor.org/issues/0907/0907_4.htm.

Bianchi, Robert. *Unruly Corporatism: Associational Life in Twentieth-Century Egypt.* New York: Oxford University Press, 1989.

Bikhchandani, Sushil, David Hirshleifer, and Ivo Welch. "A Theory of Fads, Fashion, Custom, and Cultural Change as Informational Cascades." *Journal of Political Economy* 100, 5 (1992).

Binder, Leonard. *Muslim Liberalism.* Chicago: University of Chicago Press, 1988.

Birdsall, Nancy, and Arvind Subramanian. "Saving Iraq from Its Oil." *Foreign Affairs* 83, 4 (July–August 2004).

Blaydes, Lisa. *Elections and Distributive Politics in Mubarak's Egypt.* Cambridge: Cambridge University Press, 2011.

Bocco, Riccardo, and Mohammad-Reza Djalili, eds. *Moyent-Orient: Migrations, Démocratisation, Médiations.* Paris: Presses Universitaires de France, 1994.

Bozarslan, Hamit. "Réfléxions sur les Configurations Révolutionnaire Égyptienne et Tunisienne." *Mouvements,* 17 August 2011. http://www.mouvements.info/Reflexions-sur-les-configurations.html.

Brand, Laurie A. "The Effects of the Peace Process on Political Liberalization in Jordan." *Journal of Palestine Studies* 28, 2 (Winter 1999).

Briancon, Pierre, and John Foley. "IMF Reviews Praise Libya, Egypt, and Other Nations." *New York Times,* 22 February 2011.

Brinks, Daniel, and Michael Coppedge. "Diffusion Is No Illusion: Neighbor Emulation in the Third Wave of Democratization." *Comparative Political Studies* 39, 4 (2006).

Browers, Michaelle L. "Origins and Architects of Yemen's Joint Meeting Parties." *International Journal of Middle East Studies* 39, 4 (November 2007).

———. *Political Ideology in the Arab World: Accommodation and Transformation.* Cambridge: Cambridge University Press, 2009.

Brown, Nathan J. *Constitutions in a Nonconstitutional World: Arab Basic Laws and the Prospects for Accountable Government.* Albany: State University of New York Press, 2002.

———. "What Is at Stake in Kuwait's Parliamentary Elections?" Carnegie Endowment for International Peace, May 2008. http://carnegieendowment.org/files/brown_kuwait_elections_FAQ_final.pdf.

Brown, Nathan J., and Amr Hamzawy. "The Draft Party Platform of the Egyptian Muslim Brotherhood: Foray into Political Integration or Retreat into Old Positions?" Carnegie Papers, Middle East Series, no. 89. Washington, DC: Carnegie Endowment for International Peace, January 2008.

Brown, Nathan J., Amr Hamzawy, and Marina Ottaway. "Islamist Movements and the Democratic Process in the Arab World: Exploring the Gray Zones." Carnegie Papers, Middle East Series, no. 67. Washington, DC: Carnegie Endowment for International Peace, March 2006.

Brownlee, Jason. *Authoritarianism in an Age of Democratization.* Cambridge: Cambridge University Press, 2007.

———. "The Decline of Pluralism in Mubarak's Egypt." *Journal of Democracy* 13, 4 (October 2002).

———. "Executive Elections in the Arab World: When and How Do They Matter?" *Comparative Political Studies* 44, 7 (July 2011).

———. "Unrequited Moderation: Credible Commitments and State Repression in Egypt." *Studies in Comparative International Development* 45 (2010).

Brumberg, Daniel. "Islam, Elections, and Reform in Algeria." *Journal of Democracy* 2, 1 (Winter 1991).

———. "Islamists and the Politics of Consensus." *Journal of Democracy* 13, 3 (2002).

———. *Reinventing Khomeini: The Struggle for Reform in Iran.* Chicago: University of Chicago Press, 2001.

———. "The Trap of Liberalized Autocracy." *Journal of Democracy* 13, 4 (October 2002).

Brynen, Rex. "The Dynamics of Palestinian Elite Formation." *Journal of Palestine Studies* 24, 3 (Spring 1995).

———. "Economic Crisis and Post-Rentier Democratization in the Arab World: The Case of Jordan." *Canadian Journal of Political Science* 25, 1 (March 1992).

———. "The Iraq War and (Non) Democratization in the Arab World." In Mokhtar Lamani and Bessma Momani, eds., *From Desolation to Reconstruction: Iraq's Troubled Journey.* Waterloo: Wilfrid Laurier University Press, 2010.

————. "The Neopatrimonial Dimension of Palestinian Politics." *Journal of Palestine Studies* 25, 1 (Autumn 1995).

————. "Palestine and the Arab State System: Permeability, State Consolidation, and Responses to the Intifada." *Canadian Journal of Political Science* 24, 3 (September 1991).

————. "Political Culture and the Puzzle of Persistent Authoritarianism in the Middle East." Paper presented at the annual conference of the International Political Science Association, Santiago, July 2009.

Brynen, Rex, Bahgat Korany, and Paul Noble, eds. *Political Liberalization and Democratization in the Arab World.* Vol. 1, *Theoretical Perspectives.* Boulder: Lynne Rienner, 1995.

Bugra, Ayse. "Class, Culture, and the State." *International Journal of Middle East Studies* 30, 4 (1998).

————. "Labour, Capital, and Religion: Harmony and Conflict Among the Constituency of Political Islam in Turkey." *Middle Eastern Studies* 38, 2 (2002).

Burnell, Peter. "The Domestic Political Impact of Foreign Aid: Recalibrating the Research Agenda." *European Journal of Development Research* 16, 2 (2004).

Buruma, Ian. "Lost in Translation: The Two Minds of Bernard Lewis." *New Yorker,* 14 June 2004. http://www.newyorker.com/archive/2004/06/14/040614crbo_books.

Bush, George W. *Decision Points.* New York: Crown, 2010.

Buzan, Barry. *People, States, and Fear.* 2nd ed. London: Harvester Wheatsheaf, 1991.

Carapico, Sheila. "Foreign Aid for Promoting Democracy in the Arab World." *Middle East Journal* 56, 3 (Summer 2002).

Carothers, Thomas. "The End of the Transition Paradigm." *Journal of Democracy* 13, 3 (January 2002).

————. "Promoting Democracy and Fighting Terror." *Foreign Affairs* 82, 1 (January–February 2003).

————. *Revitalizing U.S. Democracy Assistance: The Challenge of USAID.* Washington, DC: Carnegie Endowment for International Peace, 2009.

Carothers, Thomas, and Marina Ottaway, eds. *Uncharted Journey: Promoting Democracy in the Middle East.* Washington, DC: Carnegie Endowment for International Peace, 2005.

Cavatorta, Francesco. "Civil Society, Islamism, and Democratisation: The Case of Morocco." *Journal of Modern African Studies* 44, 2 (2006).

————. "The Convergence of Governance: Upgrading Authoritarianism in the Arab World, and Downgrading Democracy Elsewhere?" *Middle East Critique* 19, 3 (Fall 2010).

————. "'Divided They Stand, Divided They Fail': Opposition Politics in Morocco." *Democratization* 16, 1 (February 2009).

————. "Neither Participation Nor Revolution: The Strategy of the Moroccan Jamiat al-Adl wal-Ihsan." *Mediterranean Politics* 12, 3 (November 2007).

Cavatorta, Francesco, and Azzam Elananza. "Political Opposition in Civil Society: An Analysis of the Interactions of Secular and Religious Associations in Algeria and Jordan." *Government and Opposition* 43, 4 (2008).

Chang, Ha-Joon. *Bad Samaritans: The Myth of Free Trade and the Secret History of Capitalism.* London: Bloomsbury, 2008.

Chanin, Clifford, and F. Gregory Gause III. "U.S.-Saudi Relations: Bump in The Road or End of the Road?" *Middle East Policy* 10, 4 (Winter 2003).

Chaudhry, Kiren. "The Myths of Market and the Common History of Late Developers." *Politics and Society* 21, 3 (September 1993).

————. "The Price of Wealth: Business and State in Labor Remittance and Oil Economies." *International Organization* 43, 1 (Winter 1989).

Chhibber, Pradeep K. "State Policy, Rent Seeking, and the Electoral Success of a Religious Party in Algeria." *Journal of Politics* 58, 1 (February 1996).

Chomiak, Laryssa, and John P. Entelis. "The Making of North Africa's Intifadas." *Middle East Report* 259 (Summer 2011).

Church, Michael. "Billion-Dollar Ambition." *World Soccer,* January 2011.

Clark, Janine A. "The Conditions of Islamist Moderation: Unpacking Cross-Ideological Cooperation in Jordan." *International Journal of Middle East Studies* 38, 4 (2006).

———. *Islam, Charity, and Activism.* Bloomington: Indiana University Press, 2004.

———. "The State, Popular Participation, and the Voluntary Sector." *World Development,* 23, 4 (1995).

Clark, Janine A., and Jillian Schwedler. "Who Opened the Window? Women's Struggle for Voice Within Islamist Political Parties." *Comparative Politics* 35, 3 (April 2003).

Clark, Janine A., and Amy E. Young. "Islamism and Family Law Reform in Morocco and Jordan." *Mediterranean Politics* 13, 3 (November 2008).

Cochrane, Paul. "Are Lebanon's Media Fanning the Flames of Sectarianism?" *Arab Media and Society* 2 (Summer 2007). http://www.arabmediasociety.com/?article=206.

———. "The 'Lebanonization' of the Iraqi Media: An Overview of Iraq's Television Landscape." *Transnational Broadcasting Studies* 16 (2006). http://www.tbsjournal.com/Cochrane.html.

———. "Saudi Arabia's Media Influence." *Arab Media and Society* 3 (Fall 2007). http://www.arabmediasociety.com/countries/index.php?c_article=122.

Collier, Paul, et al. *Breaking the Conflict Trap: Civil War and Development Policy.* Washington DC: World Bank, 2003.

Cook, Steven. *Ruling but Not Governing: The Military and Political Development in Egypt, Algeria, and Turkey.* Baltimore: Johns Hopkins University Press, 2007.

Cordesman, Anthony. *Iraq Trends in Violence and Civilian Casualties, 2005–2009.* Washington, DC: Center for Strategic and International Studies, 5 May 2009. http://csis.org/files/media/csis/pubs/090504_iraq_patterns_in_violence.pdf.

———. *Saudi Arabia: National Security in a Troubled Region.* New York: Praeger, 2009.

Crocker, Chester A., Fen Osler Hampson, and Pamela Aall, eds. *Leashing the Dogs of War: Conflict-Management in a Divided World.* Washington, DC: US Institute of Peace, 2007.

Crystal, Jill. *Oil and Politics in the Gulf: Rulers and Merchants in Kuwait and Qatar.* Cambridge: Cambridge University Press, 1995.

Dajani, Nabil "The Re-Feudalization of the Public Sphere: Lebanese Television News Coverage and the Lebanese Political Process." *Transnational Broadcasting Studies* 16 (2006). http://www.tbsjournal.com/Dajani.html.

Dalacoura, Katerina. "US Democracy Promotion in the Arab Middle East Since 11 September 2001: A Critique." *International Affairs* 81, 5 (2005).

David, Assaf, and Oren Barak. "How the New Arab Media Challenges the Arab Militaries: The Case of the War Between Israel and Hizbullah in 2006." Middle East Institute, Policy Brief no. 20, October 2008. http://www.mideasti.org/files/New-Arab-Media.pdf.

David, Steven. "Explaining Third World Alignment." *World Politics* 43, 2 (1991).

Davies, Graeme A. "Inside Out or Outside In? Domestic and International Factors Affecting Iranian Foreign Policy Towards the United States, 1990–2004." *Foreign Policy Analysis* 4, 3 (July 2008).

Davis, Eric. "History Matters: Past as Prologue in Building Democracy in Iraq." *Orbis* 49 (Spring 2005).

Dawisha, Adeed, and I. William Zartman, eds. *Beyond Coercion: The Durability of the Arab State.* London: Croom Helm, 1988.

Delacroix, Jean. "The Distributive State in the World System." *Studies in International Comparative Development* 15, 3 (1980).

al-Derazi, Abdellah. "Old Players and New in the Bahraini Elections." *Arab Reform Bulletin,* 2 June 2010. http://carnegieendowment.org/arb/?fa=show&article=40903.

Desrues, Thierry, and Miguel Hernando de Larramendi, eds. *L'Année du Maghreb 2009.* Paris: CNRS Éditions, 2009.

Dessouki, Ali E. *Islamic Resurgence in the Arab World.* New York: Praeger, 1982.

Diamond, Larry. "Elections Without Democracy: Thinking About Hybrid Regimes." *Journal of Democracy* 13, 2 (April 2002).

———. "Why Are There No Arab Democracies?" *Journal of Democracy* 21, 1 (January 2010).

el-Din, Gamal Essam. "Secular Opposition Slams New Electoral Law." *al-Ahram Weekly,* 26 May–1 June 2011. http://weekly.ahram.org.eg/2011/1049/eg3.htm.

Diwan, Kristin. "Kuwait's Impatient Youth Movement." Middle East Channel, *Foreign Policy Magazine,* 29 June 2011. http://mideast.foreignpolicy.com/posts/2011/06/29/kuwait_s_youth_movement.

Doner, Richard F., Bryan K. Ritchie, and Dan Slater. "Systemic Vulnerability and the Origins of Developmental States: Northeast and Southeast Asia in Comparative Perspective." *International Organization* 59, 2 (2005).

Donno, Daniela, and Bruce Russett. "Islam, Authoritarianism, and Female Empowerment: What Are the Linkages?" *World Politics* 56, 4 (July 2004).

Dorlian, Samy. "The Sa'da War in Yemen: Between Politics and Sectarianism." *The Muslim World* 101, 2 (April 2011).

Drake, Paul, and Eduardo Silva, eds. *Elections in Latin America.* San Diego: University of California Press, 1986.

Dris-Ait-Hamadouche, Louisa. "The 2007 Legislative Elections in Algeria: Political Reckonings." *Mediterranean Politics* 13, 1 (March 2008).

Duclos, Louis-Jean. "Les Élections Législatives en Jordanie." *Maghreb-Machrek* 129 (July–September 1990).

Dunne, Michele. "The Baby, the Bathwater, and the Freedom Agenda in the Middle East." *Washington Quarterly* 32, 1 (January 2009).

———. "Time to Pursue Democracy in Egypt." Carnegie Endowment for International Peace, January 2007. http://carnegieendowment.org/files/Dunne_Egypt_FINAL2.pdf.

Dunne, Michele, and Amr Hamzawy. "From Too Much Egyptian Opposition to Too Little—and Legal Worries Besides." Carnegie Endowment for International Peace, 13 December 2010. http://www.carnegieendowment.org/2010/12/13/from-too-much-egyptian-opposition-to-too-little-and-legal-worries-besides/chf.

Durac, Vincent. "The Impact of External Actors on the Distribution of Power in the Middle East: The Case of Egypt." *Journal of North African Studies* 14, 1 (March 2009).

———. "The Joint Meeting Parties and the Politics of Opposition in Yemen." *British Journal of Middle Eastern Studies* 38, 3 (December 2011).

Duran, Burhanettin, and Engin Yildirim. "Islamism, Trade Unionism, and Civil Society: The Case of Hak-Is Labour Confederation in Turkey." *Middle Eastern Studies* 41, 2 (March 2005).

Eakin, Hugh. "The Strange Power of Qatar." *New York Review of Books,* 27 October 2011. http://www.nybooks.com/articles/archives/2011/oct/27/strange-power-qatar.

Ehteshami, Anoushiravan, and Steven Wright, eds. *Reform in the Middle East Oil Monarchies.* Reading, UK: Ithaca Press, 2008.

Eickelman, Dale F., and John W. Anderson. *New Media in the Muslim World: The Emerging Public Sphere.* Bloomington: Indiana University Press, 1999.

Eickelman, Dale, and James Piscatori. *Muslim Politics.* Rev. ed. Princeton: Princeton University Press, 2004.

al-Ekry, Abd al-Nabi. "Al-Wefaq and the Challenges of Participation in Bahrain." Carnegie Endowment for International Peace, 19 May 2007. http://www.carnegieendowment.org/arb/?fa=show&article=20932.

Esposito, John L. ed. *Political Islam: Revolution, Radicalism, or Reform?* Boulder: Lynne Rienner, 1997.

Esposito, John L., and Dalia Mogahed. *Who Speaks for Islam? What a Billion Muslims Really Think.* New York: Gallup, 2007.

Esposito, John L., and James P. Piscatori. "Democratization and Islam." *Middle East Journal* 45, 3 (Summer 1991).

Esposito, John L., and John O. Voll. *Islam and Democracy.* New York: Oxford University Press.

Fahmy, Ninette S. "The Performance of the Muslim Brotherhood in the Egyptian Syndicates: An Alternative Formula for Reform?" *Middle East Journal* 52, 4 (Autumn 1998).

Fandy, Mamoun. "Tribe vs. Islam: The Post-Colonial Arab State and the Democratic Imperative." *Middle East Policy* 3, 2 (1993).

———. *(Un)Civil War of Words: Media and Politics in the Arab World.* London: Praeger Security International, 2007.

Fathi, Schirin H. *The Palestinian Component in Jordan's 1989 Parliamentary Elections.* East Jerusalem: PASSIA, 1995.

Feige, Edgard L., and Katarina Ott, eds. *Underground Economies in Transition: Unrecorded Activity, Tax Evasion, Corruption, and Organized Crime.* Aldershot: Ashgate, 1999.

Field, Nathan, and Ahmed Hamam. "Salafi Satellite TV in Egypt." *Arab Media and Society* 8 (Spring 2009). http://www.arabmediasociety.com/?article=712.

Filiu, Jean-Pierre. "The Local and Global Jihad of al-Qa'ida in the Islamic Maghrib." *Middle East Journal* 63, 2 (2009).

Finkel, Steven E., Aníbal S. Pérez Liñan, and Mitchell A. Seligson. "The Effects of U.S. Foreign Assistance on Democracy Building, 1990–2003." *World Politics* 59, 3 (April 2007).

Fish, Steven M. "Islam and Authoritarianism." *World Politics* 55, 1 (October 2002).

Forsythe, David P., ed. *Encyclopedia of Human Rights.* Vol. 2. Oxford: Oxford University Press, 2009.

Freedom House. *Freedom in the World 2011.* Washington, DC, 2011. http://www.freedomhouse.org.

Friedman, Thomas. "The First Law of PetroPolitics." *Foreign Policy,* 25 April 2006.

Fuller, Graham. *The Future of Political Islam.* New York: Palgrave Macmillan, 2003.

Gambetta, Diego, ed. *Trust: Making and Breaking Cooperative Relations.* London: Blackwell, 1990.

Gambill, Gary. "The Iraqi Media: Free Marketplace of Ideas or Pluralism of the Powerful?" 12 June 2009. http://www.onlineopinion.com.au/view.asp?article=8982.

Gandhi, Jennifer, and Ellen Lust-Okar. "Elections Under Authoritarianism." *Annual Review of Political Science* 12 (2009).

Gandhi, Jennifer, and Adam Przeworski. "Authoritarian Institutions and the Survival of Autocrats." *Comparative Political Studies* 40, 11 (November 2007).

Garnham, David, and Mark Tessler, eds. *Democracy, War, and Peace in the Middle East.* Indiana: Indiana University Press, 1995.

Gause, F. Gregory, III. *The International Relations of the Persian Gulf.* Cambridge: Cambridge University Press, 2010.

———. "Iraq's Decisions to Go to War, 1980 and 1990." *Middle East Journal,* 56, 1 (Winter 2002).

———. *Oil Monarchies: Domestic and Security Challenges in the Arab Gulf States.* New York: Council on Foreign Relations Press, 1994.

———. "Rageless in Riyadh: Why the Al Saud Dynasty Will Remain." *Foreign Affairs,* 16 March 2011. http://www.foreignaffairs.com/articles/67660/f-gregory-gause-iii/rageless-in-riyadh.

———. "The Middle East Academic Community and the 'Winter of Arab Disontent?': Why Did We Miss It?" In *Seismic Shift: Understanding Change in the Middle East.* Washington, DC: Henry L. Stimson Center, 2011.

———. "Why Middle East Studies Missed the Arab Spring." *Foreign Affairs* 90, 4 (July–August 2011).

Gellner, Ernest. *Muslim Society.* Cambridge: Cambridge University Press, 1983.

Gerges, Fawaz A. "The End of the Islamist Insurgency in Egypt? Costs and Prospects." *Middle East Journal* 54, 4 (Autumn 2000).

Gerschenkron, Alexander. *Economic Backwardness in Historical Perspective.* Cambridge, MA: Belknap, 1962.

Ghanem, As'ad. "Founding Elections in a Transitional Period: The First Palestinian General Elections." *Middle East Journal* 50, 4 (Autumn 1996).

Ghareeb, Edmund. "New Media and the Information Revolution in the Arab World: An Assessment." *Middle East Journal* 54, 3 (Summer 2000).

el-Ghobashy, Mona. "Antinomies of the Saad Eddin Ibrahim Case." *Middle East Report Online,* 15 August 2002. http://www.merip.org/mero/mero081502.html.

———. "Constitutional Contention in Contemporary Egypt." *American Behavioral Scientist* 51, 11 (July 2008).

———. "Egypt's Paradoxical Elections." *Middle East Report* 238 (Spring 2006).

———. "The Metamorphosis of the Egyptian Muslim Brothers." *International Journal of Middle East Studies* 37, 3 (2005).

———. "The Praxis of the Egyptian Revolution." *Middle East Report* 258 (Spring 2011).

Goldsmith, Arthur. "Muslim Exceptionalism: Measuring the 'Democracy Gap.'" *Middle East Policy* 14, 2 (Summer 2007).

Gramsci, Antonio. *Selections from the Prison Notebooks.* Edited and translated by Quentin Hoare and Geoffrey Nowell Smith. New York: International Publishers, 1971.

Guazzone, Laura, and Daniela Pioppi. "Globalisation and the Restructuring of State Power in the Arab World." *International Spectator* 42, 4 (December 2007).

Hadenius, Alex, and Jan Teorell. "Cultural and Economic Requisites of Democracy: Reassessing Recent Evidence." *Studies in Comparative International Development* 39, 4 (Winter 2005).

———. "Pathways from Authoritarianism." *Journal of Democracy* 18, 1 (January 2007).

Hafez, Mohammed. *Why Muslims Rebel: Repression and Resistance in the Islamic World.* Boulder: Lynne Rienner, 2003.

Haklai, Oded. "Authoritarianism and Islamic Movements in the Middle East: Research and Theory-Building in the Twenty-First Century." *International Studies Review* 11 (2009).

Hamid, Shadi. "Arab Islamist Parties: Losing on Purpose?" *Journal of Democracy* 22, 1 (January 2011).

———. "The Islamist Response to Repression: Are Mainstream Islamists Radicalizing?" Policy brief. Brookings Doha Center of the Saban Center for Middle East Policy, Brookings Institution, August 2010.

Hammond, Andrew. "Saudi Arabia's Media Empire: Keeping the Masses at Home."

Arab Media and Society 3 (Fall 2007). http://www.arabmediasociety.com/countries/index.php?c_article=121.

Hamzawy, Amr. "The Key to Arab Reform: Moderate Islamists." Policy brief. Washington, DC: Carnegie Endowment for International Peace, 2005.

———. "The Saudi Labyrinth: Evaluating the Current Political Opening." Carnegie Papers no. 68. Washington, DC: Carnegie Endowment for International Peace, April 2006.

Hamzawy, Amr, and Nathan J. Brown. "Can Egypt's Troubled Elections Produce a More Democratic Future?" Carnegie Endowment for International Peace, December 2005. http://carnegieendowment.org/files/PO24.brown.hamzawy.FINAL1.pdf.

Hamzawy, Amr, Marina Ottaway, and Nathan Brown. "What Islamists Need to Be Clear About: The Case of the Egyptian Muslim Brotherhood." Policy outlook. Washington, DC: Carnegie Endowment for International Peace, February 2007.

Harik, Iliya, and Denis J. Sullivan, eds. *Privatization and Liberalization in the Middle East*. Bloomington: Indiana University Press, 1992.

Harram, Faris. "TV Station Stirs Sectarian Tensions." 15 June 2009. http://www.uslaboragainstwar.org/article.php?id=19536.

Harrigan, Jane, and Hamed el-Said. *Aid and Power in the Arab World: World Bank and IMF Policy-Based Lending in the Middle East and North Africa*. Basingstoke: Palgrave Macmillan, 2009.

Hashim, Ahmed S. *Insurgency and Counter-Insurgency in Iraq*. London: Hurst, 2006.

Haugbolle, Hostrup, and Francesco Cavatorta. "Will the Real Tunisian Opposition Please Stand Up? Opposition Coordination Failures Under Authoritarian Constraints." *British Journal of Middle Eastern Studies* 38, 3 (December 2011).

Hawthorne, Amy. "Can the United States Promote Democracy in the Middle East?" *Current History,* January 2003.

Hegghammer, Thomas. "Islamist Violence and Regime Stability in Saudi Arabia." *International Affairs* 84, 4 (2008).

———. "Lady Gaga vs. the Occupation." *Foreign Policy,* 31 March 2010.

Henry, Clement, and Robert Springborg. *Globalization and the Politics of Development in the Middle East*. Cambridge: Cambridge University Press, 2001.

Herb, Michael. *All in the Family: Absolutism, Revolution, and Democracy in the Middle Eastern Monarchies*. Albany: State University of New York Press, 1999.

———. "A Nation of Bureaucrats: Political Participation and Economic Diversification in Kuwait and the United Arab Emirates." *International Journal of Middle East Studies* 41, 3 (2009).

———. "No Representation Without Taxation? Rents, Development, and Democracy." *Comparative Politics* 37, 3 (April 2005).

———. "Princes and Parliaments in the Arab World." *Middle East Journal* 58, 3 (Summer 2004).

Hermet, Guy, Alain Rouquie, and Richard Rose, eds. *Elections Without Choice*. New York: Wiley, 1978.

Hertog, Steffen. "Defying the Resource Curse: Explaining Successful State-Owned Enterprises in Rentier States." *World Politics* 62, 2 (April 2010).

———. *Princes, Brokers, and Bureaucrats: Oil and the State in Saudi Arabia*. Ithaca: Cornell University Press, 2010.

Hervouet, Gérard, and Michel Fortmann, eds., *Les Conflits dans le Monde, 2010*. Laval: Presses de l'Université Laval, 2010.

Heydemann, Steven. "Authoritarian Learning and Current Trends in Arab Governance." In *Oil, Globalization, and Political Reform,* Doha Discussion Paper. Washington, DC: Brookings Institution, 2009.

———. "Defending the Discipline." *Journal of Democracy* 13, 3 (July 2002).

————, ed. *Networks of Privilege in the Middle East: The Politics of Economic Reform Revisited.* Basingstoke: Palgrave Macmillan, 2004.

————. "Toward a New Social Contract in the Middle East and North Africa." *Arab Reform Bulletin,* January 2004. http://carnegieendowment.org/2008/08/20/toward-new-social-contract-in-middle-east-and-north-africa/7k6.

————. "The Uncertain Future of Democracy Promotion." 30 August 2010. http://www.hivos.net/Hivos-Knowledge-Programme/Themes/Civil-Society-in-West-Asia/News/The-Uncertain-Future-of-Democracy-Promotion-by-Steven-Heydemann.

————. *Upgrading Authoritarianism in the Arab World.* Washington, DC: Brookings Institution, October 2007.

————. *War, Institutions, and Social Change in the Middle East.* Berkeley: University of California Press, 2000.

Hinnebusch, Raymond. "The Ba'th Party in Post-Ba'thist Syria: President, Party and the Struggle for 'Reform.'" *Middle East Critique* 20, 2 (Summer 2011).

Hofheinz, Albrecht. "The Internet in the Arab World: Playground for Political Liberalization." *Internationale Politik und Gesellschaft* 3 (2005).

Hudson, Michael. "After the Gulf War: Prospects for Democratization in the Arab World." *Middle East Journal* 45, 3 (Summer 1991).

————. *Arab Politics: The Search for Legitimacy.* New Haven: Yale University Press, 1977.

————. "Democratization and the Problem of Legitimacy in Middle East Politics." *MESA Bulletin* 22, 2 (December 1988).

Huntington, Samuel. "The Clash of Civilizations?" *Foreign Affairs* 72, 3 (Summer 1993).

————. *The Clash of Civilizations and the Remaking of World Order.* New York: Simon and Schuster, 1998.

————. *Political Order in Changing Societies.* New Haven: Yale University Press, 1969.

————. *The Third Wave: Democratization in the Late Twentieth Century.* Norman: University of Oklahoma Press, 1991.

————. "Will More Countries Become Democratic?" *Political Science Quarterly* 99, 2 (Summer 1984).

Huntley, Wade L. "Rebels Without a Cause: North Korea, Iran, and the NPT." *International Affairs* 82, 4 (2006).

Ibn Khaldun. *The Muqaddimah: An Introduction to History.* Vol. 2. Translated by Franz Rosenthal. New York: Pantheon, 1958.

Ibrahim, Saad Eddin. "Anatomy of Egypt's Militant Groups." *Journal of Middle East Studies* 12, 4 (December 1980).

International Crisis Group. "Drums of War: Israel and the 'Axis of Resistance.'" Middle East Report no. 97. Brussels, 2 August 2010.

————. "The Meanings of Palestinian Reform." *Middle East Briefing.* Washington, DC: International Crisis Group, 12 November 2002.

International Foundation for Electoral Systems. "Elections in Tunisia: The 2011 Constituent Assembly." http://www.ifes.org/~/media/Files/Publications/White%20PaperReport/2011/Tunisia_FAQs_072011.pdf.

International Institute for Strategic Studies. *The Military Balance 2010.* London, 2010.

International Labour Office. *Global Employment Trends for Youth.* August 2010. http://www.ilo.org/public/english/region/afpro/addisababa/pdf/getforyouth.pdf.

International Monetary Fund. *World Economic Outlook.* Washington, DC, 2003.

Jamal, Amaney. *Barriers to Democracy: The Other Side of Social Capital in Palestine and the Arab World.* Princeton: Princeton University Press, 2007.

————. "When Is Trust a Desirable Outcome? Examining Levels of Trust in the Arab World." *Comparative Political Studies* 40, 11 (November 2007).

Jamal, Amaney, and Mark Tessler. "Attitudes in the Arab World." *Journal of Democracy* 19, 1 (January 2008).

Jones, Toby. "Counterrevolution in the Gulf." Peace Brief no. 89. Washington, DC: US Institute of Peace, 15 April 2011.

————. *Desert Kingdom: How Oil and Water Forged Modern Saudi Arabia.* Cambridge: Harvard University Press, 2010.

————. "Seeking a 'Social Contract' for Saudi Arabia." *Middle East Report* 228 (Fall 2003).

Judis, John. "Blood for Oil?" *New Republic,* 31 March 2003.

Kamrava, Meran. *Democracy in the Balance: Culture and Society in the Middle East.* London: Chatham, 1998.

————. "The Middle East's Democracy Deficit in Comparative Perspective." *Perspectives on Global Technology and Development* 6 (2007).

————. "Royal Factionalism and Political Liberalization in Qatar." *Middle East Journal* 63, 3 (Summer 2009).

Karam, Azza M. "Islamist Parties in the Arab World: Ambiguities, Contradictions, and Perseverance." *Democratization* 4, 4 (1997).

Kardoosh, Marwan A., and Riad al-Khouri. *Qualifying Industrial Zones and Sustainable Development in Jordan.* Amman: Jordan Center for Public Policy Research and Dialogue, September 2004.

Karl, Terry Lynn. *The Paradox of Plenty: Oil Booms and Petro-States.* Berkeley: University of California Press, 1997.

Kéchichian, Joseph A. *Power and Succession in Arab Monarchies: A Reference Guide.* Boulder: Lynne Rienner, 2008.

Kedourie, Elie. *Democracy and Arab Political Culture.* London: Cass, 1994.

Kepel, Giles. *The Prophet and the Pharaoh.* London: al-Saqi, 1985.

Kerr, Malcolm. *The Arab Cold War: Gamal Abdal Nasir and His Rivals, 1952–1970.* London: Oxford University Press, 1971.

————. "Review: Edward Said, Orientalism." *International Journal of Middle East Studies* 12 (December 1980).

Khalaf, Abd al-Hadi, "Political Reform in Bahrain: End of the Road." *Middle East International,* 19 February 2004.

Khalaf, Abdulhadi, and Giacomo Luciani, eds. *Constitutional Reform and Political Participation in the Gulf.* Dubai: Gulf Research Center, 2006.

Khalifé, Khaled. *Madih al-Karahiya.* Beirut: Dar al-Adab, 2008.

Khalifé, Mustapha. *Al-Qawqa'a.* Beirut: Dar al-Adab, 2008.

Khalil, Magdi. "Egypt's Muslim Brotherhood and Political Power: Would Democracy Survive?" *Middle East Review of International Affairs* 10, 1 (March 2006).

Kienle, Eberhard. "More Than a Response to Islamism: The Political Deliberalization of Egypt in the 1990s." *Middle East Journal* 52, 2 (Spring 1998).

————, ed., *Politics from Above, Politics from Below: The Middle East in the Age of Economic Reform.* London: Saqi, 2003.

King, Stephen. *The New Authoritarianism in the Middle East and North Africa.* Bloomington: Indiana University Press, 2009.

Kirby, Owen H. "Want Democracy? Get a King." *Middle East Forum* 7, 4 (December 2000). http://www.meforum.org/52/want-democracy-get-a-king.

Knowles, Warwick M., ed. *Professional Associations and the Challenges of Democratic Transformation in Jordan.* Amman: al-Urdun al-Jadid Research Center, 2000.

Koehler, Kevin "Authoritarian Elections in Egypt: Formal Institutions and Informal Mechanisms of Rule." *Democratization* 15, 5 (December 2008).

Korany, Bahgat, ed. *The Changing Middle East: A New Look at Regional Dynamics.* Cairo: American University in Cairo Press, 2010.

Korany, Baghat, Rex Brynen, and Paul Noble. *The Many Faces of National Security in the Arab World.* New York: St. Martin's, 1993.

———, eds. *Political Liberalization and Democratization in the Arab World.* Vol. 2, *Comparative Experiences.* Boulder: Lynne Rienner, 1995.

Korany, Bahgat, and Ali E. Hillal Dessouki, eds. *The Foreign Policies of Arab States.* 2nd ed. Boulder: Westview, 1991.

Kostiner, Joseph, ed. *Middle East Monarchies: The Challenge of Modernity.* Boulder: Lynne Rienner, 2000.

Kraidy, Marwan M. "Saudi Arabia, Lebanon, and the Changing Arab Information Order." *International Journal of Communication* 1 (2007).

Kramer, Martin. *Ivory Towers on Sand: The Failure of Middle Eastern Studies in America.* Washington, DC: Washington Institute for Near East Policy, 2001.

———. "Should America Promote a Liberal, Democratic Middle East?" Lecture delivered to the Weinberg Founders Conference, Washington Institute for Near East Policy, 2002. http://www.geocities.com/martinkramerorg/Landsdowne2002.htm.

Krause, Keith. "Insecurity and State Formation in the Global Military Order: The Middle Eastern Case." *European Journal of International Relations* 2, 3 (1996).

Kuran, Timur. *Private Truths, Public Lies: The Social Consequences of Preference Falsification.* Cambridge: Harvard University Press, 1997.

Kurspahic, Kemal. *Prime Time Crime: Balkan Media in War and Peace.* Washington, DC: US Institute of Peace, 2003.

Kurtz, Marcus. "The Dilemmas of Democracy in the Open Economy: Lessons from Latin America." *World Politics* 56, 2 (January 2004).

———. "The Social Foundations of Institutional Order: Reconsidering War and the 'Resource Curse' in Third World State Building." *Politics and Society* 37, 4 (2009).

Kurzman, Charles, ed. *Liberal Islam: A Sourcebook.* New York: Oxford University Press, 1998.

———. "Structural Opportunity and Perceived Opportunity in Social-Movement Theory: The Iranian Revolution of 1979." *American Sociological Review* 61, 1 (February 1996).

———. *The Unthinkable Revolution in Iran.* Cambridge: Harvard University Press, 2004.

Kurzman, Charles, and Ijlal Naqvi. "Do Muslims Vote Islamic?" *Journal of Democracy* 21, 2 (April 2010).

Laipson, Ellen, ed. *Seismic Shift: Understanding Change in the Middle East.* Washington: Henry L. Stimson Center, 2011.

el-Laithy, Heba; and Khalid Abu-Ismail. *Poverty in Syria, 1996–2004: Diagnosis and Pro-Poor Policy Considerations.* Damascus: United Nations Development Programme, 2005.

Lamani, Mokhtar, and Bessma Momani, eds. *From Desolation to Reconstruction: Iraq's Troubled Journey.* Waterloo: Wilfrid Laurier University Press, 2010.

Langohr, Vickie. "Cracks in Egypt's Electoral Engineering: The 2000 Vote." *Middle East Report Online,* 7 November 2000. http://www.merip.org /mero/mero110700.html.

———. "Too Much Civil Society, Too Little Politics" *Comparative Politics* 36, 2 (2004).

Lesch, David W. *The New Lion of Damascus: Bashar al-Asad and New Syria.* New Haven: Yale University Press, 2005.

Leverett, Flynt Lawrence. *Inheriting Syria: Bashar's Trial by Fire.* Washington, DC: Brookings Institution, 2005.

Levitsky, Steven, and Lucan Way. *Competitive Authoritarianism: Hybrid Regimes After the Cold War.* Cambridge: Cambridge University Press, 2010.

———. "The Rise of Competitive Authoritarianism." *Journal of Democracy* 13, 2 (April 2002).

Lewis, Bernard. "Freedom and Justice in the Middle East." *Foreign Affairs* 84, 3 (May–June 2005).

———. "Studying the Other: Different Ways of Looking at the Middle East and Africa." Keynote address at the annual conference of the Association for the Study of the Middle East and Africa, 25 April 2008. http://asmeascholars.org.

Lindberg, Staffan I., ed. *Democratization by Elections: A New Mode of Transition.* Baltimore: Johns Hopkins University Press, 2009.

———. "The Surprising Significance of African Elections." *Journal of Democracy* 17, 1 (January 2006).

Lindblom, Charles. "The Market as Prison." *Journal of Politics* 44, 2 (May 1982).

Lipset, Seymour Martin. "Some Social Requisites of Democracy: Economic Development and Political Legitimacy." *American Political Science Review* 53 (March 1959).

Lockman, Zachary. *Contending Visions: The History and Politics of Orientalism.* Cambridge: Cambridge University Press, 2004.

Lohmann, Susanne. "The Dynamics of Informational Cascades: The Monday Demonstrations in Leipzig, East Germany, 1989–91." *World Politics* 47, 1 (October 1994).

Longuenesse, Elisabeth, ed. *Batisseurs et Bureaucrates: Ingenieurs et Societe au Maghreb et au Moyen-Orient, Etudes sur le Monde Arabe 4.* Lyon: Maison de l'Orient Mediterraneen, 1990.

Louer, Laurence. *Transnational Shia Politics: Religious and Political Networks in the Gulf.* New York: Columbia University Press, 2008.

Lucas, Russel E. "Deliberalization in Jordan." *Journal of Democracy* 14, 1 (January 2003).

———. "Is the King's Dilemma only for Presidents?" *Arab Reform Bulletin,* 6 April 2011.   http://www.carnegieendowment.org/2011/04/06/is%2Dking%2Ds-%2Ddilemma%2Donly%2Dfor%2Dpresidents/1uz0.

———. "Monarchical Authoritarianism: Survival and Political Liberalization in a Middle Eastern Regime Type." *International Journal of Middle East Studies* 36, 1 (February 2004).

Luciani, Giacomo. "Economic Foundations of Democracy and Authoritarianism: The Arab World in Comparative Perspective." *Arab Studies Quarterly* 10 (1988).

Lust, Ellen. "Why Now? Micro Transitions and the Arab Uprisings." *The Monkey Cage* blog, 24 October 2011. http://themonkeycage.org/blog/2011/10/24/why-now-micro-transitions-and-the-arab-uprisings.

Lust-Okar, Ellen. "Reform in Syria: Steering Between the Chinese Model and Regime Change." Carnegies Papers, Middle East Series, no. 69. Washington, DC: Carnegie Endowment for International Peace, 2006.

———. *Structuring Conflict in the Arab World: Incumbents, Opponents, and Institutions.* New York: Cambridge University Press, 2005.

Lust-Okar, Ellen, and Amaney Jamal. "Rulers and Rules: Reassessing the Influence of Regime Type on Electoral Law Formation." *Comparative Political Studies* 35, 3 (April 2002).

Lust-Okar Ellen, and Seloua Zerhouni, eds. *Political Participation in the Middle East.* Boulder: Lynne Rienner, 2008.

Lustick, Ian. "The Absence of Middle Eastern Great Powers: Political 'Backwardness' in Historical Perspective." *International Organization* 51, 4 (1997).

Lynch, Marc. "Blogging the New Arab Public." *Arab Media and Society* 1 (Spring 2007). http://www.arabmediasociety.com/?article=10.

———. "'Reality Is Not Enough': The Politics of Arab Reality TV." *Transnational Broadcasting Studies* 15 (Fall 2005). http://www.tbsjournal.com/Archives/Fall05/Lynch.html.

———. "Saving Egypt's Elections." *Foreign Policy Magazine,* 2 October 2011. http://lynch.foreignpolicy.com/posts/2011/10/02/egypt_struggles_to_change_course.

———. *Voices of the New Arab Public: Iraq, Al-Jazeera, and Middle East Politics Today.* New York: Columbia University Press, 2006.

Mabry, Tristan James. "Modernization, Nationalism, and Islam: An Examination of Ernest Gellner's Writings on Muslim Society with Reference to Indonesia and Malaysia." *Ethnic and Racial Studies* 25, 4 (July 2005).

Maciejewski, Edouard, and Ahsan Mansur, eds. *Jordan: Strategy for Adjustment and Growth.* Washington, DC: International Monetary Fund, 1996.

MacKenzie, Tyler. "The Best Hope for Democracy in the Arab World: A Crooning TV 'Idol'?" *Transnational Broadcasting Studies* 13 (Fall 2004). http://www.tbsjournal.com/Archives/Fall04/mackenzie.html.

Maila, Joseph. "The Ta'if Accord: An Evaluation." In Deirdre Collings, ed., *Peace for Lebanon? From War to Reconstruction.* Boulder: Lynne Rienner, 1994.

Makiya, Kanan. *Republic of Fear: The Politics of Modern Iraq.* Berkeley: University of California Press, 1989.

al-Malky, Rania. "Blogging for Reform: The Case of Egypt." *Arab Media and Society* 1 (Spring 2007). http://www.arabmediasociety.com/?article=12.

Mangold, Peter. *Super Power Intervention in the Middle East.* New York: St Martin's, 1978.

Mansfield, Edward, and Jack Snyder. "Democratic Transitions, Institutional Strength, and War." *International Organization* 56, 2 (Spring 2002).

Marks, Jon. "Nationalist Policy-Making and Crony Capitalism in the Maghreb: The Old Economics Hinders the New." *International Affairs* 85, 5 (2009).

Marshall, Shana. "Money for Nothing? Offsets in the U.S.–Middle East Defense Trade." *International Journal of Middle East Studies* 41, 4 (November 2009).

McFaul, Michael, and Tamara Cofman Wittes. "The Limits of Limited Reforms." *Journal of Democracy* 19, 1 (January 2008).

McInerney, Stephen. "Shifts in U.S. Assistance to Egypt Alarm Democracy Advocates." *Arab Reform Bulletin,* April 7, 2010. http://carnegieendowment.org/arb/?fa=downloadArticlePDF&article=40530.

Mecham, R. Quinn. "From the Ashes of Virtue, a Promise of Light: The Transformation of Political Islam in Turkey." *Third World Quarterly* 25, 2 (2004).

Mehaji, Jais. "Egypt Caretaker Government Passes Electoral Draft Law amid Parties' Vehement Objections." *Fair Vote,* Arab Spring Series, 8 July 2011. http://205.186.128.106/egypt-caretaker-government-passes-electoral-draft-law-amid-parties-vehement-objections.

Meijer, Roel. "Taking the Islamist Movement Seriously: Social Movement Theory and the Islamist Movement." *International Review of Social History* 50 (2005).

Meital, Yoram. "The Struggle over Political Order in Egypt: The 2005 Elections." *Middle East Journal* 60, 2 (April 2006).

Mekouar, Merouan. "The Last Moroccan King?" *Open Democracy,* 8 August 2011. http://www.opendemocracy.net/merouan-mekouar/last-moroccan-king.

Meyer, David S. *The Politics of Protest.* New York: Oxford University Press, 2007.

Midlarsky, Manus I., ed. *Handbook of War Studies.* London: Unwin Hyman, 1989.

Milanovic, Branko. "Inequality and Its Discontents: Why So Many Feel Left Behind." *Foreign Affairs,* 12 August 2011. http://www.foreignaffairs.com/articles/68031/branko-milanovic/inequality-and-its-discontents.

Miles, Hugh. *Al-Jazeera: How the Arab TV News Challenged the World.* London: Abacus, 2005.

———. "Think Again: Al Jazeera." *Foreign Policy* 155 (July–August 2006).

Miller, Judith. "The Challenge of Radical Islam." *Foreign Affairs* 72, 2 (Spring 1993).

Mishal, Saul, and Avarham Sela. *The Palestinain Hamas: Vision, Violence, and Coexistence*. New York: Columbia University Press, 2000.

Mitchell, Timothy. "Carbon Democracy." *Economy and Society* 38, 3 (August 2009).

———. "Dreamland: The Neoliberalism of Your Desires." *Middle East Report* 210 (Spring 1999).

———. "McJihad: Islam in the US Global Order." *Social Text* 20, 4 (Winter 2002).

Moaddel, Mansoor, ed. *Worldviews of Islamic Publics*. New York: Palgrave, 2005.

Mohammed, Nadeya Sayed Ali. "Political Reform in Bahrain: The Price of Stability." *Middle East Intelligence Bulletin* 4 (September 2002).

Moore, Barrington, Jr. *Social Origins of Dictatorship and Democracy: Lord and Peasant in the Making of the Modern World*. Boston: Beacon, 1966.

Moore, Pete. *Doing Business in the Middle East: Politics and Economic Crisis in Jordan and Kuwait*. Cambridge: Cambridge University Press, 2004.

———. "Making Big Money in Iraq." *Middle East Report* 252 (Fall 2009).

———. "Rentier Fiscal Crisis and Regime Stability in the Middle East: Business and State in the Gulf." *Studies in Comparative International Development* 31, 1 (Spring 2002).

Moore, Pete, and Christopher Parker. "The War Economy of Iraq." *Middle East Report* 243 (Summer 2007).

Moore, Pete W., and Bassel F. Salloukh. "Struggles Under Authoritarianism: Regimes, States, and Professional Associations in the Arab World." *International Journal of Middle East Studies* 39, 1 (February 2007).

Moore, Pete W., and Andrew Shrank. "Commerce and Conflict: US Efforts to Counter Terror with Trade May Backfire." *Middle East Policy* 10, 3 (Fall 2003).

Muasher, Marwan. "A Decade of Struggling Reform Efforts in Jordan: The Resilience of the Rentier System." Carnegie Papers. Washington, DC: Carnegie Endowment for International Peace, 2011.

Mufti, Malik. "Elite Bargains and the Onset of Political Liberalization in Jordan." *Comparative Political Studies* 32, 1 (February 1999).

Muhanna, Elias. "Deconstructing the Popular Vote in Lebanon's Election." *Mideast Monitor* 4, 1 (July–August 2009). http://www.mideastmonitor.org/issues/0907/0907_3.htm.

Muller, Edward N., and Mitchell A. Seligson. "Civic Culture and Democracy: The Question of Causal Relationships." *American Political Science Review* 88, 3 (September 1994).

Munif, 'Abdel Rahman. *Al' an . . . Huna, aw Sharq al-Mutawaset Mara Ukhra* [Now... Here, or East of the Mediterranean One More Time]. Beirut: al-Mu'assasa al-'Arabiya lil-Dirasat wa-l-Nasher, 1992.

Munson, Ziad. "Islamic Mobilization: Social Movement Theory and the Egyptian Muslim Brotherhood." *Sociological Quarterly* 42, 4 (2001).

Murphy, Emma C. "Agency and Space: The Political Impact of Information Technologies in the Gulf Arab States." *Third World Quarterly* 27, 6 (September 2006).

Najem, Tom Pierre, and Martin Hetherington, eds. *Good Governance in the Middle East Oil Monarchies*. London: RoutledgeCurzon, 2003.

Naqib, Khaldun. *Society and State in the Gulf and Arab Peninsula: A Different Perspective*. London: Routledge, 1990.

National Democratic Institute. "Final Report on the Palestinian Legislative Council Elections," Washington, DC, 25 January 2006. http://www.cartercenter.org/resources/pdfs/news/peace_publications/election_reports/Palestine2006-NDI-final.pdf.

Neuman, Stephanie G., ed. *International Relations Theory and the Third World*. New York: St. Martin's, 1998.

Newman, Edward, Roland Paris, and Oliver P. Richmond, eds. *New Perspectives on Liberal Peacebuilding*. Tokyo: United Nations University Press, 2009.

Niblock, Tim, and Emma Murphy, eds. *Economic and Political Liberalization in the Middle East*. London: Tauris, 1993.

Noman, Helmi. "Middle East and North Africa." OpenNet Initiative, . http://opennet.net/research/regions/mena.

Norris, Pippa, and Ronald Inglehart. "Islamic Culture and Democracy: Testing the 'Clash of Civilizations' Thesis." *Comparative Sociology* 1, 3–4 (2002).

Norton, Augustus Richard. *Civil Society in the Middle East*. Vols. 1–2. Leiden: Brill, 1995.

Nouzille, Vincent. *Dans le Secret des Présidents: CIA, Maison-Blanche, Élysée, les Dossiers Confidentiele*. Paris: Fayard, 2010.

O'Donnell, Guillermo, Philippe C. Schmitter, and Laurence Whitehead. *Transitions from Authoritarian Rule: Tentative Conclusions About Uncertain Democracies*. Baltimore: Johns Hopkins University Press, 1986.

Okruhlik, Gwenn. "Rentier Wealth, Unruly Law, and the Rise of the Opposition: The Political Economy of Oil States." *Comparative Politics* 31, 3 (April 1999).

———. "Understanding Political Dissent in Saudi Arabia." *Middle East Report Online*, 24 October 2001. http://www.merip.org/mero/mero102401.

Onis, Ziya, and E. Fuat Keyman. "Turkey at the Polls: A New Path Emerges." *Journal of Democracy* 14, 2 (April 2003).

Ottaway, Marina. "Women's Rights and Democracy in the Arab World." Carnegie Papers no. 42, February 2004. http://carnegieendowment.org/files/CarnegiePaper42.pdf.

Ottaway, Marina, and Julia Choucair-Vizoso, eds. *Beyond the Façade: Political Reform in the Arab World*. Washington, DC: Carnegie Endowment for International Peace, 2008.

Ottaway, Marina, and Michelle Dunne. "Incumbent Regimes and the 'King's Dilemma' in the Arab World: Promise and Threat of Managed Reform." Carnegie Papers no. 88. Washington, DC: Carnegie Endowment for International Peace, December 2007.

Ottaway, Marina, and Amr Hamzawy. "Islamists in Politics: The Dynamics of Participation." Carnegie Papers no. 98. Washington, DC: Carnegie Endowment for International Peace, November 2008.

Oweidat, Nadia, et al. *The Kefaya Movement: A Case Study of a Grassroots Reform Initiative*. Santa Monica: RAND, 2008.

Pack, Howard, and Janet Rothenberg Pack. "Foreign Aid: The Question of Fungibility." *Review of Economics and Statistics* 75, 2 (May 1993).

Patai, Raphael. *The Arab Mind*. Rev. ed. New York: Hatherleigh, 2002.

Penner Angrist, Michele, ed. *Politics and Society in the Contemporary Middle East*. Boulder: Lynne Rienner, 2010.

Perthes, Volker, ed. *Arab Elites: Negotiating the Politics of Change*. Boulder: Lynne Rienner, 2004.

———. "Syria's Parliamentary Elections: Remodeling Asad's Political Base." *Middle East Report* 174 (January–February 1992).

Peters, Anne, and Pete Moore. "Beyond Boom and Bust: External Rents, Durable Authoritarianism, and Institutional Adaptation in the Hashemite Kingdom of Jordan." *Studies in Comparative International Development* 44, 2 (2009).

Pew Global Attitudes Project. *What the World Thinks in 2002: How Global Publics View Their Lives, Their Countries, the World, America*. Washington, DC: Pew Research Center for the People and the Press, 2002.

Phillips, Sarah. "Foreboding About the Future in Yemen." *Middle East Report Online*, 3 April 2006. http://www.merip.org/mero/mero040306.

———. "Yemen and the Politics of Permanent Crisis." Adelphi Paper no. 420. London: International Institute for Strategic Studies, 2011.

Pintak, Lawrence. "Border Guards of the 'Imagined' *Watan*: Arab Journalists and the New Arab Consciousness." *Middle East Journal* 63, 2 (Spring 2009).

————. "Satellite TV News and Arab Democracy." *Journalism Practice* 2, 1 (February 2008).

Pipes, Daniel. *The Long Shadow: Culture and Politics in the Middle East.* New Brunswick, NJ: Transaction, 1989.

————. "There Are No Moderates: Dealing with Fundamentalist Islam." *The National Interest* 41 (Fall 1995).

Polanyi, Karl. *The Great Transformation: The Political and Economic Origins of Our Time.* Boston: Beacon, 2001.

Powel, Brieg Tomos. "A Clash of Norms: Normative Power and EU Democracy Promotion in Tunisia." *Democratization* 16, 1 (February 2009).

Powerhouse, Jon. *Democracy from Above: Regional Organizations and Democratization.* Cambridge: Cambridge University Press, 2005.

Pripstein Posusney, Marsha. "Multi-Party Elections in the Arab World: Institutional Engineering and Opposition Strategies Studies." *Comparative International Development* 36, 4 (2002).

Pripstein Posusney, Marsha, and Michele Penner Angrist, eds. *Authoritarianism in the Middle East: Regimes and Resistance.* Boulder: Lynne Rienner, 2005.

Przeworski, Adam. *Transitions from Authoritarian Rule: Comparative Perspectives.* Baltimore: Johns Hopkins University Press, 1986.

Ragin, Charles. "Turning the Tables: How Case-Oriented Research Challenges Variable-Oriented Research." *Comparative Social Research* 16 (1997).

Remmer, Karen L. "Does Foreign Aid Promote the Expansion of Government?" *American Journal of Political Science* 48, 1 (January 2004).

Richards, Alan, and John Waterbury. *A Political Economy of the Middle East.* Boulder: Westview, 1990.

Rise, Richard, ed. *International Encyclopedia of Elections.* London: Macmillan, 2000.

Robinson, Glenn E. "Defensive Democratization in Jordan." *International Journal of Middle East Studies* 30, 3 (August 1998).

Rodrik, Dani. "Where Did All the Growth Go? External Shocks, Social Conflict, and Growth Collapses." *Journal of Economic Growth* 4, 4 (December 1999).

Romano, David. "The Struggle for Autonomy and Decentralization: Iraqi Kurdistan." In Mokhtar Lamani and Bessma Momani, eds., *From Desolation to Reconstruction.* Waterloo: Wilfrid Laurier University Press, 2010.

Rose, David. "The Gaza Bombshell." *Vanity Fair,* April 2008.

Rosen, Lawrence. "Expecting the Unexpected: Cultural Components of Arab Governance." *Annals of the American Academy of Political and Social Science* 603 (January 2006).

Ross, Michael. "Does Oil Hinder Democracy?" *World Politics* 53, 3 (April 2001).

————. *The Oil Curse: How Petroleum Wealth Shapes the Development of Nations.* Princeton: Princeton University Press, 2012.

Rueschemeyer, Dietrich, Evelyne Huber Stephens, and John D. Stephens. *Capitalist Development and Democracy.* Chicago: University of Chicago Press, 1992.

Rustow, Dankwart A. "Transitions to Democracy: Toward a Dynamic Model." *Comparative Politics* 2, 3 (April 1970).

Ryan, Curtis R. "Jordan's New Electoral Law: Reform, Reaction, or Status Quo?" Middle East Channel, *Foreign Policy Magazine,* 24 May 2010. http://mideast.foreignpolicy.com/posts/2010/05/24/jordan_s_new_electoral _law_reform_reaction_or_status_quo.

Ryan, Curtis R., and Jillian Schwedler. "Return to Democratization or New Hybrid Regime? The 2003 Elections in Jordan." *Middle East Policy* 11, 2 (June 2004).

Sa'd, 'Abdo. *Al-Intikhabat al-Niyabiya li-'Am 2005: Qira'aat wa Nata'ej* [The 2005 Parliamentary Elections: Reflections and Results]. Beirut: Markaz Beirut lil-Abhath wa-l-Ma'loumat, 2005.

———. *Al-Intikhabat al-Niyabiya li-'Am 2009: Qira'aat wa Nata'ej* [The 2009 Parliamentary Elections: Reflections and Results]. Beirut: CIEL, 2009.

Sadiki, Larbi. "Political Liberalization in Bin Ali's Tunisia: Façade Democracy." *Democratization* 9, 4 (Winter 2002).

———. "Popular Uprisings and Arab Democratization." *International Journal of Middle East Studies* 32, 1 (February 2000).

———. *Rethinking Arab Democratization: Elections Without Democracy.* Oxford: Oxford University Press, 2009.

Safran, Nadav. *Saudi Arabia: The Ceaseless Quest for Security.* Cambridge: Harvard University Press, 1985.

Said, Edward. *Orientalism.* Rev. ed. New York: Random, 1994.

Salamé, Ghassan, ed. *Democracy Without Democrats? The Renewal of Politics in the Muslim World.* London: Tauris, 1994.

Salem, Paul, ed. *Conflict Resolution in the Arab World: Selected Essays.* Beirut: American University of Beirut Press, 1997.

———. "Documents: The Ta'if Agreement—Annotated Text." *Beirut Review* 1, 1 (Spring 1991).

Sallam, Hesham. "Striking Back at Egyptian Workers." *Middle East Report* 259 (Summer 2011).

Salloukh, Bassel F. "The Limits of Electoral Engineering in Divided Societies: Elections in Postwar Lebanon." *Canadian Journal of Political Science* 39, 3 (2006).

Salloukh, Bassel, and Rex Brynen, eds. *Persistent Permeability? Regionalism, Localism, and Globalization in the Middle East.* Aldershot: Ashgate, 2004.

Salzman, Philip. *Culture and Conflict in the Middle East.* Amherst, NY: Prometheus, 2007.

———. "The Middle East's Tribal DNA." *Middle East Quarterly* 15, 1 (Winter 2008). http://www.meforum.org/1813/the-middle-easts-tribal-dna.

Sayan, Serdar, ed. *Economic Performance in the Middle East and North Africa: Institutions, Corruption, and Reform.* London: Routledge, 2009.

Sayigh, Yezid. "'Fixing Broken Windows': Security Sector Reform in Palestine, Lebanon, and Yemen." Carnegie Papers no. 17. Washington, DC: Carnegie Endowment for International Peace, October 2009.

al-Sayyid, Mustafa. "Mixed Message: The Arab and Muslim Response to 'Terrorism.'" *Washington Quarterly* 25, 2 (Spring 2002).

Schedler, Andreas. "Authoritarianism's Last Line of Defense." *Journal of Democracy* 21, 1 (January 2010).

———, ed. *Electoral Authoritarianism: The Dynamics of Unfree Competition.* Boulder: Lynne Rienner, 2006.

Schlesinger, James R. "Quest for a Post–Cold War Foreign Policy." *Foreign Affairs* 72, 1 (Winter 1993).

Schlumberger, Oliver. *Debating Arab Authoritarianism: Dynamics and Durability in Nondemocratic Regimes.* Stanford: Stanford University Press, 2007.

Schmitter, Philippe C. "Twenty-five Years, Fifteen Findings." *Journal of Democracy* 21, 1 (January 2010).

Schumpeter, Joseph. "The Crisis of the Tax State." In Alan T. Peacock, ed., *International Economic Papers* no. 4. London: Macmillan, 1954.

Schwedler, Jillian. "Can Islamists Become Moderates? Rethinking the Inclusion-Moderation Hypothesis." *World Politics* 63, 2 (April 2011).

———. "Democratization, Inclusion, and the Moderation of Islamist Parties." *Development* 50, 1 (2007).

———. *Faith in Moderation: Islamist Parties in Jordan and Yemen.* New York: Cambridge University Press, 2006.

———. "More Than a Mob: The Dynamics of Political Demonstrations in Jordan." *Middle East Report* 226 (Spring 2003).

———. "A Paradox of Democracy? Islamist Participation in Elections." *Middle East Report* 209 (Winter 1998).

Shaery-Eisenlohr, Roschanack. "From Subjects to Citizens? Civil Society and the Internet in Syria." *Middle East Critique* 20, 2 (Summer 2011).

Sharabi, Hisham. *Neopatriarchy: A Theory of Distorted Social Change*. Oxford: Oxford University Press, 1992.

Sharp, Jeremy M. *Egypt: 2005 Presidential and Parliamentary Elections*. Washington, DC: Congressional Research Service, 21 September 2005. http://fpc.state.gov/documents/organization/54274.pdf.

Shatz, Adam. "The Native Informant." *The Nation,* 28 April 2003. http://www.thenation.com/doc/20030428/shatz.

Shehata, Dina. *Islamists and Secularists in Egypt: Opposition, Conflict, and Cooperation*. London: Routledge, 2009.

Shehata, Samer, and Joshua Stacher. "The Brotherhood Goes to Parliament." *Middle East Report* 240 (Fall 2006).

Shikaki, Khalil. "The Palestinian Elections: An Assessment." *Journal of Palestine Studies* 25, 3 (Spring 1996).

———. "The Peace Process, National Reconstruction, and the Transition to Democracy in Palestine." *Journal of Palestine Studies* 25, 2 (Winter 1996).

———. "Sweeping Victory, Uncertain Mandate." *Journal of Democracy* 17, 3 (July 2006).

Shimon, Samuel, ed. *Beirut 39: New Writing from the Arab World*. London: Bloomsbury, 2010.

Shirazi, Farid. "The Contribution of ICT to Freedom and Democracy: An Empirical Analysis of Archival Data on the Middle East." *Electronic Journal on Information Systems in Developing Countries* 35, 6 (2008).

Shrank, Andrew. "Reconsidering the Resource Curse: Selection Bias, Measurement Error, and Omitted Variables." Unpublished manuscript, Yale University, New Haven, 2003.

Shull Adams, Linda. "Political Liberalization in Jordan: An Analysis of the State's Relationship with the Muslim Brotherhood." *Journal of Church and State* 38, 3 (1996).

Silverstein, Paul. "Weighing Morocco's New Constitution." *Middle East Report Online,* 5 July 2011. http://www.merip.org/mero/mero070511.

Sisk, Timothy D. *Religion, Politics, and Power in the Middle* East. Washington, DC: US Institute of Peace, 1992.

Smith, Benjamin. "Oil Wealth and Regime Survival in the Developing World, 1960–1999." *American Journal of Political Science* 48 (2004).

Smith, Lee. "Inside The Arab Mind: What's Wrong with the White House's Book on Arab Nationalism." *Slate,* 27 May 2004. http://slate.msn.com/id/2101328.

Sotloff, Steven. "Bahrain's Shia Crackdown." Middle East Channel, *Foreign Policy Magazine,* 10 September 2010. http://mideast.foreignpolicy.com/posts/2010/09/09/Bahrain.

Stacher, Joshua A. "Post-Islamist Rumblings in Egypt: The Emergence of the Wasat Party." *Middle East Journal* 56, 3 (2002).

Stanfield, Gareth R. V. *Iraqi Kurdistan: Emergent Democracy*. London: Routledge Curzon, 2003.

Stepan, Alfred, with Graeme Robertson. "An 'Arab' More Than 'Muslim' Electoral Gap." *Journal of Democracy* 14, 3 (July 2003).

Sullivan, Denis, and Sana Abed-Kotob. *Islam in Contemporary Egypt: Civil Society Versus the State*. Boulder: Lynne Rienner, 1999.

Tabbaa, Dima Toukan. "Jordan's New Electoral Law Disappoints Reformers." *Arab Reform Bulletin,* 22 June 2010. http://www.carnegieendowment.org/arb /?fa=show&article=41040.

Telhami, Shibley. *Power and Leadership in International Bargaining.* New York: Columbia University Press, 1990.

Tessler, Mark, ed. *Area Studies and Social Science: Strategies for Understanding Middle East Politics.* Bloomington: Indiana University Press, 1996.

———. "Democracy and the Political Culture Orientations of Ordinary Citizens: A Typology for the Arab World and Beyond." *International Social Science Journal* 59, 192 (June 2008).

———. "Do Islamic Orientations Influence Attitudes Toward Democracy in the Arab World? Evidence from Egypt, Jordan, Morocco, and Algeria." *International Journal of Comparative Sociology* 43 (2002).

———. "Islam and Democracy in the Middle East: The Impact of Religious Orientations on Attitudes Toward Democracy in Four Arab Countries." *Comparative Politics* 34, 3 (April 2002).

———. "Religion, Religiosity, and the Place of Islam in Political Life: Insights from the Arab Barometer Survey." *Middle East Law and Governance* 2, 2 (2010).

———. "The View from the Street: The Attitudes and Values of Ordinary Egyptians." *Journal of North African Studies* 9, 2 (Summer 2004).

Tessler, Mark, and Eleanor Gao. "Democracy and the Political Culture Orientations of Ordinary Citizens: A Typology for the Arab World and Beyond." *International Social Science Journal* 59, 192 (June 2008).

Tetlock, Philip E. *Expert Political Judgment.* Princeton: Princeton University Press, 2005.

Tétreault, Mary Ann. "Kuwait's Annus Mirabilis." *Middle East Report Online,* 7 September 2006. http://www.merip.org/mero/mero090706.html.

———. *Stories of Democracy: Politics and Society in Contemporary Kuwait.* New York: Columbia University Press, 2000.

Tétreault, Mary Ann, and Mohammed al-Ghanim. "The Day After 'Victory': Kuwait's 2009 Election and the Contentious Present." *Middle East Report Online,* 8 July 2009. http://www.merip.org/mero/mero070809.html.

Tezcür, Günes Murat. "The Moderation Theory Revisited: The Case of Islamic Political Actors." *Party Politics* 16, 1 (2010).

———. *The Paradox of Moderation: Muslim Reformers in Iran and Turkey.* Austin: University of Texas Press, 2009.

Thompson, Allan, ed. *The Media and the Rwanda Genocide.* London: Pluto, 2007.

Tilly, Charles. *Coercion, Capital, and European States, AD 990–1990.* Cambridge: Blackwell, 1990.

———, ed. *The Formation of Nation States in Western Europe.* Princeton: Princeton University Press, 1975.

Tlemcani, Rachid "Electoral Authoritarianism." Carnegie Endowment for International Peace, March 2008. http://www.carnegieendowment.org/publications /index.cfm?fa=view&id=19176.

Traboulsi, Fawwaz. "Public Spheres and Urban Space: A Critical Comparative Approach." *New Political Science* 27, 4 (December 2005).

Traub, James. *The Freedom Agenda: Why America Must Spread Democracy (Just Not the Way George Bush Did).* New York: Picador, 2009.

Tripp, Charles. *Islam and the Moral Economy: The Challenges of Capitalism.* Cambridge: Cambridge University Press, 2006.

Turam, Berna. "The Politics of Engagement Between Islam and the Secular State: Ambivalence of 'Civil Society.'" *British Journal of Sociology* 55, 2 (2004).

———. *Between Islam and the State: The Politics of Engagement.* Stanford: Stanford University Press, 2007.

Ulfeder, Jay. "Natural Resource–Wealth and the Survival of Autocracy." *Comparative Political Studies* 40, 8 (August 2007).

United Nations Development Programme. *Human Development Report 2010.* New York, 2010.

Usher, Graham. "The Democratic Resistance: Hamas, Fatah, and the Palestinian Elections." *Journal of Palestine Studies* 35, 3 (Spring 2006).

Valbjørn, Morten, and André Bank. "Examining the 'Post' in Post-Democratization: The Future of Middle Eastern Political Rule Through Lenses of the Past." *Middle East Critique* 19, 3 (Fall 2010).

———. "Signs of a New Arab Cold War: The 2006 Lebanon War and the Sunni-Shi'i Divide." *Middle East Report* 242 (Spring 2007).

Vandewalle, Dirk. *Libya Since Independence: Oil and State-Building.* Ithaca: Cornell University Press, 1998.

Vermeren, Pierre. *Histoire du Maroc Depuis l'Indépendance.* Paris: La Découverte, 2002.

Vitalis, Robert. *America's Kingdom: Mythmaking on the Saudi Oil Frontier.* Palo Alto: Stanford University Press, 2006.

———. "The Democratization Industry and the Limits of the New Intervention." *Middle East Report* 187–188: *Intervention and North-South Politics in the 90's* (March–June 1994).

Vitalis, Robert, and Ellis Goldberg. "The Arabian Peninsula: Crucible of Globalization." Working Paper RSC no. 2002/9, Mediterranean Programme Series. Florence: European University Institute, 2002.

Volpi, Frédéric. "Political Islam in the Mediterranean: The View from Democratization Studies." *Democratization* 16, 1 (2009).

Waldner, David. *State Building and Late Development.* Ithaca: Cornell University Press, 1999.

Walt, Stephen. *The Origins of Alliances.* Ithaca: Cornell University Press, 1987.

Wannous, Dima. *Kursi.* Beirut: Dar al-Adab, 2009.

Waterbury, John. *Egypt: Burdens of the Past, Options for the Future.* Bloomington: Indiana University Press, 1978.

Wedeen, Lisa. *Ambiguities of Domination: Politics, Rhetoric, and Symbols in Contemporary Syria.* Chicago: University of Chicago Press, 1999.

———. *Peripheral Visions: Publics, Power, and Performance in Yemen.* Chicago: University of Chicago Press, 2008.

———. "The Politics of Deliberation: *Qat* Chews as Public Spheres in Yemen." *Public Culture* 19, 1 (Winter 2007).

———. "Seeing Like a Citizen, Acting Like a State: Exemplary Events in Unified Yemen." *Comparative Study of Society and History* 45, 4 (October 2003).

Wegner, Eva, and Miquel Pellicer. "Islamist Moderation Without Democratization: The Coming of Age of the Moroccan Party of Justice and Development?" *Democratization* 16, 1 (February 2009).

Weiffen, Brigitte. "The Cultural-Economic Syndrome: Impediments to Democracy in the Middle East." *Comparative Sociology* 3, 3–4 (2004).

Whitehead, Laurence. "Losing 'the Force'? The 'Dark Side' of Democratization After Iraq." *Democratization* 16, 2 (April 2009).

Wickham, Carrie Rosefsky. *Mobilizing Islam: Religion, Activism, and Political Change in Egypt.* New York: Columbia University Press, 2002.

———. "The Path to Moderation: Strategy and Learning in the Formation of Egypt's Wasat Party." *Comparative Politics* 36, 2 (January 2004).

Wiktorowicz, Quintan, ed. *Islamic Activism: A Social Movement Theory Approach.* Bloomington: Indiana University Press, 2004.

———. "Islamic Activism and Social Movement Theory: A New Direction for Research." *Mediterranean Politics* 7, 3 (Autumn 2002).

———. "The Limits of Democracy in the Middle East: The Case of Jordan." *Middle East Journal* 53, 4 (Autumn 1999).

———. *The Management of Islamic Activism: Salafis, the Muslim Brotherhood, and the State in Jordan.* Albany: State University of New York Press, 2001.

———. "The New Global Threat: Transnational Salafis and Jihad." *Middle East Policy* 8, 4 (December 2001).

———. "The Political Limits to Nongovernmental Organizations in Jordan." *World Development* 30, 1 (2002).

Willis, Michael. "Morocco's Islamists and the Legislative Elections of 2002: The Strange Case of the Party That Did Not Want to Win." *Mediterranean Politics* 9, 1 (2004).

Woodward, Bob. *Plan of Attack.* New York: Simon and Schuster, 2004.

Wright, Robin. *Dreams and Shadows: The Future of the Middle East.* New York: Penguin, 2008.

Yacoubian, Mona, and Scott Lasensky. "Dealing with Damascus: Seeking a Greater Return on U.S.-Syria Relations." Special Report no. 33. Washington, DC: Council on Foreign Relations, 2008.

Yadav, Stacey Philbrick. "Antecedents of the Revolution." *Studies in Ethnicity and Nationalism* 11, 3 (December 2011).

———. "Understanding 'What Islamists Want': Public Debate and Contestation in Lebanon and Yemen." *Middle East Journal* 64, 2 (Spring 2010).

Yadav, Stacey Philbrick, and Janine Clark. "Disappointments and New Directions: Women, Partisanship, and the Regime in Yemen." *HAWWA: Journal of Women of the Middle East and of the Islamic World* 8, 1 (2010).

Youngs, Richard. "The European Union and Democracy Promotion in the Mediterranean: A New or Disingenuous Strategy?" *Democratization* 9, 1 (2002).

Zahar, Marie-Joëlle. "Liberal Interventions, Illiberal Outcomes: The United Nations, Western Powers, and Lebanon." In Edward Newman, Roland Paris, and Oliver P. Richmond, eds., *New Perspectives on Liberal Peacebuilding.* Tokyo: United Nations University Press, 2009.

———. "Peace by Unconventional Means: Lebanon's Ta'if Agreement." In Stephen J. Stedman, Donald Rothchild, and Elizabeth Cousens, eds., *Ending Civil Wars: The Implementation of Peace Agreements.* Boulder: Lynne Rienner, 2002.

Zayani, Mohamed, ed. *The Al-Jazeera Phenomenon: Critical Perspectives on New Arab Media.* London: Pluto, 2005.

———. *Arab Satellite Television and Politics in the Middle East.* Emirates Occasional Paper no. 54. Abu Dhabi: Emirates Center for Strategic Studies and Research, 2004.

Zayani, Mohamed, and Sofiane Sahraoui. *The Culture of Al Jazeera.* London: McFarland, 2007.

Zisser, Eyal. "What Does the Future Hold for Syria?" *Middle East Review of International Affairs* 10, 2 (June 2006).

Zogby, James. *Arab Voices: What They Are Saying to US and Why It Matters.* New York: Palgrave Macmillan, 2010.

Zubaida, Sami. "Is There a Muslim Society? Ernest Gellner's Sociology of Islam." *Economy and Society* 24, 2 (May 2005).

About the Authors

Rex Brynen is professor of political science at McGill University and research coordinator at the Interuniversity Consortium for Arab and Middle Eastern Studies (ICAMES) in Montreal. He is author, editor, or coeditor of eight books on various aspects of Middle East politics, including *Palestinian Refugees: Challenges of Repatriation and Development* (2007) and *Persistent Permeability: Regionalism, Localism, and Globalization in the Middle East* (2004).

Pete Moore is associate professor of political science at Case Western Reserve University and a senior nonresident research fellow at ICAMES. His research focuses primarily on issues of political economy, state-society relations, and substate conflict in the Gulf and the Levant. He is author of *Doing Business in the Middle East: Politics and Economic Crisis in Jordan and Kuwait* (2004) and serves on the board of directors of the *Middle East Report.*

Bassel F. Salloukh is associate professor of political science at the Lebanese American University in Beirut and a senior nonresident research fellow at ICAMES. He is author, coauthor, and coeditor of a number of books, chapters, and journal articles on political science, the domestic and foreign politics of Lebanon and Syria, and Middle East international relations, including *Mapping the Political Landscape: An Introduction to Political Science* (2007) and *Persistent Permeability: Regionalism, Localism, and Globalization in the Middle East* (2004).

Marie-Joëlle Zahar is associate professor of political science at the Université de Montréal and a senior research fellow at ICAMES. Her research focuses on the comparative study of political violence and approaches to conflict management in the Middle East, the Balkans, and Africa. She is author and coauthor of several journal articles and book chapters on the dynamics of conflict and the politics of peacebuilding in Lebanon, Iraq, Sudan, and the Arab-Israeli conflict, and coeditor (with Stephen Saideman) of *Intra-State Conflict, Governments, and Security: Dynamics of Deterrence and Assurance* (2008).

* * *

Janine A. Clark is associate professor of political science at the University of Guelph and a senior nonresident research fellow at ICAMES. She has written widely on Islamist politics in the Middle East, including *Islam, Charity, and Activism: Middle-Class Networks and Social Welfare in Egypt, Jordan, and Yemen* (2004).

Merouan Mekouar is a PhD candidate in the Department of Political Science at McGill University and a graduate research fellow at ICAMES. His research focuses on the politics of North Africa and the role of informational cascades in the Arab Spring.

Index

Abbas, Mahmoud, 58, 161, 235
Abdullah II (King of Jordan), 47, 49, 50, 52, 179, 186
Abizaid, John, 53
Afghanistan, 5, 268
Ahmadinejad, Mahmoud, 260
al-Ahmar, Sadiq, 88
al-Ahram, 249
Ajami, Fouad, 101, 103
al-Akhbar, 249, 250
Alawi dynasty, 176
Alawis, 45–46
Albrecht, Holger, 134
Algeria: civil society in, 31; civil war in, 5, 31, 32, 37; colonialism in, 30, 31; constitutional reform in, 32; decentralized political leadership in, 31; decline in oil revenue, 199; defense expenditures, 263*tab*; economy of, 31–32, 151, 218, 219*tab*, 220, 221*tab*; elections, 31, 33, 147, 148*tab*, 163; electoral systems in, 160*tab*; 151; income inequality in, 227*fig*; internet filtering in, 238, 238*tab*; new constitution in, 151; nongovernmental organizations in, 31; patrimonial networks in, 33; political corruption in, 33; protests in, 30–33, 151, 219
Al Jazeera, 17, 187, 233, 235, 236, 239, 240–244
Allawi, Iyad, 55, 160
Anderson, Lisa, 6, 103, 183, 201
Annan, Kofi, 43
Arab Barometer project, 106
Arab Cold War, 268, 269, 270, 271
Arabian Peninsula: globalization in, 69, 70, 72; monarchy in, 69, 176–177; protests in, 69–89; tradition *vs.* modernity in, 69, 70. *See also* Gulf states
Arabism, 97, 102

al-Arabiya, 187, 240–244
Arab League, 43, 50, 274
Arab News Network (ANN), 236
Arab Radio and Television Network (ART), 236
Arab Socialist Union (ASU), 22
Arab Spring: defining, 10*n*2; imagination of the possible in, 111; monarchical responses to, 186–188; underemphasis on agency of protesters, 10*n*2. *See also* Protests
Arab world: bypassed by third wave of democracy, 4; civil society in, 121; common language in, 2; electoral waves in, 149–158; income inequality in, 227*fig*; lack of democracy in, 1; lack of opportunity for middle class in, 227, 228; permeability of, 2, 257, 259, 268, 269, 270; political change in, 3–8; postindependence need to construct national economies, 217; public debt in, 218; regional security issues, 257; shared cultural/linguistic connections in, 111; shared political narratives in, 2
Arafat, Yasser, 56, 57, 58
al-Assad, Bashar, 42, 43, 44, 45, 275
al-Assad, Hafez, 60
al-Assad, Maher, 45
Authoritarianism: brittle, 222–229; civil society as bulwark against, 126; economic liberalization and, 213–230; electoral engineering of, 158–162; future trajectories of, 108–109; growing crisis of political legitimacy, 101; hegemonic, 149, 156, 159; hybrid, 4, 9, 31; maintenance of through controlled liberalization strategies, 149–158; manipulation of electoral systems by, 159–162; persistence of, 1,

development of, 214, 215; direct, 27; electoral, 1, 10n1; growth of as globalized ideal, 108, 111; impact of Islamic religious tradition on, 99; neoliberalism and, 216; political, 195; pothole theory, 130, 131; procedural definitions of, 73; promotion of by West, 5, 272–277; rejection of by radical Islamists, 123; rentierism and, 193–209; representative, 197; rhetoric, 72; socioeconomic preconditions for, 214; third wave, 272; transitional, 87

Democratization: clientalism and, 159; defined, 12n16; defensive, 47; electoral, 123; importance of regional permeability for, 109–112; interlocking impediments to, 288; Islamist movements and, 119–139; links to rents, 193, 194; military expenditures and, 263; moderation and, 119, 124–137; pluralism as substitute for, 4; political, 12n16; third wave, 1, 4, 95, 188, 215; Western foreign policy emphasis on, 5

Demonstration effects, 37, 96, 236, 242, 272

Dependency theory, 195

Despotism, oriental, 193

Doha Declaration for Democracy and Reform, 61, 274

Donno, Daniela, 99

Druze, 164

Dubai: absolute control in, 70; lack of political opposition in, 70; liberal economic expansion in, 199; liberalization in, 70; al-Maktoum rulers in, 70; political participation in, 70

Economic: change, 6, 70; conglomerates, 226; deprivation, 112; development, 23, 213, 214, 217; inequality, 19, 23, 36, 213, 227, 228, 294; justice, 35; liberalization, 10, 22, 49, 150, 203, 213–230; reform, 22, 50, 123, 147, 150, 151, 182, 213, 226; sanctions, 46

Economy: global, 21, 27; market, 150, 151; petroleum, 47; political, 102, 222–229; political authority in management of, 217; rentier, 10; social market, 45

Egypt: in Arab politics, 17; Arab Socialist Union (ASU), 22; army role in protests, 24, 25; Central Security Force, 24; civil society in, 24; corruption in, 158;

cronyism in, 227; defense expenditures, 263tab, 264; economic growth, 23; economic liberalization in, 22; economic reform in, 22; elections, 22, 26, 119, 147, 148tab, 151, 156, 157tab, 163, 164; electoral fraud in, 5, 22, 23; electoral laws in, 165; electoral systems in, 157tab, 160tab; elite corruption in, 36; Farouk in, 177; Freedom and Justice Party (FJP), 26, 119; Free Officers coup in, 22; Ghad party, 23; income inequality in, 227fig; infitah policies in, 218, 219; internal challenges in, 261; internet filtering in, 238tab; internet use in, 237tab; Islamism in, 26; Islamist electoral victory in, 26, 121, 151, 156, 158, 166, 166tab, 167; Jihad in, 123; Kefaya protest movement, 23; legitimacy issues in, 36; liberalization, 219tab; limited multipartyism, 5; low electoral turnouts, 26; manufactured exports, 221tab; media coverage of protests in, 233, 236, 239, 240; military abandonment of president, 9; military coup in, 3, 22; military loyalty in, 264; monarchy in, 176, 177; Muslim Brotherhood in, 22, 23, 24, 25, 101, 131, 139, 140n8, 156, 158, 164; National Democratic Party (NDP) in, 22, 25, 26, 156, 158; al-Nour party, 26; overthrow of Mubarak in, 17; parliamentary elections in, 6; peace with Israel, 22; post-regime political differences in, 25; privatization in, 22; professional associations in, 126; promises of reform in, 24; protests in, 1, 17, 22–27, 219, 270, 271; public debt in, 219; regime change in, 22–27; rentierism and, 197tab; repression in, 24; socioeconomic grievances in, 23; source of external revenue, 197tab; state patronage in, 22; State Security Intelligence, 24; structural adjustment programs in, 220; Supreme Council of the Armed Forces (SCAF), 25; television station orientation, 247; ties with United States, 22, 224; transitional process in, 26, 27; unemployment in, 23; al-Wasat party in, 131

Egyptian Satellite Channel (ESC), 234, 235

Eickelman, Dale, 100

Elections: aimed at containing state fiscal crises/socioeconomic upheavals, 149;

for outside allies by, 265; seen through Eurocentric lens, 103; socioeconomic differences between countries in, 217; superpower military-security relationships with, 262; support for democracy in, 107; tendency to focus on personal relations rather than formal rules, 97; transnational Islamist appeals in, 266–272; United States assistance to, 204; Western efforts at democracy promotion in, 272–277

Middle East Broadcasting Centre (MBC), 235, 236

Mikati, Najib, 62

Military: authoritarianism, 9; coups, 3; expenditures and democratization, 263; loyalty to regime, 9. *See also* Security forces

Military coups, 3

Millennium Challenge Corporation, 87

Miro, Mustafa, 44

Modernization, 218; theory, 195

Mohammed VI (King of Morocco), 34, 35, 37, 159, 163, 178, 180, 181

Mohammed V (King of Morocco), 33, 176

Monarchies: ability to delay or reverse reforms by, 181; ability to undertake limited liberalization to divide oppositin, 173–188; absolute, 3, 174, 175*tab*; adaptive behavior of, 181; advantage of smaller populations to, 185; in Arabian Peninsula, 69, 80, 82–85; authoritarian, 71, 174; authoritarian-constitutional, 3; in Bahrain, 2–3, 173, 175*tab*; centralization of power in, 182; comparisons to Arab republics, 173–176, 180, 181; constitutional, 80, 174, 175*tab*; differences among, 174–176; difficulty in accommodating middle class, 182; dynamics of, 10; dynastic, 184; in Egypt, 177; failed, 184, 185; as guardians of national interest and unity, 174; Hashemite, 52, 150, 179; hereditary, 71, 183; implications of changes through accession, 178, 179; installation of perception of permanence, 185, 186; institutional flexibility and inclusiveness of, 183; in Jordan, 3, 41, 47–52, 173, 175*tab*, 178; in Kuwait, 3, 173, 175*tab*, 176, 177; legitimization of, 183; liberalization and, 173–188; managing reform in, 181; manipulation

of electoral processes by, 174, 175; modernization and, 183; in Morocco, 3, 33, 173, 175*tab*, 178; in Oman, 3, 173, 175*tab*; palace coups, 178; political-culture factors in, 183; political histories, 176–182; in Qatar, 3, 173, 175*tab*; recent, 183; removing old elites through reform, 178; with rentier-state characteristics, 184, 185; role played by oil in strengthening regime, 183, 184; in Saudi Arabia, 3, 82–85, 173, 174, 175*tab*, 177, 184; social differentiation and, 185; stability of, 178; strategies for survival of, 181–186; traditional, 182; in Tunisia, 177; in United Arab Emirates, 3, 173, 175*tab*; use of divide-and-rule tactics, 181; in Yemen, 177

Morocco: colonialism in, 30, 31; constitutional amendments in, 35; corruption in, 36; coup attempts in, 34; defense expenditures, 263*tab*; economic inequality in, 36; elections, 34, 36, 148*tab*, 159, 163, 174, 180, 187; electoral fraud in, 34; electoral systems in, 160*tab*; elimination of opposition in, 34; exploitation of nationalist and socialist rivalries by monarchy in, 34; February 20 Movement in, 163; governance strategies in, 33; Hassan II in, 33, 34, 180; income inequality in, 227*fig*; *infitah* policies in, 218; internet filtering in, 238*tab*; internet use in, 237*tab*; investments in public infrastructure in, 35; Islamist electoral success, 166, 166*tab*, 167; Istiqlal party, 33, 34; Justice and Development Party in, 123, 128, 129; liberalization, 219*tab*; manufactured exports, 221*tab*; marginalization of opposition in, 34; media coverage of protests in, 236; membership in Gulf Cooperation Council (GCC), 89*n*2; Mohammed VI in, 34, 35, 37, 159, 163, 180, 181; Mohammed V in, 33, 176; monarchy in, 3, 33, 34, 173, 175*tab*, 176, 178; Parti Democracy la Justice et du Développement (PJD), 34, 36, 159; political patronage in, 34; population, 174; prodemocracy activists in, 35; as production state, 174; protests in, 35–36, 173, 219; public debt in, 219; rentier status, 175*tab*; repression in, 33, 34; response to Arab Spring, 187;

About the Book

For years the authoritarian regimes of the Arab world displayed remarkable persistence. Then, beginning in December 2010, much of the region underwent rapid and remarkable political change. This volume explores the precursors, nature, and trajectory of the dynamics unleashed by the Arab Spring.

The authors focus on the complex forces that have sustained authoritarianism in the region, as well as the roots of popular mobilization and regime overthrow. They also examine the possibilities for democratic reform—and, where it has occurred, relapse. Their work offers a comprehensive assessment, at once sophisticated and accessible, of current developments and trends in the countries of the Arab Middle East and North Africa.

Rex Brynen is professor of political science at McGill University. **Pete W. Moore** is associate professor of political science at Case Western Reserve University. **Bassel F. Salloukh** is associate professor of political science at the Lebanese American University in Beirut. **Marie-Joëlle Zahar** is associate professor of political science at the University of Montreal.